THE NATION'S CAPITAL
BREWMASTER

THE NATION'S CAPITAL BREWMASTER

Christian Heurich and His Brewery, 1842–1956

Mark Elliott Benbow

McFarland & Company, Inc., Publishers
Jefferson, North Carolina

LIBRARY OF CONGRESS CATALOGUING-IN-PUBLICATION DATA

Names: Benbow, Mark, author.
Title: The nation's capital brewmaster : Christian Heurich
and his brewery, 1842–1956 / Mark Elliott Benbow.
Other titles: Christian Heurich and his brewery, 1842–1956
Description: Jefferson, North Carolina : McFarland & Company, Inc., 2017. |
Includes bibliographical references and index.
Identifiers: LCCN 2017041603 | ISBN 9781476665016
(softcover : acid free paper) ∞
Subjects: LCSH: Brewers—Washington, (D.C.)—Biography. | Heurich, Christian,
1842–1945. | Christian Heurich Brewing Company (Washington, D.C.) |
Breweries—Washington, (D.C.)—History.
Classification: LCC TP573.5.H48 B46 2017 | DDC 663.092 [B] —dc23
LC record available at https://lccn.loc.gov/2017041603

BRITISH LIBRARY CATALOGUING DATA ARE AVAILABLE

ISBN (print) 978-1-4766-6501-6
ISBN (ebook) 978-1-4766-2934-6

Front cover: Brewery founder Christian Heurich
(collection of Jan King Evans Houser)

Printed in the United States of America

*McFarland & Company, Inc., Publishers
Box 611, Jefferson, North Carolina 28640
www.mcfarlandpub.com*

To Annette

Table of Contents

Preface

This work is the product of not only many years' research and writing, but of my longtime curiosity about the history of brewing in D.C. I have been a breweriana collector[1] since I was a teen in the 1970s, when collecting beer cans was a fad. Like most such collectors, I lost interest in collecting when I went to college, as studies and other priorities took precedence. Graduate school left little time for such leisure activities, as did starting a new career as an analyst for the U.S. government. However, I never lost my interest as a historian in how the brewing industry developed, and the interest sparked in me as a teen eventually found fruit in my scholarly pursuits. My specialty is the 1910s, and my dissertation at Ohio University and my first book were both on Woodrow Wilson.[2] As the staff historian at the Woodrow Wilson House Museum in Washington, D.C., from 2003 to 2006, I produced an exhibit on the history of Prohibition in the nation's capital that included material from Christian Heurich's brewery. That exhibit began my digging deeper into Heurich's life and his business. It not only touched my interest in early twentieth-century American history, studying Heurich's life allowed me to pursue my interest in immigration, the temperance movement, changing gender roles in American society, and the history of Washington, D.C., my adoptive home.

Apparently, I am not alone in this interest in the brewing industry. There is growing attention being paid to the history of breweries. The growth of microbreweries in the past decade or more has ignited a renewed interest in long-gone local breweries and now-defunct local brands. New breweries have taken the names of past companies and old brand names have been reborn. In some cases, local brewers have even been able to recreate recipes of brands that disappeared from store shelves and from barroom taps decades ago. Locally, DC Brau and local beer historians Mike Stein, Joshua Hubner, and Pete Jones were able to recreate Heurich Lager Beer. They released it in 2013 and again in 2016. The second release was even in cans, whose design echoed original Heurich labels. This interest by local brewers has been mirrored by historians, professional and amateur, inside and outside academia. The German Historical Institute's Immigrant Entrepreneurship project sponsored numerous biographies and topical essays on German immigrants, many of which were brewers, including Heurich.[3] The reader will find in this work's bibliography a number of these recent histories, issued by nonacademic publishers such as the History Press, as well as by university publishers. The result is a growing flood of titles on individual breweries as well as those on the brewing industry in particular regions, states, and cities.

One of the largest hurdles in writing one of these brewery histories is the lack of records. Well over a thousand brewers were closed by Prohibition. About one-quarter of them never reopened. Between 1933 and 1980, over 600 of the 700-plus breweries that had operated in the 1930s closed their doors. Many, if not most, of these breweries' records were lost. On rare occasions some were salvaged. In the case of one Chicago brewery, for example, the brewery records were retrieved from the basement of the abandoned brewery offices. In Heurich's case, an office fire in the 1930s destroyed decades' worth of Heurich's records. Some survive, badly charred, in the Smithsonian archives. Other remaining records are held by the Historical Society of Washington, D.C. The Heurich House Museum in the DuPont Circle neighborhood has many personal papers, including Heurich's third wife's diaries and Heurich's unpublished memoirs. Fortunately, as a prominent local citizen, Heurich's activities were frequently covered by the local press, as well as in the trade press, such as *The Western Brewer*. Finally, one of Heurich's granddaughters, Mrs. Jan King Evans Houser, was very supportive of this project and not only granted me multiple interviews, but provided me with access to all the family material she has collected over the years.

In addition to a growing interest in brewing history, there has been a bit of a renaissance in studies on the history of the District of Columbia. Unfortunately, with no local state university press, there is no obvious publisher for such histories, but despite this, new works do continue to be released. I have used these studies to place Heurich within his local context. D.C. was originally intended to be a center of production as well as the seat of the national government, and Heurich established himself in D.C. to take advantage of that dream. But by the end of the nineteenth century, it was clear that D.C. was not going to become an industrial hub. As such, Heurich's brewery was somewhat of an anomaly, especially by the 1930s, as the capital's development concentrated on supporting the federal government and the tourist trade. I hope that this work will inform the reader how Heurich's brewery fit into Washington's changing economy.

Of course, any book requires a lot of support and assistance to write. I would be remiss if I did not thank Kim Bender and Erika Goergen, director and archivist respectively at the Heurich House Museum, for their support, for giving me access to any part of the house I needed, and for reviewing my draft. Erika was also very helpful in helping me locate material in their archives. The staff at the Washington Historical Society Kiplinger Library were always obliging and friendly, as was the staff at the Washingtoniana Collection at the D.C. Public Library. The staff at the Smithsonian Archives and at the numerous reading rooms of the Library of Congress were always there to assist as well. One of the benefits to living in the D.C. area is being able to rely on such wonderful resources.

Among the other scholars who helped me, I wish to thank Dr. Uwe Spiekermann from the German Historical Institute and Dr. Stafan Manz, Head of German, Reader in German at Aston University in Great Britain. Both gave me invaluable help in my research. Alan Lessoff at Illinois State University deserves thanks for his help and encouragement with my initial inquiries. Of course, my Ph.D. advisor, Dr. Alonzo Hamby, always gets my heartfelt gratitude for his support as I pushed my way slowly through Ohio University's demanding graduate program.

My colleagues in the History and Politics Department at Marymount University have been wonderful, especially my chair, Dr. Margaret Tseng. I also should recognize my friends in the English Department. Dr. Eric Norton deserves special thanks. His deep knowledge of and interest in the Prohibition literature of the nineteenth century provided me with additional sources I would have missed otherwise. Tracy Rich from the CIA's history staff was very helpful in finding me information about the uses of the Heurich Brewery after January 1956. And finally, my uncle, James Getty, passed on his memories of meetings held in the old brewery when he worked for the United States Air Force.

Thank you to local breweriana collectors Jack Blush, Chuck Triplet, Steve Gordon, and Mike Cianciosi. Each provided me with answers to questions and examples of Heurich breweriana for my research. Moreover, they were each supportive of this project. Local history author Garrett Peck was generous in sharing information and in providing support.

A huge thank-you to Mrs. Jan King Evans Houser for her support through a project that I know took much longer than originally anticipated. I could not have finished this work without her help!

The biggest thank-you goes, of course, to my wife Annette. For over twenty-five years, she has helped me through career changes and research projects. She has stood over copying machines helping me duplicate documents and articles I needed, made sure I had a quiet space and time to write, listened to my enthusiastic explanations when I found some new, cool piece of information, and never, ever asked when I would finally be finished. She also was very tolerant when I explained just why I had, *had* to buy that Senate beer can that just appeared on eBay and how it wasn't a hobby, it was for my work, honest! To my wife Annette, the love of my life, I dedicate this book.

Introduction

On November 25, 1961, sounds of explosions echoed through western Washington, D.C. The blasts came just across the street from several buildings belonging to the Central Intelligence Agency (CIA), and as the dust settled, police surrounded the area to keep curious bystanders at a safe distance. Over three hundred pounds of dynamite stacked against the walls of the icehouse of the abandoned Christian Heurich Brewery on Water Street in the capital city had felled most of the brewery's walls, leaving but one standing. The explosions were the result of a planned demolition of the old brewery to make room for the new Theodore Roosevelt Bridge and for what would become the John F. Kennedy Center for the Performing Arts. The brewery, founded in 1872 by German immigrant Christian Heurich, had long been a centerpiece of the brewing industry in Washington, and Heurich's brewery complex on the Potomac had been a city landmark since being built in the 1890s. In early 1956, the brewery was closed and sat waiting for the wrecking ball. It took multiple attempts, in the autumn of 1961 and then in the spring of 1962, to tear down what Heurich had built. According to local stories, the wrecking ball at first just bounced off the building's strong cork-lined brick walls. While the story may be apocryphal, it would be fitting if true, as Heurich's business survived a lot more over the years than just a demolition crew, including fires, the anti–German hysteria of World War I, prohibitionists, and competition from other local and national breweries. What was a one-ton steel ball compared to those challenges?[1]

Christian Heurich (1842–1945) was not only Washington, D.C.'s most prominent brewer; he was also one of the elder statesmen of the brewing industry in the United States. Born in the Duchy of Saxe-Meiningen in what is now central Germany, Heurich immigrated to Baltimore after the American Civil War to build his own brewery. He succeeded on a scale only a few of his fellow brewers would be able to match. At the peak of his success in the early 1940s, Heurich was second only to the federal government in the amount of land he owned and in the number of employees working for him in Washington. His career spanned the growth of the brewing industry from the Gilded Age of the 1870s through the Second World War. Heurich prospered during the economic turmoil of the late nineteenth and early twentieth centuries, endured the anti–German hysteria of the First World War and the Prohibition movement, and survived and even prospered during the Great Depression. By the time he died at the age of 102, he was the oldest working brewer in the United States.

Heurich was born in 1842 in Haina in the Duchy of Saxe-Meiningen, one of the numerous small states and principalities that made up what is now Germany, just a few

Having successfully resisted the wrecking ball, the Heurich icehouse finally gives way to explosives. November 1961 (courtesy the D.C. Public Library, Star Collection © *Washington Post*).

years before the outbreak of the nationalistic revolutions of 1848. The first chapter discusses Heurich's childhood and the apprentice system as it existed in the nineteenth century. His parents ran a tavern and Heurich was trained through the apprentice system as both a butcher and as a brewer. As a young man, he traveled through Central Europe as a journeyman, refining his knowledge of the brewing arts. In 1866, Heurich immigrated to the United States, initially living in Baltimore with a married sister and her husband. He also spent time in Chicago, Cincinnati and Kansas, working in breweries and on a relative's farm. Heurich's experiences as an immigrant illustrate the importance of the German immigrant community in America to the new immigrants from their homeland. Baltimore had a large, active German immigrant community in which newcomers could settle and ease their way into American society. Finally, Heurich's work experiences will be placed into the context of the brewing industry as it existed in the third quarter of the century, as more breweries opened to meet the demands of a changing American society and a growing taste for German-style lager beer.

In 1872, Heurich moved to Washington, D.C., with a business partner to open their own brewery. The second chapter covers Heurich's experiences in Washington, D.C., in the last quarter of the nineteenth century. He chose the capital city as his new home to take advantage of a town that was growing not just because of the presence of the federal government, but because city leaders, led by Board of Works head Alexander Shepherd, were promoting and rebuilding the District to become a working world-class city with industry and business opportunities outside of the realm of government work. Heurich adopted this new vision of his adopted city and found a place within the small but active German-American community along the Potomac. He married three times and worked to assimilate into American culture. His business prospered during a period in which the brewing industry expanded and then began a wave of consolidation.

Chapters 3, 4, and 5 examine Heurich's life as his business reaches its peak. He opened a new, modern brewery along the Potomac River and started a family while establishing himself among the business elite of Washington in his DuPont Circle mansion. Despite this success, Heurich also had to deal with a growing prohibition movement in Virginia, one of his business's main markets, and even in Washington as anti-alcohol congressmen worked to make the capital city dry as an example to the nation. Heurich closed his brewery in 1917, as discussed in Chapter 6, when the District went officially dry, but that was not the end of his troubles. During the First World War, Heurich was the subject of numerous rumors that he was actively aiding Germany against the U.S. Additionally, Washington was subject to increasingly stringent anti-enemy alien laws aimed at the local German population, even those who were naturalized citizens such as Heurich. He spent much of the war at his dairy farm in nearby Maryland, away from the restrictions, returning to his DuPont Circle home after the war was over.

The Heurich Brewery remained closed from 1917 until 1933. Chapter 7 examines how Heurich passed through the dry years, and how the brewery reopened in 1933 when Prohibition ended. Already in his seventies when Prohibition arrived, Heurich could have easily retired and lived off his substantial real estate investments. Wanting to remain active, and concerned about his employees, Heurich mothballed the brewing equipment and the former brewery became an ice plant, supplying Congress and the Supreme Court. Ninety years old when Prohibition ended in 1933, Heurich did not need to reopen his brewery, but he was still mentally and physically active, and the familiar smell of brewing once again filled the air along Water Street and the Potomac. Heurich's brewery was the only one of Washington's pre-Prohibition breweries to prosper after 1933 as the brewing business began a long, slow process of falling under the dominance of a few large national brewers. Heurich also had to deal with the rising issue of segregation and Jim Crow, as the African American population in Washington began to demand equal employment rights. After a threatened boycott, Heurich agreed to hire African American workers as brewery drivers. Nonetheless, despite the changing business environment, the Christian Heurich Brewing Company survived and prospered during the first post–Prohibition decade.

When the U.S. entered World War II in December 1941, Washington began a period of rapid growth of both population and infrastructure. The years from 1941 to 1945 were the last heyday of Heurich's brewery as he took advantage of the growing market. In contrast to how Heurich was regarded in 1917–1918, during the Second World War he was not treated as an enemy alien, but as the grand old businessman of the city. He remained active and working until shortly before his death in March 1945. The concluding chapter examines Heurich's life and legacy as one of the senior businessmen of the nation's capital. The brewery continued operating under his son, Christian Heurich Junior, but under pressure from the increasingly powerful national brewers and with changing popular tastes in beer, the brewery lost much of its market share. It closed in early 1956. The brewery building was torn down to make room for the Theodore Roosevelt Bridge and the Kennedy Center. Heurich's DuPont Circle mansion became headquarters for the local historic society until reacquired by the family in the early twenty-first century, and is currently a museum.

Heurich's efforts to adapt to his adopted country and to find a promising location for his new brewery demonstrates how immigrant entrepreneurs could succeed by finding an economic niche to fill. Heurich found his by taking advantage of the rapid growth of the nation's capital and the growing taste for the lighter German-style lager been he had been trained to make in Europe. Heurich's business prospered in the late nineteenth and early twentieth centuries like many other small and medium-sized breweries, and like so many other brewers, he searched for a way to survive Prohibition. After 1933 Heurich was successful in the short term, but his brewery faced the same pressures from increasingly powerful breweries such as Anheuser-Busch, Schlitz, and Pabst. Over four hundred breweries that reopened after 1933 had closed again by 1960, approximately two-thirds of the total breweries in the country. Like so many of his peers who immigrated to the U.S. in the last half of the nineteenth century, Heurich built a business that prospered while the founder was alive, but which could not survive the changing business conditions of the twentieth century.

1

Youth and Immigration: 1842–1870

Christian Heurich was born on Monday, September 12, 1842, in a castle overlooking the small farming village of Haina in the Duchy of Saxe-Meiningen. He was the third of four children, two boys and two girls. His parents, John Casper Heurich, Jr. (1806–1861), and Anna Marguerite Fuchs Heurich (1807–1856), ran an inn in the village and were tenants in what Heurich later described as "an old castle" belonging to the University of Würzburg. The eldest Heurich child was August Friedrich (born 1835). Next came Elisabeth Adelipa (born 1839). Christian was the third child and second boy. After Christian, the Heuriches had one more child, Emilie, born in 1844.[1] While the Heurich family was Lutheran, Christian Heurich was not particularly active in church activities. In a 1927 letter to a clergyman who was asking for a donation, Heurich noted that he was "educated in the Lutheran belief" and that he was "well acquainted with real Christian teachings and with the Life and Teachings of Dr. Martin Luther."[2]

Politically the Duchy of Saxe-Meiningen was stable, but it was an isolated and economically backwards region. There was no railroad communication with the other German states until 1870. The Duchy was part of the German Confederation, formed in 1814 at the Congress of Vienna in part to replace the defunct Holy Roman Empire, which had ceased to exist in 1806 during the Napoleonic Wars (1803–1815). With a population of about 160,000, it covered approximately 2,500-km stretched out along the Werra River. A bit less than half was wooded, with much of the rest agricultural land. Three-quarters of the people were rural, mostly peasant farmers and woodsmen.[3] The Duchy was one of thirty-eight mostly small states represented in a parliament, the "Diet" in Frankfort. The Confederation was dominated by the handful of large states that were members, especially Austria and Prussia. One of the Saxon duchies, Saxe-Meiningen was ruled by Duke Bernhard II[4] (1803–1866) as a constitutional monarchy. An 1829 constitution created a legislature, the Diet, with twenty-four members. Voting was restricted to all "domiciled male" taxpayers over age twenty-five.[5] There was a free press in the Duchy, and Duke Georg I (reigned 1782–1803) occasionally gave refuge to liberal dissidents, including Johann Wolfgang von Goethe and Friedrich von Schiller. Georg I also expanded educational opportunities for the children of his realm, both boys and girls alike, and Heurich would benefit from this opportunity. Georg I died in 1803, when his son, Bernhard Erich Freund, was only three years old. The boy's mother, Louisa Eleanora, acted as regent and preserved the Duchy's independence through the turmoil of the Napoleonic Wars, joining the Allies in 1813. Bernhard took the throne for himself in 1821.[6]

During Europe's 1848 "Springtime of the Peoples," demonstrations often led to revolution throughout the continent and would even touch Heurich's small village in the forests of southern Germany. In France, King Louis-Philippe was forced to abdicate, and the short-lived Second Republic was formed. In Denmark, growing demonstrations forced the new king, Frederick VII, to adopt a constitution. Hungary, long a part of the Hapsburg Austrian Empire, attempted to win first its autonomy within the empire and then its independence. Riots in Vienna forced the conservative Austrian government to resign, to be replaced by pro-reform ministers. In Germany, demonstrators in several states began demanding not only reform but also the formation of a unified German government. The Pan-Germanic movement soon showed some success as a German parliament began meeting in St. Paul's Church in Frankfort in May 1848. Most of the smaller principalities in the area had popular governments, and demands for reform were sometimes granted, at least temporarily. The People's Spring was felt in Saxe-Meiningen the same as in other parts of Germany when a small number of radicals demanded extensive reforms. Although revolutionary Friedrich Hecker's march in April from Konstanz to Karlsruhe did not come anywhere near Saxe-Meiningen, it inspired at least some supporters. In his memoirs Heurich recounted that as a boy he watched the revolutionary Heckerites drill in his home town. When celebrating his one hundredth birthday in 1942, Heurich recalled that as a six-year-old he had "worn the Hecker hat" and "drilled with my schoolmates." Despite the Heckerite popularity with small boys, a citizen's militia formed to support Duke Bernard, and the reform movement quickly faded. Heurich, however, had fond memories of the revolution, noting, "Hecker and Carl Schurz were great revolutionists, and afterwards came to this country and became good American citizens."[7]

The great events occupying the rest of Europe—the revolutions of 1848, the growth of railroads, industrialization—washed over Heurich's boyhood home but left few permanent marks, at least while Heurich was young. Future events, such as the unification of Germany in 1871 and both world wars, would have a greater impact on the area, but occurred after Heurich had immigrated to America. In the late 1850s and 1860s, Saxe-Meiningen was a pleasant enough place to grow up, and Heurich revisited it many times as an adult. Later in life, he boasted about the famous Germans who came from "my section of Germany, including Rudolf Diesel, Johann Sebastian Bach, and Martin Luther." Nonetheless, for an ambitious young brewer in the 1860s, it was not a place where he could make his mark on the world. His home's isolation from most of the turmoil of the period made for a safe environment in which to grow up, but as a young man, Heurich was not as interested in finding a safe place as he was interested in finding a place to succeed and take risks.[8]

Heurich's education was not extensive, but it provided him with enough of the basics he'd need. In his first school in Haina, Heurich had one teacher, Rektor Jung,[9] who taught approximately fifty students ranging from six to fourteen years of age. No doubt doing his best not to be overwhelmed by the sheer number of students, the teacher covered the basics—reading, writing, and mathematics. The latter was Heurich's best subject, and he noted in his memoirs that "figures came [easily] to me," which made up for "deficiency along other lines."[10] When he was not in school, Heurich worked in his father's tavern, serving customers, washing serving ware, and helping the family business. This made for exhaustingly long days, something Heurich grew used to.[11]

Heurich's father, Casper, as the local innkeeper, was both brewer and butcher–two essential skills for innkeepers. He was also an unofficial community leader, a local advisor to peasants, and, according to Heurich, an "easy mark" for a "sob story." As such he was not as well-off as he could have been. Heurich implied that this generosity put a strain on the family. He noted that had his father not been so generous, his mother "might not have worn herself out as early in life as she did."[12] In 1854 the Heurich family moved a few kilometers away to Römhild, where his father purchased another inn. Heurich attended a new school, excelling in mathematics.

His mother, Anna, did not enjoy her new home long. She died on March 8, 1856, only forty-eight years old. Heurich does not mention a cause, but implied in his memoirs that it was overwork and exhaustion. Copies of undated German records in Heurich's personal papers stated that she died from "nervous fever." An 1850 German health text noted that "nervous fever is ushered in by disturbances in the nervous pains, feverish pulse, loss of appetite, and or at least the sleep is unrefreshing and beset with fantasies [dreams]."[13] Archaic medical terms can be difficult to translate to a modern diagnosis, but "nervous fever" sometimes refers to typhus. It could also refer to what was later known as a nervous breakdown due to exhaustion, an illness her son was also vulnerable to as an adult. Whatever the cause, Anna Heurich's death left Casper to raise four children without his wife.

Soon after, Heurich's father fell ill, and he died in 1861 at age fifty-five. According to family stories, he died from "a broken heart." Records in the Heurich family papers note that he died from "consumption" or pulmonary tuberculosis. Management of the inn "passed into other hands," and although Casper Heinrich had arranged for the family to continue living there, the children began to depart one by one.[14] Heurich's older brother, August Friedrich, was barely twenty-one. He married, and he and his wife took in his younger sister, Emilie, only eleven when their mother died. However, it was Heurich's older sister, Elisabeth Adelipa, who seemed to have the greatest influence on Heurich's decision to move to the United States to find opportunity. She was sixteen when her mother died, whereupon she immigrated to the United States with family friends. Once in America she met and married a Baltimore ship's captain, Hermann Jacobsen.[15]

After his mother died, Heurich graduated from his local school in 1857 at the top of his class. At fifteen, he was the age when adolescent males in central Europe usually began their apprenticeships, and Heurich followed his father's path by learning to brew beer and butcher. His apprenticeship came at a time when the guild system was starting to decay due to industrialization. During the early industrial revolution, skilled tradesmen had to compete with factories and the "putting out system" in which workers, essentially subcontractors, worked in their own homes manufacturing goods for their employers. Light manufacturing, such as making shoes, locks, and textiles, were the most affected. Other trades, including brewing, continued to follow the apprenticeship and journeyman system for a bit longer. Heurich was apprenticed to an innkeeper named Freund in the town of Themar, about fifteen kilometers north of his home.

Heurich's life as an apprentice would not have been easy. Apprentices ranked at the bottom of any industry, and physical discipline and even abuse were not only common, but were expected. Masters varied in terms of how they treated their apprentices, and although Heurich did not say much about his master in his memoirs, he never complained about his treatment. Heurich did not praise him either, unlike the fond way he remembered his schoolmaster, noting proudly that he told Heurich's parents that their son was a "'born' mathematician." "The teaching was," Heurich remembered, "good and through."[16] He learned how to brew several styles of beer, including light and dark lagers. Traditional

German beers were made with barley, but weiss beer, made with wheat, became popular beginning in the sixteenth century. Since these lighter-colored lager beers developed in Bavaria and Vienna in the early nineteenth century were quite well-liked at the time, these beers may have been among the first he learned to make, and were the types of beer that he would later brew to his great advantage in the United States.[17]

The German brewing industry was also changing due to technological advances that affected how beer was made. Brewing was losing some of its character as an art as research into the brewing process made scientific measurements possible. These changes were not limited to Germany, as technological advances in other parts of Europe, such as Britain, were soon introduced to the rest of the continent and then to the United States. For example, in the late eighteenth century, brewers in Britain began using thermometers to keep their product at a steady temperature. German brewers soon adopted the same practice. In 1834 several Munich breweries began using a saccharometer, which measures the amount of sugar in a solution, an innovation soon adopted elsewhere. Brewers in Bavaria gained a reputation in the neighboring German states as among the most advanced in central Europe, and young brewers, like Heurich, began to travel to the region to learn the newest techniques. More formal schools would be established, but not until later in the century, after Heurich had already migrated to America. As a result, while he probably was taught the most modern brewing methods for the time, Heurich learned them via the traditional apprentice-journeyman system just as it was beginning to evolve into a formal system of schools.[18]

In 1859 at age 17, after two years as an apprentice, Heurich went on his journeyman trip, or *Wanderjahre*, new brewers who had just finished their apprenticeship took in order to learn their trade. Heurich spent the next two years traveling and learning from master brewers while following the traditional trade routes through central and western Europe. In this tradition, a journeyman would travel with a small set amount of money in his pocket, approximately equivalent to five marks, and would return with the same amount after two or three years. He carried identification with him as he crossed multiple borders between states, which would help guarantee food and shelter from other members of his guild while searching for a job. Even if a master tradesman could not offer the wandering journeyman a job, he was supposed to give him shelter, food, drink, and perhaps a small amount of money, then send the young man on his way with a traditional blessing, "God give you happiness and blessing. Our best greeting to the job you will eventually get." In reality, by the time Heurich went on his trip, the ritual was not often followed, as there were more journeymen than jobs, and there were complaints about journeymen who were little more than beggars.[19]

A journeyman had to carry a *Wanderbuch* with him, a small book that recorded his movements and employment history. It had to be shown to border guards when crossing from one territory to another. It also had to be shown to the local police and approved by the authorities, who might keep the journeyman waiting for a few hours or a few days. Often the local police kept the book and returned it to the journeyman when he moved on. Each job the journeyman held was recorded, as was the name of the master for whom he worked and comments from his employer on his performance. If the journeyman got in trouble with the police, that would also be recorded. Some destinations, such as Switzerland, which gave refuge to political dissidents after the 1848 revolutions, were suspicious to the authorities. Stamps showing that the journeyman worked there, as Heurich did, could cast suspicion upon him as being a radical. The young man on his *Wanderjahre* might claim to have "lost" his book to avoid showing it, but that created suspicion as well, even if the journeyman had, indeed, actually lost it. If the journeyman did get in trouble, he could be sent back to his home, which was listed as well, effectively ending his career. Taking a job outside of one's trade, such as in one of the new factories being created all over Europe, would mark the journeyman as a deserter to his trade, and that would have ruined his career as well. The harsh routine was a form of initiation that new members of the group were expected to endure in order to enter the ranks of the masters. Only then could they open their own shop, marry, and start a family if they wished.[20] Traditionally the journeyman stayed with his master's family and lived as one of them. How well, or poorly, he was treated depended upon the whims and personality of his employer. Masters were permitted to physically discipline both journeymen and apprentices, which often included beatings, and journeymen could treat apprentices the same way.[21]

This journey, sometimes referred to as a "waltz," was required for all journeymen before they could apply to be a master craftsman. It allowed the journeyman to learn more aspects of his craft from a variety of masters, and it spread innovations and new techniques among the guild from one area to another. It also provided an accepted means for unemployed tradesmen to look for new work. These young workers would trade notes on employers, and their network provided information on who was good to work for and whom to avoid, as well as what specifics about the trade they might learn from whom. They could also stay in a *Herberge*, or hostel for journeymen. Workers from different trades might stay in the same place, but would generally eat with those who worked in the same trade. Conditions on the road were often harsh. The food, living conditions, and hygiene standards varied from place to place, but because they spent so much time on the road, journeymen had a reputation for being unclean. In some areas the local police were required to check the skin of entering journeymen for infectious diseases such as scabies, an examination that was humiliating and uncomfortable, as the journeyman had to strip and put up with any jokes or teasing from the police lest he get a beating. Journeyman guidebooks often advised putting up with the humiliation because the police could make it impossible to work in the area. Local authorities often saw a journeyman, unmarried and an outsider to the community, as a possible source of trouble. Journeymen associations, which sometimes set up meeting rooms or arranged for boarding houses, provided a safe haven for the young workers, but they also sponsored revels with drinking, singing, and general carrying-on. Heurich would have participated along with other journeymen. In his late teens, single, and working hard, he no doubt played just as boisterously as the others when given the chance.[22]

During his trip, Heurich put his training as a butcher and a brewer to good use. He worked as a butcher in Basel for several weeks and then walked to Munich, roughly 400 kilometers to the northeast. From there, he traveled north to the Danube, and then rafted to Vienna, approximately another 400 kilometers. Here he found work as a brewer. He worked in Vienna for two years and then traveled through Graz, Trieste, Venice, and Milan. He wanted to see the source of the river Danube, so he followed it to its beginning, two disappointing small streams in what is now Baden-Württemberg. A rough map from a translation of his memoirs shows the routes he took from 1859 through 1863. He traveled through what is now Germany, Austria, Slovenia, Italy, Switzerland, France, and Hungary. At the time, he stayed largely within the various German states (prior to the 1871 unification) and the Austro-Hungarian Empire, along with France, Italy and

Switzerland. According to the map, these are the places he visited, listed in the order he reached them.

1859	Verona	Oldenburg
Römhild	Trento	Bremen
Basel	Bolzano	Kassel
Lindau	Brixen	**1863**
Kempten	Through Brenner Pass	Römhild
Munich	Innsbruck	Lyon
(by raft up Isar River	Tegernsee	Geneva
and then up the	Munich	Lausanne
Danube)	Ingolstadt	Interlaken
Linz	Regensburg	Through Susten Pass
Vienna	Nuremberg	Altdorf
1861	Erlangen	Flüelen
Vienna	Bamberg	Brunnen
Graz	Dresden	Feldkirch
Trieste	Leipzig	Innsbruck
(by boat)	Berlin	Salzburg
Venice	Hamburg	Vienna
Padua	Bremervörde	Budapest
Vicenza	Bremerhaven	Back to Vienna

There is no mention of how long he spent in each place, and in many cases he may simply have passed through. It was not always an easy walk, either. The Susten Pass was not open to vehicular traffic until the late 1930s. From the list, however, it's clear he was attracted to Vienna. He stayed there from 1859 until 1861, and returned in 1863.[23]

In his memoirs, Heurich did not spend a lot of time discussing the experience, except for remembering all the places he traveled and how much he fell in love with Vienna. Nearer the end of his life he revisited some of the places he worked as a teen and met one of his former colleagues. Of course, remembering events from his teen years fondly while in his eighties and nineties does not necessarily mean he enjoyed the experience as it was happening. Most likely the experience confirmed his desire to open his own brewery and to be independent in his work. During a strike in the 1880s, he snapped, "I did not come to this country to be in slavery," which suggests he resented the controls exercised over him as an apprentice and journeyman.[24]

In April 1863, after more than 3 years as a journeyman, Heurich returned home to Römhild, where he reported for mandatory military service, normally three years on active duty and four in the reserves. "Faulty vision" released him from having to serve, and he resumed his travels, working his way through Germany, France, and Switzerland before returning to Vienna on what he would later call "the poor man's 'grand tour.'"[25] By the time he was done, he had walked, ridden, and rafted through much of west-central Europe, working in numerous breweries along the way. Heurich learned a variety of ways to brew beer and made invaluable contacts among his fellow brewers in the region. He also, no doubt, learned to rely on himself, which would be a useful skill as he immigrated to America. For young men in the apprentice system, such as Heurich, the journeyman period marked the traditional transition from youth to adulthood.[26]

Of all the cities he visited during his *Wanderjahre*, Heurich loved Vienna best. He later wrote of that "wonderful city" and said he "warmed to its beauty, its leisure, its culture." He noted in his memoirs that he had "passed 'the most beautiful time of my life in Vienna.'" According to family tradition, he fell in love twice in Vienna. That certainly would not be unusual. Apprentices and journeymen were supposed to remain single, but could marry as soon as they finished their *Wanderjahre* and then settle down as fully responsible adult members of society.[27]

One of Heurich's loves, however, was Vienna itself. Contrasted with the tiny isolated towns in Saxe-Meiningen, the Austrian capital was no doubt a tremendously exciting city for a young man in the early 1860s. The lights,[28] the arts, the music he loved, and the atmosphere of the city cast a spell on Heurich that never wore off. Night must have been especially enchanting to the young man. Heurich was used to the dim candlelight of a small town: "When I was born the only light we had were small tapers on oil in a glass of water. My mother sewed by this light and my father read by this light." Even though gas street lighting was dim by modern standards, the streets of Vienna must have seemed magical. Although night is sometimes seen as mysterious and a bit dangerous with a hint of a promise of physical pleasures, Vienna at night would have been especially seductive to a young man experiencing his first taste of adult freedoms and would have been even more enticing after the restrictions of life as an apprentice.[29]

To contribute to his awe of this glamor, young Heurich arrived in the Austro-Hungarian Empire's capital city at a time when it was transforming itself into a beautiful, modern city. Heurich first arrived in Vienna just as the *Ringstrasse* was being built. In 1857 Emperor Franz Joseph I ordered the medieval city's walls and moats, which were no longer of any use, to be torn down and replaced by a grand avenue around the heart of the city to serve as a showcase for the empire. Among the grand new structures that arose along the *Ringstrasse* were the town hall, the parliament, university buildings, and theaters. In 1871, when Heurich chose Washington, D.C., as his new home, it was also in the midst of a vast project to remake itself into a world-class modern city to compete with the grand European capitals, including Vienna.[30]

Heurich worked in several Viennese breweries as a brewer and a cellarer for three years, probably cleaning and pitching barrels, which was hard, dirty, and often dangerous work requiring the use of molten pitch to seal the barrels. He continued to learn different ways to make beer and planned to eventually open his own brewery. It was this dream, in fact, that prompted him to leave Vienna. Encouraged by his sister Elisabeth, he began to think about moving to the U.S. His sister's role in shaping this part of Heurich's life was crucial. After immigrating to the United States in 1859, Elisabeth met and married her husband, Captain Hermann Jacobsen, in Baltimore. From there, she wrote to Heurich often, trying to persuade him to move to the U.S. to start his own brewery. In his unpublished memoirs Heurich noted, "I really believe her main object was to gather in another young German recruit for the armies of the North ... she never said so, but I think that if I had landed in Baltimore between '61 and '65 instead of in '66 she would have marched me pronto up to the first recruiting officer."[31]

After the American Civil War ended in 1865, Elisabeth "became more insistent," noting that "Germans ... were opening breweries all over the country. Americans were ... going in for the lighter, healthier and more sustaining beverages introduced and almost daily being improved on by my own countrymen." In other words, Americans were drinking more lager beer. She told her brother that he might never be able to open a new brewery in Vienna, but there was ample opportunity to start his own business in America.[32]

Elisabeth's letters to Heurich were typical of the "America letters" that immigrants sent home for generations. According to one estimate, by the 1870s well over two million letters a year crossed the Atlantic to Germany, many of them urging friends and relatives at home to immigrate. Like many new immigrants to the United States, Heurich's sister praised her new country, stressed that the new world offered greater opportunity than the old, and undoubtedly promised to help him start a new life. The common goal shared amongst journeymen like Heurich was to open their own shop. For Heurich this would have been difficult if he stayed in the Old World. While journeymen were expected to travel and work in different places, once they reached the status of master they would generally be restricted to setting up their own business in their home state. For Heurich this meant returning permanently to Saxe-Meiningen. There were approximately 178,000 people in his home duchy, compared to a bit over a half million in his beloved Vienna. The ambitious young man wanted to move on to bigger things.[33]

Heurich did not record why he picked the United States, but having family there already was a particularly important inducement. According to family stories, Heurich considered immigrating to Russia, which was also industrializing at a rapid pace, and where the existing German minority would provide a market for beer. After the Napoleonic Wars (1803–1815), British merchants, as the main foreign competitors, had been active in Russia, but tended to focus on expanding into London's colonial holdings, leaving more opportunities for German merchants to explore the expanding Russian market. Germans tended to concentrate in the larger cities and in areas within Russian territory that already had large German immigrant populations such as near the capital, St. Petersburg, and in the Black Sea region. German firms included banks, merchant houses, textile firms, and breweries, the latter of which were appearing at a rapid rate.[34] According to *The American Brewers' Gazette* in 1878, breweries in Russia numbered "about as many as in the States," and moreover, "some of them are of very fair proportions." The *Gazette* specifically mentioned the Kalinkin Brewery in St. Petersburg, which produced 100,000 barrels a year and would have ranked among the five largest breweries in the United States at the time. An 1885 U.S. State Department commerce report referred to the Kalinkin Brewery as one of the largest in the world, noting, "Large breweries now exist in Moscow, Odessa, Kief [sic], Warsaw and other cities, and an excellent (although for the people still too expensive) article is turned out. In 1879 there were 2,592 breweries, whose total production was about 191,000,000 gallons." Heurich's consideration of Russia as a possible place to start a new brewery demonstrated a sound judgment on where his chosen industry would grow. Nonetheless, given the history of Russia in the twentieth century, his descendants were, no doubt, happy he moved to Washington instead of St. Petersburg.[35]

As he contemplated moving to America, Heurich most likely considered both the drawbacks and advantages. The United States was in the post–Civil War recession in 1865–1866, but if this worried him or if he was even aware of it, he did not mention it in his memoirs. His sister was waiting, along with a large, established German community in Baltimore, so that might well have eased any anxieties about future employment. Moreover, even in a recession, Heurich had a better opportunity to begin his own brewery in the United States than back home.[36] He would not be alone in making such a calculation. A majority of German immigrants to the United States in the middle of the nineteenth century, like Heurich, were skilled workers or artisans who were drawn to America to put their skills to good use.[37]

By early 1866 Heurich had saved approximately three hundred dollars in gold. He took his sister's advice and left for America as part of the second great wave of nineteenth-century German migration to the United States.[38] He traveled via Hamburg. At the time Hamburg and Bremen were both making "conscious efforts" to "develop their emigration business," so young Christian Heurich had plenty of company.[39] Over 90 percent of all German immigrants leaving for America in the 1860s and early 1870s departed from one of these two major German ports.[40] Once in Hamburg, Heurich caught a freight steamer "filled with cattle" to the British port of Grimsby, near Hull on the eastern English coast.[41]

From there he took a train to Liverpool, where cheap passage to the United States could be purchased. The British port was a major transit point for German immigrants heading to the U.S. This route had become popular with German-speaking immigrants by the early 1850s, so it was well established by the time Heurich made the trip. Once in Liverpool, travelers would wait days or even weeks for their scheduled ship, and inexpensive boarding houses in the port city catered to the immigrant trade. As soon as they got off the train in Liverpool, Heurich and his fellow immigrants would have been set upon by "runners" for these boarding houses. The runners were usually boys who would carry travelers' luggage. Paid according to how many tenants they brought to a boarding house, runners were notoriously aggressive, often grabbing luggage from the owner's hands, who would then be forced to follow the runners and their luggage to the house. Runners would fight each other for customers and tried to steal them from each other.[42]

Whether Heurich carried his own luggage, he probably followed one of these boys to a large boarding house that may have originally have been a warehouse. Rooms cost, at most, about one shilling a night, and the price often included food. Cleanliness depended upon price, the cheaper places not being as fastidious about their cleanliness. The streets Heurich walked along would have been dirty and crowded with travelers, immigrants, sailors, runners, dockworkers, and probably a few others, including prostitutes and tavern owners who were there to serve, or prey upon, the sailors and immigrants. There would have been crates, barrels, rope, lumber and supplies stacked along the way. Posters advertising ships to American, Canada, and Australia were pasted along the walls of the buildings. No doubt Heurich would have heard multiple languages, not just English and German, but Celtic, Welsh, and many others. Some of the sights, sounds, and smells of a big city would have been familiar to Heurich from Vienna, but the hectic British port would have been much more chaotic, simultaneously frightening and exciting for a young man on his way to start a new life in a country far away from home.[43]

After a few days in a crowded rooming house with little to do, Heurich was likely eager to set sail for America. The trip would take, on average, about ten to fourteen days. And he took passage in steerage, probably to save money. Heurich did not note his ticket price in his memoirs, but a 1940 newspaper article claimed that his ticket cost seventy-five thalers.[44] Heurich booked passage on the passenger ship *Helvetia*, a three-masted steamship that made regular trips between Liverpool and New York for the National Steam Navigation Company, a passenger shipping line that specialized in carrying emigrants. Their ships left Liverpool, stopped in Queenstown in Ireland, and then sailed for America. The *Helvetia* was launched in 1865, so she was still a new ship when Heurich sailed on her to America. Part of a new generation of steam-powered vessels, *Helvetia* boasted a clipper bow for speed and sported just one funnel, but with "three masts rigged for sail." The sails were to aid the engines, not to entirely replace them. In one voyage, rough seas rendered her engines useless, and *Helvetia* ended up being blown across the

English Channel to France because "she was not designed for sailing." With an iron hull, which was a bit safer than wood in the North Atlantic when ice floes moved south, the *Helvetia* was powered by a single screw propeller. Later ships had two, as those with the single screw often noticeably rolled and pitched in poor weather, making a hellish trip for the poor passengers. *Helvetia* had a top speed of about ten knots. When Heurich sailed on her, the ship was commanded by Captain William Ogilvie, an experienced seaman who had commanded vessels since 1832.[45]

Heurich would have expected and found crowded conditions on the ship. He described the voyage, noting that although he never again had to travel steerage, "the *Helvetia* treated us right well.... The food was coarse but well-cooked and plentiful." Steerage passengers were crowded below decks, sleeping in shared bed racks and coming to the deck perhaps once or twice a day for fresh air. Heurich remembered that he "slept on a straw mattress on boards with just blankets and no feather beds as in Germany." Multiple passengers shared the same bunk. When one turned, "we all turned."[46] Toilet and cooking facilities would have been present but primitive, and ventilation would have been poor, although the conditions would not have been anywhere nearly as hellish as on the infamous "coffin ships" two decades before, in which so many Irish immigrants had perished.

Liverpool was also the most popular departure point for Irish immigrants leaving for America, so the *Helvetia* was filled with both Irish and German immigrants, the two representing the two largest groups of immigrants to the United States in 1866. That year 68,047 Irish entered though New York, a slightly lower number than had entered in 1865. Heurich was one of 106,716 Germans that entered the United States through New York that year—the highest number since 1854—and most of those came through Liverpool. However, unlike Heurich, the majority of German immigrants came from Prussia and the northeast, where changes in agriculture were pushing people to migrate to the western

The *Helvetia*. Taken from a trade card (author collection).

German states as well as overseas. Migrants from Heurich's home in middle Germany made up a relatively small proportion of the total, although, as noted above, many were, like him, artisans or skilled workers.[47]

The *Helvetia* departed Liverpool on May 2, 1866, with 925 passengers, "a full compliment [*sic*] of German and other emigrants on board." The first day out, the ship was immediately beset by rumors of cholera. Cholera can strike quickly, sometimes less than a day after exposure, running through a range of symptoms including profuse watery diarrhea (often described as "rice water"), vomiting, cramps, and severe dehydration. The rumors quickly proved true. Two passengers died soon after leaving port and the *Helvetia* was refused entry into Queenstown (now Cobh, on the eastern Irish coast) and ordered back to Liverpool. Cholera had indeed established itself on the ship, and in Heurich's words, "most of the passengers were completely beside themselves."[48]

Back in Liverpool, authorities could not keep all the passengers on the crowded *Helvetia*. The stricken ship was anchored at the Sloyne, an area in the river Mersey where the tides and currents were mild, and where the ship could be kept isolated from the rest of the harbor. Two ships in the harbor, the *Jessie Nunn* and the *War Cloud*, were moved near the *Helvetia* as extra space for the passengers. The *Jessie Nunn* was reserved as a hospital ship with a staff of nurses and doctors to treat those with cholera. Five hundred of the passengers were "British subjects" (probably mostly Irish), and they were assigned to the *War Cloud*. The remaining immigrants, including Heurich, mostly Germans but with a few other nationalities as well, remained for the time being on the *Helvetia*. A few passengers were moved to a nearby workhouse.[49]

Trying to contain the outbreak, Liverpool authorities sent word to authorities at the Dutch port of Rotterdam warning them not to send more immigrants to Hull who would continue by rail to Liverpool. Many immigrants from central Europe left from Hamburg, as had Heurich. However, the city officials at Hamburg likely were not helpful in temporarily stemming the flow of emigrants from their country, as their policy to deal with cholera outbreaks was designed to reduce public panic and disorder rather than suppress the disease's spread. One historian described their procedure as "its now traditional policy of suppression and inaction."[50] Focused on suppressing news and rumors of an outbreak, they provided no warnings to travelers. As a result, travel continued unabated. Back in Britain, to deal with immigrants who were already in transit, Liverpool health officials inspected the local boarding houses looking for those with the disease. Unfortunately, there was a significant loophole in local sanitary laws. Lodging houses were subject to inspection and restrictions on the number of occupants, but public houses with liquor licenses, and businesses listed as "hotels," were not subject to the same inspections and could be overflowing with migrants, making them prime breeding grounds for disease.[51]

Cholera continued to spread among the passengers as well as among other German immigrants in the port city, some of whom were lodged in the local poorhouse. The *Helvetia*'s crew panicked as passengers continued to sicken and die. When the mayor refused their pleas to be let ashore, the crew, forty in all, seized a tug and tried to escape. When stopped, one crewman told police that passengers were "dropping off" [dying]. Thirtynine of the crew agreed to return, and the lone holdout was held by police. Their fear was not unreasonable. One of the ship's stewards as well as the young ship's doctor both died from the disease before the month was out. The outbreak was blamed on the Germans, and as the disease progressed, German immigrants in Liverpool found themselves stranded as they were sometimes refused permission to board ships leaving for the United States. Some ships forcibly removed Germans who tried to board.[52]

Those under quarantine on the shore had to sit and wait. Their luggage was brought ashore, but Liverpool authorities were horrified that some of the immigrants, probably seeking the comfort of eating familiar food, insisted on eating the food stored in their luggage, even if it had gone stale. Passengers were commonly expected to bring food with them for the trip, but the quarantine began to last longer than the voyage had been scheduled to take. According to one press account, "the provisions were stale butter, cheese, brown bread, black-pudding, etc., altogether unfit for food. Although the emigrants were cautioned of the danger of eating some of the provisions found, it is said in some cases they persisted in doing so." The *Liverpool Mercury* tried to put the best face on their situation, claiming that the "majority of the emigrants appear in good spirits, they heartily engage in various amusements, singing, dancing, and music." Those who needed exercise were taken for walks, escorted by police to keep them away from the city's inhabitants. Heurich spent his time beginning to learn English and "picked up some."[53]

The *Helvetia* remained in quarantine in Liverpool for three weeks,[54] and over three hundred passengers died from the disease, although it is unclear how many of those were among the original nine hundred passengers. Despite precautions, the disease, which began among the German immigrants, rapidly spread between ships' passengers, newly arriving German immigrants, and the population in Liverpool. Some of the mattresses used by the ill on the *Jessie Nunn*, stained by feces, urine, and vomit, were not properly disposed of and were instead simply tossed overboard into the harbor. Local residents found them and reused them, further spreading the disease. Many passengers lost much of their clothing and bedding, which was burned, although Heurich seemed to have kept his. Many items were only damaged, however, and despite warnings, poor locals salvaged some of these items as well. The harbor water, which doubled as a sewer for the ships, provided another way for the contagion to spread to locals wading in the water trying to salvage material.[55]

The 1866 cholera epidemic in Liverpool was part of the Fourth Cholera Pandemic (1863–1875), one of several such pandemics that killed millions during the nineteenth century. The First Pandemic (1816–1826) hit mostly Asia. The Second (1829–1851) affected Russia, Europe, the Middle East, and the United States. The Third (1852–1860) spread from south Asia east as far as Japan and west as far as the United States. It hit Vienna in 1854 and 1855, a few years before Heurich lived there, although it would have an effect on him nonetheless as he heard stories from the older employees at the breweries where he worked. Unfortunately for many of Heurich's shipmates, as well as many of Liverpool's poor, the incomplete understanding of how cholera spread meant that the measures taken were woefully insufficient to stop the spread despite lessons learned from earlier outbreaks. The Fourth Pandemic's spread, including its appearance in Liverpool, was aided by the Austrian-Prussian War of 1866, which spread cholera through the Austro-Hungarian Empire, including to immigrants from the German states passing through the British Isles on their way to the United States.

Faced again with their enemy cholera, local medical authorities in Liverpool were still uncertain how the disease was transmitted, although it was understood to be carried by individuals rather than being a disease of entire communities. British physician John Snow had discovered that contaminated water spread the disease in 1854, but the exact nature of the contamination was not yet known and the connection with the water supply was not universally accepted. The idea that disease was spread by miasma, or bad air, was still widespread. Medical historian Stephen Halliday noted that "the 'miasmatic' explanation of the cause of disease figured prominently in the long debates among the people who were responsible for combating the cholera epidemics that afflicted Britain … between 1831 and 1866." The miasmatic explanation was not as outdated as it may seem. It did recognize that cholera was associated with "conditions of filth and overcrowding." Fortunately, some of the health measures passed before 1866 that were intended to reduce foul odors and miasma, such as installing glazed water-flushed drainpipes for waste, also helped prevent cholera-infected feces from entering the water supply.[56]

Heurich survived because he remembered an account about the 1854–1855 outbreak in Vienna. According to the story as Heurich remembered it, the city's brewery workers were fearful that they were about to die, so they drank the beer they had made instead of water. By inadvertently avoiding contaminated water, they survived. Remembering this story while quarantined, Heurich limited himself to beer and made it through the outbreak without contracting the disease. He was not, however, overly fond of English beer and later wrote that it "did not do me any harm except to almost persuade me to remain in that country to teach them how to make good German lager." There was likely no real temptation for him to stay. Britain was suffering a bank panic in May 1866 as hundreds of banks failed. There were runs on banks in Liverpool while Heurich was there, so a combination of a sick economy and sick people made Britain an unattractive place to settle for the young German immigrant.[57]

The *Helvetia* was finally emptied of passengers and crew. It was disinfected, its bedding destroyed or cleansed. Once the outbreak seemed to be contained and passengers were no longer falling ill, those who were sent to other ships or to the city's poorhouse were allowed to reboard the ship. Some passengers, including Heurich, had remained on the ship the entire time except for when it was being disinfected. On May 29, a little over three weeks after the first passengers fell ill, the *Helvetia* left Liverpool the second time. It arrived in New York on Monday, June 11, 1866.[58]

Landing at the entry depot at Castle Garden at the foot on Manhattan Island, Heurich was not impressed with New York. Castle Garden was an old fortress which had served as a concert hall (Jenny Lind performed there in 1850) before being converted into the city's official immigration entry point in 1855. Previously, immigrants arriving in New York had simply entered the city from wherever their ship happened to dock. This not only prevented federal, state, or local government officials from keeping track of who was entering, but also allowed easy access to the new immigrants by local confidence men, thieves, prostitutes, and other criminal undesirables. In part to control the immigrants and in part to protect them, New York funneled them through the stone walls and high fences of Castle Garden, out of sight of the city. At first, labor agents were allowed access to the newcomers, as were ticket sellers for railway lines. But after unscrupulous labor brokers tricked some German immigrants into signing abusive labor agreements with a landowner in Virginia, officials tried to keep a closer watch on the greenhorns, not always with success.[59]

When Heurich arrived at Castle Garden in June 1866, immigration officials were finalizing a formal procedure for processing new arrivals. First the Boarding Department would send an officer to each newly arrived ship at the Quarantine Station six miles out

Castle Garden, the Labor Exchange: Emigrants on the Battery in front of Castle Garden, New York. An 1868 engraving showing the facility and the crowd outside. Wood engraving after Stanley Fox (*Harper's Weekly*, 1868 August 15. LC-USZ61-366).

of New York. The officer would check the number of passengers, collect reports on illnesses and deaths, and make sure that there was no unauthorized contact between the ship and shore as it continued into New York Harbor to the docks. Once the ship was in the harbor, a landing agent and a customs inspector would take a tug to the vessel, check the passengers' luggage, and escort the immigrants to the landing pier. Non-immigrants would accompany the ship to its regular pier to disembark. Once they had landed, immigrants were quickly checked by a medical officer. Those who were sick would be transferred to hospitals on Ward's Island or Blackwell's Island. New York's newspapers had reported the cholera outbreak, so it is likely that the medical office paid careful attention to the passengers on the *Helvetia* after its bout with cholera.[60]

Having passed the medical exam, Heurich and his shipmates would have proceeded into the Rotunda, the center of the complex, and divided into English and non–English speakers for processing. Heurich had picked up only a handful of English words, so he would have been moved to the latter group. The Registering Department would review each immigrant's paperwork, recording name, nationality, former residence, and intended destination. After that, the immigrants could, if they wished, buy tickets from an approved railroad company agent. First, however, they had to talk to a "booker," who often had to try to decipher scrawled, incomplete, misspelled names of towns or cities in the U.S. Some immigrants did not have enough information, such as the Swedish immigrant who wanted to go to "Farmington, U.S." but did not know which of the over two dozen towns with that name he wanted.[61] Fortunately, Heurich knew he wanted to go to Baltimore.

The booker would have given him a slip of paper listing the destination and number of tickets needed, and Heurich would have bought them from a ticket seller within the same facility. Immigrants would pay more inside Castle Garden than if they purchased the same tickets sold outside, which led to frequent complaints, but immigration officials noted that this procedure protected the newcomers from being defrauded by confidence men selling fake tickets outside. Immigrants who were staying in New York, which included Heurich for the short term, could pick up their luggage or have it sent to a local address. They could also exchange currency, another step in the immigration process that the state had taken over because immigrants had frequently been taken advantage of in the past. The rates changed frequently, however, and many immigrants did not understand why their money's value changed seemingly in an instant.[62]

Newcomers being met by friends and family could go to the Information Department and wait until their names were called as their contacts came to pick them up. Immigrants also could write and mail letters to family and friends telling them of their arrival or asking for funds. Destitute immigrants waiting to be sent money from family or friends would be sheltered at Ward's Island along with the ill. Licensed boarding-house keepers were allowed into the Rotunda to offer rooms to newcomers. A Labor Exchange set up in an office inside Castle Garden for those immigrants looking for work.[63] Heurich passed though the health inspection and checked his trunk to be delivered to one of the nearby licensed boarding-house keepers. Having been given directions to the boarding house

The Labor Exchange. Interior view of the office at Castle Garden, New York City. Wood engraving after Stanley Fox (*Harper's Weekly*, 1868 August 15. LC-USZ61-367).

and finished with the processing regimen, Heurich would simply have walked out into the city, a new arrival in America.[64]

Castle Garden is small compared to the vast Ellis Island complex that replaced it in 1892. A visitor can easily walk around the entire structure in less than three minutes. The building is made of red brick and stone, and the original ports for cannon are still visible in the walls. In 1866 the entire one-acre site was surrounded by a wooden wall to keep the immigrants separated until they were processed and to protect them from con men and criminals waiting to prey on new arrivals. Heurich would have walked through the gateway on the north end. Trinity Church's steeple would have been visible over the wall. Small wooden buildings and sheds outside the old Castle served as offices and storage. Families would have crowded around outside the wall waiting for their related newcomers to emerge from the building. The enormous wood and metal gates, installed in the original fort when it was built to defend the city from the British in the War of 1812, were still there, but were left open as smaller gates were now sufficient.

Heurich would have been surrounded by sounds and smells of the people, the city, and the sea behind him. Ships' bells, seagulls, shouting sailors, and the sound of the water would have gradually been drowned out by the sounds of the city in front of him. The smell of the sea, whatever was not overcome by the smells from the crowds of people in such a small space, similarly would have quickly given way to the smells of the city: people, food, garbage, and horses. As in Liverpool, runners would have grabbed his arms to pull him towards a particular boarding house. "Come with me! I know a nice place you can stay!" His clothing probably identified him as a German, so they would have shouted in German, or some form of it at least, "Komm mit mir!" Perhaps still getting his land legs back after having spent so much time at sea, Heurich headed into the city full of three-, four-, and five-story wood and brick buildings set alongside muddy streets and wooden sidewalks. There were numerous saloons nearby serving sailors, dockworkers, and immigrants alike. Prostitutes would have been working in and near the saloons trying to entice new customers. Heurich may well have stopped to have a drink, excited to finally be in his new country and relieved that the voyage was over. It had been over a month since he left Germany.[65]

When Heurich arrived in New York City it had a population of 900,000. It was only three years since the July 1863 Draft Riot, the largest riot in American history. As many as 2,000 people died when rioters protesting the Union draft were put down by federal troops returning from Gettysburg. Heurich undoubtedly saw men in the blue federal uniform, as the Civil War had just ended the year before and Union troops were still being discharged. One familiar sound probably met his ears: he would have heard a lot of German spoken in the city. New York City had one of the largest German populations in the world, second only to Berlin and Vienna. *Kleindeutschland*, on the Lower East Side, was an easy walk from Castle Garden, and it was where about 75,000 Germans lived, approximately 60 percent of the total number of Germans in New York City at the time.[66]

In his memoirs Heurich noted that it had been raining heavily and the unpaved streets were thick with mud. He stayed in a "rather dilapidated boarding house" not far from Castle Garden, a bit disappointed in his new temporary residence. Heurich later remembered that "everyone seemed to be chewing tobacco–and expectorating wherever it pleased them." Saloons were "everywhere" and, to his apparent chagrin, advertised "all brands of whiskeys" but "no beers." Heurich noted that he "passed a dozen drunken men in my journey from the Garden to the boarding house." The son of innkeepers was not impressed by the boarding house food either: "steak as tough as leather, watery cabbage, even more watery potatoes." After three disappointing days as a tourist, Heurich boarded a train for Baltimore. After a painfully slow thirteen-hour, one-hundred-fifty-mile trip that passed through Philadelphia and Wilmington, Heurich arrived in his sister's new home city about ten o'clock at night.[67]

Elisabeth and her husband, ship's captain Hermann Jacobsen, lived on Canton Avenue in Fells Point, a waterfront area on the north side of Baltimore Harbor. It had been home to mariners and those who built, repaired, and supplied ships since the early eighteenth century. In the 1860s about a quarter of Baltimore's 200,000 residents were either German immigrants or of German ancestry. The area where Heurich's sister lived was a ward with one of the heaviest German populations, where they mixed with other immigrants and African Americans on the streets and on the docks. By 1900 the area was considered a slum, but in the 1860s it was a busy port area and, if not rich, was working class. Captain Jacobsen was the master of a small sailing ship, the schooner *Lucy W. Alexander*, which carried grain, flour, and fruit between Baltimore, New York City, and the West Indies. Transporting commodities between the Caribbean and Baltimore was a prosperous trade arrangement that had thrived for over a century. In the 1870s Baltimore was second only to New York City in the amount of breadstuffs exported, including millions of bushels of corn and wheat. Moreover, schooners such as Jacobsen's were common, although considerably outnumbered by the generally larger barques.[68]

Heurich had not sent a message from New York telling Elisabeth of his arrival, but was somehow surprised that she was not waiting for him. "I walked into the lamp lit depot expecting to find her there and was surprised and disappointed when I saw no sign of her." He noted later with some embarrassment that he had "no explanation" for "all this foolishness." "Apparently," he confessed, "I took it for granted she would know all about me and my movements." All Elisabeth knew was that her brother intended to come to America, but not when he might be expected. A stranger noticed the young man standing in the dark, no doubt looking somewhat lost, and asked if he could help. Heurich asked if the man knew Captain Herman Jacobsen. The stranger did, and directed the twenty-three-year-old immigrant to his brother-in-law's house. Fortunately the train station was on President Street, just a few blocks away from where Heurich's family lived on Canton Avenue. Grabbing his trunk, Heurich set off through the dark streets hoping for a warm family welcome from a sister he had not seen in almost a decade. Instead he found that his sister and her husband were not home. He was greeted at the door of the two-story home by a "middle-aged colored woman," the Jacobsens' cook and housekeeper, who probably initially wondered who this young stranger was, knocking on her employers' door. Heurich had picked up a few words in English in Liverpool, and living in a heavily German area, the woman may have understood a little *Deutsch*, so the two strangers stood in the entryway trying to communicate. Both resorted to hand signals, Heurich using gestures that he later described as probably being "wholly inappropriate." The woman finally made Heurich understand that his sister and her husband were at sea and not expected to return for six weeks. The *Lucy W. Alexander* had departed for Kingston, Jamaica, on May 23, while Heurich was still in quarantine in Liverpool. Fortunately, Elisabeth had left a letter with her housekeeper in case her brother arrived while they were gone and giving him free rein of their home.[69]

Heurich settled in and became a full-time student of the English language. This

Engraving by D.C. Baxter (taken from page 24 of the Philadelphia, Wilmington & Baltimore Railroad guide. This is the station where Heurich arrived in June 1866 (Library of Congress, Prints and Photographs Division, HAER MD,4-BALT,25—1).

became his main priority. Although he undoubtedly heard a great deal of German in Fells Point with its German-speaking immigrant population, he was determined to learn English. He signed up for classes at a nearby language school and attended three classes a day. While on the *Helvetia*, Heurich had made friends with some fellow Germans who lived in the United States, but who had gone back to Germany for a visit and were now returning to America. In their conversations, he was surprised and disappointed that they had learned so little English. He thought that immigrants who did not learn their new home's language "were not going to go very far in the matter of advancement." Heurich even turned down a job offer from a local brewery so he could spend his time learning his new language. He spent seven and a half hours a day in class and then spent the rest of his time wandering around Baltimore getting to know his new home.[70]

Heurich found the Maryland port city to be far more enjoyable than New York. He especially liked the cooking, which he described as "southern cooking and not at all good for me." His sister's servant was, he happily remembered, "an excellent cook." He also took advantage of some of the local Chesapeake Bay cuisine. One night he indulged himself at the "Eutaw Tavern" with the sixty-cent "special" on a meal of oysters, terrapin soup, fried chicken Maryland,[71] a dozen fresh vegetables, a dozen spiced vegetables, hot rolls, and apple pie, "washed down with a jug of beer." The "Eutaw Tavern" was the Eutaw House, described in an 1866 visitors' guidebook as an "immense structure of brick on the corner of Baltimore and Eutaw streets and celebrated as one of the best hotels in this country." Heurich noted that it was one of the biggest meals he had ever eaten. He remembered it fondly and found it a pleasurable way to learn more about his new adopted country's foods.[72]

The building where Heurich's sister and her husband lived in 1866. The bar on the corner was the Jacobsens' home in 1866 (photograph by the author, 2016).

Heurich also walked to Greenmount Cemetery to read the inscription on the statue of John McDonough, a Baltimore native born in 1779 who became a wealthy businessman and planter in New Orleans. Upon his death in 1850, McDonough left his two-million-dollar estate split between Baltimore and New Orleans to expand their public educational systems. In 1860 his body was moved to Baltimore, and the statue Heurich went to view was dedicated in August 1865, not quite a year before Heurich arrived in the city. Heurich's English teacher told him that "every ambitious immigrant boy should learn by heart the inscription" on its base. In his unpublished memoir, Heurich quoted the inscription found on one side of the pedestal, bragging, "I can still quote the words without a hunt through my scrapbooks.

> Remember that labor is one of the conditions of our existence. Time is gold. Throw not one minute away but place each one to account. Do unto all men as you would be done by. Never put off till tomorrow that which you can do today. Never bid another do what you can do yourself. Never covet what

is not your own. Never think any matter so trivial as not to deserve notice. Never give out that which does not first come in. Never spend but to produce. Let the greatest order regulate the transactions of your life. Study in the course of your life to do the greatest possible amount of good.

He noted that McDonough had written those rules in 1804 when he was 25 years old, and added, "I resolved that, in so far as I was able, I would follow all the days of my life, John McDonogh's [sic] 'rules'; I, too, was twenty-five and practically penniless." Heurich did, in fact, quote the words accurately in his memoirs, although the "penniless" was an exaggeration, as he still had about two hundred of the three hundred dollars in gold he started with when he left home. The passage to America did not deplete his savings, and he was living in his sister's house rather than renting a room. So he probably still had the equivalent of several months' wages. Nonetheless, he was not a wealthy man even if he was not "penniless," and he invested much of his remaining money in a local "building association" and later made enough money from his "job in a brewery for very good pay" to be able to make "additional monthly deposits."[73]

When his sister returned with her husband from their voyage to the West Indies on August 4, 1866,[74] Heurich was able to greet them in "grammatical though somewhat stilted English, much to their surprise and gratification." Reunited with his older sister and meeting her husband for the first time, he continued to attend night classes while looking for a job.[75] Baltimore was a good place for Heurich to refine his brewing skills. In 1867, the U.S. had an estimated 3,700 breweries, and Baltimore was home to as many as forty-five. The number was in constant flux as breweries opened, merged, closed, and reopened. At the time, Baltimore was the fourth-largest city in the country, and its large population of German immigrants was well represented in the local brewing industry.[76]

The German community took an active role in greeting new arrivals. For example, the Baltimore German Society, established in 1783, distributed food and clothing to new German immigrants, and helped them find housing and doctors. Additionally, its employment agency, founded in 1845, helped newcomers find jobs. Heurich quickly found a job at Röst's brewery, one of the first lager breweries in the U.S. Unfortunately Heurich's memoirs are silent on how he found his job, only noting where he began work. It is likely that Heurich used the German society to find the position at Röst's because the brewery was not in the immediate neighborhood where his sister lived. The brewery's owner, Bavarian-born George Röst, was an established member of Baltimore's German community and, according to one local historian, the "father of Baltimore brewmasters." Röst established his brewery in 1851 between East North Avenue and Gay Street, about two and a half miles north of Fells Point. As his lager beer gained in popularity, Röst built a beer garden, George Rost's Meadow, next to the brewery. In 1866 he added a shooting range, a *Schützenverein*, along Gay Street. His *Schützenfest* (shooting festival) became a popular event, drawing not only the local German immigrant population, but other Baltimoreans as well as city officials to watch men demonstrate their skill with a rifle. The winner was crowned "king" and a local woman was picked as "queen." The event was so popular that another similar event was held in Carroll Park in western Baltimore. Röst's event then became known as the Eastern *Schuetzen*.[77]

Heurich spent a little over a year in Baltimore. In the spring of 1867, he received his first citizenship papers, in which he declared his intention to become a U.S. citizen. Soon after, he began working as the foreman of the malt house at Jacob Seeger's Brewery in the western part of the city. He believed that he owed this job largely to his "good grasp" of English. This job was a long several-mile walk from Fells Point, but there were horse-drawn trolleys that Heurich could have used. Of course, given his extensive *Wanderjahre*, Heur-ich may not have been bothered by the walk. Like Röst's business, Seeger added a beer garden for music and dancing as well as a hall for community meetings. The brewery's main building was described in an 1858 guide book:

> Jacob Seeger's Brewery, at Pratt Street and Frederick road, is on a site 300 by 300 feet. It is constructed principally of blue free stone. The brewery fronts 90 feet and has a depth of 40 feet. It has a steam engine. In its malt mill the first process is employed, that of grinding the malt which is then conveyed into water vats containing 150 barrels.... The vaults [for aging, or laagering, the beer] are probably the best constructed in the country. Their archway is two feet thick, the side walls three feet. The prin-cipal ones are cemented, and well ventilated, and have an atmosphere peculiarly favorable for the desired purpose.... There are several vaults for the preservation of summer beer.... In one of the cellars is a spring of excellent water, which is pumped to the upper portion of the building.... In the rear of the brewery are several buildings which are used as carriage houses, stables, coopering shop, cask sheds, etc.[78]

Heurich never specified how long he worked at Seeger's brewery before heading west. However, in the summer of 1867 he left in search of better opportunities and a chance to move outside the immigrant community that he said he thought was preventing him from perfecting his English, which he wanted to do before starting his own business. His first stop was Chicago, where he worked briefly for Seipp and Lehmann, a rapidly growing brewery that produced about 48,000 barrels a year in 1867, making it the city's largest brewery. However, in Chicago, with its large German-American population, Heurich was still working in an area dominated by native German speakers. He decided to keep moving west, "to become familiar with American life and to perfect my English." After only a few months in Chicago he left to go live with a cousin near Topeka, Kansas. There were few Germans in the area where his cousin and his family lived, so he antic-ipated being able to constantly hear and practice speaking English.[79]

Heurich's cousin and his family had been living in Kansas since the mid–1850s. They had been supported, Heurich claimed, by a New England abolitionist group during the struggle to determine whether Kansas would be a free or a slave state. There were numer-ous such groups created in 1854 and 1855 after the passage of the Kansas-Nebraska Act, which allowed voters in Kansas Territory to determine if it were to enter the union as a slave or free state. Both pro- and antislavery forces quickly began organizing to recruit and subsidize supporters to settle in Kansas. At least one group, the German Kansas Set-tlement Society in Cincinnati, Ohio, recruited German immigrants to add to the anti-slavery numbers. There were many such groups in New England, New York, and Ohio. Heurich noted that Eli Thayer's New England Emigrant Company sponsored his aunt and cousins in their move to Kansas, probably in the mid–1850s. Thayer, a Boston abo-litionist, was one of the leaders of the migrant aid movement, speaking and raising money throughout the northeast, sometimes working with Horace Greely's *New York Tribune.* Thayer's group helped found Lawrence, Kansas, as a center of free Kansas support. It was sacked by pro-slavery forces in May 1856. Heurich's cousins had moved into a violent and chaotic area. In Heurich's words, Kansas was "no place for timid people," noting that he had "blundered onto a Kansas which was, apparently, still in the throes of the ill-feeling brought about, fourteen years before, by the passage of the Kansas-Nebraska bill [*sic*]." He wryly noted that he was only a twelve-year-old schoolboy in Haina when the bill passed, but "here I was twenty six, had come from afar—and the argument was still going on."[80] By 1867 his cousin was prospering and Heurich enjoyed living there, but the violence lingered after the recent Civil War. The "wild men of both sides of the argument," Heurich remembered, "still found excuses for cattle-stealing, holdups, crop burnings and bank robberies."[81]

Heurich was now a farm worker, not a brewer, but he later remembered this time fondly. Most of the people in the area were native English speakers and his language skills improved. He worked from four in the morning until six in the evening with time after work for fun. "Life was a round of spelling bees, quilting bees, and husking bees," Heurich remembered, "with dances thrown in for good measure." He saw buffalo and Indians and claimed to have met men who survived being scalped by Indians: "they were all bald-headed." Some victims did survive being scalped, but it's likely the "survivors" were having some fun with the young newcomer.

Heurich's time in Kansas was at the beginning of a wave of migration into the Great Plains from Europe, including from Germany and Bohemia. By the early twentieth century, Germans comprised the largest immigrant group in the Plains states. This wave was driven by factors in the United States and in Europe. One major reason was war. Heurich reported for military service but was excused because of poor eyesight. Other draftees simply left to avoid service, which often required a commitment several years, including time in the reserves. Industrialization in Europe reduced the need for labor on farms and promoted immigration not only to America but also within Europe. More-over, technology, especially the growth of the railroads and faster steamships crossing the Atlantic, helped spur the flow of immigration to the American West.[82]

Of all his Kansas experiences, Heurich was most proud of casting his one and only vote for president, that vote being for Republican Ulysses S. Grant in the election of 1868. At the time, some states allowed immigrants to vote if they had begun the process to become citizens. In 1868 Grant easily defeated Democrat Horatio Seymour. He also carried Kansas easily with almost 69 percent of the vote. Heurich would spend most of the rest of his life as a resident of Washington, D.C., and as such, he was unable to cast another vote in a presidential election; residents of the "federal city" were excluded from voting in presidential elections until 1964. Heurich could not even vote for President Grant when he ran for re-election in 1872, as Heurich was living in D.C. by then.[83] Heurich remained fond of Grant, describing the 18th president in his memoirs as "my favorite among the presidents of the United States."[84]

Heurich left Kansas in the spring of 1869 complaining of a recurring fever that may have been a symptom of malaria. He lived for a time with family members[85] in Belleville, Illinois, where he worked as a maltster in a brewery, probably either Loeser & Hartmann or Philip Neu & Peter Gintz, the two breweries operating in that city at the time. He also spent time in nearby St. Louis, Missouri, where he heard a young Joseph Pulitzer speak at a rally. It was probably a local Republican gathering. Heurich had apparently decided to support the Republicans, as he was already a fan of Grant. German-Americans were numerous in the Republican Party. Ironically, Pulitzer was part of the Liberal reforming faction, which opposed Grant, while Heurich remained a fan of the eighteenth president the rest of his life.[86] Whatever Pulitzer's opinion of the former Union general, Heurich was so impressed with the young newsman that he decided to translate Pulitzer's articles from the *Westliche Post* into English for practice. While in St. Louis, as he had in Baltimore and Chicago, Heurich found work at a local brewery, although he does not mention in his memoirs which one. Heurich's health did not improve, however, and he "reluctantly" returned to Baltimore in the spring of 1869. By then, he had spent three years in the U.S.,

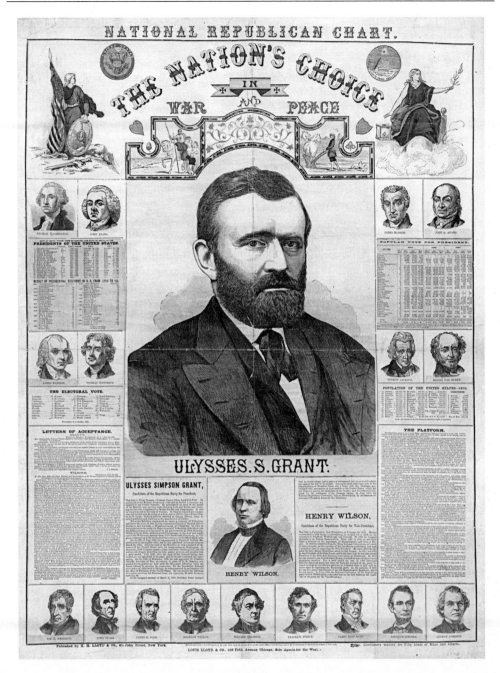

Republican campaign poster, 1872, shows all the presidents including Grant, as well as his running mate, Henry Wilson (Library of Congress).

had seen several major cities in the eastern half of the country, had worked in multiple breweries, but had not yet found a chance to open his own.[87]

Back in Maryland, his brother-in-law suggested that he might regain his health at sea, so Heurich signed on as a common seaman, a "banana roustabout," on his brother-in-law's ship, the *Speculator*.[88] The schooner left Baltimore for Bermuda on May 28, 1869.

From Bermuda they sailed to Kingston, Jamaica. From there they probably went to the San Blas Islands in Panama and then to New York, where they arrived on August 26. Given the normal length of Captain Jacobsen's trips, they probably returned to Baltimore from New York, although it's possible they returned to the Caribbean and then to their home port.[89] Heurich had a miserable trip. He suffered severe seasickness, but kept at his work. By the time the ship returned from its Caribbean run after several months, Heurich's fever was gone and he had visited several new places. Still, he gladly abandoned his brief career as a sailor to restart his interrupted career as a brewer.

He accepted a position as brewmaster at a new brewery in Ripley, Ohio. The brewery only operated for a few months because it was, in Heurich's words, "not run properly and came to a 'blow-up.'" The poorly run brewery failed and was purchased by another in nearby Cincinnati. After returning to Baltimore he went back to work at Seeger's Brewery as the foreman of the malt house for thirty-five dollars a month and board, a respectable if not overly generous salary.[90] The young brewer was gaining more experience and responsibility as he slowly worked his way up in the brewing industry.

While at Seeger's, Heurich was approached by its brewmaster, Paul Ritter, who suggested that they go into business together and buy a brewery. Paul Hugo Ritter was two

Banana boats unloading in New York, circa 1890–1910. A common route for ships such as Captain Jacobsen's went from Baltimore, to the Caribbean, to New York, then back to Baltimore (Library of Congress).

years older than Heurich and a native of Rottweil in Baden-Württemberg in southwestern Germany. Ritter had learned the brewing trade in Rottweil, so he likely went through much the same apprenticeship experience as Heurich. Ritter had immigrated to the United States in 1864 and moved to Cincinnati, Ohio, another city with a large German community and part of the triangle of three Midwestern cities with large German-American populations: Cincinnati; St. Louis, Missouri; and Milwaukee, Wisconsin. Ritter married Katherine Föbel in Cincinnati in about 1866 and they had two sons before moving back to Baltimore. Ritter became brewmaster at the Seeger Brewery, where he met Heurich. The two young men were clearly both interested in advancing in the American brewing industry, but Ritter also had a young, growing family to support.[91] Heurich agreed to go into business with Ritter. He had already been scouring the mid–Atlantic area for a suitable location and had settled on Washington, D.C., just 40 miles south of Baltimore. He had been saving his money, and must have felt he had enough set aside that he could set out on his own. It had been five years and one short-lived attempt to become a brewmaster since he landed in New York, but Heurich was ready to set out on his own in partnership with another young, ambitious German brewer.

The District of Columbia was an attractive opportunity. The national capital's population had increased dramatically during the Civil War; the city boasted 131,000 residents in 1870, compared to 75,000 in 1860. The city was undergoing a burst of new development sparked by the creation of a territorial government in 1871. The most important member of this new government was vice-chair of the D.C. Board of Public Works, Alexander Shepherd. During his tenure as vice-chair (1871–73) and his subsequent term as Washington's second governor (1873–74), Shepherd rebuilt the city, paving roads, adding sewer and gas lines, installing street lights, and filling in the old canal—where Constitution Avenue is now—that had become a fetid sewer. He established the city's first public transportation system (horse-drawn trolleys) and planted 60,000 trees. The city began creating parks and filling the wet areas south of Pennsylvania Avenue to create much of what is now the western area of the National Mall. As a result, early 1870s Washington must have looked like an attractive place to establish a new business. Moreover, there was the added incentive of not having to compete with powerful already established brewers. It seemed an appealing choice for two young German immigrants determined to set out on their own.[92]

2

Early Years in D.C.: 1871–1879

In 1871 Heurich had been in the United States for five years. He had spent much of that time in Baltimore, but had also worked in breweries in Chicago and St. Louis, was a crewman on a ship hauling fruit to the Caribbean, and worked on a farm in Kansas. He had applied for U.S. citizenship and had voted for president for the one and only time in his life, for Ulysses S. Grant in 1868. Now closing in his thirtieth birthday, and having made one aborted start as a brewmaster in Cincinnati, Heurich again began looking for a place to establish his own brewery. While at Seeger's in Baltimore, Heurich was approached by its brewmaster, Paul Ritter, who suggested that they go into business together and buy a brewery. Heurich agreed.

Heurich was about to enter the American brewing industry just as it entered an age of rapid expansion and change. Lager beer, which is aged in cold storage and made with a bottom-fermenting yeast, was introduced sometime about 1840, when ships were at last able to cross the Atlantic in only three weeks, quickly enough that the sensitive brewing yeasts could be transported to America and remain viable. Before lagers came to the U.S., Americans drank ales, which were darker, heavier, and contained more alcohol. Ales also soured easily, and so were less popular than cider, rum, or distilled liquor. Lager was lighter in color and taste than ale, although the early Munich-style lagers were not as light and effervescent as the Bohemian variety that would become popular in the United States about the same time that Heurich's brewery was beginning to grow.

The number of breweries was rapidly growing as beer production leaped after the Civil War, rising from 2.5 million barrels in 1863, to six million in 1867. Breweries existed in every state and territory. By the early 1870s approximately 3,700 breweries competed with one another in the U.S. Although many of them were short-lived, new breweries would pop up to replace those that closed. Moreover, these were largely local businesses with a small capacity compared to the largest breweries a decade or two later. The largest of them, George Ehret of New York, produced 138,449 barrels of beer in 1877. Phillip Best of Milwaukee was second, making 121,634 barrels. By 1900, however, Best (by then named Pabst Brewing) and St. Louis' Anheuser-Busch would top a million barrels a year, but that was still a quarter century in the future. In 1871 Christian Heurich was entering a market crowded with newcomers all competing for a growing market without, as of yet, having to worry about being crowded out by established major brewing corporations. For now, at least, the young German immigrant could fulfill his dream of starting his own business.[1]

Heurich had been making short day trips to nearby cities and towns on his day off

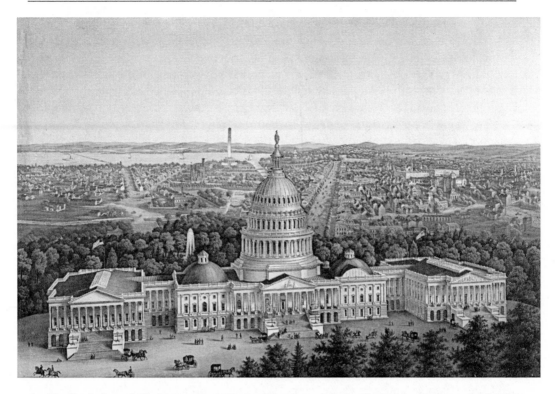

An idealized view of Washington in 1870. Looking east with the Capitol in the foreground. The Potomac River is in the distance. The unfinished Washington Monument rises up in the center. The main street moving away at a right slant is Pennsylvania Avenue. Heurich's first brewery would have been off to the right at the edge of the built-up area. E. Sachse & Co., Lithographer. *View of Washington City* (Library of Congress).

to scout for a location. He decided upon Washington, D.C., rejecting Philadelphia, Pennsylvania, and Wilmington, Delaware, as well as Frederick and Ellicott City in Maryland. Heurich preferred the east coast, he later wrote, "because opportunities in my line were more likely to occur in long-populated areas than in the mushroom-springing towns and cities of the mid-west and the west." He doesn't note why he made this judgment, although his experience with the abortive attempt to start a brewery in Cincinnati may have influenced him. He also seems not to have considered New York. He visited the city "with the idea of studying the breweries [rather] than of opening up my own." Of course, Heurich had not liked New York when he landed there in 1866. He thought the city dirty and full of whiskey rather than beer drinkers. There were also a lot of breweries in the city, well over fifty in 1871, plus another two dozen in Brooklyn.[2]

Despite the presence of a large German population, New York was just not attractive to Heurich. He instead concentrated on areas near Baltimore, where his sister and her family lived. Again, his experiences in 1866 may have influenced him: the rail trip from New York to Baltimore took him all day because the lines was in poor shape. He also considered Richmond, Virginia, as well as several small cities in western Maryland. However, Washington, D.C., topped the young immigrant's list of possible sites for a new brewery.[3]

Why did Heurich and Ritter choose Washington, D.C., as their new home? There is little evidence to guess at Ritter's motivation, but we can look at what may have attracted Christian Heurich to the United States' capital city. There are several relevant factors: the business climate, including potential competitors; D.C.'s geographic location; and finally, personal and aesthetic factors that may well have swayed Heurich. The first matter is to look at the city itself. What was it about Washington as a city in 1871 that attracted Heurich?

The capital's population seemed sufficient to support a brewery. Though Washington's population had increased dramatically during the Civil War, it was still only about one-half the population of Baltimore.[4] But D.C. was home to only four operating breweries in 1870, compared to well over forty in Baltimore. Many of the Baltimore breweries were no doubt small, providing their beer and ale to a single saloon or hotel, but nonetheless, there appeared to be a comparatively severe deficit of breweries in the national's capital. Brewers other than Heurich must have noticed the same thing, because over a dozen new breweries opened in Washington in the 1870s. Some failed quickly, but others sprang up to replace them. Additionally, there were two breweries across the river in Alexandria, Virginia, one of which, Robert Portner's, became one of the largest breweries in the South.[5]

In the 1870s, however, beer was not easily transported long distances. Over 90 percent was sold on draft. Bottles were heavy and expensive to ship. Some breweries would ship kegs of their beer to distant locations, where it was bottled by a local bottler, but this was an added expense, especially since refrigeration was cumbersome and expensive. As a result, most beer was made and consumed locally. What did this mean for Heurich and Ritter? Cumberland, Maryland, which had five operating breweries in 1870, was over one hundred and thirty miles away, too far away to easily compete with those in the District. Towns close to D.C. were generally too small to support a brewery on their own. There were about 29,000 people in Alexandria City and Alexandria County combined, but Fairfax and Falls Church numbered barely in the hundreds. Richmond was an industrial center, but it was a hundred miles away and still recovering from the war. So any new brewery in Washington had only Baltimore's breweries as their most likely competitors, and even though Baltimore was only forty miles to the north, that still meant its breweries were hampered by the cost and difficulties of shipping. Of course, Heurich and Ritter still had more than enough local competitors with which to contend, since other eager local brewers were entering the market, but there was a business opening to exploit here. No other city in the east combined a significantly-sized population with a lack of large established breweries.

Moreover, as Heurich himself noted in his memoirs, D.C. was undergoing a burst of new development:

> [I]n 1870, in which year I made several trips, [Washington] seemed to be on the way up. True enough, I stood on the step of the Capitol one autumn afternoon and saw ahead of me nothing but Virgin forest, but I came back again in a very few weeks and the change was, to say the least, startling; streets were being laid out, trees were being planted by the hundreds, sewers were being put in and buildings were going up so fast I could see them actually growing![6]

This growth was sparked by the creation of a territorial government in 1871 that established self-rule for the city for the first time since its founding. The District of Columbia and Washington City had for seventy years undergone a series of different governments. The District of Columbia Organic Act of 1801 placed the territory under the control of the U.S. Congress, but that body was never certain how best to handle the federal district.

As a result, they largely neglected the District's needs. Moreover, the District and Washington City were not originally the same thing. There were two counties and three cities in the District of Columbia. Washington County lay to the north and east of the Potomac River, while the Virginia side was Alexandria County. The cities of Alexandria and Georgetown maintained their existing governments. In 1846 the Virginia section was ceded back to Virginia via retrocession. During the Civil War the U.S. Congress considered, but rejected, the idea of re-annexing the Virginia portion.[7] The District remained in three parts, Washington City, Georgetown and the county of Washington, until they were joined in 1871 by the Organic Act, creating a new territorial government for the District. The entire area was now Washington, the District of Columbia.

The most important member of this new government was not the first governor, but the vice-chair of the D.C. Board of Public Works, thirty-six-year-old Alexander Shepherd. That made Shepherd the effective head of the D.C. Board of Public Works, a position he held from 1871 to 1873, before serving as governor of the District of Columbia until 1874. Shepherd was one of a group of reformers who wanted to make Washington into a world-class showcase city. Although Shepherd was a native of the District, many of the other members of the Committee were from elsewhere. Historian Allan Lessoff traced those he labeled "improvers" and found that many of the members were newcomers from the North. They were also young; the mean age was forty-one, compared to the mean age of forty-eight for the District as a whole. Lessoff describes the improvers as "young entrepreneurs, overly infused with the 'Northern' spirit of the Gilded Age." Their adversaries in the Citizens Executive Committee opposed the new territorial government and large-scale expensive improvements, and complained that Shepherd's supporters were "carpetbaggers." This echoed the Southern states' "redeemer" campaigns during Reconstruction. The Redeemers wanted to return to a whites-only government and to eliminate the power and influence of industrialist newcomers from the North as well as to disenfranchise the newly freed slaves. The same struggle would be repeated in many respects in Washington in the 1870s, including opposition to African American voting rights, but during the short life of the territorial government, Shepherd and his allies rebuilt the city.[8]

Shepherd responded to the post–Civil War movement in Congress to relocate the U.S. capital to St. Louis. He did so by rebuilding Washington—paving roads, adding sewer and gas lines, and installing street lights. Shepherd finally dealt with the old Washington City Canal, which ran through the center of the city (along what is now Constitution Avenue) following Tiber Creek. The canal had never been of much use: it was too shallow, silted up quickly, and ended up being an open sewer. Shepherd finally had the canal covered over and the start of a new, modern sewer system built. Residential streets were graded to make them uniform, and railroads with lines into the city were forced to grade their tracks to match the streets. Finally, Pennsylvania Avenue, arguably the center street of the city, was dealt with. The street's surface was in terrible condition. Its cobblestones were falling apart and it was prone to flooding. Wooden blocks specially treated to delay rot seemed to be the answer, and in early 1871, as Heurich and Ritter were looking for a suitable city to start their new business, Washington held a festival to celebrate the repaving of Pennsylvania Avenue. At last Washington looked as if it might start to resemble a world-class capital city.[9]

The improvements were expensive—Shepherd built up more than ten million dollars in debt—and although Congress abandoned the idea of moving the capital, Shepherd's spending shocked Congress and they revoked D.C.'s territorial status. Of course, this was not especially challenging, as Congress tended to resent spending any money on the city, and cutting the District's budget became a favorite way for Congressmen to demonstrate their "frugal" ways to the folks back home. Shepherd went into self-imposed exile in Mexico, where he managed silver mines. He returned to the District in September 1887, where he was greeted by the locals with dinners. The *Evening Star* noted, "So many visitors and old-time friends came to see him at his Washington retreat that it was impossible for him to obtain the rest and quiet necessary to his complete recovery" from a head injury suffered in his Mexican mine.[10]

Heurich was impressed by Shepherd's efforts, later calling him "God's gift to Washington at a sorely needed time." A 1942 Heurich beer advertisement called him one of "Washington History's Heroes." Shepherd's rebuilding not only changed the areas of the city inhabited by the federal government, which lawmakers and their staffs often occupied for only part of the year, but also for the city's fulltime residents and businesses. Washington's founders had intended the city to be a place not only for the government to function, but also for businesses to thrive as well. Despite these hopes, Washington always lagged far behind nearby Baltimore economically. With the infrastructure built by Shepherd, it seemed as if the city might be able to fulfill the dream of making it a business center. However, as Alan Lessoff points out, Shepherd turned Washington away from a possible future as an industrial city, into one where the economy centered on serving the U.S. government. Fortunes in D.C. were to be made, not in manufacturing, but in utilities, real estate, and high-end retail. As the city spread north from the area centered on the White House and Capitol, the new areas were dominated by residential development, while industry was pushed west and south towards the Potomac and Anacostia Rivers. Heurich's career exemplified these trends—his brewery ended up on the western edge of the city, along the Potomac, while his mansion was in a wealthy neighborhood north of the White House. Moreover, he made much of his fortune investing in real estate.[11]

There were other factors besides the business climate and Shepherd's improvements to attract Heurich. As noted earlier, Washington was close enough to Baltimore to make visiting his family there relatively easy. Moreover, as in Baltimore, there was a German-speaking community in the District. Washington's small but lively German-American population included 5,000 residents, roughly between 3 and 4 percent of the city's population. There were a number of active German-American organizations, such as the *Columbia-Turn-Verein* (a gymnastics club), which hosted balls, theater productions, English classes, and other courses. There was also a *Sängerbund*, or singing club, and two *Schützenverein* (shooting clubs), each of which owned a park. In addition, the German-American community supported boating clubs, a fishing club, and other organizations that entertained the general public as well. Washington, D.C., was also home to a German newspaper and numerous Catholic and Protestant churches, as well as a Jewish synagogue. Thus, Heurich and Ritter were moving to a city where they would find an established immigrant community.[12]

Cities are also part of larger networks, connected by trade, finance, established business and family ties, communications, and travel networks, as well as through political connections. Washington was on the southeastern periphery of the growing but already extensive railroad network that connected the industrial Midwest and the northeast. D.C. was connected economically to Baltimore, western Maryland, and parts of Virginia via railroad and a canal. The city also had a small port, and there was regular ship traffic through the Chesapeake Bay region stretching from Baltimore to D.C. to Norfolk. The railroads, however, were especially critical at this time, and once Heurich expanded his business, it would be into Virginia and Maryland, eventually adding branches in Norfolk and Baltimore, the cities at the ends of the local transportation network.

Finally, Washington under Shepherd may have struck a familiar and welcoming chord within Heurich as having something of the flavor of Vienna, a city the young immigrant loved. Of course, Washington was exceptionally crude compared to the Hapsburg capital, even though both cities were national capitals; but both were rebuilding as Heurich visited them. Vienna was constructing its famous *Ringstraße*, a wide tree-shaded thoroughfare lined with opulent public and private buildings reflecting the glory of the Hapsburg Empire. When Heurich was surveying Washington, Shepherd was creating a central federal area surrounded with wide, tree-lined streets that would also be lined with impressive public and private buildings. Vienna was more successful than D.C. in limiting commercial traffic in the city's center, as railroads continued to operate along Washington's main streets, although the stinking sewer of the canal was finally covered over. It's possible that Heurich saw in Washington some echoes of the pleasures of a fine capital city, or at least the potential to eventually echo the grace and charm of his beloved Vienna.

The two partners agreed on Washington as their new home, and in September 1872, they put up about $1,000 each (approximately $18,400 in 2010) to form Ritter and Heurich. They rented the Schnell Brewery and Tavern on 20th Street NW between M and N Streets for $1,600 a year (approximately $29,500 in 2010). Their landlord asked for six months' rent in advance, in case the new business failed. Founded by George Schnell in 1864, the brewery produced about 500 barrels of wheat (or weiss) beer per year, much of which was sold at its adjacent tavern and beer garden. According to Heurich, the brewery was "run-down." He later remembered, "Of the five breweries operating in the capital ... the worst of these, I came to be informed, was the Schnell Brewery." Heurich described that part of D.C. in 1872 as "sparsely inhabited and a little cluster of buildings in the neighborhood stood sort of by themselves. All around were fields, many of them cultivated ...

The George Schnell Brewery that Heurich and his partner turned into their own in 1872 (courtesy American Breweriana Association).

cornstalks of the last harvest lay on the edge of DuPont Circle." Besides the brewery, there were two small houses and a beer saloon connected to the brewery. Heurich disliked whiskey, and took the trouble to make it clear: "I mean a beer saloon."[13]

They were far from the city center. In 1872 the area was on the outskirts of the city and there were still farmer's fields nearby.[14] A paving map from the period shows many of the streets around the brewery would just have been paved in 1873. The paving material varied, but included wood, stone and concrete, 20th Street would be the latter. Just two blocks west, the roads remained dirt. Some of this land was owned by August Mueller, Schnell's father-in-law. Heurich noted that Mueller "farmed the land from DuPont Circle to the edge of my brewery." DuPont Circle, then known as Pacific Circle, had just been constructed by the U.S. Army Corps of Engineers in 1871, and Shepherd's improvements included the first water and sewer lines in the area. Besides Mueller's farm, Heurich's neighbors included a brickyard and slaughterhouse, both businesses often found on the industrial zones on the edge of cities.[15]

Heurich would live the rest of his life in this same area, although he also spent time in a farm he built in suburban Maryland. The mansion he would build in the 1890s, and where he died in 1945, was less than two blocks from where his original brewery stood. However, the area itself changed dramatically in those decades, and Heurich's life mirrored those changes, reflecting the evolving nature of the place where he chose to live and work. In sociology there is a difference between "space" and "place." Space is abstract, taking form in "the structural, geometrical qualities of a physical environment," while "place" is particular, a community created by its residents. They define the "place" and delimitate its boundaries through use by those who live, work, and travel within it. The residents of a specific place set their own "identity boundaries," as individuals and as groups, and they protect their "space" from incursion by outsiders, physically as well as in the form of claims made on the place by the wider community.[16] For Heurich, the "space" he occupied beginning in 1872 was along New Hampshire Avenue and 20th Street. However, the definitions of that same "place" evolved over the last quarter of the nineteenth century. When he moved to the area with Ritter, they were on the boundary of Washington City. What later became Florida Avenue was named "Boundary Street" at the time, marking the border between the developed area and the undeveloped. Like many border spaces, it was a place to put businesses and people that were only marginally welcome. As such, it was an area of light industry, including the brewery and slaughterhouses as well as brickyards. There was farmland there and the residents would have been classified as working class. However, the area was beginning to turn more and more residential, and so while Heurich's brewery remained in the same "space," it gradually began to no longer fit into how the area defined itself as a "place." That still lay twenty years in the future when Heurich began, but his actions in the 1870s, including improving his own economic circumstances, lay the foundation for that very transformation.

A month later they were busy brewing. Ritter worked as salesman and bookkeeper and Heurich brewed the beer, getting up at 3:00 a.m. and working until nightfall, making "a good mild German lager" that he only aged for a week before selling. In his memoirs, Heurich noted that "Frank," described as an "aged colored man," did most of the work at the brewery for the original owner. He was kept on as deliveryman and porter: he "remained a faithful employee of mine until his death." Ritter and his family lived in a small house at 1231 20th Street next to the brewery, while Heurich rented a room from

The Heurich brewery sometime in the 1870s. From the brewery tour pamphlet, "A See Trip through a Great Brewery," circa 1937 (author collection).

them. Ritter's wife tended to the small attached barroom where their beer was sold. Their production started small. Heurich made at most only five barrels a day at first, sometimes as few as three, but as the beer became better known around the area, demand grew.[17] He remembered later that lagers were still new. "Many still brewed top fermented beers," much of which "was dark, cloudy, [and] heavy-bodied."[18]

Heurich and Ritter's choice of Washington as a good market for a new brewery was apparently shared by others. Between 1873 and 1876 at least twelve breweries opened in the District. Not many were long-lived. Six closed in a year or two. Four of the remainder went out of business by 1885. One lasted into the 20th century, but closed before the capital went dry in 1917. The multitude of new breweries was not a unique situation to D.C. in the 1870s. A study of brewery opening and closing from 1633 to 1988 demonstrated that a "density dependence" operated with brewers as it did for other businesses. Density dependence asserts that as different examples of a particular type of business open, that creates a sense of "legitimacy" which attracts other businesspeople to open similar businesses. This sense of legitimacy does not necessarily include a moral sense, although with breweries that played a role as well. Instead, legitimacy refers to a business's demonstrating that it is viable. This will attract competition. In the case of breweries in the 1870s, a second, moral sense of the word also applies in the wake of the antebellum temperance movement. The temperance movement had reached a peak in the 1850s. In 1851 Maine passed a law banning alcoholic beverages. Twelve other states followed with their own "Maine Laws." The movement stalled as it became clear that these laws were unpopular and unworkable. Maine, for example, suffered numerous anti-temperance riots. The Civil War further weakened the temperance cause as soldiers drank to fight cold and boredom and the U.S. government began to increasingly rely on taxes on whiskey and beer to finance the war. These taxes continued to be an important financial resource for the federal government even after the war. However, the temperance forces still existed, and there was still strong suspicion that making and selling alcoholic beverages was not a legitimate business among parts of American society.[19]

Not all new breweries prospered. Carroll and Swarminathan's study of breweries found that the mean longevity of a brewery was 14.6 years. The median length of time a brewery stayed in business was only eight years. The situation was a bit better in Washington, D.C., in Heurich's era. The average length of time a brewery that operated between the Civil War and Prohibition remained in business was 17.9 years. The median was four years. If you include the three breweries from this period that operated in Alexandria (county and city both), then the numbers improve. The average time a brewery operated was 20.8 years and the median was nine, but of the breweries in the area, only a handful dominated the local market in the 1870s and 1880s into the beginning of the 20th century.[20] Heurich's was one of them, along with John Albert's, George Juenemann's, and the Adt family brewery in D.C. Heurich's three main competitors changed ownership multiple times, operating under different names, but, along with Heurich, remained in business until 1917. Moreover, two of his competitors across the river in northern Virginia were still operating when Virginia went dry in 1916.[21]

Of Heurich's longest-lasting D.C. competitors, what would eventually become the National Capital Brewing Company was the oldest. It was founded in 1850 by George Beckert, a German immigrant who came to the United States with his wife in 1844. In 1850 they opened "Beckert's Garden" in the Capitol Hill area. It was a beer garden with picnic grounds along with a restaurant and the requisite saloon. Beckert died in 1859 and the brewery changed hands several times over the next decades. In 1872 Beckert's beer garden was run by a son-in-law, Hermann Richter. Alexander and Francis Adt owned it from 1874 until 1882. John Guethler operated the brewery and an even larger beer garden until 1886. Henry Rabe purchased the brewery and expanded its capacity to 30,000 barrels a year. In 1890 Rabe sold out to Albert Carry and Robert Portner. Carry (originally Carri) owned several breweries in D.C. over several decades. He was also a German immigrant, although his family had moved to Germany from Italy earlier. He came to the United States in 1872, working in Cincinnati, as Heurich briefly did, before coming to Washington in 1886. Carry and Portner renamed their new firm the National Capital Brewing Company, a name it kept until closing in 1917. Portner sold his interests after a few years, but Carry continued running the brewery, and under him it expanded and modernized further. National Capital Brewing had a capacity by the end of the nineteenth century of 100,000 barrels. The five-story structure produced several different lager beers and, like most breweries at the time, sold mostly draft beer for local consumption.[22]

The second of Heurich's longtime competitors to open was the Washington Brewing Company, one of several breweries to use that name. Founded in 1858 by Owen Humphrey and George Juenemann, it was originally known as the Juenemann Brewery. Juenemann was another German immigrant, coming to the United States in 1851 and working in D.C. as a tailor before starting his brewery. Renamed the Mount Vernon Lager Beer Brewery and Pleasure Garden, it was the largest brewery in D.C. before being overtaken by Heurich's. Juenemann died in 1884. His widow ran the brewery until selling it to Albert Carry in 1886. Carry modernized this brewery, as he would the National Capital Brewery later, increasing its capacity to 100,000 barrels. Juenemann's old brewery was Carry's for only a brief time, as he sold it to a British syndicate in 1889. The syndicate rechristened it as the Washington Brewery, featuring George Washington the centerpiece of its logo. It operated under this name until 1917.[23]

The last of Heurich's main D.C. competitors was founded by John Albert in 1870. Albert & Company was located in Foggy Bottom, near where the Watergate Complex would eventually be built. In 1897 Albert's son sold the company to Edward Abner, whose uncle was active in local breweries, including Portner's. Abner's business partner was an Irish immigrant, Peter Drury. The Abner-Drury brewery expanded along the Potomac waterfront, not far from where Heurich's brewery operated from the 1890s until 1956. The Drury family ran the brewery until D.C. went dry in 1917, and it was the only local brewery aside from Heurich's that reopened in 1933 after Prohibition.[24]

There were also three additional close competitors in northern Virginia: Robert Portner's and Henry Englehardt's breweries in Alexandria, and the Arlington Brewery in the Rosslyn area of Alexandria County. Englehardt's Shuter's Hill Brewery was founded in 1858. Englehardt, at first its brewmaster, purchased it in 1872 and operated it until it burned down in 1893. It was always a small brewery, concentrating on a small part of the local market.[25] The most prominent of Heurich's Virginia competitors was Robert Portner's Tivoli Brewery. Portner, a German native from Westphalia, began his brewery in Alexandria in 1862, providing beer for the thousands of Union troops occupying northern Virginia during the Civil War. After the war he expanded his Tivoli Brewery, and through adopting the newest technology, his business grew to become one of the largest in the South. Portner, one of the first brewers to take advantage of the new refrigerated railcars to ship his beer, had over fifty depots in Virginia, the Carolinas and Georgia. He also invested in the National Capital Brewing Company, described above, and Portner and co-investor Albert Carry divided the local market between themselves. National Capital would sell their product north of the Potomac River and Tivoli would sell south of the river. Portner died in 1906 and his brewery closed when Virginia went dry in 1916.[26]

The newest of Heurich's major local competitors was the Arlington Brewery, which began as the Consumers Brewery in 1895 in Rosslyn, Virginia. Built overlooking the Potomac River across from Georgetown, it was renamed the Arlington Brewery in 1902. With a capacity of 100,000 barrels, the brewery was modern, if short-lived. When it was built, Rosslyn was filled with legal and illegal saloons, as well as gambling houses, brothels, and a popular race track. After a short-lived attempt to survive on the D.C. market alone,[27] it closed when Virginia went totally dry in 1916.

As Heurich and Ritter began their new business in 1872, their task was not so much competition with the other area breweries, but simply to get their own brewery operational. With Heurich as brewmaster, they switched from weiss beer to the barley-based, light lager he had learned to brew as a journeyman in Europe. The brewery began to catch on, but the partnership quickly dissolved, and Heurich bought out Ritter on August 2, 1873, to become the sole proprietor.[28] Heurich never specified why the break occurred, but he noted in his memoirs that "right was on my side." The Ritter family history claims that Heurich was "jealous of Paul [who] was out meeting the public and selling the product while Christian was stuck back in the brewery." It is possible that Heurich may have thought that Ritter was taking too much credit for the brewery's excellent beer, since Heurich always stayed behind making the beer while Ritter went out to sell the product. Ritter did start his own brewery in western Maryland, but it was never as successful as Heurich's, which suggests that the latter was in fact making the better beer. Whatever the reason for the break, Heurich bought out Ritter and started running the business by himself. At the time, he was producing two beers, a light lager and "a full bodied dark brew." He often worked eighteen-hour days to meet the demand for his product, which proved so popular that he had to put customers on a waiting list.[29]

Heurich's long days were not as far outside the norm as it might seem today. Working in a brewery like Heurich's in the 1860s and early 1870s demanded long hours and hard work. Days were long; fourteen to eighteen hours a day, six days a week, plus six to eight hours on Sundays, was common. As one union publication noted:

> [I]t might be said that they were always working except when they were asleep. A foreman malter from Buffalo reports as follows concerning the hours of labor in malteries in the year 1863: "Work began at five o'clock in the morning, and, with the exception of an hour for breakfast and for dinner, it lasted until six in the evening. At eight the men went to work again, in order to finish their floor and kiln work, which lasted until half-past nine or ten o'clock."

This description was written in 1910, after decades of workers fighting for better hours. In the 1870s and 1880s the day often began at four in the morning, and sometimes as early as two a.m., with the workday continuing until dark the following evening. It's telling that in 1889, when St. Louis brewery workers got a new contract, their union succeeded in reducing their work week to twelve hours a day, six days a week. Wages for these long hours were not generous. In the 1860s they averaged about twenty to twenty-five dollars a month, which increased to about fourteen dollars a week by the 1880s. One benefit was the *sternewirth*, the beverage privilege, or all the free beer the worker could consume. This supposedly made up for the long hours, but it could also lead to alcoholism. Some breweries included room and board, which in a small brewery might simply mean that the workers lived with the brewery owner's family. Larger breweries could contract with local boarding houses, which also sold the brewery's beer. Some brewers charged for room and board, often about five dollars a week, which could significantly decrease a worker's salary. Sometimes the "room" in "room and board" was simply allowing the exhausted worker to sleep on a hops sack in the brewery. Finally, violence in the workplace was not uncommon, as managers could strike workers as a disciplinary measure.[30]

Most breweries were still tiny; five or six workers were the norm, including the owner/brewer. Seeger's, where Heurich worked in Baltimore, was a somewhat larger brewer, so it would have had more workers. The number of employees on average in American breweries doubled from 1870 to 1880 and then doubled again from 1880 to 1890, when the average was twenty-six workers per brewery. These larger numbers included foremen, but not necessarily the owner except in the smallest firms. Working conditions varied, although the work was always hard, and the conditions often unpleasant. The brew kettles had to be kept hot, which could lead to stifling conditions. In 1888 ten brewery workers died of heatstroke in St. Louis alone during the hot summer. On the other extreme, working in the cold lagering vaults and icehouses could lead to rheumatism. Workers who were too old to work elsewhere might find themselves in the bottle shop, at least after 1880 when bottling became more common. This could also be dangerous, as over-pressurized bottles could explode into the worker's eyes. It says something about this period of industrialization, however, that conditions in other industries were often worse, and breweries rarely, if ever, lacked for workers.[31]

Breweries were also a common form of immigrant business. Historian Cindy Lobel's study of food and culture in New York in the nineteenth century, *Urban Appetites*, discusses how immigrant businesses dealing in food and beverage served immigrant communities. They provided food and drink that were familiar to immigrants. They provided economic opportunity, they helped ease the assimilation process for newcomers, and they often provided other services, such as information centers, post offices, translation services, etc. Lobel's model fit breweries in cities such as New York and Cincinnati, but Heurich's business did not fit this model well largely because Washington did not have the large immigration population necessary to create immigrant-dominated neighborhoods. As noted earlier, there was no *Kleindeutschland* in D.C. The existing German population in the city probably welcomed Heurich's lager beer, which was still being introduced to American drinkers, but the newcomer's customers would have to come from somewhere other than the local immigrant society. So who did make up Heurich's customer base?[32]

The federal government created Washington, and its presence has always shaped the city, from its geography to the local economy, to the makeup of its population. However, Washington's inhabitants, while ultimately dependent upon the presence of the federal government for their town's economic life, also had to include the types of workers necessary to keep any city operating. Moreover, Washington's society was divided along lines of class and status. Heurich noted that the upper classes preferred wine and whiskey to beer. Accordingly, his very first customers came not from the city's elite, but rather from the working and middle classes who, along with African Americans, comprised the city's permanent, full-time population. They included lower-ranking government functionaries, such as clerks and secretaries, as well as those nongovernmental workers. As Heurich later bragged, "It was mighty good beer and the Washington of that day, full of workmen on the projects initiated by … Shepherd, needed good German lager."[33] In his memoirs he noted that the "lower [classes] when their day of toil was done, clung closely to the little beer taverns and restaurants of their neighborhoods," including his brewery and saloon on 20th Street. Historian Jon Kingsdale noted how saloons acted as a "poor man's club." "In its most encompassing function," he explained, "the saloon served many workingmen as a second home [and the] middle-class male [could retire] to the corner saloon to meet his friends." Heurich tapped into this market in what was a rapidly growing urban area. He also tapped into the growing restaurant and hotel scene, which was expanding along with the city.[34]

The saloon or tavern was also markedly an adult masculine space in the early 1870s, a far cry from the more family-oriented beer gardens of Vienna or the beer gardens common in so many German-American communities, including Washington's. Saloons ran the range from exclusive and well-appointed to dives with little more than a board stretched across two barrels. Heurich's initial saloon was attached to his brewery and served only his own beer, and not distilled beverages with a higher alcohol content, such as whiskey. No descriptions survive of the interior of Heurich's first establishment, but if it fit the typical model, there would have been tables and chairs set around the room, along with a bar where customers would stand. Sawdust would have covered the floor (to soak up spit tobacco juice) and pictures of favorite sporting figures may have been on the wall. Paintings of a pretty woman *dishabille* were also common, although since Ritter's wife originally worked at the bar, followed by Heurich's sister Elisabeth and then his first wife Amelia, it may have lacked this feature. The lack of whiskey sales not only reflected the influence of the traditional German beer garden, it reflected Heurich's own dislike of the liquor.

Single men dominated the working-class saloon of the era. The saloon acted as a social club, and early on, Heurich's fit this criterion. In addition, as a brewer, Heurich himself fit into the working class, even though he was also the firm's owner. In terms of class ranking, artisans, including brewers, generally were numbered among the working or lower-middle classes in the 1860s and 1870s. Status, of course, would vary somewhat by trade and according to the artisan's personal income. Some generalizations can be made for brewers in large urban areas of the United States in the mid-nineteenth century. In the 1840s and 1850s they were roughly equal socially with saloonkeepers. By 1870 their status would have been about the same, but just as Heurich was entering the competition with his own brewery, an opening had begun to appear, allowing brewers to climb in status. A major cause of this opening was the technological changes that were beginning to affect the brewing industry, allowing for a much great production volume. The small brewer who hired a half dozen or fewer workers who lived with the brewer and his family would continue to exist, but was being eclipsed professionally and socially by the emergence of the beer barons or "Brewer Princes." Men such as New York's George Ehret and Jacob Ruppert became wealthy industrialists. Their breweries' sales would jump from the tens of thousands of dollars annually into the millions, and their production from a few hundred or a few thousand barrels, into the hundreds of thousands. Eventually Christian Heurich would follow the same path.[35]

Heurich was part of a larger trend in his choice of a trade, as German immigrants dominated the American brewing industry. German immigrants and their first-generation children made up 11 percent of the male workforce, according to the 1880 census. However, they were notably dominant in several skilled trades, especially brewing. Slightly over 80 percent of those identified in the 1880 census as brewers (15,449) were German. Seventy-six percent of pork butchers and sausage makers were also German. These two trades were still somewhat intertwined with brewing in the nineteenth century. Remember that Heurich apprenticed to learn both trades, before concentrating on brewing. Knowing how to make beer, and how to turn a pig into sausages, would have been useful for someone who was going to operate an inn in a small village or town, where beer and food were served. Heurich's father was an innkeeper, so it is possible he had learned both trades as well, or at least was familiar with them. In addition, 44 percent of saloon employees were German, as were a third of those listed as bartender, both certainly occupations associated with brewing.[36]

Heurich was still a long way off from entering the city's elite in 1872, separate not only in status, but set apart geographically. The Washington elite tended to live and work near Pennsylvania Avenue and in expensive neighborhoods such as parts of Georgetown. Heurich's brewery was slightly north of the area where the wealthy and powerful lived in 1872, and his customers came from the local neighborhood. By the 1890s, however, the area where Heurich settled would shift from borderland working class to upper-class. By then he was welcome as a residential neighbor, but, as we shall see, his brewery was increasingly out of place, and he moved his business to an industrial area near the Potomac River south of Georgetown.

Because Heurich had to run the brewery himself, his sister Elisabeth came down from Baltimore to help. She also encouraged Heurich to find a wife. Heurich told his sister that he had a girl in mind, but thought he was too busy to be married. Elisabeth suggested that he ask the girl anyway. Heurich agreed, mustered his courage, and, after being literally pushed out of his house by Elisabeth, "dashed" to his next-door neighbor, August Mueller, who farmed the land by DuPont Circle next to Heurich's brewery. Mueller was a German immigrant, and was listed in an earlier city directory as a brewer and bottler, as well as a florist and gardener. Heurich proposed to Mueller's daughter, Amelia, who immediately accepted. Amelia was not only Heurich's neighbor, she also was the widow of George Schnell, who had leased the brewery to Heurich. Schnell had died in November 1872, leaving everything to his wife. Heurich and Amelia were married on September 9, 1873. Heurich was a few days shy of his thirty-first birthday, and his bride was almost a year older.[37] It was by all accounts a happy marriage, although a nephew later noted that it was "not born of misty-eyed romance. It was a practical solution to a pressing problem."[38]

September 1873 was a month of both personal and historical turning points; it saw not only Heurich's wedding, but also the beginning of a global depression. Changes in the worldwide silver market had already weakened the U.S. economy when American financier Jay Cooke's Northern Pacific Railway was forced to declare bankruptcy that month. Cooke's bank was subsequently forced to close, then more banks failed, and the New York stock market collapsed. Throughout the nation, businesses went bankrupt and closed. Heurich noted in his memoirs that his business did not seem to suffer: he continued selling about eight barrels a week and making about $100 weekly (approximately $1,880 in 2010), one third of which was profit. That translated into an average a profit of about $1,700 a year (approximately $32,000 in 2010) at a time when the average annual wage for a U.S. worker was about $384 a year (approximately $7,220 in 2010). So Heurich's business—still small-scale and local in nature—was doing well. He continued to do much of the work himself, acting as brewer, salesman, and deliveryman. He lived at his 20th Street brewery with Amelia, a female servant, and several workers. In his second year of business, Heurich added six more employees, who, in the German craft tradition, lived with the family. As his business expanded, Heurich not only hired more workers but also brought relatives and others over from Germany, including some of his brother August Friedrich's sons. They sometimes paid their passage with their labor upon arrival.[39]

Heurich actively promoted his business. In the summer of 1875 he sponsored a bar stand at the Washington *Schützverein's* 10th Grand *Schuetzenfest* at the society's park, although the *Evening Star* identified him as "Charles" Heurich. The park was on Seventh Street (now Georgia Avenue) just above Florida Avenue in what was then a "sparsely settled" area. Stretching between Hobart and Kenyon Streets, it stretched back about 400 to 500 feet and was surrounded by a wood fence. Most of the activities occurred outdoors, although there were buildings for meetings and dinners. Several thousand people could attend events at the park. Small boys would sneak in using "return passes" given to people as they left and then passed from one boy to another through holes in the fence. Once inside they could earn money by running errands such as delivering ice cream and, probably, rushing a few growlers of beer. Veterans from the local Soldiers' Home would come to the park to relax and have a beer with friends; there would be shooting contests and circus acts, and sometimes one of the club members would pull out a cannon to set off to thrill the crowd. No doubt Heurich and Amelia enjoyed time at the park with their friends from the German community, strolling through the park, dodging running children, and, given Heurich's desire for children of his own, perhaps discussing starting their own family.[40]

This was not the only way Heurich participated in local society. He was also a member of the Washington delegation to a national brewers' convention in Cincinnati, along with two other D.C. brewers and Alexandria's Robert Portner. Thirty-three years old, Heurich was the youngest of the four men, and of the three brewers, had the newest brewery. Fellow delegate George Juenemann had opened his D.C. brewery in about 1850, and Portner's had started in 1862. The fourth member was Louis Schade, a local lawyer whose clients included the brewer's association. All four were German immigrants.[41]

Not everything was calm for Heurich. In 1875 his 20th Street brewery survived the first of three fires. A chimney spark set some of the roof on fire and caused "several thousand in damage." Fire was a common hazard in breweries. Of course, brewing required heating the product, which was often done with an open flame. As steam boilers became more popular, they added to the fire hazard. Moreover, malt dust is flammable, so the malting rooms were a known hazard. Breweries were commonly constructed of wood, but in the latter part of the nineteenth century they were replaced by steel, brick, and concrete structures. In the 1890s Heurich would oversee not only the construction of a new fireproof brewery, but also a fireproof home.[42]

Besides fire, Heurich had other work troubles at times. On February 9, 1878, he had two of his employees arrested for stealing copper pipe. That morning a policeman approached Heurich and asked if he was missing any copper pipe. He was. Some pipe that had just been stored in the cooper's shop on the brewery grounds was missing. The officer told Heurich that a bag full of copper pipe had been found nearby, along with a man's coat. The coat smelled of beer, and was identified as belonging to Charles Coleman, a workman at the brewery. Coleman and his half-brother William Neil had moved the pipe to the shed where it was stored. The shed was locked and guarded by a "fierce dog within the brewery enclosure" at night, but was open in the day. Coleman and Neil had already been arrested and were in custody, probably at the nearby station at K and 20th Streets. Heurich thought the men looked "suspicious" and asked the policeman and a justice of the peace at the station their opinion, and upon being told that it would be proper to swear out a warrant, he did so. The two men were charged with the theft. The next day Heurich's wife paid their bail, upon her husband's request. The charges ended up being dismissed and Coleman and Neil then sued Heurich for $10,000 each. After a jury trial, Neil was awarded $50 and Coleman got nothing. An appeal went to the Supreme Court of the District of Columbia, and in 1883 the Court found for Heurich. The advice he had been given by the policemen and the justice of the peace to press charges was not legal justification, as neither were legally competent to give such advice. But the court ruled his decision was reasonable, and that "given the array of facts," a reasonable man "would have been fully justified in suing out the warrant."[43]

In July 1878 Heurich was attacked by "two roughs" in the restaurant attached to his brewery. According to the *Evening Star*:

> Henry Tanner, alias Henry Goldsmith, and John Curran ... went to Heurich's place and forced themselves into his windows in the daytime, after having been refused an entrance, and assault[ed] the proprietor, acting in a very disorderly manner. Blows were struck and a general melee followed, until the [police] officers came upon the ground.

Tanner and Curran were each sentenced to sixty days in jail, and Tanner was fined an additional $10 or thirty days for "assault and battery on Sergeant Perry in attempting to arrest him." Less than two weeks later Heurich had to leap from his carriage when his horse ran away from him on Virginia Avenue. Heurich was not injured, but his carriage was "demolished by colliding with a pump." Unfortunately for Heurich, this was not the end of his troubles in 1878.[44]

In 1874 Heurich was invited to join the officers of Washington's German-American

German American Savings Bank,

No. 632 F Street, Cor. Seventh, nw.

WASHINGTON, D. C.

CHR. HEURICH,	JOHN HITZ,	CHARLES E. PRENTISS,
R. B. DONALDSON	JAMES M. LEWIS,	CHRISTIAN RUPPERT,
	WM. F. MATTINGLY.	

BANK HOURS—Ten o'clock A. M. to Three o'clock P. M. Open on Saturday evenings from Six to Eight o'clock to receive deposits only.

INTEREST PAID ON DEPOSITS.

Small Safes for rent in fire and burglar proof vault. Government bonds and other securities and valuables received for safe keeping, at special rates.

JOHN HITZ, *President.*   C. E. PRENTISS, *Treasurer.*
WM. F. MATTINGLY, *Secretary.*   S. L. MATTINGLY, *Asst. Treasurer.*

An advertisement for the German-American Bank, prominently listing Heurich. *Boyd's Directory of the District of Columbia,* 1878.

National Savings Bank, which had been founded the year before. He was exceptionally proud of the fact that, after only a few years in business, he had entered the ranks of the city's leading businessmen. In letters to his family back in Germany, he bragged of his success, not only as a brewer, but also as a bank director. On this last point, he might well have overstated his success, given that it was a small bank.[45] Whatever the case, his good fortune was fleeting, as the bank collapsed in the autumn of 1878. Heurich and another board member, Christian Ruppert, assumed responsibility for covering the bank's losses to its depositors. Heurich held $2,000 in bank stock. In an interview with the *Washington Post,* B.U. Keyser, the receiver of the failed German National Bank, described the debts and obligations left when the bank failed. He noted that the bank had $130,000 invested in capital, but $120,000 was in the bank building, which he described as very overpriced. There were about $200,000 in deposits, and between two and three thousand depositors. The "largest has $7,000 on deposit; the next largest, $6,000, and the rest range from $1,000 down to $5, and there is due to depositors about $270,000." Keyser estimated there were approximately $349,000 in assets such as real estate and furniture. This figure turned out to be exceptionally optimistic.[46]

The bank president and a cashier were tried on embezzlement charges. Heurich was one of those who testified, and, although convicted, the two culprits were released on account of mistakes made by the prosecution. In his memoirs, Heurich claims they were acquitted, but hints that he disagreed with the verdict. Heurich took out insurance on his businesses, borrowed from the insurance company to pay off creditors, and then worked even harder to expand his business to pay back the loans from the insurance company. Heurich bragged in his memoirs that he "literally saved that bank with a tidal wave of beer." Throughout the rest of his long life, Heurich refused to serve on another bank board. In one of his scrapbooks he later wrote of his philosophy "to be saving and take little risks; to lend no money to others, nor endorse for others; for my experience tells me so." From then on, Heurich primarily invested in local real estate. One of the area's largest landowners, second only to the federal government, he capitalized on the city's growth by purchasing scattered plots of land, including several in the southwest quadrant, where he built his brewery in the 1890s. He also bought enough land in Maryland, just outside the D.C. border, to build a dairy farm and a second home.[47]

Real estate was a common investment among brewers. Often it was done to secure a place to build a saloon. Frederick Pabst, of Milwaukee's Pabst Brewing empire, followed this model, as did the Busch family in St. Louis and Heurich's competitor in Virginia, Robert Portner. Real estate was a safe place to invest to assure a steady stream of income from "rent." In economics, "rent" may be defined as "any excess payment above that required for production."[48] Sociologists John Logan and Harvey Molotch's classic study, *Urban Fortune: The Political Economy of Place*, notes that as urban development proceeds, a class of "active entrepreneurs" purchases land, "gaining control over locations likely to be strategic over time." They "strive to put themselves in the path of the development process." Heurich's strategy fits this criterion. He had the advantage of living in the District of Columbia, where development was spreading in every direction, and the land he purchased ended up allowing him to not only earn "rent" but would also, in the 1890s, allow him to move his brewery to a suitable location when the changing nature of the space where he operated compelled him to find a new spot for production.[49]

Much of the property Heurich purchased at first was simply needed to expand his brewery. For example, in 1876 he bought two lots adjacent to his brewery and used the extra space for carriage sheds. He also quickly learned to be careful. In 1876 he bought two building sites, but did not purchase title insurance after being assured by a friend, "a German ... who passed as a very rich man," in the city's recorder office, that there was no problem with the property. In 1878 Heurich was startled to see five building sites for sale, including these two properties, on which he had already constructed buildings. He bought all five lots, including the two he thought he had already owned. In his published memoirs he referred to this episode as his "second lesson," the first being to not serve on a bank's board of directors. Heurich's friend who had so poorly advised him in 1876 apologized and "gave [Heurich] other papers to cover [the] loss." Alas for Heurich, those papers also turned out to be worthless. Fortunately, Heurich noted, "since the brewery was flourishing, I easily recovered my loss."[50]

Real estate was, in some respects, a somewhat old-fashioned investment by the 1870s in the U.S. This is not to imply that it was not a good investment. Indeed, Heurich's investments in land paid off quite handsomely. However, the nineteenth century was marked by a growth of the idea of risk. To be a "free man" meant that one took responsibility for your own personal risk financially. This, in turn, led to a growth in financial instruments such as insurance and investments in mortgages. Previously, personal wealth and the independence of being a free man were linked to ownership in land, reflected in American history with ideas such as Thomas Jefferson's idealized nation of yeoman farmers. The land idea was never abandoned, as may be seen in the popularity of the Homestead Act and the twentieth-century ideal of the suburban home. Heurich was building his fortune at a time when investments in railroads, followed by large-scale industries such as steel, were increasingly popular. The potential payoffs were huge, but so was the risk of failure and bankruptcy. His experience with the failure of the German-American bank, however, no doubt shaped his view of how to manage his investments. Historian Jonathan Levy noted in his history of the idea of financial risk that "the Panic of 1873 was a profound cultural event, the coming-out party for the economic chance world." It was also a warning to Heurich that he never forgot about risk and responsibility.[51]

Despite the economic strain of the Long Depression (1873–1878), Heurich continued to expand his brewery. He was successful enough to indulge his fondness for President Grant when he purchased for five hundred dollars a unique wooden three-sided roll-top desk that was intended to be a gift for the Union war hero from F.E. Shultze, a supporter in Bozeman, Montana. However, the federal government refused to pay the shipping costs, so the desk was placed on auction. Heurich purchased it and used it for the rest of his life, and it is still on display in the Heurich House in Washington.[52] He could afford some luxuries such as the beautiful desk. His customer base was growing. Heurich bragged that the White House had begun to buy his beer. However, he noted that this was not the case during the administration of President Rutherford B. Hayes (1877–1881). Hayes was a temperate drinker and his wife, Lucy, was an ardent prohibitionist. Later known as "Lemonade Lucy," she avoided serving alcohol at White House functions. Still, she was not quite as "dry" as later prohibitionists would be. She did not object if her husband enjoyed a beer with friends in their hometown of Cincinnati, and when Hayes was in the Union Army during the Civil War, he celebrated promotions along with other officers with a drink of liquor (Heurich insisted it was beer). Lucy's mother even drank wine for health reasons. Still, they did not serve alcohol at official functions, and Hayes worked to keep the Prohibitionist faction within the Republican Party.[53]

This tolerance had limits, however. In July 1878, the Washington *Schützverein*, of which Heurich was a member, held a five-day festival with shooting contests and parties at the headquarters. The festivities began with a parade past the White House, observed by President Hayes. The society's president, Simon Wolf, a local attorney and the District's recorder, had also arranged for the club to be presented with a bouquet of flowers from Mrs. Hayes. That an organization known for enjoying good German lager received a public gift from the First Lady was enough of an outrage to local Drys, but Wolf went further. When a *Washington Post* reporter asked Wolf about how recent rainy days would affect the fest, Wolf could not resist tweaking the local Drys in his answer: "You may say the *Schuetzen-fest* will continue until we have five good days; so you can tell the temperance people to pray for good weather, or they may have to endure our festival until next October." Faced with the demands of an enraged local temperance society, Hayes asked Wolf for his resignation. Later that same year, to placate the local German community, Hayes offered Wolf a municipal judgeship. Moreover, the temperance people must not have prayed for good weather, as the next day the scheduled celebrations were delayed by a heavy rainstorm that required the shooting contests be postponed.[54]

After Hayes was replaced by James Garfield (1881) and Chester Arthur (1881–1885), Heurich's beer returned to the White House. According to Heurich, "With Mrs. Hayes

Heurich began expanding his brewery in 1877. It was dedicated with a gala celebration in the summer of 1878 (courtesy American Breweriana Association).

out of the presidential residence Christian Heurich's beer was again permitted inside the walls, there to remain as an almost standing order for eight presidents until the arrival of national prohibition in the District of Columbia—November 1917."[55] Whichever presidents did or did not drink his beer, Heurich continued to thrive. He purchased additional property between M and N Streets NW along 20th Street in June 1877. In October he applied for a building permit to build a new four-story brewery building on this land. The permit application noted that the brewery would cost $15,000. Brewery operations continued at the existing facility while the expansion was built. When it opened, the original small two-story facility had been replaced with a much larger building topped with a clock tower. There was an attached building for an ice machine and another with coolers. It had a capacity of 30,000 barrels.[56]

On a warm summer night in July 1878, he celebrated the opening of his expanded brewery on 20th Street with a party for 1,000 guests. The *Washington Post* gushed over the new facility:

> [T]he brewery was]the largest and most complete of any this side of New York, and it will favorably compare with any in the country. The structure is the result of the personal industry, intelligent management and sound business principles of Mr. Heurich. It is an improvement and enhances the value of all the surrounding property, and gives Washington the credit of having the champion lager beer brewery south of New York.[57]

Heurich was becoming part of a growing Washington business establishment that hoped to finally fulfill the original idea of making the capital a center for industry as well as the seat of government. That idea had stalled, as discussed earlier, but Alexander Shepherd's improvement campaign increased hopes that D.C. might, at last, grow into a world-class capital with an industrial sector. A local Board of Trade floundered in the late 1860s, but in 1878 a group of local businessmen formed the National Fair Grounds Association. They formed what Logan and Molotch term a "growth machine" and a "growth coalition." A growth machine is, in their usage, centered on a collection of entrepreneurs "in similar situations" that unite to help promote their interests in general. Their interests are not limited to a single scale. The "geographical unit" of their interest may be "as small as a neighborhood shopping district or as large as a national region." Together these businessmen unite with relevant "progrowth associations and governmental units" to form the "machine." A "growth coalition" is formed when the machine forms an alliance with local leaders, whether governmental or otherwise, to promote a particular region, such as Washington. The coalition includes entrepreneurs, political leaders, local professionals, and businessmen. Local newspapers often sign on as partners. Local labor leaders may also join in, concerned that new growth provide jobs.[58]

The National Fair Grounds Association was such a "growth machine," and members used their individual ties to members of Congress to successfully push for official sanction. Approved by Congress in June 1878, HR 4616 chartered the Association, permitting it to buy up to two hundred acres of land in the cities of Washington or Georgetown, and to erect "suitable buildings" to exhibit "products of the soil, of domestic animals, and of the products of mechanical, scientific, and artistic skill, ingenuity, and invention." A five-man board of directors would oversee the organization, and they could sell up to 200,000 dollars of stock at one hundred dollars a share. The list of the organizers is long and includes several notable names, such as Elisha Francis Riggs, from the prominent local banking family. However, none of Washington's brewers' names appear. Indeed, many of the investors were not even Washington locals, but investors from elsewhere probably hoping to take advantage of an opportunity.[59]

The nineteenth and early twentieth centuries were the height of industrial and agricultural fairs designed to promote a region's or local community's products, and to encourage further industry, investment and development. The Centennial Exposition in Philadelphia in 1876 had drawn almost nine million visitors, roughly equivalent to about one-fifth of the total population of the U.S. This total came in spite of the ongoing Long Depression. The industrial displays at the Centennial exposition were particularly notable, especially the giant Corliss steam engine that powered much of the machinery at the fair. For Washington businessmen, this type of fair made perfect sense to promote their own city. The Association eventually settled on a one-hundred-thirty-acre site in Ivy City in northeast Washington. There were four main buildings: the Main Building, the Art Building, Machinery Hall, and the Grandstand facing a horse-racing track. There were also over twenty smaller structures, including an icehouse and refreshment stands. It was far smaller than the Centennial Fair, which covered almost four times as many acres and had over two hundred buildings, but the organizers still hoped it would be a success, drawing attention to D.C. and, of course, making a profit for the investors.[60]

The National Fair opened on October 29, 1879, with a four-hour parade, described by the *Washington Post* as a "monster mercantile and mechanical" procession. Heurich was named one of the assistant marshals. His brewery was represented by six wagons,

The entrance of the fair grounds for the National Fair. From *The National Fair Exhibition Buildings Illustrated,* **1879.**

probably carrying barrels of his beer. Heurich's was not the only brewery in attendance. Rival George Jeuneman contributed a wagon carrying a "mammoth cask and Gambrinius [*sic*]." King Gambrinius is a figure in European folklore, the patron saint of beer and brewers, although he is not an actual saint. His figure appeared on numerous American breweries and beer labels. The parade was judged too long to go all the way to the fairgrounds, so it circled around downtown Washington, and then guests and exhibitors made their way to the fairgrounds to hear a dedication speech by President Hayes.[61]

The fair itself seems not to have been a success, even though an estimated ten to fifteen thousand attended opening day. Open for only two weeks, the fair's total visitor figures are unavailable, although opening in late October turned out to be a poor decision. Washington weather in October is sometimes mild, but it can also turn bitterly cold quickly, and poor weather, including freezes and high winds, discouraged attendance. The fair closed on November 8. Many of the buildings were dismantled immediately, although the race track and grandstand remained, and the organizers immediately began to improve them in hopes of making the facility an ongoing business. Indeed, the small scale of the fair reflects the struggles of those trying to promote D.C. as an industrial location. Their hopes were greater than their capabilities. Certainly a fair the size of the 1876 Philadelphia celebration was never possible, but the short duration of the National Fair, and the fact that the racing facilities were the only real permanent structures, suggests that perhaps the entire enterprise was a way to get Congress to approve a new race track for Washington. However, even if the fair was meant as a subterfuge, it allowed Heurich to promote his business and to show off how successful he had become in only seven years, although the fair's prize for best beer went not to one of the locals, but to Peter Doelger's from New York City.[62]

By the end of the 1870s, Heurich was an established member of the Washington community. His brewery was successful and expanding. He was acquiring real estate in the city and was one of the leaders of the German community. He was happily married and bragged in letters to family back in Germany of his successes. The rest of the nineteenth century would see Heurich's brewery continue to expand, and his place in the city would continue to evolve as he faced challenges both professional and personal.

3

Moving Up in Business and Society: 1880–1894

As the tenth anniversary of Heurich's move to D.C. approached, he had become a prominent member of Washington's business community, and local civic boosters bragged about his brewery as an asset to the city. An 1884 guide, *Historical and Commercial Sketches of Washington and Environs*, extravagantly praised the brewery, noting, "The excellence and purity of Heurich's beer is universally known." The guide, produced by the E.E. Barton Publishing Company, was meant to promote the city to attract new businesses, so it was not unbiased, but the guide's claim that "in its manufacture nothing of a deleterious character is used, while the best malts of Canada, Wisconsin, and Ohio are manipulated in its production," does fit the remaining records, which record his purchase of grain and hops. Heurich was also modernizing his plant. The guide reports that the brewery has "two of the larger sized ice machines to furnish the refrigeration for the cellars and the fermenting rooms." Capacity had also expanded: "The brewery has a capacity of 50,000 barrels per annum, and during the last twelve months the sales reached almost its full brewing capacity."[1] Heurich had twenty men working for him, along with a half-dozen delivery teams, and he had built an addition next to his home and the brewery to house the extra workers. His hard work paid off as his brewing business and real estate investments continued to grow.[2]

In 1881 Heurich opened a German-style beer garden next to his brewery, which he later described as the "first distinct beer garden known in the nation's capital." No whisky or other hard liquors were served there. It was a place for people to drink beer with friends and family, and to listen to music and relax. He even argued at brewers' national meetings that their industry should distance itself from whiskey, to adopt a stance of "dis-association with that which makes disreputable saloons—whiskey. Beer is a beverage, whiskey never was." (He did accept whiskey had medicinal uses.) Heurich ran the beer garden for fifteen years. After he sold it, the new owner began to serve whiskey, much to Heurich's disgust.[3]

Heurich was even then planning on expanding further. The *Historical and Commercial Sketches of Washington and Environs* reported on his plans to build a new brewery on another location:

> The site for its construction is upon a lot of ground owned by Mr. Heurich, embracing five acres, at what is known as "Isherwood," located on Sixteenth Street Northeast. The brewery will occupy an entire square in block eight. The capacity of the new brewery will be 100,000 barrels of beer per annum,

and so arranged that double that amount can be produced if required. There are several large and never-failing springs upon the grounds owned by Mr. Heurich, and adjacent to it the "Federal" spring, which became somewhat historic during the war. The material to be used in the new structure will be brick, and the brewery will be supplied with all the latest improvements as well as with all of the latest appliances known in mechanical science.[4]

Heurich would build a new brewery but on a different spot, along the Potomac on Water Street. He did not indicate why he abandoned his idea of building in Isherwood, but it may have simply been that the Water Street location was in a more appropriate industrial area. Nonetheless, the description from the 1884 account showed the type of structure which Heurich wanted to build.

A new kind of competitor entered the Washington market to compete with Heurich, but they were not local. Several large "ship-

Christian Heurich's portrait in 1883 as published in the *Western Brewer*. Heurich was then 41 years old. From the collection of Jan King Evans Houser. Used with permission.

This drawing of the expanded 20th Street Brewery appeared in the *Western Brewer*, August 1883.

ping brewers" began moving into Washington as well as numerous other cities throughout the country. These companies took advantage of several new developments. First was the expansion of the railway network, which gave them access to more parts of a national market. Second was the development of the refrigerated rail car to transport lager beer. The first such cars had been developed before the Civil War, but they did not come into common usage until the 1880s, prompted by companies such as Swift Meats, which needed a reliable way to ship their product cold.[5] They also depended upon reliable ice-making machinery, both for use in the cars (which could not produce their own cold temperatures at first) and for the depots at the destination, so the beer could be stored cold. This took an enormous amount of ice. A 40-foot railcar needed 10,000 pounds, and this needed to be topped off if not completely replaced daily.[6] In short, it required an investment in resources to establish and maintain a large distribution network that would be daunting to smaller breweries. Only the largest breweries could establish more than a small network to expand their distribution area. However, this also protected small breweries from all but the biggest breweries, as few had the means to distribute their products on a large scale across a large region. For example, in Washington at least a half-dozen distant breweries set up a distributorship, and only three of them lasted more than a few years. Some of the shipping brewers that established distributors in Washington included (listed in the order they opened):

Bergner & Engel (Philadelphia, PA) 1881–1900

Christian Moerlein (Cincinnati, OH) 1886–1901 (dates approximate)

Pabst Brewing (Milwaukee, WI) 1887–1917

Joseph Schlitz Brewing (Milwaukee, WI) 1887–1917

Anheuser-Busch (St. Louis, MO) 1888–1917

Gerhard Lang Park Brewing (Buffalo, NY) 1889–1896

Val Blatz Brewing (Milwaukee, WI) 1896–1897[7]

One of the major national shipping brewers, Lemp Brewing of St. Louis, did not have a branch in Washington, but may have been sold in bottles locally after 1900 once bottling became easier. The three largest, Pabst, Schlitz and Anheuser-Busch, remained until the District went dry in 1917.

Distance shipping allowed brewers such as Schlitz and Pabst to ship kegs of beer to areas well outside of their home market. This expansion went beyond just selling in saloons. The development of bottling technology allowed them to expand into the home, restaurant, and hotel markets as well. There were limitations. Bottles were not yet a major part of beer sales, and at first bottling was a laborious process done mostly by hand. Washed bottles were filled by means of a rubber hose attached to an ordinary keg, then a cork was inserted into the foaming neck of the bottle, driven in by a single pressing machine, and wired on by hand. A hand-glued label and a tin foil wrapper on the neck made the bottle ready for its heavy wooden case. Beer bottled at the brewery, or by a nearby bottler, was generally for local consumption. Bottles were too heavy for a brewer to ship economically to distant cities. Often they'd be filled locally by bottlers once they reached their destination. So, for example, once a keg of Pabst reached Washington, its contents would be bottled by a local branch of the producing brewer, or an independent bottler under contract.[8]

There were numerous bottlers in D.C. Some bottled just beer from one brewery, some switched between breweries, some bottled beer and soft drinks alike. Groceries sometimes bottled their own drinks, including whiskey. Moreover, some breweries used multiple bottlers, muddying the picture further. An 1881 local business directory published by the *Washington Post* had fifteen entries under "Breweries." Of these fifteen, three were actually producing their own beer—Heurich, George Juenemann, and George Kernwein (in business from 1874 to 1884). There were eleven breweries open in D.C. during 1881, but the others were, for whatever reason, not listed. The rest of the fifteen businesses listed were actually bottlers.[9] Three listed themselves as bottlers of Heurich's beer. One, James Butler, claimed to be the "only bottler of Chr. Heurich's Lager Beer," a claim which was not entirely accurate, as the very next entry, for Julius Eisenbeiss, boasted as being a "Lager Beer bottling depot of Chris. Heurich's celebrated premium beer." Of the rest, four were bottlers for Philadelphia's Bergner and Engel's brewery. Two bottled the products of New York City's George Ehret's, which was at the time the country's largest brewery. Three did not specify which brewery's products they bottled, and one was unclear, noting only that they bottled "Philadelphia Lager Beer." Four also bottled soft drinks or water.[10]

Bergner and Engel's and Ehret's were early example of shipping breweries, but they were quickly surpassed by the larger Midwestern shipping breweries listed earlier. Both Pabst and Schlitz opened their own depots in Washington by the decade's end. Note that there were no bottlers listed for Baltimore, only one from New York City, and one (possibly two) from Philadelphia.[11] New York and Philadelphia at this time both had dozens of breweries. Why were they not shipping more of their product south to D.C.? In other words, why did Heurich not have more competition? Simply put, most of the biggest breweries did not think they needed to ship much outside of their home area. New York was the largest city in the United States with a population of 1.2 million. Philadelphia was second with 847,000, and Brooklyn was third with 566,000. Washington was fourteenth with 147,000. Given the existing difficulties to ship large amounts of beer and having it remain palatable, whether in bottles or barrels, Heurich's home territory was simply not big enough to make the effort for most of the breweries of New York and Philadelphia. They had plenty of customers closer to home. In contrast, the breweries in Milwaukee, Cincinnati, and St. Louis had to travel farther to find customers away from their home areas. That, in turn, forced them to create the skills and infrastructure to effectively ship their product, including a trained workforce of salesmen to get their product into saloons and hotels. Once they were experienced at shipping their beer around the Midwest and West, and had a trained sales force, shipping their beers into D.C. was not so much a leap into a new area as it was a logical next step. The company first expanded close to home, then, as they gained experience, moved further afield. For example, Pabst's Washington, D.C., branch opened in 1889, the fifteenth branch office the Milwaukee brewers opened. Their first branch office was in Chicago in 1878. They opened their second in 1879 in Kansas City. Most of the rest of the branches they opened in the 1880s were in Wisconsin, Michigan, and Illinois. They established a branch in Pittsburgh in 1884 and reached New York City in 1888.[12]

The shipping brewers had several hurdles to overcome in entering local markets, D.C. as well as others. Some of the obstacles were technological, as noted earlier, while others involved regulations and entering existing markets. The technological changes between 1870 and the end of the century helped the brewers overcome not just logistical problems transporting the beer to distant markets, but also in dealing with financial and marketing issues. One of the most vexing of these difficulties was the process for taxing beer. Beer taxes were a major source of income for the U.S. government during the Civil War. Only a minuscule percentage of beer was bottled when the tax began in 1862, so taxes were paid on each barrel. Brewers purchased tax stamps, which had to be affixed to each barrel. Federal revenue agents oversaw the process, making sure a canceled stamp would be applied to the barrel to show the tax had been paid. Because there was no provision for bottled beer in the law, brewers had to first fill the barrel, then pay the tax, then siphon the beer from the barrel to the bottles, and this had to be done in a separate building. In 1889 two employees of Milwaukee's Pabst Brewing developed a system using a pipeline that measured the beer, so that it could be moved from the brew kettles to the bottling room without being put into barrels. In 1890 Congress amended the excise tax law to allow breweries to bottle their own beer inside the brewery itself using this system. Despite these changes, draft beer sold in saloons still accounted for a large majority of the beer sold. For example, after Pabst began putting resources into bottling beer, the share of their sales for bottled beer out of their total sales doubled, but this was only an increase from 5 to 10 percent.[13]

By 1900, bottling technology had also improved. Bottles were too expensive not to be recycled, so the brewers wanted them returned, which required they be washed and sterilized. To keep other companies from reusing bottles that belonged to someone else, breweries used embossed bottles with their company name and logo prominently displayed. New machines were developed to wash and pasteurize bottles, and to attach labels. One of the biggest developments was the crown-top bottle that used a crimped bottle cap. Developed by Baltimore's Crown Cork and Seal Company, and still in use over a century later, the crown cap eliminated a plethora of various stopper mechanisms that complicated washing and filling bottles. Earlier methods, including corks, rubber stoppers, and porcelain caps held on with wires, generally worked, but often made cleaning bottles after use difficult, especially those methods that physically attached the stopper to the bottle so that both were returned together. The development of the crown cap solved this technical problem, but bottling was still a labor-intensive operation that required significant financial outlays by brewers. Nonetheless, bottling beer became increasingly necessary for any brewer hoping to compete beyond its immediate local market.

The final major technological changes to alter the brewing industry at this time included pasteurization and the discovery of pure yeast. Louis Pasteur's book on fermentation and beer *Etudes sur la Bière* ("Studies on Beer") was published in 1876. By heating beer to a temperature just below its boiling point, brewers killed harmful bacteria that could affect their beer. In addition, in 1878, Danish chemist E.C. Hansen discovered that certain strains of yeast hurt the beer's flavor, but that by cultivating a strain from a single good cell, brewers could avoid unintentionally making inconsistent batches of beer spoiled by undesirable types of yeast mixed in with the good. Together these changes made storing and shipping beer over distances while maintaining its flavor more practical.[14]

What did these changes mean for Heurich? He had essentially eight major competitors: the other three large D.C. breweries, two across the river in northern Virginia, and at least three large national brewers with local distributors. Smaller brewers would enter and exit the market from time to time, but these eight breweries had the advertising dollars and production capacity to compete for the D.C. area. Moreover, they also had the ability to invest in new technology to keep up with advances in production and packaging. Brewers had to keep pace with the changing technology or risk losing out to competitors. Heurich was successful, at least in part, because he did keep up with these changes, using first local bottlers to package his beers, and then adding bottling machinery to his Water Street brewery, which opened in 1896.

It was the changes in bottling that were probably most visible to the consumer, and were key to understanding how beer was marketed and consumed in this era. Brewing historian Martin Stack argues that bottled beer held five specific attractions for the shipping breweries in particular, although they could also apply at least in part to local brewers such as Heurich:

1. It allowed them to bypass saloons.
2. Bottled beer could be shipped to dry areas.
3. It helped construct brand loyalty.
4. They could target more affluent customers.
5. The profit rates were higher than selling beer by the barrel to saloons.[15]

Even with the technology to transport beer, the shipping brewers had to find a way to find an outlet to sell their beer. The first advantage for brewers was the ability to bypass locally held, i.e., "tied" saloons. Most saloons at the time were "tied," meaning they sold beer from one specific brewer only. Most commonly they had a contract with one of their local brewers, who may have fronted the money for furnishing, signs, mirrors, the bar, tables, etc., in exchange for the saloon only selling that brewery's products. Any saloonkeeper who tried to violate this agreement would soon find himself out of business. Local brewers would not welcome the entry of an out-of-town competitor, so the shipping breweries had to find a specific market niche to fill.[16] Bottled beer allowed them to present a more expensive, higher quality beer to middle-class consumers for consumption at home, as well as in restaurants and hotels. The shipping brewers in effect created a new market in order to bypass the obstacles of entering the established one. This new customer base would not help Heurich a great deal immediately, as he already had a large group of saloons selling his product. However, the business model created by the shipping brewers would help Heurich at the end on the nineteenth century as he expanded into new markets, establishing branches in Norfolk and Baltimore in 1896 and 1898 respectively.

Another benefit for brewers who shipped their products was made possible by a loophole in federal and state laws—alcoholic beverages could be shipped into many dry jurisdictions. The shipping breweries, as well as wineries and distilleries, could ship their product into areas where customers had no legal place to buy alcohol. This would not have affected the D.C. brewers much in the 1890s, but by 1900 Virginia did begin to go dry, county by county, which constricted possible marketplaces for Heurich's beer. Note that when Heurich did establish a branch office in Virginia, it was in Norfolk, a wet city surrounded by dry territory. State dry laws often allowed, as Virginia's did, residents to transport alcohol for their personal use from wet territory into dry. The amount was limited, so trying to bring a wagonload of beer in barrels would have quickly raised suspicions and prompted a visit from law enforcement, but a case or two of beer in bottles was generally allowed. This exception to prohibition laws was not closed until the Webb-Kenyon Act of 1913, which forbad interstate shipping of alcohol into dry areas.[17]

The third advantage was that brewers could use their bottle labels to help create and maintain brand loyalty. The idea of companies producing a specific brand instead of a generic product was a new development in the nineteenth century. Luxury goods tied to certain producers, such as Wedgeworth china, predated the idea of a brand. However, many products in the nineteenth century were sold by producers in bulk to wholesalers, who then dealt with merchants. A cracker or a pickle, sold from barrels, was simply a cracker or a pickle. Beer was often identified as being produced by a particular brewer, and customers might look for beer made by a brewer with a reputation for producing a good product. A customer in Washington in 1876 might ask which saloons sold "Heurich's beer" but would not expect to ask for Senate Beer—one of Heurich's most popular brands after 1890. The idea of a specific brand representing a particular product made by a specific producer, though, had several advantages in overcoming some of the issues with which shipping brewers had to deal.[18]

Looking at the ads for brewers in the late 1870s and early 1880s, the modern consumer might be struck by how little detail is given. The bottlers listed in the Washington 1881 directory discussed earlier would simply note that they bottled "Heurich's Lager Beer" or "George Ehret's Beer." This worked for local companies and even for shipping brewers, such as Ehret's, who depended upon a local reputation and the tied saloons for customers. A man walking into a Washington saloon in 1881 might ask whose beer he was drinking and, if he enjoyed it, could look for other saloons serving the same beer. However, a man who liked Heurich's beer could not walk into just any saloon in D.C. and ask for that beer again. If the saloon was tied to another brewer, then that's whose beer that saloon sold. Saloons, of course, would advertise whose beer they sold with large signs outside their business. Shipping brewers without a local saloon network aimed to

The George Bauer Saloon at Water Street and M Street SW, date unknown. George W. Bauer owned a saloon or restaurant on either 7th Street or M Street SW from 1872 to 1902. The street sign in front of the building appears to read "Water Street SW" and "M Street SW" (Library of Congress, Prints and Photographs Division, LC-DIG-npcc-00188).

A close-up of the photograph shows two Heurich signs on the front of the building. The men outside are mostly African American, as that area of Washington was largely a working-class, industrial area in the late 19th century and a center for the city's black population (Library of Congress, Prints and Photographs Division, LC-DIG-npcc-00188).

get around this bottleneck by selling their beer in outlets such as hotels, groceries and restaurants, and that required educating the potential customers to ask for their beer specifically. Creating a brand got around this problem. Pabst created "Blue Ribbon" beer and Anheuser-Busch "Budweiser," and then, through advertising, convinced the consumer to go into a retail outlet and ask for that product by name. This tactic was heavily used initially by companies selling beverages and food. The National Biscuit Company was a pioneer in this method, selling Uneeda Biscuits. Congress helped facilitate this method in 1870 by passing the first trademark law, which prevented other companies from copying a registered brand name or symbol. The original law was challenged in court, and it took until 1905 to stabilize the system, but the basic ground rules were laid down starting about the time Heurich was looking for a place to start his own brewery. The trademark system also allowed a single company to sell multiple products of the same type. Once he began using brand names, Heurich could sell Heurich's Lager, Senate, and Maerzen instead of a solitary product.

    While brand names were a useful innovation, they also created their own problems; how was the producer to educate the consumers so that they knew to purchase a specific brand, and how best to convince the buyer that your brand was superior to others? Newspaper advertisements were one solution, but most newspapers were local, and most cities had multiple newspapers. In 1880, for example, Washington had the *Daily Critic*, the *National Republican*, the *Sunday Herald*, the *Washington Post*, the *Evening Star*, the *Washington Sentinel*, and, just across the Potomac, the *Alexandria Gazette*. All carried advertising, and even though many people read multiple papers, an advertiser hoping to reach the largest segment of the city's population had to advertise in most of them. Moreover, this same problem, multiple places to advertise, would repeat itself in every large city, dramatically raising the advertising costs to brewers trying to expand into multiple marketplaces.

National magazines such as *Harper's* provided a solution by providing a single place to advertise over a wide region. Patent medicines were among the very first to see the potential of national advertising, and other companies soon copied their examples. Between 1871 and 1891, *Harper's* jumped from five pages of advertisements to over one hundred pages of ads per issue.[19] This did not mean national producers would skip advertising in newspapers—the Washington papers have ads for many of the shipping brewers—but using magazines did help create a widely distributed customer base. This also created a problem for smaller, local companies such as Heurich's. To compete, he also had to create specific brands, the two most popular of which were Senate for his lighter lager, and Maerzen, which was a darker beer. By early 1883 ads began appearing in D.C. newspapers for "Heurich's Superior Maerzen Lager Beer." Within ten years the local D.C. breweries were all advertising individual products by their brand names.[20]

There is a difference between a trademark and a brand, although the two often overlap, at least when referred to informally. Trademarks, such as Heurich's "H" superimposed over a hop leaf and the Washington Monument, were designed to indicate an origin. Business historian David Higgins notes that they developed in cotton textiles and in metal fabrication such as making tableware, to indicate which tradesman or firm produced them. In this form they were, in his words, "protobrands." Brands, such as Senate or Maerzen, were designed to carry more information than just the producer. They implied specific attributes of the product, carrying a specific image.[21] Heurich's use of Senate as one of his brand names was perfect for D.C. Named after the upper house of the American legislature, the name "Senate" implied the product was dignified and superior to other beers. "Maerzen" was named after a specific type of beer that could vary from dark to light. Heurich was no doubt faithful to this type's original style, which was dark and somewhat bitter. Copying the darker German style, as opposed to the lighter Austrian version, allowed Heurich to set it apart from his Senate to gain a greater share of the market.[22]

Stack's fourth advantage in bottling for brewers was that bottles were appealing to "affluent, middle-class drinkers." Their effort to shift their prime customer base from saloons, often catering to the working or lower classes, to a more prosperous and more respectable middle-class home market would accelerate in the 1910s as the temperance movement gained momentum. However, the beginnings of this strategy could be seen in the later part of the nineteenth century, especially in the advertising and marketing of the shipping breweries. Bottled beer was sold in some groceries (although so were some distilled liquors), as well as in respectable hotels and restaurants. Many breweries also offered home delivery of their beer in bottles by the case. All of these outlets allowed the customer to avoid contact with the saloon.[23]

Many in the brewing industry were beginning to realize that the ills of the saloon were affecting the reputation of the entire industry. For his part, Heurich worked to distance himself from salons that served distilled liquor. The restaurant attached to Heurich's first brewery served only his own products and no hard liquor. Moreover, unlike many bars in the area, Heurich's saloon was furnished with tables and chairs. In this respect, it more closely resembled a traditional German beer hall than an American saloon, since many of the latter did not provide seating for customers. Despite these efforts, Heurich was frustrated by how the brewing industry was tied together with those making whiskey and other distilled liquors. "The prohibitionists," he complained, "refused to see a difference and it seemed to be a case of all or nothing with them." Of course, this wholesome atmosphere would not necessarily apply to every saloon that sold Heurich's beer, but, as will be discussed in a later chapter, by the end of the century Heurich was also explicitly marketing beer for home use.[24]

The fifth and final advantage Stack attributes to the shipping brewers' strategy was that "bottled beer offered a much greater profit potential." The data for Pabst and Blatz, both Milwaukee shipping breweries, are incomplete, but there is a noticeable trend beginning in 1881 and lasting until Prohibition. During the 1880s beer sold in a saloon from a keg offered a greater profit than that sold in a bottle. The data for the 1890s are fragmentary, but strongly suggest that bottled beer was far more profitable than that sold on draft. For example, in 1893 Pabst made a profit of $1.29 per barrel of keg beer, versus $1.83 per barrel of bottled beer. The profit per barrel of keg beer for Blatz is not available, but they made $2.20 profit per barrel of bottled beer. Assuming that saloons selling Blatz's keg beer charged about the same amount as those selling Pabst, a not unreasonable assumption as price wars between brands kept saloon prices fairly uniform, then Blatz probably made approximately the same amount of profit per barrel of keg beer as Pabst, about $1.29. By the beginning of the twentieth century the gap was even larger as continued "beer wars" over prices drove the price of beer sold to saloons even lower. In 1904 Pabst made about $.39 profit per barrel of keg beer, compared to a $3.43 profit per barrel of bottled beer, roughly nine times greater.[25]

Of course this profit margin, as well as the other benefits Stack identifies, were not limited to the big shipping breweries. Regional and local brewers, including Heurich and his D.C. competitors, also began to pay even more attention to bottling for many of the same reasons, although not every advantage applied equally for the local breweries as they did for the shippers. For example, Heurich already produced about one half of the beer sold in Washington, so he had little need to penetrate a saloon market dominated by existing brewers. He was the existing brewer who dominated the local saloons. Being able to ship legally into dry areas was useful, as much of Virginia was dry after 1910. Note that the first branch office Heurich established was in Norfolk, which was not only home to a naval base, but was a wet island in a sea of dry counties, and it was legal for consumers to bring a limited amount of beer for personal use to their homes if they lived in a dry county. The profit potential is of obvious benefit. Heurich was a successful businessman who was not likely to pass up such an opportunity.

Finally, there was the chance to expand brand loyalty and find a middle-class home market. Heurich's efforts to position his products as appropriate for home use accelerated after 1900, but some of that emphasis was already present. As noted earlier, when he established his first brewery, it followed the German model, with places for patrons to sit and no hard liquor, rather than the coarser saloon model. No doubt many saloons that sold Heurich's beer were not middle-class and did not follow the German family-friendly beer garden model. And, as was noted earlier, many of his initial patrons were working, not middle-class. Still, Heurich always insisted that his product was healthy and in the 1890s was advertising his beers as a healthy beverage.

Aside from his role selling a great deal of beer, Heurich was also participating in D.C. society as a benefactor, active in numerous local organizations. Perhaps the most notable was the German Orphan Home, founded in 1879 as the "German Protestant Orphan Asylum Association of the District of Columbia." In 1882 the "Protestant" was dropped. Heurich was one of the founders, along with Simon Wolf and other members of D.C.'s German-American community. Heurich was himself an orphan, his mother having died when he was fourteen, and his father a year later. Despite the name, the Orphan Home did not just take in orphans. Like many other such establishments, it also took in abandoned children as well as those whose parents could not afford to take care of them. The Home purchased a thirty-two-acre farm in rural Anacostia, in the southeastern part of the District. They began with a dozen children, but quickly expanded, taking care of more children and adding a library and a pharmacy. Young children attended school at the Home, while older ones attended a local public school. Residents could leave once they reached legal age, eighteen for girls, and twenty-one for boys. Congress appropriated some money for the Home, including $16,000 to build a new brick building in 1890. An additional $14,000 was raised from supporters, including Heurich. The new facility could house up to eighty children.[26]

Heurich's public activities included fun activities as well. In January 1880 the Washington *Schützverein* lay the cornerstone for a new building for its events, the previous building having been destroyed in an 1879 fire. Heurich was one of the dignitaries at the ceremony and was one of those who contributed items to place inside the cornerstone.[27] A year later, in January 1881, he was made an honorary member of D.C.'s Union Veterans Corps. That same month he had one of the displays during a winter carnival featuring a huge beer vat, "astride of which was an image of Gambrinius." Heurich was a member of the Committee on Illumination and Fireworks for the city's celebration of the centennial of the American victory over the British at Yorktown in 1881. In 1882 the National Brewers' Association met in Washington, and Heurich hoisted a tour of his expanded brewery and a celebratory dinner for the delegates.[28] He clearly was now a prominent figure in D.C. society, an accepted member who fit into the "space" created by local society.

Even in the best of times, Heurich also had to deal with occasional accidents and problems. In May 1881 his brewery suffered its second fire. At about 9:00 on Sunday morning, May 1, a fire began near the brewery's stables. It spread to the stables and the carriage house. The brewery's ten horses were rescued, although three were injured. Three delivery wagons were damaged and a "light wagon" was destroyed. Other material in the stables, such as harnesses, were damaged. There was $3,000 in damage. The *Washington Post* report suggested that some boys playing with matches started the fire. Heurich claimed it was caused by a careless smoking worker. Most of the news coverage of the fire was not about the cause, or the damage, but about an altercation between City Commissioner Thomas P. Morgan and the fire department's Chief Engineer Martin Cronin. Morgan happened to be near the brewery when the alarm was sounded and hurried to the site. When Chief Cronin arrived, he thought that Morgan, who had previously served as a fire commissioner, was infringing on fire department responsibilities. Morgan claimed that the chief was rude to him when asking him to leave, and demanded that he be reprimanded. Chief Cronin was forced to apologize.[29]

Heurich thrived, but his workload began to take a toll on his health. He suffered from unspecified breakdowns and "dizzy" spells. In 1881 he suffered from what he later described as "a serious breakdown in health due, according to my doctor, to nothing more nor less than hard work." The doctor advised Heurich to "take an immediate rest, counseling as the most satisfactory cure a sea-voyage." This surely hit a nerve with Heurich. In 1869 he suffered from a lingering illness, which may have been malaria. He regained his health by signing as a seaman with one of his brother-in-law's voyages to the Caribbean. While his health was restored, the voyage was not among Heurich's most pleasant memories. He later described that trip as having resulted "in physical and mental suffering never to be forgotten." When his doctor suggested another sea voyage Heurich burst out laughing, then had to explain to his offended physician about his earlier experience. His doctor assured him that he need not sign up as a seaman, but as a passenger. Heurich agreed and decided to take his wife to see his homes in Römhild and Haina, as well as to "take the [water] cure" at Karlsbad.[30]

In June 1882, Heurich, his wife Amelia, and his sister Elisabeth left Baltimore for Germany on the SS *America*, operated by the Norddeutscher Lloyd company. It was the first trip back to his home since coming to America, but many more would follow. Heurich continued to return to Germany regularly throughout his life. Before he died he claimed to have made seventy-three trips across the Atlantic, but the 1882 trip was only his second. Certainly his accommodations had improved since his first rip. Heurich could afford to travel first class at this time, and may well have done so. The *America* was twenty years old when Heurich sailed on her. As was common for passenger liners going between Europe and the United States at the time, it had far more space for steerage passengers (room for 480) than for first class (76) and second class (107). The Norddeutscher Lloyd line operated weekly departures between New York and Baltimore to Bremen and back with eight ships.[31] The Heurich family would have left from New York and arrived in Bremen from seven to ten days later. From there they took the train, which now reached Heurich's old home town. In his memoirs Heurich remembered how he felt when he stepped off the train back in Römhild for the first time in at least sixteen years:

> Here is the moment I have been waiting for since 1866—these twenty five years [*sic*]. I have come home a successful man. The innkeeper's son is a prosperous American merchant. Look at this throng of old friends gathered around to welcome you.[32]

Heurich and his wife spent a month in Germany, and he noted that he suffered a "flash of homesickness for the land of my adoption!" Heurich describes how happy he was to see his old hometown, "the lovely old weather-beaten houses, the quaint, narrow, crooked streets." He saw childhood friends and one childhood sweetheart, now a "comfortable looking hausfrau with children tugging at her skirts." He remembered her as "a pretty little thing with long flaxen tresses, the child belle of my early schooldays." Heurich and his wife were childless (he would not father any children until his third marriage), so the sight of his old sweetheart with children of her own may have struck him as particularity poignant.[33]

After leaving Römhild, the Heuriches went on to Karlsbad, as Heurich had found that taking the "cure" did improve his health. The fact that he chose Karlsbad is interesting, given the speculation about the causes of Heurich's ill health in 1869–1870. He complained of a recurring fever and general ill health. One possible explanation was malaria, which could be found in the river valleys of the Midwest where Heurich lived for a time. A short biographical article published in 1932 claimed that it was malaria, as did a 1940 newspaper article about his career. The latter claimed that he suffered two bouts with the disease while in Kansas.[34] Heurich described his illness in only limited and general terms, but suggested that his illness left him weak and unable to work, and that it reoccurred throughout much of his life. An 1879 medical journal described the symptoms of those suffering from what the author labeled *malarial cachexia* in this way:

> There is a general sense of malaise, or a feeling of being constantly tired; breathlessness on exertion; ability to do but a fractional part of the manual labor formerly possible; and the fatigue after labor is profound, and slowly recovered from. Want of energy is very common, and there are often hypochondria and irritability; all these without any apparent organic disease. In many cases there are frequent attacks of sick headache, or migraine, evidently the result of this cachexia, as they occur in persons who were not naturally disposed to them.

This is a wide description, and could fit multiple conditions. However, the same medical journal article recommends as a treatment "Carlsbad salts" and "the hot springs."[35] Again, this is only suggestive. Carlsbad salts could refer to mineral water or salt from the specific Bohemian town, but was also sometimes used generically. However, there were hundreds of spas in Europe, with the largest concentration of them in Switzerland and Bohemia and neighboring parts of Germany. One historian counted ninety-nine spas and mineral springs just in Westphalia. Of all these options, Heurich picked Karlsbad, which was recommended by one medical guide, stating:

> Cases of malarial cachexia and anaemia, from long residence in tropical countries, are often benefited by waters and baths, varied according to individual indications.… For cases with hepatic and splenic enlargements the Bohemian spas, and especially Karlsbad, have a high reputation.[36]

The cost of treatment at the spa was not listed in the medical guidebooks, but would have been beyond the reach of anyone who was not, at the very least, comfortably middle-class. Nonetheless, spas crossed economic and social boundary lines, much as did Heurich at the time, occupying multiple spaces simultaneously. The spa culture had been developing for over a century even before Heurich's first visit in 1882. Spas in central Europe, France, and England had catered first to royalty and nobility, and then to the wealthy. Even lower-born persons could experience the benefits of drinking and bathing mineral waters at many spas, although well-off peasants and wealthy patrons were kept separate at the facilities. The societal aspect of the spa was, as discussed earlier, a particularly important part of the experience.

Many German spas in particular profited more by their casinos than from the health benefits of their waters. While Austria had not allowed the formation of casinos, and France had banned them in 1837, Germany did not rid the spas of their profitable side businesses until 1870–1871, removing not just an income stream, but a focal point for guests' socializing. As a result, spas began to re-emphasize the health benefits rather than the social. This did not mean that all gaming disappeared. If a few well-to-do gentlemen wanted to play a game of cards of their own volition and some money changed hands at the end, well, that was their business. Heurich loved to play skat all his life, but for small stakes at most. If he indulged while at Karlsbad, it was part of the relaxation that was a crucial part of the process. No doubt he had little trouble finding two partners (it was a three-person game), but the rules were not yet finalized and games varied by region in Germany, so some settling of the ground rules would have come first. At home in D.C. while playing skat, Heurich enjoyed drinking a bottle or two of his brewery's beer, served warm. At Karlsbad, though, the beer might well have been replaced by the local mineral water, which was, after all, the point of going there, although light beers were allowed.[37]

Unlike other spas in central Europe, Karlsbad was not an old Roman spa town. It had been discovered in the fourteenth century, according to legend by Emperor Charles IV. It is not entirely correct to say King Charles "discovered" it, as the area was already known as "Wary" (from "warm"), but the town was named after Charles and he may well have spread the word of its existence to other nobility. Karlsbad, like much of the rest of the region, was part of numerous kingdoms, and political control varied as wars and dynastic battles swept over the area repeatedly. It was sacked during the Thirty Years' War. However, by the seventeenth century it was being used by royalty, including Russian Czar Peter the Great in 1711 and 1712, to "take the cure." Visitation dramatically increased beginning in the late eighteenth and early nineteenth centuries, from 445 visitors in 1785 to 28,600 in 1885. By the 1880s there were over a dozen springs ready for visitors, as well as numerous hotels. An 1885 guide lists nine "hotels of the first class" and four "of the second class."[38]

Spa guests followed a daily routine, and visits were intended to be long enough to allow them to get settled into it. Schedules could vary between different spas and during different eras.[39] Heurich's routine at Karlsbad probably looked like this, described in the 1885 guidebook:

1. Wake up call at his door at 5:30 a.m.
2. At 6:00 begin taking "his morning goblet" of spring water "from the hands of the neatly dressed little maid who presides over the fountain." The guide warns visitors not to be late, as there will be a line of two to three hundred people, many of whom will have to wait in line more than once, depending upon how many glasses of the water their doctor prescribed. Guests could hire someone to wait in line for them and bring them their water, however, for 20 krona.
3. After drinking the water, "a promenade is taken, enlivened by the strains of the band." Guests take their walk after every cup—water, walk, water, walk, water, walk—until they have taken all of their prescribed dosage of spring water.
4. After the walks and watering, guests had a light breakfast, usually coffee and a hard roll, no butter. The guidebook warns American and English visitors that this may take some acclimation if the guest is used to a more "substantial morning meal."
5. After breakfast guests have free time for walking or taking a ride until dinner.
6. Dinner (lunch) is "simple." The guest is served "soup, fish, a roast joint, green vegetables, stewed fruit," and may enjoy light alcoholic beverages, including, no doubt to Heurich's relief, "light German beer."
7. After lunch, guests were encouraged to take another walk, perhaps find a quiet place to sit and talk. Napping was "strictly forbidden." They could enjoy coffee at a local café "cheerfully served by the young and pretty coffee-girls." A band would play from 4:00 to 6:00.
8. After 6:00, guests would enjoy a light supper, probably similar to the lunch menu.
9. After supper, Heurich could have enjoyed the theater, a concert, or even a dance at a ballroom, although formal attire was discouraged.
10. Guests retired to bed by 10:00, a bit later if attending a dance, although 5:30 a.m. would come quickly.[40]

The Karlsbad routine fits the pattern of this type of spa treatment with its emphasis on consuming the waters, sometimes in daunting amounts. (Patients walked for 10–15 minutes between glasses; no doubt their walks took them past a restroom before the end.) The social aspect was also key. Note that the activities center on an orderly middle-class regimen. The attached gambling house at some German spas pre–1870 were obvious exceptions, but also note that not every spa allowed gambling, and that it was banned in large part because it seemed to be overshadowing the healthy, more respectable middle-class activities. Spa life centered on a carefully balanced mixture of discipline and amenities, and as the spas' customer base transitioned from nobility and the most wealthy to a middle-class clientele, the daily routine evolved to fit.[41] Even the special diet, the "simple" food, fit this increased emphasis on the middle class. Thinness in men had come to signify self-control rather than hunger or want, at least for the middle class. This "self-control" indicated "moral fitness," and the latter was linked to physical fitness and health.[42]

A major part of the spa experience was the music, which was probably a major reason why Heurich so enjoyed visiting them. Heurich loved music. Seeing one of the premier performances of Richard Wagner's *Parsifal* and then meeting the composer was one of his favorite memories of visiting Karlsbad. Of course he was also a longtime supporter of the Washington *Sängerbund*. Spas used music as part of their treatment because music affected the guests' emotions, and restoring an emotional balance was as crucial a part of spa experience as the physical treatment. Music could not only stimulate particular emotions, it could "provide a rhythm that would sustain those emotions."[43] As such, it was not mere background noise, nor was it only solemn, serious music, although a chorale would not be out of place. Cheery light music, such as waltzes, was favored. The German term was *Tafelmusik*, lunch-time music, although at a spa it would play before breakfast and before supper, to set the emotional mood. It could also set a leisurely walking pace for guests strolling preferably with other guests.

Light music also helped establish the sense of sociability, which was a critical part of spa treatment. Guests were expected to find "congenial yet appropriate company." The *Partie*, or small social group, was "the most important emotional institution of a spa." Consisting of small groups of guests, a *Partie* would get together in mid-morning or afternoon to go walking in the countryside, or take a short tour of the sites in the local town. After dinner the *Partie* might enjoy music together, play cards, or dance. Being by yourself was frowned upon, so Heurich, like other guests, would be under pressure to find a congenial group to spend his time with. If you were with family or friends, such as Heurich traveling with his wife, there was less pressure to find company with strangers. There was some mixing of classes, as well as nationalities. Of course the cost of the spa would deter the poor or working class from attending, but middle class, upper class and nobility might mingle, if only for a time. Families might go together to introduce adolescent daughters to society in an unpressured atmosphere. Perhaps the "congenial but appropriate company" might include a future spouse. Heurich was with his wife on his first trip to Karlsbad, but on later trips when he was by himself, a few parents undoubtedly looked him over as a possible match. He was by then a well-off, handsome man, still on the young side of middle age, with a respectable, successful business.[44]

There was a central paradox to the spa life, however. Was it primarily medicine, or was it a pleasant vacation? Many would have said it was both, but the spa treatment was about balance, and there was a necessary balance between medical treatment and relaxation that was not always maintained. The pre–1870 casinos in German spas are the most blatant example of an imbalance, but they were not the only cause for concern. What was the overlap between "guest" and "patient"? Were they the same thing, or were guests only there to enjoy the relaxing atmosphere, with any health benefits an agreeable side effect? There was a nationalistic aspect to this question as well. The latter quarter of the nineteenth century was an era of German advances in science and medicine. This was a great source of pride among Germans, and the spas reflected this as they worked to professionalize their medical treatments. Their advertising, including pamphlets in English sent to the United States for the public as well as directly to physicians, emphasized the science behind "hydrotherapy." Spa doctors worked, unsuccessfully in the end, to have "balneology" ("*balneum*" is Latin for "bath") recognized as a legitimate specific discipline in German medical schools. However, as the twentieth century grew closer, the health aspects of the spa life became more important than the social. As one historian noted, by the 1890s, "Patients voluntarily submitted themselves to a curative regimen under the direct supervision of a physician and paid for the privilege." The medical aspect, the "curing," had "assumed the unquestionably dominant position." As the 1885 guidebook proclaimed, "The goddess of health reigns supreme, and all must yield to her sway."[45]

Heurich also managed to do some work while in Europe. One of his old friends, a fellow apprentice, was now running a brewery in Pilsen, then in Austria-Hungary. Heurich studied how his old colleague made Pilsener beer. From there, Heurich and Amelia traveled through Frankfurt, Wiesbaden, Koln, and then to Hamburg. Not everything went smoothly. While preparing to leave Munich for Stuttgart, Heurich asked the train conductor for an empty compartment for privacy. He tipped the man a mark and was led to an empty compartment where he and his wife settled in and fell asleep. Sometime after dark, Amelia thought something seemed wrong. Heurich checked and found that the car they were in had been decoupled from the Stuttgart train, and had been left behind in Ulm, leaving them to try to find a hotel room in the middle of the night.

The next morning they visited the "Ulm Cathedral," where Heurich discovered that he was recognizably American. After a tour of the cathedral he tipped the guide a mark coin. "You are from America," the astonished guide said. Heurich said yes. "Then I must show you what you have not yet seen," the guide continued, "and what is very interesting." A bemused Heurich later noted, "In other words the tip of a mark [about twenty-five cents in American currency at the time] could only come from an American." To add some perspective, a small tradesman might make five to six marks a day. The Heuriches reached Stuttgart safely, then went to Frankfort am Main and saw the Goethe festival. Finally they reached Bremen and sailed for New York and then home. He remembered the trip fondly for the rest of his life. In a handwritten comment in the draft of his unpublished memoirs, written about 1940, Heurich wrote "Glorious memories!" by the section describing his trip.[46]

What did this mean for Heurich? He found himself in a transitional space, much as he occupied one in Washington. Traditionally spas were a playground for royalty, or at least for those of noble birth. Peasants were allowed within specific limits, restricted as to time and place. In the nineteenth century, however, the middle classes were admitted within spa society, initially under restrictions, and then with increased access. Eventually the spa culture itself changed to fit a middle-class view of orderly, healthful relaxation for medicinal purposes. The closing of the casinos was a part of this transition. So was the music, which reflected middle-class tastes: popular, accessible, and certainly not avant-garde. Heurich was himself in a similar space, both economically and socially. Certainly he was better off financially as a brewery owner than he had been as an apprentice. However, his transitional status went beyond such superficial changes. Note how the tour guide remarked that Heurich "must be an American" because of his generous tip of a full mark. As both an immigrant and as a tourist, Heurich resided in a borderland between those who are fully members of a group and those who are fully outsiders. Heurich was visiting his homeland, but now was discernable as an "other," even if being defined as a generous, wealthy American was a positive definition of otherness. His hometown of

Römhild apparently greeted him warmly, but twenty years of changes that had occurred in his absence meant that he no longer quite totally fit, certainly not in the role he had filled as a young man when he left home. In Karlsbad, Heurich and his wife would have been placed into roles as tourists, temporary, if necessary, visitors.

This does not mean that Heurich would have necessarily been uncomfortable occupying this borderland between native and outsider. He continued to visit spas throughout the rest of his life; he thought they promoted his health, and he and his wife enjoyed their stay in 1882. As noted earlier, Heurich loved music, and while visiting Bayreuth he was able to "plunge into such an orgy of music as had not been my privilege—and my joy—since the period of my journeyman apprenticeship in my beloved Vienna." He was especially delighted to see "the first performance of Wagner's dedicatory festival play, *Parsifal*," on July 26. There were sixteen performances that summer of Wagner's three-act opera, which had taken him twenty-five years to finish. Heurich enjoyed an orchestra of 107, a chorus of 135, and 23 soloists, some performing multiple parts. He also got to meet Wagner himself, noting, "It was unforgettable."[47]

The Heuriches had not been able to have children. However, some of Amelia's family, and Keyser, had seven children and struggled to support them. Heurich and Amelia suggested that they adopt one of the children, perhaps Amelia Keyser, Amelia Heurich's little niece who came and played at the brewery. Keyser refused and the idea went nowhere. In one of the odd twists history sometimes takes, in 1899 the younger Amelia Keyser became Heurich's third wife. That still lay two decades in the future, but in the autumn of 1883 the elder Amelia began to suffer from poor health. She went through a long series of illnesses and temporary recoveries. A nephew later noted in a family history that Amelia caught a "bad cold" while Heurich was taking the *kaltwasserkur* (cold water cure) in Germany. Her health failed enough that her doctor forced them to cancel another trip to Europe for the summer. Instead she went to Baltimore to stay with family. In September 1884, too weakened to travel back to Washington, Amelia died of pneumonia at age forty-four. Her tombstone read "Ach sie haben, Eine gute Frau begraben, Und

Top: Amelia Keyser as a baby, circa 1866. The niece of Heurich's first wife, Amelia. The Heuriches offered to adopt her as their own (courtesy Jan King Evans Houser). *Bottom:* Amelia Mueller Schnell (1841/2–1884), Heurich's first wife. This is a memorial photograph framed by flowers in the Christian Heurich home. Photograph by Mark Benbow (courtesy the Heurich House Museum).

dem Gatten war sie mehr." ("Oh they have Buried a good woman, And to the husband she was more.") Her photo still hangs in the Heurich mansion, in a glass frame surrounded by preserved white flowers.[48]

A distraught Heurich buried himself in his work. Heurich described how he would "just crowd out misery with prolonged and continued activity so that you go to bed at night just tired out and fall into dreamless, restful sleep." However, once again there was a cost to his health, and on his doctor's orders, he made another trip to Germany to take the "cold water cure" at Elgersburg, in Saxe-Gotha. Heurich did so in the summer of 1885, but noted that he couldn't work himself to exhaustion for ten months, then try to "balance nature's book with two months of a complete laydown." So his doctor also suggested that Heurich purchase a farm so he could enjoy fresh air while still remaining close enough to the District to keep an eye on his business. He ended up purchasing a 376-acre piece of land near Hyattsville, Maryland, only eight miles from his brewery on 20th Street NW. Heurich named his new farm Bellevue, and it remained his country home and refuge for the rest of his life. Heurich had the farm's silos—a frequent fire threat in farms of that era—built out of concrete to make them fireproof. At the time, building with concrete was still relatively new. In the early 1890s, he would take a similar approach when he built a new home in the city and a new brewery. His country home was "comfortable, unpretentious ... the typical gabled frame house of the eighties, with high ceilings and good-sized rooms." It would remain the beloved country retreat for Heurich and his family for the next seventy years.[49]

Heurich also had to deal with unions for the first time in 1885. He was doing business with W.S. Jenks & Company, a local business that sold stoves, fuel, and hardware.[50] Jenks was a nonunion business, and the Knights of Labor threatened to boycott Heurich's business unless he stopped doing business with Jenks. Heurich had already promised that the contractors working on buildings which he owned, such as a boarding house across the street from his brewery, would use only union workers. At least one contractor had failed to abide by this restriction, so several of the city's trade unions called for a boycott of Heurich's beer.

Brewery unionization was just regaining momentum in 1885 after earlier setbacks. The Brewery Workers Union had attempted a strike against the entire New York City brewing industry in 1881. The new union did not have enough resources, so the strike failed and the union collapsed. By 1884 brewery workers in New York were reforming a new organization as part of the Knights of Labor. In the spring of 1885, the Peter Doelger Brewery, one of the largest in New York, fired several workers for union activity. The union called for a boycott of the brewery's products, and the brewery was forced to back down. Peter Doelger agreed to the union's demands and even paid $1,000 to reimburse the union for some of the boycott's cost. The 1885 success against Doelger was unusual, especially as the major breweries in New York City after the strike actually encouraged workers to join and went so far as to threaten workers who did not. By 1886, 90 percent of the city's brewery workers were members. The unions in D.C. were not nearly as strong, but they were active.[51]

Boycotts were a powerful weapon for unions. The Knights of Labor organized workers across an entire industry rather than concentrating on workers with a specific skill. This allowed the Knights to mobilize a wider range of support for a boycott than the craft unions that organized workers according to skill rather than industry. While the Knights used strikes to gain leverage, they also were able to use several types of boycotts.

Primary boycotts were against a particular individual company. Secondary boycotts were used to stop others from doing business with the company being boycotted. A "materials" boycott involved refusing to use material for a job that was made by a specific company, such as bricklayers not using material made by a brick manufacturer being boycotted. Boycotts of brewers, including this action against Heurich, were known as "buy only union beer" campaigns and were a common form of secondary boycott. Of the 1,339 boycotts in this period, almost 40 percent were against two types of firms, construction companies and bakers. Among the other industries commonly targeted were breweries.[52]

There were limitations to this tactic, however, when targeting businesses such as Heurich's. They were difficult to organize against multiple businesses in the same city. This was an issue in New York, as the brewery workers struggled to convince workers not to buy from the companies being boycotted, which provided most of the beer for the entire city. That meant getting support from not only those workers immediately affected, but by different groups of consumers—workers and middle class alike. In extreme cases this meant having to provide for importing union-made beer from out of town so consumers had an alternative. Boycotting a single company, or a small group of companies, was more practical, and statistics from New York between 1885 to 1892 show that boycotts were most frequently employed against smaller-scale producers that had sufficient competition to allow consumers to take their business elsewhere.

If workers for one business were represented by several different unions, a successful boycott meant getting support from each individual group, as well as from workers in the same industry at other companies, and from workers in general. Finally, for a boycott to succeed, it sometimes had to gain support from other businesses. For brewery boycotts this meant winning support from saloonkeepers, bartenders, and liquor dealers. The Washington unions could not expect such unprecedented levels of cooperation. When the Knights of Labor called for a boycott of saloons selling Heurich's beer, the brewer fought back. He radically lowered the price of his beer so those saloons could sell his beer at half price or less.

The boycott continued, so Heurich called for a public meeting at D.C.'s Cosmopolitan Hall, a popular public meeting place, on June 1, 1885. Union members were invited, as were the beer sellers. The hall was full, and on Heurich's suggestion, attendees elected Charles Walter as meeting chair.[53] Heurich defended his record, claiming that only a tiny fraction, $2,000 of a total $100,000, spent on construction had been for nonunion work. Only one nonunion workman had been hired, and that "was by mistake." According to the *Evening Star*'s account, Heurich "said that he was a laboring man himself, and in sympathy with them." However, he "did not propose to surrender his personal liberty and allow others to dictate to him about his private affairs." "Every cent of money he now possessed," Heurich continued, "would be devoted to resisting this attack upon his rights as a free man." His architect, Mr. Dutton, then spoke, noting that Heurich "inevitably favor[ed] union men and union prices." A discussion between Heurich and labor leader "Mr. Blake" got into a discussion that the *Star* reporter described as "animated" but "temperate." Simon Wolf, a local lawyer and anti–Temperance supporter, tried to steer the meeting towards a resolution, noting that everyone present seemed to want "to do what was right." A committee of beer sellers and union representatives would form a committee to work out an arrangement to end the boycott.[54]

This would seem to have ended the meeting with an agreement, but Heurich again noted that he would fight the boycott with all of his resources. This started an even more animated discussion with the union representative.

> "If you defy the trade unions," exclaimed Mr. Blake, "I warn you, Mr. Heurich, that you will go under."
>
> "All right," said Mr. Heurich, "I am satisfied to go under."
>
> "Unless you come down from your high horse," continued Mr. Blake, with some warmth, "I predict that you will come to poverty."
>
> "Very well," responded Mr. Heurich, "I did not come to this country to be in slavery. It is not a question of dollars and cents with me. It is a question of principle. I will stake all I have on this question."

The meeting, noted the *Star*, "adjourned without appointing the committee" of beer sellers and union representatives.[55] In his published memoirs, Heurich noted simply that he attended a meeting, where he recorded "there was talk, pro and con," but "I could not make heads or tails out of it."

The boycott continued, and Heurich left for what was becoming his regular summer trip to Europe. Ten weeks after the Cosmopolitan Hall meeting, the boycott was still in progress, and the beer sellers were getting nervous. On August 11, eighty-nine local saloon keepers who sold Heurich's beer met to consider what to do. The Washington Saloon Keepers Association had been in existence before the boycott, although it had originally been named the German Saloon-Keepers Association. Such groups were common in the late nineteenth and early twentieth centuries, and operated to jointly fight the prohibitionists and to police their own members so as to prevent scandals that might aid the temperance forces' calls to close the saloons. German-Americans were the predominant ethnic group among saloonkeepers in many cities, so such associations often started as all-German groups. Widening the membership to include other members, however, gave the groups more influence. The D.C. association met again on August 14 with representatives of the Knights of Labor and the Federation of Labor Unions. Colonel Tim Lee, who had a saloon on D Street near 10th Street, claimed that his sales of beer were down by about a third. The saloonkeepers had their own issue with the unions, especially about selling cigars made in nonunion shops. The saloonkeepers agreed to sell only union-made cigars and to pressure Heurich to settle the dispute.[56]

Heurich was represented by Charles Jacobsen. One of his nephews, son of Heurich's sister Elisabeth in Baltimore, he had begun working for Heurich in the summer of 1873 when he was only thirteen years old. He filled growlers, tins of beer that customers could carry home to drink. He began working for his uncle full time as a salesman and bill collector when he turned twenty. Heurich did not yet have any children, and was unmarried at the time, so he relied on his nephew to run the brewery business while he was away. Jacobsen agreed to send a cable to Heurich asking him if he would agree to the unions' terms, to hire none but union men and to use nothing but union-made material in his construction projects, "or in any other kind of work he may want done." The unions insisted on getting a signed agreement. The saloonkeepers balked, They had good relations with Heurich and did not want to seem distrustful. They agreed that a cable from Heurich would suffice. A message was sent to Heurich in Hamburg, and he replied: "Contents of your dispatch accepted. Heurich." This was "taken as an acceptance of the terms" and the boycott was lifted.[57]

Heurich remembered later that his "reply stopped the battle until my return." Once home again, Heurich "agreed to this compromise" as a "favor to my customers."[58] His competitors probably had mixed feelings. Heurich at that time claimed to be selling fully half of the beer sold in D.C. Given that he had approximately two hundred dealers selling his beer, that is likely a reasonable estimate. Had those selling Heurich's beer abandoned him for other suppliers, his local rivals would have been the obvious beneficiaries. However, they would also have been wary of giving the unions a victory. If Heurich, the city's largest brewer, turned out to be vulnerable to union pressure, then they would be even more so.[59]

Heurich's reaction to the union demands was interesting. His sharp reaction to the union, comparing his acquiescence to union demands to slavery, would not have been out of place in the other industrial union battles of the era. His experiences first as an apprentice, then as a journeyman, and finally as an employee of other breweries before starting his own business, left him with sympathy for laborers, but also a determination not to allow such dominance of his own fortunes by others again. There is more than a trace of this in his experience with the failed German-American Bank, in which he found himself in debt to others, forcing him to take out insurance to borrow money to pay back his creditors. He never again put himself in a financial situation where that might recur, and avoided serving on another bank board. In contrast, however, he was willing to place such demands on those contractors and supplies with which he regularly dealt. Was this sympathy for workers and unions, or simply a business decision by a successful businessman? Heurich could make hard decisions that left bruised feelings when he felt it necessary and justified, such as his buying out Paul Ritter, his first business partner in D.C. He was willing to defy the boycott even if that meant possibly hurting the businesses of the dealers selling his beer. So while Heurich did show sympathy and concern for his own employees through his long career, his requiring other businesses to hire only union labor while escaping that requirement himself was likely a purely business decision.

While nephew Charles Jacobsen dealt with the union while his uncle was away, another of Heurich's nephews, Hugo Julius Heurich, supervised the brewery operations as foreman. The son of Heurich's brother, August Friedrich, Hugo had come to the U.S. from Germany to work for his uncle. In early 1886, however,[60] Hugo was badly injured during barrel pitching, coating the inside of the barrels with pine resin to seal them from leaking as well as to sanitize them. It was a dangerous procedure: the resin was applied while boiling at 350 degrees, and the resulting vapors could be explosive. A contemporary guide to brewing described it:

> The pitch is brought to the boiling point in an open boiler of sheet-iron or copper, which is bricked in over a furnace. The barrel is laid obliquely against a block of wood, the open side being somewhat raised, the necessary quantity of pitch is poured into it with a ladle, and thus is ignited by a red-hot iron. The head which has been taken out is turned towards the barrel, so that only sufficient air can enter for keeping up the burning, and the smoke can pass out. The pitch should burn briskly, because if the smoke is not carried off well the beer will afterwards acquire a disagreeable, smoky taste.... After a few minutes, the head is pressed tightly against it to extinguish the fire, the pitch is scraped out of the grooves of the chime, the head is quickly put in, the hoops are driven up, the barrel is turned over several times to distribute the pitch uniformly, and finally the plug is knocked out to allow the air and smoke to escape. The barrel must then be rolled for some time until the pitch has become cold, and then the bung is also taken out.[61]

After the accident, Hugo could no longer work. He died in February 1886 from his injuries, only twenty-eight years old. Heurich does not spend much time discussing the accident in his memoirs, and does not even refer to Hugo by name, simply referring to him as "my nephew." This does not mean that Heurich was uncaring about his young family member's death, but it does suggest that he tried to emotionally distance himself from the accident and his nephew's death.[62]

In February 1887, Heurich married a second time. His new wife was Mathilde Daetz, sister of August Daetz, the brewery's secretary and treasurer. Mathilde had moved to the U.S. from Bremervoerde (near Bremen), Germany, in 1886 and spoke little English. She was described as a tall brunette, "with perfect features and brown hair and eyes."[63] A surviving photo at the Heurich House Museum shows a delicate young woman. At the time of their marriage, Heurich was forty-five and Mathilde was twenty-five years old. Married at the Concordia Lutheran Church in Washington, D.C., they set up house in a home built at 1218 19th Street NW, just behind the 20th Street brewery. It was a stand-alone three-story brick townhome, and Heurich and his wife soon expanded it. In 1889 he hired a young local architect, John G. Meyers, to add a second story to the kitchen and to build a glass conservatory as an addition for $1,500. After the Heuriches moved out in 1894 to live in their new home, they rented it to the Washington Fencers' Club. The young architect, John

Heurich's second wife, Mathilde Daetz (1865–1895). From a painting hanging in Heurich's home. Photograph by Mark Benbow (courtesy the Heurich House Museum).

Meyers, must have made his clients happy, as the Heuriches chose him to design their new, much larger home a little over a block away in 1892.[64]

Heurich and his new bride traveled to Europe in June, visiting Marienbad, a popular spa town in Bohemia that was at its height of popularity between 1870 and 1914.[65] The marriage was happy, but Mathilde's health was "not good," according to Heurich. In 1889 she was pregnant. Heurich noted in his unpublished memoirs, "At last I believed I was to become a father; the prayers of years were to be answered." Unfortunately, Mathilde lost the child during an unspecified "operation" which left her bedridden. On doctor's orders, Heurich purchased a home in Atlantic City so that she could enjoy the fresh sea air and breezes. The seaside resort was a popular destination, and certainly would have been more pleasant than Washington in summer. They also traveled to Wiesenbaden and Schlangebad in Germany, making trips to Europe in late 1889 and in the summer of 1890. In 1891 Heurich and Mathilde traveled throughout the American west, including a trip to the hot mineral springs at Pas de Robles, California. Mathilde's health, however, remained poor. Heurich noted that "she never did wholly recover from the strain and the pain of those weeks in Atlantic City" when she lost her unborn child. The memory remained painful for Heurich. When he edited the draft of his unpublished memoirs fifty years later, he crossed out the paragraph describing Mathilde's illness and their loss.[66]

Despite his beloved wife's illnesses, Heurich had to continue focusing on his brewing business, and the late 1880s were busy. Beginning in 1884, the Department of Agriculture began to run a long series of tests for adulterants on foods, condiments, spices, and beverages. Earlier tests had shown contaminants such as lead in products such as butter, oleomargarine, alcoholic beverages and coffee berries. The series of tests were supervised by Agriculture Department chemist Dr. Harvey Wiley, an Indiana native and Civil War veteran who was concerned not just with harmful additions such as lead, but with consumer fraud by manufacturers substituting cheaper ingredients without their customers knowing. Such adulteration also put honest competitors at a disadvantage, giving rise to support for the efforts from farmers and state agriculture agencies. Moreover, such adulterants could cause American exports to be refused in Europe, which would also hurt producers.

The series of reports, published as parts of *Bulletin 13: Foods and Food Adulterants*, began to come out in 1887, published by the Department of Agriculture. Each bulletin listed the "normal characteristics of the product" being tested, then gave the specifics of how each was tested. Products came from all over the U.S., but many were simply purchased by the government chemists themselves in the markets in Washington. They included local products, but also those from national companies, such as the shipping brewers. The first three parts of the bulletin were issued in 1887. Others would soon follow. These first reports covered dairy products, spices and condiments and, in Part III, "Fermented Alcoholic Beverages, Malt Liquors, Wine and Cider." The reports were not as horrific as one might expect, given later stories such as Upton Sinclair's *The Jungle*. For example, milk was most commonly adulterated by removing cream and by watering it down. Oleomargarine was sold as real butter, although this was not a health issue. Spices were more of a problem, especially in ground form. Some "pepper" did not actually contain much actual pepper, having been stretched with rice, corn, mustard hulls, and even dirt. The alcohol report indicated that American wines were often watered down, and in many cases did not have much actual grape in them, consisting largely of alcohol, sugar and water. The problem, so far as the Department was concerned, was not necessarily health concerns, but that some companies were selling products covertly made with cheaper ingredients, defrauding the consumer.[67]

What about the beer? The report tested thirty-two different beers, in bottles and draft, "about all the different brands and varieties of beers of domestic manufacture obtainable in Washington."[68] According to the report:

> The malt liquors used as samples were all purchased in Washington, D.C., and included the various popular brands made in Milwaukee, Cincinnati, Philadelphia, New York, &c., which are sold all over the country, as well as the product of the few local brewers. Some were obtained from wholesale dealers, but the majority were purchased in retail saloons and groceries, without statement of the purpose for which they were intended. All the draft beers were obtained in this way. A few English and German beers and ales were analyzed for comparison.

The report announced that some of the beers used other materials as substitutes for malt, such as sugar, which added no nutritional value. The possible additives of most concern, however, were preserving agents.[69]

The report named no specific beers, but Heurich knew that his beer did not contain these additives or other "impurities." He complained to Norman Colman, Commissioner of Agriculture, that by not naming the beers examined, the report cast a doubt on all the beers produced in the city. At first the commissioner refused to act, then he promised he would release the results showing that Heurich's beer had no adulterants, then he again refused. Frustrated, Heurich took his complaint to the U.S. Congress. It took the intervention of a friendly congressman and fellow German immigrant, Jacob Romeis (R–Ohio),[70] to force the Department of Agriculture to release the results for Heurich's beer. Even then it was not until late 1891 that the results were released. The Department of Agriculture chemists had tested two bottles of Heurich's beers and neither contained any impurities or malt substitutes. Beginning in 1891, Heurich ran advertisements boasting that his beer had "a record of purity that challenges the world." This advertising campaign continued for several years.[71]

Concern over the health of food and drink also affect Heurich's dairy. Bellevue was also a working dairy farm, although according to family lore it never turned a profit and was more of a hobby for Heurich than a serious business. He used Holstein-Friesian cattle (known as Holsteins in America), the familiar black and white dairy cows. They dated in the United States back to the seventeenth century, but were imported in numbers starting in the 1860s. They became popular enough that breeders maintain lists (herd books), and founded the Holstein-Friesian Association of America in 1885. The herd books list Heurich as among the members of those who bred and kept Holsteins. Heurich did not just keep the one breed, however. Federal records show Heurich importing German Red Angler cattle through Hamburg to Baltimore. Red Anglers are another type of milk cow, less popular than the Holsteins. Newspaper accounts also attest to his owning Jersey and Guernsey cows as well.[72]

In the early 1890s tuberculosis (TB) in both humans and cattle was a major health concern in the U.S. The disease can jump from one species to another, so fears that people might get TB from cattle was not totally unreasonable. Nor was it appetizing to think of eating meat or drinking milk from tubercular cows. In June 1894 Heurich invited representatives from the U.S. government, including the Secretary of Agriculture, the District's Health Office, representatives from the U.S. Army, and doctors and veterinarians to Bellevue to demonstrate a new test for TB in cattle. A "miserable rain" kept some from attending, including several members of the House of Representatives, but a half-dozen invitees did come to see the demonstration. Dr. David E. Buckingham, a prominent young local veterinarian, administered the test for tuberculosis to ninety of Heurich's cattle. Previously he had injected a culture, "Koch's tuberculin,"[73] made from tubercle bacilli mixed with glycerin, into the shoulder of the animal. After twelve hours, if the subject had tuberculosis, its temperature would rise several degrees. If it did not, its temperature would remain normal. Twelve of Heurich's cattle reacted to the test, indicating that they had the disease. Five of these twelve were killed with the visitors as witnesses, and each animal was examined. All five were confirmed to have tuberculosis. The remainder of the twelve were sent to Virginia for further tests. Heurich did not mention the event in his memoirs, but it's likely he was trying to not only help publicize the test's reliability, but also demonstrate his willingness to take a financial loss by destroying the diseased animals. According to the *Evening Star*, "The animals killed represented a money value of over $1,000 and at the commencement of the test [Heurich] announced his determination of slaughtering his entire valuable herd if it was found necessary to prevent the milk from his farms from exercising a dangerous effect upon those who used it." Of course, this was good publicity. Newspaper advertisements in 1894 advised consumers to buy "Bellvue [*sic*] Dairy Farm" milk because "this is the only herd of cows within one hundred miles of Washington that can show a clean health certificate." Even aside from the good publicity, Heurich demonstrated a constant concern for the healthiness of his products, beer as well as milk. He was also always interested in exploring new technologies, which was evidenced not only on his dairy farm, but in the technology he used in his brewery and in his home. The sales value was an important factor, but not the only one, in Heurich's estimation.[74]

In January 1891 Heurich legally incorporated his brewery. He registered it in Alexandria, Virginia, however, not in the District of Columbia. He did not explain this decision in his memoirs, nor was it mentioned in the press. One possible explanation is the deserved reputation Congress had in running the District of Columbia. It was notoriously unresponsive to the needs and desires of the everyday residents of the city, including businesses. There are other possible explanations, including taxes. However, incorporating in Virginia did not seem to save Heurich money. His brewery and home were still subject to Washington's taxes, and he frequently noted how he was one of Washington's biggest taxpayers. Nor was there a heavy corporate tax in the District. In Congressional testimony given in 1912 about the tax situation in the District as established by Congress in 1878, Charles C. Lancaster testified that the city received little money from taxing corporations, and that the tax burden fell upon taxing "135,000 self-supporting citizens," including Heurich.[75] There was, however, a corporate tax in Virginia.[76]

Whatever the reason for Heurich's incorporating in Alexandria, his brewery was capitalized for $800,000 dollars, and Heurich controlled 90 percent of the stock. Heurich was president and general manager of the new company. Heurich's vice-president was Augustus B. Coppes. A local restaurateur who ran the Oriental, a hotel and restaurant on 7th Street, Coppes was also a local land investor.[77] The brewery's secretary and bookkeeper, Charles Meyer, was with Heurich from 1880 until his death in 1914. Treasurer August Daetz migrated to the United States in 1871 and worked for Heurich for years. His sister, Mathilde, was Heurich's second wife. The rest of the board consisted of local businessmen, most of whom had ties to either food retail or to land speculation. Frank Hume was a native Virginian and a Confederate veteran who lived in Alexandria. He ran a successful grocery in Washington, which included selling his own brand of whiskey. Hume was partners with fellow board member L.G. Hine, investing in new printing technology, specifically mechanical type composition. A Union veteran from Illinois, Hine had a thriving law practice in the District in the 1860s and 1870s and served as district commissioner from 1889 to 1890. Charles C. Duncanson was a D.C. native and vice-president of the Duncanson Brothers, an auction company that dealt in land sales. He may well have known Heurich, an active land investor, through his auction house. Charles Jacobsen was Heurich's nephew from Baltimore. He worked in Heurich's brewery as a young man, then started his own business, the Arlington Bottling Company, which, despite the name, operated in D.C. Among his customers was his uncle. Until Heurich opened his own bottling plant in 1897, Jacobsen's company bottled Heurich's beer. Later Jacobsen would become vice-president of the Washington Baseball Club.[78]

The board was a cross-section of various members of the Washington business community. A few were members of the District's German community, including, of course, Heurich, but they were a minority. There were two family members, but one, Daetz, was a brewery employee before he became Heurich's brother-in-law. Both sides of the Civil War were represented by veterans. None of the board members were Heurich's business rivals. Several of the other local brewers, especially Albert Carry and Robert Portner, invested in each other's firms, but Heurich remained determinedly independent. The board represented a diverse[79] group of influential local business leaders, and each had shown a talent for rising in society, becoming well-off financially through their own efforts. None were born into wealth.

By the early 1890s, there was growing local pressure on Heurich to move his brewery. When Heurich and Paul Ritter had purchased the Schnell Brewery in 1872, it was on the outskirts of the city, in a region known as "the Slashes." An 1861 guidebook described the area as "mere surfaces for the production of malaria and as proper cemeteries for the dead animals of the city." It was the borderlands of the city, with farmland, woods, a slaughterhouse, a brickyard, and a few homes occupied by the poor. In the previous chapter, it was noted that there is a difference between "space" and "place." Space is abstract, taking form in "the structural, geometrical qualities of a physical environment." In contrast, "place" is particular. It's a community created by its inhabitants who define it, and limit it within boundaries through its uses. It provides a template for its own use by those who live, work, or travel through it.[80] By the late 1880s, the neighborhood was changing, and as the place changed, so did the idea of it as a "space" for its residents. The area evolved from the city's frontier to a working-class neighborhood as families moved into the area, setting up both homes and businesses. According to an analysis of the 1880 census, the DuPont Circle area had about 3,100 residents. Approximately one-half of them were African American, and "about 250 immigrants from Ireland, Germany and Great Britain were counted among the white residents." Heurich and his family would have counted among those 250.[81]

Wealthier residents had begun flowing into the DuPont Circle area—although at first in small numbers—at the same time Heurich was expanding his brewery. Alexander Shepherd's home was just a few blocks south of what was still named Pacific Circle.[82] In 1873 noted local architect Adolph Cluss built Nevada Senator William Morris Stewart's "castle" on the Circle itself. From 1886 to 1893 it was the Chinese Legation. The British Legation opened in 1874 at Connecticut Avenue and N Street, very near Heurich's brewery. As local real estate agents promoted the area, and local investors, including Heurich, purchased land and built new homes, the population doubled between 1880 and 1892. This led to an unstable mixture of homes and residents that was unlikely to last. Heurich recalled the story of a conflict between two such neighbors, William C. Whitney, President Grover Cleveland's Secretary of the Navy (1885–1889), and "an Irish teamster," Pat Rigney. Whitney rented a mansion on I Street near 18th Street NW. Across the street was Rigney's home, "a weather beaten and much patched cabin." The teamster, his wife, and their eleven children were described by Heurich as "husky, healthy, but extremely dirty." Dismayed upon first seeing his new neighbor, Whitney tried to buy the Irishman's home, but was rebuffed repeatedly. When Whitney gave his first official party, which would have been part of D.C.'s society's official "season," the Rigneys threw their own, somewhat less opulent party. Ladies and gentlemen in the finest fashions paraded to the Whitneys' event even as much more poorly dressed celebrants paraded to their own affair across the street. The sounds of waltzes from the Whitneys' ball mingled in the warm September night air with the "piercing strains of Irish bagpipes and fiddles" from Rigney's. This burlesque continued all through the winter social season. Come the spring, Rigney agreed to sell—for five times the declared value of his home.[83]

Heurich retold this story in his unpublished memoirs with more than a little amusement, but the conflict between classes in the area was undoubtedly real. Heurich's personal life reflected the changes in the area. As the area moved from poor boundary land, to working class, to middle class, to an area for the wealthy, so Heurich's status also grew, a development not matched by the status of his business. While Heurich's reputation increased as a successful businessman, leader in his community, and benefactor, the fact remained that his main business produced beer, an alcoholic beverage at a time when an increasing number of people in the United States viewed alcoholic beverages as poisons, not only physically, but morally. Such opinion was still a minority in the U.S., but it was a noisy minority, and even those who did not see anything wrong with beer for either health or moral reasons might object to the idea of a manufacturing plant in their neighborhood. A brewery did not fit the changing idea of DuPont Circle as an elite "space."

Heurich was puzzled by this attitude. In his unpublished memoirs he sarcastically referred to those who "objected to the healthy smell of good hops and barley." In both his memoirs, published and unpublished, he blamed the "'good' people" in the Temperance movement for their efforts to "'bless' the District of Columbia with prohibition." The "complaints all emanated from the offices of the professional drys now centering on Washington in the fight for a dry law." There was an active chapter of the Women's Christian Temperance Union (WCTU) in Washington, with their accompanying rallies and prayer meetings. So Heurich's laying the blame on them is not totally unreasonable. However, his 20th Street brewery no longer fit into how some members of the local community, at least the most influential members, viewed the appropriate uses of what they now saw as "their" place. The smell of hops and barley may be pleasant, but that is beside the point. The smell was a reminder that a workplace, an industrial plant, was active in the area. Wouldn't the residents of Foggy Bottom be expected to object to the smell as well? Since they were poor and working-class, no. A sensitive nose was considered a virtue of the middle and upper classes. Lower classes were thought to be too coarse to be offended by bad odors.[84]

The changing nature of the D.C. neighborhoods meant that the longer Heurich stayed on 20th Street, the less his business would fit into the area and the more conflict would grow. Heurich decided to move. He did not attribute this decision entirely to the objections of his neighbors, although this was an important part of his decision. An equally important factor was that his existing brewery was not fireproof. Heurich had suffered through three fires since the first in 1875, the previous ones having been started by a chimney spark and by a worker smoking in the stables. The third fire at the 20th Street brewery in 1892 made it clear that a new, fireproof structure was needed.[85] By far the most devastating of the three, it began about 2:20 a.m. on Saturday, July 23. The fire began in the malt section as malt was being loaded into hoppers for the grinders. The night crew had begun pouring some new malt into the hopper when they noticed sparks, probably from small stones in the malt being ground against the metal of the grinding mechanism. The sparks were followed by flames. The malt dust ignited and flames "leaped several feet into the air." The men stopped the machinery, but the fire was already spreading. The workers tried using the fire hoses within the brewery, but malt is highly flammable and the fire was out of control. A newspaper account claimed that "flames burst forth from the top of the building with great fury, illuminating the whole northwest section of the city." The fire department took an hour to get the fire under control, keeping it from spreading to nearby buildings and homes. The brewery's horses were all saved from the stables, but the fire gutted the inside of the brewery and even damaged some of the beer in storage. Thousands of people turned out to watch the scene as police from a half dozen stations were called to control the crowds. Probably neither the fire nor the crowds watching it improved the brewery's reputation among some of his neighbors.[86]

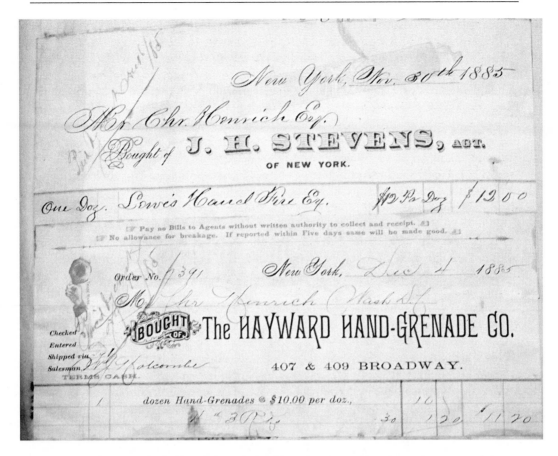

A bill for a dozen fire-extinguisher "hand grenades" from 1885 (Christian Heurich Brewing Company Records, 1883–1913, Archives Center, National Museum of American History).

The loss to the stored malt and stock alone, not to mention the rest of the brewery, totaled approximately $35,000 (approximately $494,000 in 2010), while losses to the building totaled about $65,000, enough to put the survival of the business in doubt. Heurich, however, announced that there was six weeks' worth of stock in the aging cellars and that the brewery would rebuild. The next day crews began cleaning out the wreckage, preparing to rebuild. The fire, however, prompted Heurich to rethink his operating in the old location long-term. Pressure from neighbors to move the brewery was increasing, and the recurring fires, three in less than twenty years, prompted Heurich to build a fireproof facility in a different part of the city. The time had come to move and expand capacity.[87]

Heurich's plans for expansion came just as the economy was plummeting into depression. Like the Panic of 1873, the Panic of 1893 was due in part to overbuilding and shaky financing of railroads, along with bank collapses in the United States and in Britain. A run on the gold supply, in part caused by the poorly written Sherman Silver Purchase Act of 1890, sparked bank runs and a disruption of the U.S.'s international trade. Heurich weathered the depression that lasted from 1893 through 1897 as he had that of the 1870s, as well as the shorter economic downturns of the 1880s. Heurich attributed this in part to the nature of his business: a "lowly glass of beer," he wrote years later, "is something

so steadying and so heartening as is the Rock of Gibraltar.... Come good times or bad
... I have always sold my product, steadily, increasingly. In fact, during several panics,
my business improved." Of course, Heurich had other investments as well, especially in
land. During the various depressions all he had to do, he wrote, was "let land lie and to
wait." The Panic of 1893, in which approximately five hundred banks in the United States
failed, must have reassured Heurich's earlier determination not to invest in banks after
his experiences in the 1870s. And so, still selling great quantities of beer, and with his
real estate investments waiting out the bad times, Heurich weathered the depression and
continued plans for a new brewery and a new home.[88]

In 1893 Heurich and Mathilde traveled to Chicago to visit the World's Fair. In 1867
Heurich had worked in the city briefly at the Seipp and Lehmann Brewery, but had not
stayed. He wanted to polish his English and thought that effort would be hindered by
working in an environment surrounded by other German speakers. In recalling his trip
to the 1893 Fair, Heurich noted, "I often think that but for the circumstance of my desire
to learn the language of my adopted country I might be living in Chicago today." He continued, "I am quite certain I would have done as well for myself there as I have done in
Washington."[89]

Some Washingtonians had pushed for the District of Columbia to host the Fair, but
it depended on private funding, and the city lacked sufficient resources. Nonetheless,
D.C. was considered as a finalist when a congressional committee met in early 1890 to
decide which city would get the official charter. Washington was vying for the honors,
as was Philadelphia. St. Louis was not initially included, prompting complaints from
Missouri's congressional delegation. The House of Representatives voted in February
1890, and although it was clear that Chicago was the favorite choice, it took nine ballots
for it to win the majority of votes over New York, Washington, and St. Louis, with one

A bird's eye view of the Chicago Fair, 1893 (Library of Congress).

vote for the Cumberland Gap in Maryland. The deciding factor was the amount of private pledges of funds via subscriptions from Chicago. Initially totaling five million dollars, it was less than the ten million New York City had pledged, but Chicago's lobbyists quickly matched New York's total.[90]

The Chicago Fair, officially named the World's Columbian Exposition, celebrated the 400th anniversary of Columbus's "discovering" America, and it was designed to be educational as well as celebratory. Nicknamed "the White City," the fairgrounds centered on a temporary neoclassical-designed city along the shore of Lake Michigan. One attendee described it in romantic terms:

> The long lines of white buildings were ablaze with countless lights; the music from the bands scattered over the grounds floated softly out upon the water; all else was silent and dark. In that lovely hour, soft and gentle as was ever a summer night, the toil and trouble of men, the fear that was gripping men's hearts in the markets, fell away from men and in its place came Faith. The people who could dream this vision and make it real, those people … would press on to greater victories than this triumph of beauty—victories greater than the world had yet witnessed.[91]

Heurich was not as lyrical, but he did describe it as "this mammoth production," a "wonderful thing for Americans."

The Smithsonian Institution was responsible for many of the exhibits, which included small villages of Native Americans for visitors to studiously gawk at. There was a World Parliament of Religions, and numerous academic organizations held meetings as well. Future President Woodrow Wilson, then a professor of political economy at Princeton University, gave a presentation, and Frederick Jackson Turner, a young professor from Wisconsin, delivered his landmark paper on the significance of the frontier in American history.[92] Not everything at the fair was so high-minded. The Midway was billed as educational, but it included entertainment such as side shows. Fair visitors, most of whom were white Americans, could stare at Africans in a recreated Dahomeyan village. They could sip the new Welch's Grape Juice while munching on a new snack, Cracker Jack. Heurich could have tried Pabst Blue Ribbon Beer, were he so inclined. In *I Watched America Grow*, Heurich noted two things that made an impression on him, the Ferris wheel and Fatima. The former, designed by George Washington Gale Ferris, Jr., was 264 feet high. Ferris's giant ride had thirty-six enclosed cars, each of which could handle sixty people. It took twenty minutes to make two complete revolutions, which cost the rider fifty cents to be lifted into the air to look over the park grounds, the lake, and Chicago. Fatima, also known as "Little Egypt" (real name Fahreda Mazar Spyropoulos), appeared on the Midway in the "Street of Cairo" show, where she danced what became known as the "Hoochee-Coochee," a mildly suggestive version of a belly dance. The Syrian-born wife of a Chicago Greek restaurateur, she was billed as one of "The Algerian Dancers of Morocco," appearing along with snake charmers and camel rides. Heurich does not mention if he went up in the Ferris wheel, or saw Little Egypt dance, but they were both exceptionally popular attractions at the fair, so it's certainly possible, especially since they are the two things he thought to mention in his memoirs.[93]

Back in Washington, workers started construction on a new, larger brewery by the Potomac River at 26th and D Streets in 1894. Heurich supervised the pouring of the concrete himself, using the experience he had gained from building the concrete silos at his dairy farm in Maryland. The new brewery would be far larger than any other brewery in D.C. and was to be not only as modern as possible, but would allow Heurich to expand his capacity when needed. He would no longer be constricted by space the way he was

Left: **The huge Ferris wheel at the Chicago World's Fair, 1893. Each of the 36 "cars" on the wheel could hold up to 60 people (Library of Congress).** *Right:* **There were several dancers going by the stage name "Little Egypt" who performed in the late 19th century. This is probably one of the two who performed at the Chicago Fair in 1893 (Library of Congress).**

on 20th Street. The new brewery included an ice-making plant that could produce up to one hundred and fifty tons a day, five large aging cellars for lagering his beer, and a brewing capacity at full production of 500,000 barrels of beer each year, up from 30,000 at his 20th Street facility. His business did not take immediate advantage of the extra capacity, but Heurich was evidently prepared for greater sales volume in the future. While the new brewery buildings were being built, the old facility was used to age the beer previously brewed until it was ready for sale, thus reducing the disruption in business. Once the new brewery was ready, the original one was closed.[94]

Heurich's neighbors would not be able to complain, either. He picked an area that was, as he later remembered, "not considered a 'nice' neighborhood." When Heurich purchased his 20th Street brewery it was on the fringes of D.C., geographically, economically, and socially. The site in Foggy Bottom where he put his new brewery was likewise on the fringes on the city. Geographically it was along the Potomac River near undesirable swampy land, hence the name "Foggy Bottom." Before Washington was founded, a small town named "Hamburg" had been laid out and a few homes built where the Heurich brewery would stand. One of D.C.'s first breweries, Coningham's, operated there in the late 1790s. The area was so unhealthy, however, that a disease known as the "Foggy Bottom chills" (probably malaria) deterred most people from living there. Indeed, when the gas plant opened there in the 1850s, it was seen as an improvement, as it was thought that the fumes would chase away the disease.[95] Economically and socially it was also on the fringes. The area included a large African American population, as well as poorer Irish and German immigrants. In the 1890s a small Italian population also established itself there. They largely worked in local businesses, and unskilled laborers outnumbered skilled workers. Alley housing, which lacked not only running water and sewers but also adequate access to light and air, was common throughout D.C., but especially so in this area. Besides Heurich's brewery, Foggy Bottom was also home to the Albert Brewing Company, better known by its later name, Abner Drury Brewing. The two rivals were among the larger area businesses, but Heurich's neighbors also included the Crawford Paving Company, the Godey Lime Kilns, the Clapp Ammonia Company, another lime kiln, coal dealers, and the Arlington Bottling Company run by Heurich's nephew, Charles Jacobsen. The industrial works most people associated with Foggy Bottom was the Washington Gas Company, which owned several lots just a couple of blocks north of Heurich's property. People who lived near a gas plant were not likely to complain of what Heurich called "the healthy smell of good hops and barley." The brewery fit both the physical space as well as the abstract idea of a proper place for such a business.[96]

Back in the DuPont Circle neighborhood, Heurich began building a new home for himself and his wife Mathilde. To design his new home, Heurich picked a local German-American architect, John Granville Meyers (1834–1902). The son of German immigrants,

The Heurich Brewery as seen from the Washington Monument, circa 1906–1915. The rival Arlington Brewing Company is visible just behind the Heurich brewery on the hilltop on the other side of the Potomac River (Library of Congress).

A close-up of the Heurich brewery shows that the area was still heavily industrial, with some residential (Library of Congress).

Meyers was born in Pennsylvania, but moved to D.C. in about 1863 with his wife and family. He was a carpenter, and it's possible that he came to D.C. as one of the many skilled workers who built the series of forts that protected the capital during the Civil War. By 1871, as Heurich was investigating D.C. as a possible site for his new brewery, Meyers was working as an architect. He had no formal training, but it was common practice at the time for architects to learn by reading books on the subject and working with those already experienced in the trade. He also was advertising that he worked with artificial stone, a skill he would use in building Heurich's mansion. Meyers became a supervising architect for the Treasury Department, working on the State, War and Navy Building (later named the Old Executive Building). The Treasury Architect's office was ready known for being "filled with German draftsmen," so he would have fit into the local German community in D.C. just as Heurich was getting himself established in the same. It's likely that the two men met around this time. Meyers followed this job with a contract at the new "College for the Deaf and Dumb" (now Gallaudet University). He lived in Brightwood in northeastern D.C. in an area then known as Schuetzen Park, a reflection of the German immigrant community in the area. By 1879 Meyers was designing his own buildings and was established as a local architect. During the 1880s Meyers was busy. Biographer Susan Mason noted that "during that period he designed almost three-quarters of the total one hundred fifteen buildings he designed during his entire career," specializing in "fine dwellings." He also took out several patents, including a process to make artificial stone as well as a fireproof floor and ceiling. Meyers's advertisement in an 1892 city directory even claimed "fireproof buildings a specialty." This would have been especially appealing for Heurich as he looked for the right architect to construct his new home.[97]

Designing fine homes for the upper middle class and the wealthy would have provided abundant opportunities for a D.C. architect in the 1880s and 1890s. Despite the efforts of Washington businessmen, including Heurich, to promote D.C. as an industrial location with events such as the 1879 Washington Fair, the city's local economy was already moving towards an emphasis on office work instead of industry, notably work connected with the U.S. government. As Heurich found, the areas available for industrial development were shrinking as housing developments spread through the city. That's why Heurich finally had to abandon his 20th Street facility for Foggy Bottom in the 1890s. What commercial development did exist was more likely to be retail selling rather than industrial manufacturing, as consumption superseded production. As newly wealthy Americans discovered that D.C. was open to social advancement not available in the closed elites of New York, Boston, or Philadelphia, D.C. became a popular winter home for the *nouveau riche*. Successful businessmen moved to Washington as newly elected Congressmen or appointed officials, and this fluidity made high society more open. Heurich commented on this in his memoirs: "The city was practically invaded by well-to-do midwesterners and westerners of the millionaire type [who had] just about nothing to do but spend [money] ... in some fashion it became known that 'society' could be reached and climbed aboard easier in Washington than anywhere else in these United States."[98]

Mark Twain made fun of the pretenses of the newcomers his novel *The Gilded Age* (1873) with a family named Oreillé "pronounced O-re*lay*" (emphasis in original). "The Hon. Patrique Oreillé was a wealthy Frenchman from Cork."[99] The Civil War played a role in this openness, as it destroyed the antebellum social structure based upon the families that had established themselves in the first two decades of the nineteenth century, those Twain labeled "the antiques."[100] Many of these families, such as the Bealls and the Corcorans, were Southern sympathizers and either left the U.S. capital during the war, or maintained a low profile. The dominance of the Republican Party in government in the years after the war, and the resulting incoming flood of officials who had been Union veterans, prevented the old prewar aristocracy from reestablishing itself. Heurich arrived in D.C. in 1871, just as this new social order was establishing itself, and his rise in influence kept pace with the new social elite in the city.

The growth of this newly wealthy society in turn led to a growing market for merchants and others selling luxury goods, including opulent homes. Meyers found many of his clients among the wealthier residents, including Heurich, as well as with a growing upper middle class which copied the lead of the wealthy. He also found a natural market in the close-knit local German community. Besides Heurich, his clients included merchant Christian Ruppert, confectioner Herman C. Ewald, Doctor Charles Christiani, furniture dealer Herman Burkhart, and department store owner James Lansburgh. Many of his customers were dry goods merchants, in which the local German community was well-represented.[101]

The new house Meyers designed for the Heuriches was built at 1307 New Hampshire Avenue NW, on lots 37 and 38 of square 115. The land had been purchased by Heurich's first wife, Amelia, and Heurich inherited it in 1884 when she died. An odd-shaped lot that featured a triangular point, it sits at a three-way intersection of New Hampshire Avenue, Twentieth Street and Sunderland Place, less than two blocks from Heurich's original brewery. The four-story home was built of poured concrete and steel. The *Evening Star* reported on some of the fireproofing measures: "There are no wooden joists in the house. The floors are supported on iron joists which are filled with Portland cement, a device which was invented by the architect, Mr. J.G. Meyers." The New Hampshire

Avenue–facing front was covered with dark, rough-hewn stone. The side facing Sunderland was faced with a contrasting orange-red smooth brick. Both featured wrought-iron decorations and railings, with two gargoyles on the top of the New Hampshire side. A tall stone tower connected the two street sides at the corner, which allowed Meyers to utilize the odd corner of the lot.[102] The Heuriches paid Meyer $40,000 in four equal payments, and the contract stipulated that "none but union men in good standing shall be employed."[103]

The Heurich Mansion looking across New Hampshire Avenue, circa 2010 (courtesy the George F. Landegger Collection of District of Columbia Photographs in Carol M. Highsmith's America, Library of Congress, Prints and Photographs Division).

Mathilde furnished the interior. There were four main floors and a basement. The main floor was designed for entertaining and it was the showcase for the Heuriches. One local writer described the interior of the main floor in glowing terms:

> The interior of the palatial Heurich home is well worthy of mention. The spacious hallway, triangular in shape, is of beautiful proportions, and leads to a library, on the left of the entrance, whose rich walls are covered by many fine canvasses of the modern school. Back of this large room rises the stairway of brass, marble, and onyx, whose graceful curves greatly enhance the beauty of the hall. Opposite the library is the drawing room, a lofty apartment of noble proportions, whose richly decorated ceiling, done by a master hand, of exquisitely delicate tints, fade to a handsome and richly carved ivory frieze, which, in turn, blends into the softer tints of the paneled side walls. The reception room is next to the drawing room: then music room and dining room. The drawing room opens into the music room, a smaller apartment, which is over-hung by a mezzanine gallery, and is also visible from the front hallway. Another reception room, in the rear of the music room, is beautifully proportioned, furnished, and lighted, and opens into the large, stately, superbly paneled dining room. In the rear of this room the conservatory, rookery, fernery, and aviary, wherein the plash of an electric fountain lends an enchantment to the charming environment.[104]

The family lived on the second floor of the thirty-one-room house. The basement contained the kitchens and, most notably, a *bierstube*, a beer room designed to look like a traditional rathskeller. On the walls were paintings and sayings in German related to drinking, such as "*Raum is in der kleinsten Kammer/Für den größten Katzenjammer*" (There is room in the smallest room for the biggest hangover).[105] Heurich used this room to meet friends and play his favorite car game, skat. Heurich wanted the most modern house possible, so it not only had indoor plumbing, it also had a central vacuum system,

The front parlor in the mansion (courtesy the Heurich House Museum).

Top: The Bierstube in the Heurich House. *Bottom, left:* Detail from the wall of the Bierstube. The motto *"Vom Durst Dich niemals quälen laß Im Keller liegt noch manches Taß"* roughly translates to "Never let yourself be pained by thirst, there is many a keg left in the cellar." In Heurich's Bierstube. The slogan reads "There is room in the smallest chamber for the biggest hangover." Katzenjammer in German means the yowling of cats. It also means a hangover. Photograph by Mark Benbow (three photographs courtesy the Heurich House Museum).

A close-up of the salamander on the top of the Heurich Mansion. Photograph by Erika Goergen (courtesy the Heurich House Museum).

electric and pneumatic communication systems, and both gas and electric lights. There was an elevator shaft attached, but it was never used, as Heurich never stopped using the stairs. The unmarried female servants, generally German immigrants, lived on the top floor. Heurich tapped into the local community of German craftsmen for the woodwork, masonry, and ironwork that decorated the home. His fear of losing another building to fire prevented him from using any of the mansion's many fireplaces. Heurich even had a sculpture of a salamander placed atop the mansion's roof because, according to classical Greek myths, salamanders were resistant to fire.[106]

Unfortunately, Mathilde Heurich's health was still poor. In 1893, she was seriously injured after being thrown from a horse-drawn carriage. In 1894 Heurich sent for his wife's mother and sister to come from Germany to be with them in D.C. Mathilde died at age thirty-three in January 1895, leaving Heurich a widower for a second time.[107] Heurich again lost himself in his work. His huge new home must have seemed as empty as a tomb, a daily reminder of his loss. It had been decorated by Mathilde, so everything in the house bore her touch as well. It wasn't totally empty. There were servants living there who ran the home, but their presence was just another reminder of how much Heurich had lost. Work at the brewery, and with local institutions such as the Orphans' Home, was no doubt more pleasant than going home to a space that reminded him of his late wife.

Despite his family losses, Heurich was clearly advancing economically and socially. By the early 1890s he was a part of the Washington business elite. He was active as a businessman and a philanthropist in both the German immigrant community and in Washington society as a whole. He served on the boards of directors of both the German Orphan Asylum and the Eleanor Ruppert Home for the Aged and Indigent Residents. He was also active in the Chamber of Commerce and the D.C. Board of Trade. These latter two are of particular importance because, in the absence of an elected District government, these businessmen's organizations acted as unofficial lobbyists for Washington in Congress by promoting the city's financial and business interests.[108] He also donated two acres of land he owned south of Alexandria, along the Potomac River. They bordered on Mount Vernon's property and were part of a swamp George Washington named "Hell Hole." The Mount Vernon Ladies' Association wanted to drain the land, but needed the section owned by Heurich to make it work. Heurich donated the land in 1893, the land was drained, and is now a meadow near the Mount Vernon wharf. For the price of some land of little value, Heurich got some favorable publicity, the gratitude of members of local society, and a burnished reputation as a local benefactor. In the meantime, as the twentieth century approached, Heurich's business would continue to prosper; he would marry for a third and final time, continue making regular trips back to Germany, and deal with the growing problem of the prohibition movement, which threatened his successful business.[109]

4

High Point for Heurich Brewing: 1895–1900

The last years of the nineteenth century saw Heurich building upon what he had already accomplished, as well as changes in his personal life. He built a new brewery in a different section of town, moved into his new mansion in the now-exclusive DuPont Circle area, and married for a third time, having lost his two previous wives to illness. He also had to deal with his fellow D.C. brewers and the growing unionization of his workforce. By the time the twentieth century began, he would be well established as the city's biggest brewer, dominating the local marketplace, and would be starting the family he'd always wanted.

The devastating 1892 fire at his 20th Street brewery, along with pressure from neighbors in the DuPont Circle neighborhood, convinced Heurich that it was time to find a different spot to build a new brewery. This would allow him to build a larger plant with greater capacity, and to design a fireproof building. No doubt, in his view, the three fires he'd suffered on 20th Street were enough for one lifetime. He actually considered three new locations. The first was Isherwood, a little over a mile east of the U.S. Capitol. Heurich noted that there were mineral springs in this area. The second was in southwest D.C. close to the tidal basin, near where the Bureau of Engraving and Printing building was built in 1914. The third choice was Block 22 at 26th and Water Streets, Northwest, the location he finally chose. The new location was only a mile down New Hampshire Avenue from where Heurich and his wife lived and from his original brewery location. That single mile made an enormous difference, however, in the character of the neighborhood. Foggy Bottom was not, as Heurich wryly noted in his memoirs, a "nice" neighborhood. It was, however, an appropriate place for industrial buildings.[1]

Work began quickly. In May 1894, a building permit was issued to erect "one seven-story and two two-story brick buildings, on square bounded by Twenty-fifth, Twenty-sixth, D, and Water streets, to cost $200,000."[2] Two months later, the *Washington Post* reported the ceremony celebrating the laying of the new brewery's cornerstone: "The corner-stone of the new brewery of the Chris. Heurich Brewing Company, corner of Twenty-sixth and Water streets northwest, was laid under auspicious circumstances yesterday afternoon shortly after 4 o'clock." About one hundred friends and employees attended, the celebrants enjoying kegs of beer afterwards. The *Washington Post* reported that the brewery's capacity would be 250,000 barrels a year and it would cost $400,000 to build the "absolutely fireproof" brewery.[3]

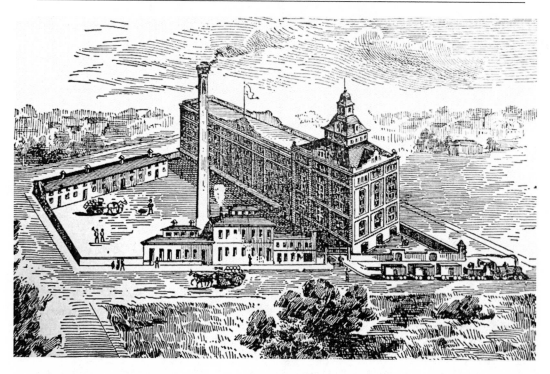

A drawing of the Water Street brewery published in 1895, as the brewery was being built. The final complex would have more structures than shown here. From the collection of Jan King Evans Houser. Used with permission.

The construction was not without incident. In February 1895 the Carpenters' Union accused Frederick Chandler, a contractor supervising construction at both the brewery and Heurich's new home, of withholding pay from some of his workers, carpenters and a watchman, paying them $2.80 a day instead of $3.00, presumably pocketing the rest. Heurich expressed doubt that Chandler was skimping on the agreed wages, but the builder was placed on the union's blacklist for twenty years. Chandler stated that the claims he had shorted workers came from disgruntled workers that he had fired. Heurich apparently accepted the explanation, as he continued using Chandler.[4] Not every problem threatened to slow the brewery's construction: police broke up a craps game in the unfinished brewery in May 1895. District police conducted an early morning raid at 1:00 a.m. and found "about forty negroes diligently engaged in 'throwing the bones.'" One of the watchmen, Charles Fantroy, was arrested. Oddly, he was one of those who had earlier claimed to have been cheated by Frederick Chandler. Such "floating" games commonly took advantage of abandoned or unfinished buildings, and unfortunately, the *Post*'s story would have appealed to its largely white readership as a reinforcement of common stereotypes about African Americans and craps games.[5]

As 1895 turned into 1896 and Heurich's new brewery neared completion, a local strike threatened to shut down Washington's brewing industry. The 1896 labor war in D.C. turned not on working conditions, wages or hours, but on the issue of which employees at the breweries would join the local union affiliated with the Knights of Labor. As an added complication, the American Federation of Labor stepped in to organize the workers under their organization's umbrella so that the struggle also became one between unions. The local Knights of Labor chapter was organized in late 1895 as Gambrinius Assembly No. 1349. They announced that they would organize all of the city's brewery workers, and would boycott the products of any brewery that refused. Washington's breweries agreed, and the workers were organized in the Gambrinius Assembly. Difficulties arose, however, when the Knights attempted to include the brewery wagon drivers. The breweries refused, arguing that the drivers were office workers and should not be included among the other workers. Indeed, the drivers' job did straddle the roles of laborer and office worker. They not only drove the wagons, loaded and unloaded the beer, they also worked as salesmen and collection agents. The National Capital Brewery's Albert Carry refused to cooperate. According to the *Post*, the "company held that the drivers should not be compelled to join the union when the other office employees were exempt." The Knights countered by noting that the drivers in other cities were members of their companies' unions. Heurich went along with his fellow brewers, probably agreeing with their position on the drivers. However, he generally had good relations with the local unions and used only union labor to build his new brewery.[6]

Three D.C. breweries—Heurich, National Capital, and Washington Brewery—had already begun to cooperate in dealing with the unions so that they could not be divided and played against one another. They were joined by Arlington's new Consumer's Brewery, founded in 1895. Portner's sold their product south of the Potomac, and so while they sometimes acted in concert with the others, in this case they remained detached from the struggle. Fearing a strike, on Saturday, January 4, 1896, the four cooperating breweries laid off all of their workers as they collected their weekly pay. The workers cleaned up their work spaces and left, and the breweries closed while new employees could be found. A union spokesman noted that the workers' fight was "not so much against the Heurich and Washington Breweries as against the National Capital." They also sent word to brewery unions in nearby cities, hoping to prevent the breweries from importing workers. With most of their workers gone, the breweries shut down while they found new workers in New York and Philadelphia. On Tuesday the breweries prepared to resume operations.[7]

Heurich clearly resented the boycott. He placed an open letter in the *Washington Post* along with National Capital Brewing and Washington Brewing, claiming that their firing workers was not the result of differences over wages, working conditions, or other labor issues, but over the demand by the Knights and the Gambrinius Assembly that the drivers, firemen, and engineers be required to join their organization. As noted earlier, the drivers were considered office employees because of their sales and collections duties, and the engineers and firemen had their own unions. In a statement to the *Post*, Heurich issued an additional reminder as well as a threat. He noted that his new brewery had cost "$1,000,000 for its plant, and it was all put up by union labor." He could, Heurich reminded the Knights, "have had the work done at less cost by non-union men." Moreover, he noted, there was still more work to do:

> We are now going to put up an ice storage house, blacksmiths' shops, stables, bottling house, flats for the men, and houses for others, and have all the wiring done for the electrical plant. All this will cost from $250,000 to $500,000 and we shall be guided in making our contracts by the actions of the District Assembly and the Federation. We don't intend to feed the asp that tries to kill us. If we are fair or unfair is not the question.

Heurich's threat had little immediate impact. That same day the engineers at each brewery went on a sympathy strike, which meant no more union labor was working in the breweries. However, the construction workers, which were members of the American Federation of Labor, the "Federation" in Heurich's statement, remained at work on the new brewery. The Knights and the Gambrinius Assembly, meanwhile, lobbied the union workers at local bottling companies, and the saloonkeepers, to join the boycott. If the bottlers could not bottle the breweries' products and the saloons refused to sell it, then it would little matter if the breweries found replacement workers.[8]

Heurich's statements and actions, those of his fellow brewers, and those of the Knights and Gambrinius Assembly were part of what can be viewed as a performance for multiple audiences. Each faction designed their actions not just to send a message to the other parties directly involved, but to their allies, as well as those groups whose support they wished to gain, especially consumers. Heurich's statement, for example, was designed to reassure his fellow brewers that he would not break ranks. It was a sign of his resolve to the Knights and their supporters. To saloonkeepers who might support the Knights' boycott of Heurich products, it was a reminder that Heurich would remove his patronage from those he had done business with before if necessary. To other union members in D.C. and their supporters, his statement was a reminder that he could take away their business, but also a reassurance that he was not anti-organized labor. This last point is especially important because the beer boycott of 1896 was not just union against management, but was part of an ongoing struggle between industrial unions, as represented by the Knights of Labor, and trade (or "craft") unions, especially the American Federation of Labor (AFL).

Industrial unions represented all the workers in an industry regardless of their jobs or their skill levels. In a brewery this meant that all workers, whether they were skilled, semi-skilled, or unskilled, or whether they worked in the malting section, with boilers, in the bottling room, or anywhere else in the brewery, would be members of the same union. Thus an issue involving one worker would require a response by all. Trade unions, such as the AFL, organized workers by their jobs and skill levels. So workers in the bottle shop would belong to a different union from the firemen who maintained the boilers. Trade unions pre-dated their industrial rivals, which evolved along with mass industrialization. Industrial unions also reflected a difference in assumptions about the role of class solidarity in an industrial society from their more conservative rivals. In 1909 Eugene Debs noted:

> Whereas, the trade union occupied itself mainly with establishing and maintaining satisfactory wage scales, hours of labor and working class conditions, industrial unionism, based upon the mutual economic interests of all workers and the solidarity arising therefrom, aims not only at the amelioration of the industrial condition of the workers, but at the ultimate abolition of the existing productive system, and the total extinction of wage-servitude.[9]

Indeed, the Knights, the industrial union, did want to refashion the political and economic structure of American society, to create a "workingman's democracy," while the trade union AFL, under Samuel Gompers, was more interested in, as Debs noted, "establishing and maintaining satisfactory wage scales, hours of labor and working class conditions." The AFL's more limited vision would win out, for reasons beyond the scope of this study, except that in the D.C. union struggle of 1896, the Knights struggled to find sufficient allies even among other organized workers. They were unable to make a convincing case that their cause affected all workers in Washington, that the sacrifices necessary to force the brewers to concede to win long-term gains would be worth the cost of work lost in the short run. Heurich in particular found that his general pro-union stance in hiring labor won him a hearing, and support, against the Knights.

After only a few days, Heurich started brewing again, now with new workers. The battle now moved to two new areas, the bottlers and the saloons. The Knights lobbied the local bottlers not to bottle the products of the boycotted brewers and threatened to call the workers out of any bottler that handled "local beer." Those companies that handled the products of out-of-town companies, the shipping breweries, were willing to accede to the Knights' demand, which would not affect their businesses. The companies that handled the local breweries, however, refused, as they would be idle if they could not package Heurich and the others' beers. Complicating the situation was Charles Jacobsen, who owned Arlington Bottling Company (which was actually in D.C., despite the name). Charles was Heurich's nephew, the son of Hermann and Elisabeth Jacobsen, Christian Heurich's sister and her husband, and had worked in the Heurich brewery as a boy. No doubt he was arguing for his uncle's interests in the bottlers' meeting. Meanwhile, the Knights looked for other breweries that would ship their beer into D.C., thus giving saloonkeepers another product to sell other than the boycotted companies' products. However, they ran into difficulties, as other brewers did not want to aid the union in a battle with their fellow owners. A third hurdle for the strikers was overcome when the local labor assembly, which had good relations with Heurich, and so was reluctant to back the boycott, finally decided in favor of the boycott. They did so largely because the other breweries, especially Albert Carry's National Capital Brewery and Robert Portner's Alexandria brewery,[10] were hostile to labor rights, and the unions were reluctant to hand them a victory. The local assembly agreed that their members would back the boycott.[11]

The situation stalemated, but the Knights' position was weakened when local saloons were unable to find other beers to sell, and so continued to sell Heurich's and the other local beers.[12] By mid–January some brewery workers, discouraged, began to return to ask for their jobs back. The brewers often refused, making exceptions "in a few cases of old employees—men who have always been faithful to their employers in the past and who went out with the assembly only in a lukewarm manner."[13] Those remaining loyal to the boycott renewed their efforts, still pressuring saloons to stop carrying the boycotted breweries' beers. Two-thirds of local saloons carried the local beers, so if the Knights could convince them to join the boycott, it would leave little outlet for the companies' sales.[14] On January 22, the strikers succeeded in bringing outside beer into D.C., from the Cincinnati Brewing Company, which was quickly supplied to saloons supporting the boycott.[15] Most saloons, however, wanted no part of the boycott, as it placed them in a difficult position, between their suppliers and the workers who made up most of their customers. The strikers seemed to have viewed Heurich as a possible mediator in the struggle, probably because of his general pro-labor stance. Representatives of the National Brewery Workers met with Heurich's lawyers, including Leon Tobriner, but were told that any communication they made had to be in writing, and would be answered in writing, to avoid any misunderstanding, a reflection of the problems Heurich had ending the 1885 strike against his company. The union representatives refused, claiming this was unworkable. Workers continued to return to Heurich's brewery to reclaim their jobs, as did some from National Capital. This was in contrast to those from the Washington brewery, who remained on strike. Indeed, most of the boycott's leaders were workers from the latter company.[16]

By the end of January 1896, the boycott appeared to be losing support. The brewers refused to compromise, and rebuffed the saloonkeepers' efforts to mediate. Other local unions were growing uncomfortable, fearing that they would lose work if they supported the boycott, but not wanting to abandon their fellows. As one non-brewery union representative told the press, "We are trying to devise a means to let the boycott die easily." With this the boycott effectively collapsed, although it officially continued for months. The Building Trades Council acted as arbitrator along with the Bricklayers' Union. The agreement noted that workers could return to their jobs if the brewers agreed they could stay organized. Heurich's lawyer, Leon Tobriner, representing the brewers, agreed. The Building Trades representatives told the press that they had no quarrel with the brewers, since "they had always found them just, honorable, and more liberal than the union scale in the matter of wages." The brewers agreed to take back the striking men, but only as positions opened. They also agreed that if the drivers wanted to form their own association they would be allowed to do so. The Trades Union then held their own meeting, at which they issued a statement that the boycott was "ill-advised" and a "sad mistake" made by inexperienced union leaders.[17] One worker told the *Washington Post* that "the boycott has ended."[18]

The officers of the Knights and the Gambrinius Assembly refused to concede defeat despite the reports. They refused to accept the settlement unless the drivers were forced to join the Gambrinius Assembly. They found little support from the other local unions. As soon as the agreement arbitrated by the Building Trades representatives had been reached, Heurich had let the contracts to raise the wrought iron gates for his new brewery's entrance. The contract to make and erect the gates, measuring 24 × 31 feet, went to a local union. So did Heurich's contract for electrical work at the brewery. In all he let $12,000 in contracts, all to local organized labor. As a result the strike supporters found little support among the Building Trades unions. Then the bottling companies formed an agreement similar to the brewers' arrangement. Should one of the bottlers be boycotted by the strikers, then all the bottlers would fire their union employees. As an additional blow to the strikers, the Bricklayers' Union, which was working on Heurich's brewery, again refused to join the strike. One by one the strikers were losing possible allies.[19]

A new player entered the conflict in late February as the American Federation of Labor (AFL) began its efforts to organize local trade unions. While the Knights had been severely weakened from their strength a decade before, they were still strong in D.C., where their national office was located. Not surprisingly, the first unions the AFL began to work with were the same trade unions that opposed the Knights' brewery boycott, including the Bricklayers' Union, which was expelled from the Knights' own District Federation of Labor in retaliation. The Building Trades unions joined the AFL at the same time they entered an agreement with the local brewers that guaranteed them all of those companies' work contracts. This affected mostly Heurich at first, but the other breweries promised that they would soon be hiring workers for improving their own facilities. Building Trades unions that remained with the Knights, such as the local tinners, would be denied work. In short, the battle between the Knights and the breweries became a struggle with the Knights on one side and the brewers and the AFL on the other.[20]

The Knights continued into the spring and summer, trying to expand their boycott, but with little success. The Gambrinius Assembly's delegates to the District Federation of Labor resigned and had to be replaced. Rumors of final agreements appeared in the local press, but quickly fell apart. Washington Capital Brewery was removed from the "unfair" list, but Heurich and the others remained on it. Individual local unions that had supported the boycott, such as the Typographical Union, continued to abandon the

Knights. As summer turned to fall, the Knights gave up their fight, reaching an agreement that the brewers would not discriminate against workers who belonged to their organization in favor of those who had joined the AFL. In October they agreed to attend one of the dinners celebrating the opening of Heurich's new brewery.[21] The strike had little effect on Heurich's business in the long run, and by making agreements with the Building Trades unions and the AFL, he maintained his generally good relations with local workers. This would prove to be especially useful in a few years when the local unions refused to side with Heurich's brewing rivals in the D.C. "Beer War" which ran from 1904 to 1908. The amount of work he provided the local construction unions proved to them that he was a reliable ally to most workers, especially those who performed skilled labor.

There were problems with workers beyond his relationship with the Knights of Labor. In April 1896, a worker fell down an elevator shaft, falling twenty feet and landing on his head and shoulders. Amazingly, although he was battered and bleeding, he did not suffer any broken bones and was sent home to rest. In late July a lineman for the Mutual District Messenger Company, John Dorsey, saw a four-horse team running away with one of Heurich's delivery wagons near what is now Scott Circle. The newspaper description sounds like something from a movie. Modern readers may be excused if they suspect the story was somewhat exaggerated:

> Dorsey jumped from his wagon and overtook the run-away, and jumped into the wagon from behind, and got over the front of the wagon and out upon the tongue, picked up the reins of the two nearest horses, and by pulling them to a dead stop, the four horses were arrested just in time to save the line of herdics standing at Connecticut avenue and M street.[22]

The most serious incident was the murder at the brewery of one of Heurich's employees by another employee. On August 12, 1896, one of Heurich's coopers, Conrad Plonk, was hit on the head with a brick by a junior fellow worker, John Sites. Plonk had been teasing the younger man, soaking him with a hose about a week before the attack. Sites did not take the teasing well, throwing a glass at Plonk, and a week later attacked him with a brick after an argument. Having struck his tormentor in the back of his head with the brick, Sites fled town. The stricken cooper was rushed to hospital, but the injuries did not appear to be severe—a cut on the head, but no skull fracture or concussion— and he was sent home. Plonk grew worse once he was at home, however, and two weeks after the attack, he returned to the hospital, where he fell into a coma and died. No one saw Sites carry out the attack, but witnesses claimed that he had promised to get revenge on Plonk for soaking him, and one witness claimed Sites boasted of having taken his revenge. There is no mention of Plonk's telling others what happened, but he was conscious and lived for two weeks after the attack, so it's probable that he gave his own testimony. Sites was captured in Maryland near Rockville, brought back to D.C., and indicted for murder. In May 1897 he withdrew a plea of not guilty to murder, but instead pleaded guilty to a charge of manslaughter. He was sentenced to eight months in the District jail and fined $50.00, an astonishingly light sentence.[23]

The leniency may have been due to several factors, but the most likely reason was that Plonk, like Sites, was African American, so his death was not taken particularly seriously by the courts. One newspaper account noted that when the police were called to get an ambulance for Plonk after he had relapsed, the police sergeant did not bother to make the call until the following morning. Plonk's death, like the craps game raid earlier, was played in the press as evidence of the criminal nature of African Americans. As for

Sites and Plonk, to outside observers it appeared as if horseplay—something associated with the young and immature—between two African American employees led to a violent attack and a death. This played naturally into stereotypes of African Americans being childlike and naturally violent. Sites claimed he only hit Plonk with his fist, but the press began describing him as having "a vicious nature." He had "frequently been arrested for assault" and "served a term in the penitentiary at Baltimore for assault."[24] Whether the accounts of Sites's criminal record were true or not, he was immediately cast as a violent criminal. Interestingly, despite the temperance campaign's efforts to portray alcohol as a prime cause of crime, especially on the part of black men, the D.C. press made no effort to tie Sites's actions to his employer. To the press, Plonk's murder was simply another example of the violence one encountered among African Americans. As the *Washington Post* noted a few years later:

> We still have in the National Capital a colored population which is by no means desirable. It is thriftless, prone to theft, lacking in moral sense, and contributes largely to the throngs which crowd the prisoners' pen in the Police Court.[25]

With such assumptions common, it is not surprising that Sites received such a light sentence. Plonk's death was considered only a slight loss, and the fight a natural occurrence for two men of their race.

Plonk's murder came in the midst of a killer heat wave that stifled the eastern part of the United States for two weeks, from late July into August. D.C. hit 94 degrees on July 27, and the heat remained, with temperatures in the upper 90s and low 100s, until finally breaking on August 14. People and animals alike suffered. There were fears of a milk shortage as cows stopped producing. Most streetcars were electric by 1896, but some of the few horses left that pulled trolleys collapsed, forcing the Eckington & Soldiers Home line to cut back on service. This was exceptionally poor timing as people began riding the open streetcars just to catch a breeze. Reporters besieged the poor employees of the Weather Bureau, which had nothing but bad news to report. No cold fronts were anywhere in sight. People began sleeping outdoors. Local businesses advertised ice boxes on sale. One drugstore advertised talcum powder, warning that "Little Babies Will Die" without relief from the heat. Newspapers warned people of the dangers of drinking cold drinks. One Civil War veteran died after chugging a pitcher of ice water. People began putting wet sponges, and even wet cabbage leaves, under their hats. Heurich's new brewery had a substantial ice plant, and he took advantage of the demand, placing advertisements in the local papers. They began as small classified ads before the heat wave, but while the normal summer demand was still high: "Notice to ice dealers. You can buy all the ice you want here—made from pure distilled water—in blocks weighing from 300 to 315 pounds each—for only 50¢—or about 16¢ a hundred." Shortly before the heat wave arrived, Heurich began using larger display ads, and they were targeted not just at ice dealers, but also to druggists, confectioners, hotels, and boarding houses: "Send your wagon over in the morning. Heurich's Ice Depot, cor. 26th and Water Sts." The price, however, remained the same, 50¢ for a 300- to 315-pound block. Heurich was not one to price gouge, and there was no need. There was plenty of profit to be made by selling at the normal price to meet an increased demand.[26]

In the midst of all this turmoil—strikes, a runaway wagon, accidents, a historic heat wave, and a murder—Heurich's new brewery was already producing beer. They began in the autumn of 1895 even as the brewery was still being constructed. A grand official opening was scheduled for November 1896. The book *100 Years of Brewing*, published by the industry journal *The Western Brewer* in 1903, described Heurich's new facility:

> The brewery is absolutely fireproof, every portion of the premises being of brick, stone and concrete. No insurance is carried.[27] This is probably the only large brewery in the country of which this can truly be said. The brew-house is equipped with a so-called double brewing plant, the five cellars of the stock-house being in direct connection with the brew-house. In connection with the brewery there is an ice-making plan of a daily capacity of one hundred and twenty tons, with ample storage facilities."[28]

The descriptions of the new brewery reflect the American industrial-age fascination with size and modernity. Trade journals regularly ran articles, sometimes several pages long, often the longest articles in each issue, with drawings and descriptions of the new facilities emphasizing their modernity and scale.[29] New factories became bigger and bigger, and technological advances represented more than just a vague sense of "progress." They flirted with a sense of a sacred space, representative of an assumed American leadership of western civilization.

The same sense was evident in the World's Fairs of the period, including Chicago in 1893, which Heurich attended. What did Heurich remember about that event decades later? He remembered the Ferris wheel, which was, at the time, the world's largest. A 264-foot-tall revolving wheel of iron and steel that could carry over 2,100 sightseers in thirty-six passenger cars, it represented the industrial and engineering power of the United States. New factories had the same type of meaning, even if it was limited to a local audience. Prominent local architects designed the new structures, company advertising prominently featured the facilities, and their openings were the occasion for local celebrations. Such festivities were signs of pride shown for any successful local business, but in part also commemorated the evidence of modernity that the new factory brought to the community.

The local press also celebrated this pride in Heurich's new brewery. A *Washington Post* article, describing the public open house to celebrate the official opening of Heurich's new brewery in November 1896, described the facility as "a model establishment" and as a "magnificent new brewery." They quoted Heurich's own claim that it was the "model brewery of the world." The article's author then described the sheer scale of the brewery,

The Heurich letterhead shows the Water Street brewery, the Paris medal, and the hop leaf logo (author collection).

A view inside the Heurich Brewery's ice plant. Circa 1919–1920, the facility was no longer making beer, just ice (Library of Congress).

before going into details about each section, indicating that he thought the plant's modernity and status as a "model" was the most important of its aspects, followed by its size:

> As it stands today it has a capacity of 500,000 barrels per annum [*sic*], and this, Mr. Heurich says can be quadrupled if necessary. In connection with the brewery is an ice manufacturing establishment with a capacity of 250 tons daily, which can, if necessary, be increased as to supply the whole District.

Visitors could follow the production process from beginning to end, following "a torrent of beer" from the time "it starts next to the roof until it finds its way to the immense fermenting and storage tubs in the cellar." There were so many "immense" tanks and vats and tubs, the author noted that it was "bewildering." Even amid this jumble of machinery, which was chaotic to the visitor but understandable to those trained in the brewing process, what was most "striking" was the "perfect cleanliness apparent everywhere. There is polish on every scrap of metal," the reporter noted, "and not a speck of dirt to be seen anywhere." The laagering cellars were described as appropriately scaled to such a large enterprise:

> The cellars on the ground floor and below give the best idea of this great beer-making enterprise. In one cellar alone seventy giant fermenting tubs are ranged with a capacity of 90 to 120 barrels each. In another there are seventy storage tubs with an aggregate capacity of 16,000 barrels. The storage tank for the malt is 54 feet deep, and has six bins, its capacity being 35,000 bushels.[30]

Detail of the Heurich Brewery used in advertisements in the early 1900s. As was so often the case, the depiction was a bit fanciful, especially with the sailboat on the Potomac so close to the brewery. The black smoke coming out of the smokestack would not have been welcome after D.C.'s anti-smoke law was passed (author collection).

Only after this admiring description is anything human-scaled described, "a cozy apartment" overlooking the river. It "is handsomely fitted up in antique oak, and the walls are adorned with frescoed burlaps in which hops were received, the result being a close imitation of tapestry. Old German mottos and some English ones, as well, extolling the virtues of good beer are scattered here and there. It is here that Mr. Heurich entertains his friends." They could, the author suggested, "sit and sip the foamy beverage, which is as plentiful in that vicinity as the water in the river, flowing noiselessly almost at the entrance of the building."[31]

The story in the *Evening Star* took a similar tone. The brewery was "a model in every way." The same production statistics were reported, including the 250 tons of ice. Reporters taken on a tour of the plant saw the "immense vats" and "immense fermenting room" where "scores of great tanks hold the yeasty compound that rises as it ferments and overflows the sides of the tanks, hanging in festoons of amber-colored foam." The "ceiling and walls ... are lined with pipes, thickly covered with ice." The accompanying line drawing of the brewery emphasizes its size. It dwarfs the tiny human figures pictured on the street next to the brewery, and it even dominates the Washington Monument and Capitol dome in the background. No other man-made structures are visible. The peak of the brewery's tallest portion is even higher than the hills and trees seen in the background. Heurich's new plant seems to rise from the bank of the Potomac to dominate the scene.[32]

This emphasis on size and scale of the brewery and its production capacity evokes and echoes earlier descriptions of natural wonders, but the overall effect gives the impression of an immense complex system rather than of a simple, understandable, discreet thing. The system is "bewildering" to the observer, but still somehow wonderful. The emphasis on the man-made flow of beer is echoed by the description of the flowing river in the *Post* story and by the illustration in the *Star*'s account. The latter's descriptions of the beer, "flowing amber," "refreshing beverage," "wholesome," and "yeasty," emphasize the naturalness of the brewery's product, just as does the comparison with the neighboring river. The brewery then may be a product of man's labor, but it become a part of the natural landscape, and the beer it produces is seemingly as much a part of a natural process as the river water.[33]

David Nye calls this an American sense of the "sublime" which in the nineteenth century turned from natural wonders to man-made structures. The "sublime" is something that inspires awe, a sense of greatness that is too big to be measured. Natural wonders such as Niagara Falls or the Grand Canyon could invoke this sense. Particular structures might also. Nye uses the example of the textile plants in Lowell, Massachusetts, as an early example of this tendency. For the latter part of the nineteenth century he might well have used the Brooklyn Bridge, which towered over the New York City skyline. Popular printmakers such as Currier and Ives produced prints of the bridge, as well as other large structures, for people to frame and admire just as they might admire a mountain range or a huge waterfall. The power and complexity of modern industry "combined the abstraction of a man-made landscape with the dynamism of moving machinery and powerful forces." Like the power of a Niagara Falls, it evoked both fear and wonder. As Nye notes, it "threatened the individual with its sheer scale" such as the tiny figures in the *Star*'s drawing of Heurich's new brewery, as well as with its "noise, its complexity, and the superhuman power of the forces at work." Yet it "reaffirmed the power of reason." It "forced onlookers to respect the power of the corporation and the intelligence of its engineers."[34]

In the era in which Heurich was expanding his 20th Street brewery, and then building his new facility on Water Street, this same type of admiration could be found in brewing industry journals, such as *Brewers' Digest*. They would publish detailed, admiring drawings of new breweries spread over two or three full large pages. The drawings would emphasize the brewery's size, usually by including a handful of diminutive human figures much as the *Star* did in its illustration of Heurich's brewery, the people dwarfed by the size of the structure. Neighboring structures, if they were shown at all, would also be shown as smaller than the brewery. Heurich's brewery advertising in city directories and in newspaper ads followed the same model, as did his brewery letterheads. Heurich's serving trays, made for servers to carry bottles and glasses of his products in a saloon, featured images of the new brewery. Many breweries used this type of tray to show the idealized vision of their facility. In each case, the design perspective chosen by the artist was used to invoke some sense of the enormous scale of the building or complex of buildings, as if the brewer is asking the viewer to admire what a magnificent structure he created.

Heurich also used his just-completed facility to cement his place as a local leader for the community as a whole, not just among the German-Americans. From November 10 through November 13, 1896, he held a series of open houses to show off his new brewery, and each day was set aside for a specific group. On Tuesday, November 10, he hosted other brewers. They came from cities throughout the eastern half of the U.S., including

Baltimore, New York, Cincinnati and Chicago, along with wholesale and retail beer dealers. Over 5,600 guests toured the facility, then enjoyed a luncheon in which one of the first kegs of beer produced at the brewery was tapped. On Wednesday the 11th, guests came from the business community, as well as diplomats, Army and Navy officers, and other professionals in the city. President Grover Cleveland and his cabinet were also invited, although there is no mention of their attending. On Thursday over 6,000 visitors came, including members of local German societies from D.C. and Baltimore. The week's events ended on Friday, when over 9,000 visitors came to take the tour, including soldiers from Fort Meyer and the Washington Barracks, local labor groups, and bicycle clubs. Note that military officers came two days before the regular soldiers were given their tour, reflecting their different social status in D.C. The *Post* reported that the brewery had to "close the gates, owing to the crush" of people. If the *Post*'s attendance figures are correct, then over 23,000 people visited the brewery in four days. Unusual for the time, the groups invited included African Americans, such as the Hod Carriers' Union.[35]

The celebratory tours were not finished, however. Monday the 16th was set aside as "Ladies Day." An announcement appeared in the *Washington Post* on the 12th, noting that:

> [S]o much interest having been shown by the ladies of Washington in the operation of the model brewery plant of the world that the Christian Heurich brewing Company have decided to set aside Monday, November 16, from 2 to 5 o'clock, as a day for ladies exclusively. Ladies can come to the brewery in parties and will be conducted through the large plant in the same manner as were the parties of men, being shown the brewing of beer from the arrival of the raw material to the final shipment to the consumers.[36]

A following article noted that male escorts would be allowed as well, although no men would be admitted alone. Guests were reassured that "every precaution is being made to prevent the presence of objectionable characters." In addition, the brewery ran free busses from Washington Circle to the brewery for guests.[37] Over 4,200 women and their male escorts attended, with two D.C. policemen at the entrance to keep out the aforementioned "objectionable characters." There were, according to the *Post*, "about three hundred carriages, many of which had coachmen and footmen in attendance," a sign of wealth, rank and status. Guests were given a tour of the brewery followed by a light lunch—"salads, frankfurters, cold meats, and rolls were served in abundance." Every guest was also given a glass of Heurich's beer. The anonymous *Post* reporter observed with evident amusement, "About 90 percent of them drank it. The other 10 percent looked as if they wanted to."[38]

Heurich's "Ladies' Day" was probably designed to counter objections by the local Drys. The Temperance Movement was active in D.C., including a chapter of the Woman's Christian Temperance Union (WCTU). By making certain that local women were able to enjoy their tour, followed by a ladylike light lunch in a safe, friendly atmosphere, Heurich asserted his brewery's respectability. The *Post*'s comment on the number of carriages outside, "many of which had coachmen and footmen in attendance," emphasized that the brewery was appropriate for upper-class women to visit and, by extension, that the brewery's beer was therefore also an appropriate beverage for women above the working class. Ladies' Day also allowed Heurich to define the meaning of his facility's "space," preventing the WCTU from doing so.

The various groups Heurich hosted were chosen to reinforce his position in the community as an important local business leader. President Cleveland and his cabinet did not appear to have attended, which suggests that Heurich was not included in the highest ranks of local society, but the presence of those who did attend indicates that he was accepted as a local figure of some importance. An earlier chapter discussed the different parts of D.C. society. The president was the center of the most exclusive part of Washington social scene. Other government officials made up a somewhat lower circle. Wealthy residents, both those who lived fulltime in the city and those who wintered there, were another group, as were local diplomats. Finally there were the "Antiques," families who had been part of upper D.C. society from the beginning. Of course there were other groups—workers, African Americans, low-level government clerks, etc.—but the upper classes revolved around wealth and rank in the government. Heurich's successful opening ceremonies indicate that he was a part of the local business elite, with enough status to be noticed by those within higher official circles. Soon after his arrival in D.C. he was selling beer to be consumed by the local elite, but now he was freely mingling with them socially.

During the tours, visitors were asked not just to enjoy the beer, but to admire the modern technology used to produce it. This showcasing of modern equipment and processes was designed to illustrate how progressive and efficient Heurich was as a businessman, a key virtue in this period of industrialization. Heurich's use of innovations, such as his large, modern ice plant, represented progress, a term that itself conveys meaning deeper than mere innovation. Advances in technology signified an advancement of civilization and an assurance to those touring Heurich's new brewery that they were citizens in one of the most advanced societies in the world. Heurich's individual celebration was to some extent also a celebration of his adopted nation's power and status.[39]

The tours also emphasized how clean and sanitary the brewery was. As one reporter commented, there was "perfect cleanliness apparent everywhere. There is polish on every scrap of metal … and not a speck of dirt to be seen anywhere."[40] Heurich's tours were part of an increasingly popular trend, a way for businesses to emphasize the hygienic conditions of where food or beverages were produced. For example, Pittsburgh's H.J. Heinz Company offered tours beginning in the 1890s. Hour-long tours were scheduled four times a day. Visitors could admire the modern facilities, as well as the preserving kitchens, the "Baked Bean Building," and the "Pickle Bottling Department." In the latter, visitors saw "several hundred women in identical white caps and aprons stuffing pickles into glass bottles." Such tours reassured customers that the plant's foods were safe to consume, as well as building brand-name recognition and good will. Other factories copied Heinz's model, and Heurich also began to hold regular tours.[41]

The cleanliness of the brewery reinforced Heurich's ongoing advertising campaign emphasizing that his beer was healthy and pure. He had long stressed his beer's purity. When his new brewery opened, Heurich began a newspaper advertising campaign that emphasized the health benefits of drinking his beer. Some of the slogans included:

"Pale Thin Folks Should Drink Heurich's Beer"
"You'll Live to a Ripe Old Age"
"You'll Have No Troubles With Your Kidneys"
"Impure Beer Is a Poison"
"Heurich's Beer Is A Good Friend to the Stomach"
"There is Health in Every Drop"[42]

One advertisement bragged that Heurich's Beer was "the best of tonics. Builds up the system, creates an appetite, aides the digestions, brings back strength and vitality. Best

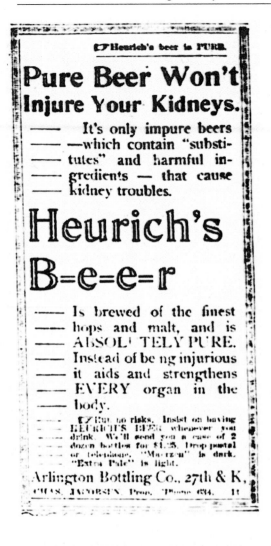

Left: "Pure Beer Won't Injure Your Kidneys" (Heurich advertisement from August 18, 1896). *Right:* "Pale, Thin Mothers." This Heurich ad in *The Evening Star,* December 12, 1896, promises health benefits for new mothers.

physicians prescribe it." The description of the ingredients is simple and straightforward: "Brewed of the finest hops and malt, and, being absolutely pure, is not injurious to the kidneys."[43]

This cleanliness campaign was designed to counter the prohibitionist effort to convince the American public that all alcoholic beverages were poison. By the last years of the nineteenth century, the Drys' efforts reached into public schools around the country in the form of required "temperance education." The Woman's Christian Temperance Union included temperance education as one of its goals from its beginning in the 1870s. However, it wasn't until Mary Hanchett Hunt took over the campaign in 1879 that it made its biggest impact. Hunt attended Patapsco Female Institute, near Baltimore, then stayed to be a science teacher, writing science textbooks. She put together a series of class lessons on the physiological effects of alcohol and convinced a school board in Hyde Park,

Massachusetts, to adopt the lesson. She then convinced several other school boards in Massachusetts to adopt her material. In 1879 Hunt was asked to address the national meeting of the WCTU and was made chair of the scientific temperance committee. This promotion gave Hunt the platform she needed to promote temperance education across the entire country, an effort that became her life's work until she died in 1906.[44]

Hunt's efforts to require temperance education were so successful that by 1900 every state, plus Washington, D.C., and the U.S. territories, required such classes in their schools and textbook companies were publishing dozens of texts to capitalize on this market. One can only imagine Heurich's reaction if he had read the following passage from a high school health textbook published in 1904:

> Would King Beer be king at all if it were not for the alcohol or some other poison equally strong,– enough, at least, to excite the system to the first stage of inebriety? The first stage of inebriety is, according to authorities, when the vital organs are stirred into a warm commotion, the heart beats beyond the normal, the nerve centers at the brain are more or less hushed, the restraining influences of will and judgment are more or less released from duty, and the animal instincts are more or less assertive.[45]

Heurich probably knew the author, as she was one of his neighbors, Mary Foote Henderson. The wife of a former Republican senator from Missouri, she and her husband built a large mansion on 16th Street NW in D.C., and were among those who encouraged the development of northwest D.C. into an upscale residential neighborhood. As such, Henderson was likely one of those who complained about the presence of Heurich's 20th Street brewery in the early 1890s.[46]

Despite the ongoing efforts of the Drys, Heurich continued to prosper as the nineteenth century entered its last years. In 1896 he registered trademarks that would become familiar to D.C. area beer drinkers. First was a logo that would be used by Heurich's brewery until it closed in 1956, described in the trademark application as "a diamond containing a representation of the Washington monument partially obscured by a hop leaf having a representation of the letter 'H' on its surface." The others included the brand names "Maerzen" and "Senate," the latter of which would become the brewery's flagship brand for many decades.[47]

Heurich also had an opportunity to sell his business. Throughout the 1880s and 1890s, British investors looked to American companies for opportunities for a safe profit. Rates of return for British companies were often low, and investments in South America and South Africa could often be unacceptably risky. As one reporter in London noted, they were "tired of investments in oriental bonds, African mining stock, colonical [sic] promotions.... American brewery stock is a more stable commodity."[48] By 1889 there were fourteen syndicates registered in London that were buying American companies, and by 1889 twenty-three British brewing and liquor firms were operating in the United States. Because many breweries were consolidating into larger companies, as Peter J. Buckley and Brian R. Roberts noted, the actual total was well over twenty-three, perhaps as high as four times as many. Moreover, many were profitable at first, although as the nineteenth century gave way to the twentieth, their profitability began to decline. Buckley and Roberts noted several reasons for this loss of profitability, including overpaying for American firms at the start, buying breweries during a boom period when there were more brewers than needed to fill consumer demand, and the difficulties in managing companies from a distance.[49]

A number of American investment houses took advantage of this opportunity to promote sales of established American businesses, among which were some of the biggest breweries in the country, such as New Hampshire's Frank Jones Brewery, the largest producer of ale in the United States. At the same time, American firms in numerous industries were merging and consolidating to form larger, hopefully more efficient and more profitable corporations. The two trends often came together as British investors joined the newly merged companies. Breweries were a popular investment for several reasons. Investments in British breweries were popular at the time, so such stock issues were a known quantity. American production was increasing, although it would soon hit a stable level of about 33.2 million barrels a year in 1895. Beer price wars had not yet become a popular feature of the industry.

Moreover, two of the main promoters, or "boomers," of American stocks were Samuel and Isaac Untermeyer. Samuel was a successful lawyer in New York City, representing many of the city's biggest brewers, as well as acting as counsel for the United States Brewers' Association (USBA). The USBA represented only 29 percent of all American brewers (including Heurich), but those companies produced 81 percent of the beer made in the United States. Thus the Untermeyers knew the American brewing industry intimately and could act as a go-between for the brewers and overseas investors. Between 1888 and 1890 the brothers successfully promoted ten companies' stock on the London market. Six of the ten were breweries, and an additional one was a granary, a business with close ties to the brewing industry.[50]

Washington's breweries were not immune to this tendency. British investors established the City of Baltimore United Breweries Limited in late 1889. The company lasted for ten years until it was itself purchased by the Maryland Brewing Company, which dominated the Baltimore market. At the same time the Baltimore syndicate brewery was being established, foreign investors entered the D.C. market. Heurich refused to sell, but Albert Carry agreed to sell his concern, which had been the Mount Vernon Brewery and before that the Juenemann Brewery.

The negative reaction in Washington to news of the sale seems to have caught Carry by surprise. When a reporter went to Carry's home to ask if the rumor that he had sold to an English syndicate was true, Carry denied it: "There is not a word of truth in the report and I do not know how it originated." The next day the *Post* ran a second report quoting a story from the April 13 issue of the London *Economist* giving the details of the sale. The story noted that Carry would continue for one year as the director of the company and that he agreed not to "engage in the brewery business for ten years within 1,000 miles of Washington." The story ended with a jab at Carry: "It will be remembered that Mr. Carry recently denied to the *Post* reporter that he had sold out his brewery." Carry and the other businessmen listed as directors of the new company denied that the report was accurate, saying it "looks like a swindle." Carry denied that any of the reported story was true, but when the reporter noted that one of his fellow board members had admitted that he had been in initial talks for such a sale, Carry admitted that he had been negotiating with British investors, but claimed he had been unable to reach a deal.

In early June the story took yet another twist as one of the British investors filed suit against Carry for refusing to complete the sale. The plaintiff claimed that he had the money to finish the sale, but that the brewery owner refused to finalize the deal as stipulated in their contract. When the case reached court, the plaintiff claimed that Carry refused to sell because he had received an even larger offer from a second English syndicate. Carry stated in an affidavit that the plaintiff only had an option to buy, not a signed contract, and that he could not sell to "English subjects, since they could not acquire title to property under the laws of the District." The sale even became an election issue in Ohio, as the syndicate's lawyer was the Democratic candidate for governor in Ohio that fall. The suit failed, and Carry sold his brewery, supposedly to a group of New York investors, for $400,000. Still, rumors that it had been sold to the English persisted. Decades later he admitted that, yes, in fact the investors were British. The New York group was a front for the foreign group, possibly to get around the District's land ownership laws. British ownership was apparently an open secret, as the trade journal *The Western Brewer* included Carry's old firm in its reports on the returns for investors in British-owned breweries.[51]

One year later, Carry and Robert Portner opened their jointly owned National Capital Brewery with a new brewery that could produce up to 100,000 barrels of beer a year. Apparently, in whatever contract Carry did end up signing when he sold his interest in the Mount Vernon Brewery, the requirement that he remain out of the local brewery business for another ten years was dropped. Portner's brewery in Alexandria was one of the largest in the South, and he and his new partner divided the local market. Portner's Tivoli Brewery would not sell north of the Potomac River, and the new National Capital Brewery would not sell south of the river. The end result of the Carry sale was one more well-financed rival for Heurich. However, unlike Heurich, this new brewery never installed a bottling line, relying on a local bottling company. They also made most of their sales in saloons as draft beer, as did Heurich and every other brewery, but as Heurich gathered more of the D.C. market for himself, this would tighten the beer market for Carry, Portner and his other local rivals.[52]

Now in his fifties, Heurich continued managing his brewery, participating in local activities such as the *Sängerbund*, and living in the mansion he had built for his late second wife. In his unpublished memoirs he described himself as "lonely and alone."[53] In the summers of 1896 and 1897 he returned to Karlsbad for the water cure. Heurich had remained close to the Keyser family, to which he was related through his first wife, Amelia. Lonesome, and still hoping for a marriage with children, he was in Germany taking the cure when he began courting Emmeline Marie Dilger, a pretty thirty-year-old related by marriage to his first wife. (Emmeline's sister Josephine was married to Amelia's nephew, Adolph.) Em, as she was known, must have been receptive at first, but then on the ocean voyage home from Germany she fell in love with a Boston doctor she met on ship. Heurich did not know that he had a rival, eight years younger than the fifty-five-year-old brewer, or why Em was still debating accepting his offer to marry. Nor would he have been happy to know why she hesitated, aside from her shipboard romance. Emmeline's family struggled with money. Indeed, Heurich had purchased their mortgage so that they would not lose their farm. In a letter to a sibling, Em poured out her emotional state in terms that would have horrified Heurich had he known her true feelings:

> If the man were not rich I never would have given him a thought again. Shame on me for this. But I thought of home and all I could do for those I love if I could make up my mind to get used to Mr. Heurich and learn to love him. He may not be a good looking man, but one of noble character.... He may also lack education ... and social polish, yet he is a perfect gentleman. I don't dislike him, but I cannot love him as I ought.[54]

Fortunately for Heurich, who seems to have been genuinely smitten with Fraulein Dilger, Em turned him down, and his eyes turned to a woman he had known since she was a child. Thirty-three-year-old Amelia Louise Keyser was the niece of his first wife,

Amelia Keyser Heurich, circa 1900 (courtesy Jan King Evans Houser).

Amelia, and the Keyser daughter that the Heuriches had tried to adopt over twenty years before. She was a native of Richmond, Virginia, where her father had briefly operated a general store after the Civil War. After it failed, the family moved back to Washington, where he operated a rathskeller, perhaps selling Heurich's beers.[55]

Twenty-one years Heurich's junior, Amelia wrote warm letters to her uncle from December 1897 through May 1898.[56] While the letters maintained a proper emotional distance expected at that time, signs of a growing affection show through. The letters show her obvious fondness for her uncle, signing them "I am, yours, Amelia L. Keyser." On March 11, 1898, Amelia wrote, "I assure you uncle that if any secret you should disclose to me will never be repeated, no-one will know of it through me." There is no hint of what such a "secret" might be. A few days later, on March 15, she noted that "in August last you so kindly invited us to visit your country home. I made several attempts to go out last fall, but always something prevented me from doing so." Undeterred, Amelia asked if she could visit on Easter: "I would so much like to go out on Easter if weather permits, and providing you will be there." She finishes the letter with a note of concern: "Are you working so hard yet? If so, why do you do that? You should not do it. Is there anything that I can do for you to help you along with your work? If there is anything that I can do, I hope, uncle, you will not hesitate for one moment to say so."[57]

The two became engaged on the evening of Sunday, December 11, 1898. Heurich and Amelia attended a lecture by Robert G. Ingersoll at the National Theater. Ingersoll was one of the most popular orators of the era, and his speeches, which could be up to three hours long, often attacked religion, an attitude which gained him the nickname "The Great Agnostic." As noted earlier, Heurich was raised as a Lutheran, but he was not especially devout. Certainly Protestant churches in the U.S., which at the time were increasingly supporting the temperance movement, held no strong attraction for him. Given Ingersoll's fame, some might say notoriety, Heurich most certainly knew what type of speech he'd be attending. Heurich and his niece heard a new lecture by Ingersoll titled "Superstition." The speaker claimed that "the enemy of progress" was superstition. "We have outgrown the Jehovah of the superstitious," a newspaper account of his speech quoted, "by reason of the object lessons of nature and her teachings as they spring from science." The article described the crowd as a "numerous, thoughtful, and miscellaneous assemblage."[58]

After the presentation, Heurich proposed to Amelia and she accepted. The wedding was scheduled for but a month later, and only the family was informed. Amelia's diary shows that every day but one until their wedding, Christian came to visit her at her home on Massachusetts Avenue not far from Heurich's mansion. They married on the evening of January 11, 1899, then honeymooned in Asheville, North Carolina, as well as St. Augustine, Jacksonville, and Orlando, Florida. They returned to D.C. on January 22, and Heurich, Amelia noted, "turned the entire house over to me." The new house was, she fretted, "O, so large" with numerous servants. In her diary the new bride noted her impressions of the servants. The cook, Anna, "did everything to please me." Minnie the chambermaid "was good," as was Jim Muir, the coachman. However, Oscar the butler she judged to be "fresh and impudent."[59] There were two minor complications. Friends could not come to welcome the newlyweds back home, as the Great Blizzard of February 1899 buried Washington under twenty inches of snow and set a record low temperature of -15 °F, trapping the family in the new home. The second complication set a somewhat warmer note: Heurich had to remind his new bride that she should no longer call him "uncle."[60]

In the summer of 1899, Heurich and his new bride traveled to Europe to visit family. Heurich's new in-laws, Amelia's parents Laura and Peter Keyser, traveled with them to New York, along with Amelia's siblings Carl, Gussie, and Anna. The latter two sailed with Amelia and Christian to Europe on the *Graf Waldersee*. One of the Hamburg-Amerika Line's newest passenger ships, she was launched in 1898, so was still new when the Heurich party sailed. The *Graf Waldersee* and her three sister ships—*Pennsylvania*, *Pretoria*, and *Patricia*—regularly sailed between Hamburg and either New York or Philadelphia. The Heuriches undoubtedly traveled first class; the ship had accommodation for 162 in first class, 184 in second, and 2,200 in third. The exceptionally large number of spaces in this

The *Graf Waldersee* (author collection).

latter group shows that the ship was designed to carry large numbers of immigrants from Hamburg to America as part of the enormous wave of immigrants crossing the Atlantic between 1890 and 1914. Second class was intended for those migrants who made repeated trips between Old World and New, as well as for less well-off tourists, young couples (it was known as the "natural habitat of the blushing bride"), and students going abroad for the summer. The Heuriches could easily have afforded first class by the time they began to make their frequent trips back to Europe, and they would have been comfortable journeys. Heurich saved a clipping from columnist Dr. Frank Crane titled "The Ship Cure." It noted, "It is impossible to look at the problems of life [when at sea] the same way you look at them when you are at home."[61]

Surviving postcards and photos of the *Graf Waldersee*'s interior show that the first- and second-class passengers would have had a comfortable trip on a well-appointed ship, with a wide promenade for passengers to stroll along, sit and read, or just watch the sea. Whereas British ships called everyone to eat at a specific time, German ships began offering tickets "without meals," which allowed the passenger to order *à la carte* at the time of his own choosing. This might have appealed to Heurich, as he was by this time beginning to carefully watch what he ate. The ship made about nine round trips a year. Mrs. Heurich's diary noted that it was a thirteen-day voyage, which was a rather long trip. Ten days was closer to the average on a slower ship, six days on the fastest vessels.[62]

Heurich usually chose to travel on German-flagged ships when he crossed the Atlantic. No doubt a major reason he picked a German ship was his pride in his native land. However, one did not have to be a German partisan to sail on their liners. From the 1880s until World War I began in 1914, German and British shipping lines competed

to provide the fastest ships with the most welcoming and luxurious décor for travelers. Some observers noted, not always positively, that it was actually possible to cross the Atlantic and never be aware that you were at sea. The main British lines, Cunard and White Star, competed for the trans-Atlantic business with the two largest German lines, Hamburg-Amerikanische Paketfahrt-Aktien-Gesellschaft (HAPAG) and Norddeutscher Lloyd. From 1898 until 1907, German ships held the trans-Atlantic speed record (the Blue Riband). However, while building ever-faster ships brought bragging rights to the companies and their home countries, sometimes it made for uncomfortable voyages for their passengers due to vibrations and noisy engines. As a result, the White Star Line, and then HAPAG, began to emphasize their ships' décor and service standards rather than speed. Instead of a race for the Blue Riband, there began a contest of decorators to create the best-decorated ship.[63] As a result, Heurich and his family would have found many German ships decorated in a way that would have felt comfortably like their home on New Hampshire Avenue, at least in inspiration if not in scale. One author described the German liners' décor as fitting "lovers of ease and Wagnerian artifacts," the latter of which would have appealed to Heurich, who was always proud that he had met the composer in person. The self-consciously German nature of the decorating was not only a matter of appealing to customers, but also was a deliberate assertion to the rest of the world that Germany belonged on the seas as a dominant power. They were not simply aping the British lines; they created their own definition of a proper ship space as German, asserting their rights to their place among the great naval powers. In 1912 HAPAG launched the SS *Imperator*, then the largest ship in the world. At her bow was a figure of an eagle and in its claws it clutched a globe with the inscription, "*Mein Feld ist die Welt*" (My Field is the World).[64]

While in Europe, the Heuriches visited Amelia's grandmother in Rüdesheim am Rhein. They traveled throughout Germany, visiting Berlin, Cologne and Karlsbad. Heurich introduced them to the cold water cure in Elgersburg in Thuringia, the region where Heurich was born. The total trip lasted only a week and a half, so it was a whirlwind tour, suggesting that Heurich did not feel the need to take the full water cure regimen, which took longer than a few days. Back in Hamburg, the family (minus Anna, who remained in Leipzig to study music) boarded the *Fürst Bismarck* for the U.S. The *Fürst Bismarck* was also part of the Hamburg-Amerika company's express line, along with *Normannia*, *Auguste Victoria* and *Columbia*. Twin-screwed liners, they were faster and more stable than single-screwed ships, which helped propel HAPAG to a dominant position among the German lines, bypassing Norddeutscher Lloyd. Notably faster than the *Graf Waldersee*, the *Fürst Bismarck* normally made the trip from Hamburg to New York in five or six days, setting a record for the Atlantic crossing several times. When the *Fürst Bismarck*'s crew spotted New Jersey's Navesink Highlands, marking their sighting of the American coastline, Heurich and his new wife would have heard the ship's crew ringing a replica of the Liberty Bell presented to the ship and its captain by the Daughters of the American Revolution in 1894.[65]

The 1899 quick tour was but the first of many to Germany for Heurich and Amelia. In 1900, Heurich, his wife, and her two sisters traveled to Karlsbad. They saw the "unforgettable" Oberammergau Passion Play.[66] The Heuriches witnessed an impressive spectacle.

Opposite, top: The *Graf Waldersee*'s **ladies' salon.** *Bottom:* The *Graf Waldersee*'s **smoking lounge (both from postcards in the author's collection).**

Christ leaving the tomb, from the 1900 Oberammergau attended by the Heuriches (Library of Congress).

According to tradition, in 1633 the citizens of Oberammergau, Bavaria, promised if God spared them from the plague then devastating the region, they would regularly celebrate the life and death of Jesus with an elaborate play.[67] When plague deaths subsided, the town honored their promise. The play was first performed in 1634, but because it is so elaborate and complicated, it is only performed once every decade, in years ending in zero. Evolving over the centuries, it is broken into sixteen acts, plus a prologue, covering the last week of Jesus' life through his crucifixion and resurrection. The acts mix a variety of artistic forms: spoken text, music, choral accompaniment, and *tableaux vivants*. The latter use motionless actors to create Bible scenes for the audience, usually accompanied by a narrator's verbal description. The 1900 version, the one the Heuriches enjoyed, was the first to be held in a new theater built especially for the production, which can last for as long as seven hours. The theater, which seats over 4,000, is still in use over a century later, although it has been modified in the decades since Heurich attended. The play was modified after World War II to reduce the many anti–Semitic aspects present in the version Heurich saw, including removing a villain simply called "Rabbi," and emphasizing the role Pilate and the Romans played in Jesus' death.[68]

Besides the Oberammergau Passion Play, another highlight for Heurich of his 1900 trip was visiting the 1900 Paris World's Fair, where two of his beers were competing for recognition among the beers from throughout Europe and North America. Heurich had left Germany in 1866 as a craftsman, an individual skilled in a specific trade. At the 1900 fair, he was competing not as an individual craftsman, but as an industrialist. The medals awarded at the fair harked back to an earlier time of individuals competing against one another to measure their skills, but now it was a competition between groups, corporations comparing their products against those of other corporations. The success of Heurich's beer in winning a silver medal reflected not just his skill as a brewer, which was certainly part of it, but of the skill of his employees, especially his brewmaster, as well as Heurich's skill as a manager, overseeing the mass production of his products. That aspect of groups competing against groups was true of the fair as a whole. Nations represented in Paris in 1900 competed at numerous levels, and their individual pavilions celebrated the works of the nations as organized groups. It wasn't until the fairs of the mid–twentieth century, such as New York in 1939–1940, that pavilions were dedicated to individual corporations. In 1900 it was still the case that even when an individual was celebrated, such as a businessman like Heurich, he was taken as being a representative of an entire nation, the individual standing for the whole.[69]

These international fairs were intended not just to spread culture, but to promote industrialization and colonialism.[70] The Paris World's Fair, officially L'Exposition de Paris 1900, was designed to showcase the accomplishments of the nineteenth century and celebrate the beginnings of the twentieth century. The French capital had hosted numerous world's fairs before—in 1855, in 1878, and in 1889. The latter, held on the centennial of the French Revolution, gave the city the Eiffel Tower, which, although an icon now, was often treated as an eyesore in the years after its creation. The 1900 fair was designed to outdo that of 1889, just as the previous fairs had all been designed to outdo their predecessors. As in 1878 and 1889, the 1900 fair was situated at the Champ de Mars, on the left bank of the river Seine. Formerly swampland, the park had become "the prototypical

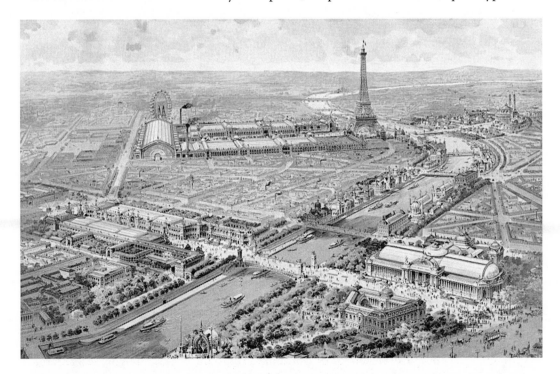

Vue panoramique de l'exposition universelle de 1900 by Lucien Baylac, 1851–1913 (Library of Congress).

exhibitionary space." In 1900, however, the Champ de Mars was too small to hold the entire exhibition, which organizers expanded to the north bank of the Seine, and some areas were even established outside of the city limits as part of the Bois de Vincennes became a fair annex. The latter, segregated from the main part, was used to display transportation-related exhibits, such as automobiles and railroads, and some of the largest machinery, as well as agricultural exhibits. It was also the site of the 1900 Olympics. The latter may be best forgotten, as they "attracted so little public attention, were so poorly organized, and proved ... a complete failure."[71]

The fairgrounds were so close to the center of the city and so extensive that the fair seemed to blend in with the city itself; one contemporary noted that it was often hard to tell where the fair ended and the city began. Heurich had visited Paris as an apprentice, but that had been over thirty years earlier, before the 1870 Franco-Prussian War, the siege of Paris (September 1870–January 1871), and the street fighting of the Paris Commune (May 1871), so the city had undoubtedly changed. There was no single architectural marvel marking the 1900 fair, unlike in 1889 when the Eiffel Tower was the centerpiece. The 1900 event did feature a moving sidewalk, the *trottoir roulant*, which Heurich and his family could have taken to travel around the fair. About four kilometers long, it had three tracks, two of which moved at different speeds around the grounds. The slower track moved at four kilometers an hour and took an hour to go one full circuit, while the quicker traveled at eight kilometers an hour and took one-half hour to go one full trip. (The third track did not move at all.) Fare was fifty centimes per person, about ten cents. The Heuriches may also have taken a small steam railway that followed the same path as the sidewalk, although traveling in the opposite direction. Unlike the 1893 Chicago Fair, there was no segregated midway set aside for purely entertaining exhibits and attractions. There were numerous restaurants and cafes, as well as attractions such as an aquarium, so not everything to see had to be "educational."[72]

About half of the fair's total space was reserved for different national exhibits. Commercial exhibits made up the other half. The latter were divided into eighteen groups, which were further subdivided into one hundred twenty classes.[73] Products from different nations were mixed together by type rather than nationality, and the groups reflected the judgment of the French organizers. Heurich was one of twenty-eight American exhibitors in Group X, Class 62, "Various Beverages." One of the twenty-eight American displays came from the Division of Chemistry in the Department of Agriculture, which presented a "collective exhibit of ales, beers, ciders, fermented drinks, and mineral waters." Their presence at the fair was a reminder that the United States participated, as did the other nations, at least in part to promote exports of the exhibiting nation's products.

In an article published in early 1899, Ferdinand W. Peck, commissioner-general for the United States to the Paris Exposition of 1900, lamented that American exports were far below their "full possibilities," especially in comparison to Great Britain: "That kingdom, with one-thirtieth the area and little more than one-half the population of the United States, enjoys double our foreign trade." "These facts," he complained, "are positively discreditable" to the U.S. "Commerce is the one thing that had made Great Britain great," Peck claimed, "and it is the important factor of public wealth." The world's fairs were one way to correct this imbalance. Peck noted that the 1893 Columbia Exposition led to the "beginning of negotiations which have led to the closing of many recent large orders for American goods." By encouraging as many American companies as possible to participate in Paris, they could present American-made goods before not only the

French population, but to the many visitors expected from around the world. To this end, Peck pleaded for an increase in the money allocated by Congress to build the United States' pavilion, from $650,000 to at least one million. This amount, equivalent to "one half of the sum that would be necessary to build one second-rate battleship, would be sufficient to ensure a victory that would prove of vastly more benefit to the people of the United States than did the recent success of their arms," a reference to the just-concluded Spanish-American War.[74]

Of the twenty-seven commercial entries for the United States in Class 62, sixteen, including Heurich, exhibited beer or ale. The remainder promoted cider, sodas, mineral water, ginger ale, and malt extract. The only D.C. brewer to display at Paris, Heurich entered both Maerzen and Senate. Other breweries among the American exhibitors included Liebmann's of Brooklyn, Indianapolis Brewing from Indiana, Goebel of Detroit, John Gund from Wisconsin, Ballantine & Sons of Newark, New Jersey, and Seattle Brewing and Malting from Washington state. Also included among the American brewery entries was Joaquin Ramos of Havana, Cuba. Combined there were 76,000 exhibitors from around the world, and five different levels of awards were given from Grand Prix to Honorable Mention. There were 45,905 total awards, so roughly 60 percent of exhibitors earned some recognition. The total awards were broken down as follows:

Grand Prix: 3,156

Gold: 8,889

Silver: 13,330

Bronze: 12,108

Honorable Mention: 8,422

Medals were automatically awarded to the Grand Prix winners, but every winner could order as many medals as he wished at his own expense.[75]

In Heurich's division, Class 62, twenty-six countries and the "colonies of France" were represented by 631 exhibits. Of these, 531 won prizes. American companies won one gold, nine silver, eight bronze, and nine diplomas (honorable mention). Indianapolis Brewing won the sole gold for the U.S. The American judge, Julius Schuller, an Indianapolis wine expert, complained that the American entries had several disadvantages. He noted that the European breweries tended to use better ingredients, "more malt, and hops and less rice, corn and other substitutes." This would not have applied to Heurich, as he did follow the higher European standards. Schuller also noted that the foreign entries "were in wood and kept well in temperatures, while the American beers were all in bottles, and of course had been boiled" (pasteurized). He said they "would have shown up far better if kept well upon exhibition."[76] Heurich later complained that his entry had been delayed in shipment and that his beer had been bottled for months. Otherwise, he claimed, he would have won a gold medal.[77] Nonetheless, Heurich could justifiably be proud of earning a silver medal in an international competition. It was his first such award, but it would not be his last. One important reason for competing in these events, in addition to finding international markets, was for bragging rights back home. Heurich took advantage of his 1900 medal, and the ones he would win later, in his advertising in the District and surrounding areas. As will be noted in the next chapter, he pictured his medals on his beer labels and in his advertising, and could brag that his beers were the only ones made in D.C. that had won such awards.

The Senate label shows the 1900 Paris medal (author collection).

Heurich returned to Washington from Paris as the nineteenth century was giving way to the twentieth. Washington was now the capital city not just of a nation, but of a new world power. The United States had defeated Spain in a matter of months in 1898 and took the last remnants of the European state's old empire, including Cuba, Puerto Rico, and the Philippines. There was fighting still in the latter, but the American economy was healthy, President McKinley was popular, and America was looking forward to the new century with confidence and a bit of a swagger. Heurich's mood matched that of his adoptive nation. He was newly married and the new century would be blessed with the children he had long wanted. His beers dominated the local market, and he would successfully face down a combined effort by the other D.C. breweries in a price war, cementing his place as leading brewer in the capital. The new century, however, would also present Heurich with new pitfalls, including the increasing strength of the prohibitionists and an anti–German panic that ended with Heurich's living in a short, self-imposed exile from D.C.

Heurich's prize desk, made for President Ulysses S. Grant. Photograph by Mark Benbow (courtesy the Heurich House Museum).

A Heurich Lager label, probably meant for a keg or case, as it is too large for a 12-ounce bottle (author collection).

A

A Senate Beer label from the mid–1930s (author collection).

The Heurich's Lager can from 1955 (author collection).

B

Introduced in 1914, Home Brew contained less than 2 percent ABV. Intended as a beverage aimed at the home market, it was revived in the 1930s (author collection).

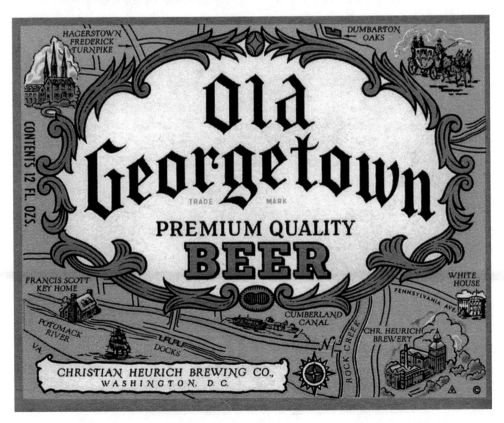

The second Old Georgetown label, used from 1950 to 1956. Note the Heurich brewery and the White House are prominent landmarks on the lower right corner (author collection).

C

Cans of Heurich's beer from the years 1939–1942 (author collection).

A Senate Beer can made into a drinking mug. Breweries sometimes turned cans into mugs for customers (author collection).

D

Left: Senate Beer bottle from 1940 with a 75th anniversary neck label (author collection).
Right: Champeer bottle (author collection).

E

Pre-Prohibition Maerzen label shows the 1900 Paris Medal (author collection).

A Senate beer bottle from the 1940s (author collection).

The Heurich Mansion, 2010 (courtesy the George F. Landegger Collection of District of Columbia Photographs in Carol M. Highsmith's America, Library of Congress, Prints and Photographs Division).

A label from the Picnic Bottle, a half-gallon of unpasteurized beer sold in the 1930s (author collection).

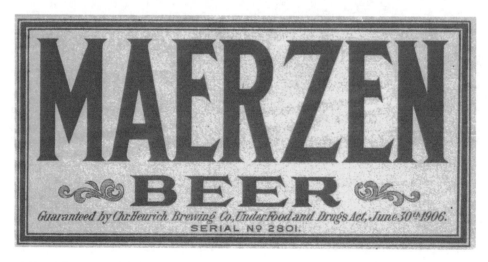

A Heurich Maerzen label, probably meant for a keg or case, as it is too large for a 12-ounce bottle (author collection).

A label from the seasonal Senate Bock Beer, circa late 1930s (author collection).

The redesigned postwar Senate Beer can. The blue can was abandoned for the white design, to which the "250" was later added (author collection).

I

J

Olde Georgetown cans. The can at left was the initial design, which was quickly replaced by the design at right (author collection).

Opposite: The dining room. Heurich's chair was at the end of the table furthest from the viewer. Amelia sat at the near end closer to the servant's stairs (courtesy the Heurich House Museum).

A Heurich matchbook from about 1938–1940, probably when Senate Ale was still a new brand (author collection).

A Heurich matchbook from the short-lived "Extra Fine" campaign of 1949 (author collection).

A Heurich matchbook advertising just Senate Beer, the brewery's flagship brand (author collection).

5

The New Century, 1901–1914

The years 1901 to 1914 were marked by continued success for Heurich and his brewery. He expanded his business and won a "beer war" with his local rivals. Heurich, having remarried in 1899, now began the family he'd long desired, and enjoyed increasing prestige as one of the leaders of D.C.'s German community. Well into middle age and approaching an age in which many wealthy men considered retiring (he turned fifty-nine in 1901), he could enjoy the results of his hard work. Once a young journeyman brewer traveling around central Europe looking for a spot to settle, Heurich had found a permanent home. By 1914, however, a series of challenges, including the First World War and Prohibition, would start to test Heurich, generating enough turmoil to threaten to undo all of his life's work.

Having returned to the United States from the 1900 Paris World's Fair, the Heuriches settled into married life. Christian had long wanted children and had mourned when his second wife Mathilde had lost her unborn child during an illness in 1888. On December 11, 1901, Amelia gave birth to a baby boy, Christian Junior (who would go by Chris). Heurich was delighted. "My cup of rejoicing was full and brimming over," he remembered. "What I had prayed for over years had at last been granted to me—in the Good Lord's own time." The happy father was fifty-nine years old. More children would follow: Anna Marguerite in 1903, Anita Augusta in 1905, and Karla Louise in 1907.[1]

Heurich and his growing family lived in the New Hampshire Avenue mansion in the DuPont Circle neighborhood, a fashionable district for the city's elites, including the local wealthy, senators, and diplomats. Nonetheless, all of his children attended Washington's public schools, and their home life was a mixture of American and German customs. The children's governess was German, but the entire family spoke both German and English at home.[2] The family followed the old German custom of erecting a Christmas tree, but by 1900 many wealthy and middle-class American families did so as well. The family also kept dachshunds as family pets, which slept at the top of the staircase at night, watching over the family.[3] At dinner the family ate together, the parents sitting at either end of the dining room table, the children arranged by age, the eldest, Christian Junior, sitting closest to his father. Amelia sat at the end closest to the servants' stairs to keep a close eye on the kitchen.

Amelia did the shopping not only for the family's clothes, but for the groceries as well. The pantry shelves were locked, and the cook had to have Amelia unlock them to retrieve such items as flour or spices. She also maintained and oversaw the household staff, maids, a cook, a gardener, a laundress, and the children's governesses. Amelia's

diary is full of comments about the household staff coming and going; she was a demanding employer, and turnover was high. Heurich visited a Turkish bath every two weeks and had a barber trim his beard frequently, until one day he caught "barber's itch." From then on, Amelia trimmed her husband's beard herself every day. However, while Amelia ran the household, Christian kept the only key to the front door. When he got older, Christian Junior got one as well. The women of the family, Amelia and her two daughters, never got a key to their own home so long as Heurich was alive. As the family's husband and father, Heurich had the ultimate responsibility, to be shared only by the son once he was old enough. Moreover, Amelia was not allowed to change the decor Heurich's second wife, Mathilde, had chosen. So it was within those limitations that Amelia was allowed to run the home on New Hampshire Avenue. The farmhouse at Bellevue, however, was hers to do with as she saw fit.[4]

In February 1899, Congress passed an anti-smoke law for the District. Designed to reduce the black smoke from burning coal that fouled the air, it proclaimed that the "emission of dense or thick black or grey smoke or cinders from any smokestack or chimney used in connection with any stationary engine, steam boiler, or furnace of any description within the District shall be deemed a public nuisance."

Top: **Karla, Anita, and Chris, circa 1910.** *Bottom:* **Chris and Anita in a toy car in the conservatory, circa 1906–1907 (both photographs courtesy Jan King Evans Houser).**

The law was to be enforced by the District's public health officials, and those convicted would face fines from $10 to $1000 a day. Private residences were exempt.[5] Businesses objected to the law, which was judged to be vague, and because of the expense of trying to find a way to reduce the smoke emitted from their businesses. Some of the local press, however, lobbied for the law. The *Evening Star* began calling for the law a year before it passed. In 1898 they noted, "The District is comparatively free at present from smoke-banners in the sky, owing to the lack of large manufacturing establishments, but there has been a marked increase in the number of these disfiguring and soiling streams of smoke in the past few years."[6] This was a remarkable change for the attitude of the city leaders a generation before, when the city was trying to encourage manufacturing to come to Washington. Heurich had participated in the 1870s fair promoting D.C. products. Now, however, the city was becoming the capital of a world power. The *Star's* call for an anti-smoke law appeared the same day the paper's front page showed the wreckage of the USS *Maine*, lying in Havana Harbor. The United States was about to become an empire, and Washington an imperial city, a showcase for a powerful nation. Increasingly there were calls for the capital city to be cleaned up and for the city to strive to make itself an international showplace. Smoke-producing industries were becoming increasingly out-of-place.

Washington was following the example of a number of other cities in passing an anti-smoke law. The term "air pollution" was not yet in common use, so the laws often relied on descriptions such as "dense or thick black or grey smoke or cinders." Heavy coal smoke from factories was referred to as "the smoke evil," "the smoke plague," or "the smoke nuisance." The laws were based upon the concept of "public nuisance," the idea that one's use of their own personal property did not allow them to have a negative effect on another person's property. The health effects of smoke were not yet known, and efforts to prove smoke caused health problems sounded too much like the discredited idea of "miasma," that bad smells carried diseases. Anti-smoke forces instead relied more on arguments of cleanliness, that smoke dirtied its surroundings and that this environment affected others, that "the city enveloped in a sooty fog is a gloomy city," and so would stunt the growth of its children. The anti-smoke laws reflected the same sensitivity to surroundings that Heurich faced when his brewery was on 20th Street as his neighborhood gentrified. Frustrated in those days by people who "objected to the healthy smell of good hops and barley," he had moved his brewery to the industrial zone of Washington, but the areas where manufacturing was welcome was shrinking. With the anti-smoke law in effect, the area for business was contracting even further.[7] Heurich fell afoul of the law in early 1902. The regulation had been enforced irregularly by health inspectors, and several companies had taken the city to court to try to have the law annulled. Heurich's trial was held in early March and a jury found him not guilty, not because his brewery was not emitting smoke, but because the brewery was owned by a corporation, and he was charged as an individual.[8] Congress considered modifying the law to allow the emission of dark smoke, provided it did not last over three minutes. The amended law, however, died in committee, and the law remained as it was. Enforcement increased, but Heurich was never brought to court again for having his brewery issue dark black or gray smoke.

That same year, 1902, Heurich was again bothered by dizzy spells, "the only form of real sickness during my close to a century of active life," he remembered.[9] Apparently he had forgotten, or did not count, his bout with malaria in the 1860s. The dizzy spells may actually have been from a recurrence of the disease, although Heurich did not note suffering from a high fever, which can also occur during a malarial relapse. Once again he traveled to Europe to "take the cure." This time he went with his wife, their son, a nursemaid, two sisters-in-law, and "two old friends, a married couple."[10] This trip would be one of Heurich's most memorable, and it illustrated the fine line he followed as an immigrant between loyalty to his birthplace and loyalty to his adopted homeland. It also followed a pattern that the Heurich family would follow for the next three decades, with interruptions for the world wars. They would live in D.C. most of the year, but come warm weather in summer, the family would spend more time at the farm in the Maryland suburbs, with trips to Cape May and Atlantic City. The highlight of the season, however, would be a long trip to Europe with a visit to a spa and resort in Germany along with side trips in central and western Europe. The family always took German-flagged liners, with a handful of exceptions, due mostly to the world wars. Heurich did not record which ship he took in 1902, but did note that they sailed on the Hamburg-Amerika line because they were now using twin-screw steamers, which had the reputation of being more stable.[11]

They traveled to Weiße Hirsch just outside Dresden, for the cure at the facility run by physician and naturopathy advocate Heinrich Lahmann (1860–1905).[12] Lahmann professed belief in an "air cure." Heurich described it as "exercise in the fresh air in 'Adam's costume.'" In his memoirs he noted his routine for the "successful, six-week cure."

> After breakfast there were electric heat treatments, massages and cold baths. After lunch we alternatively walked in the forest or sunbathed. For our diet, we had easily digestible food, plenty of garden salad without vinegar and ripe cherries. Beyond the grounds of the sanatorium, there was no objection to having a glass of beer or wine. My dizziness disappeared.

Heurich had taken the water cure before, and would again, but Lahmann's sanatorium was based on the idea that, while the water cure was occasionally useful and the correct treatment for some ailments, it could be overused. In some cases it was worse than useless, and was actually harmful. In his book, *The Airbath as a Means of Healing and Hardening the Body*, Lahmann noted, "I know many hundreds of water fanatics but not a single healthy one." "Man is not an amphibian," Lahmann sniffed; his "proper element is air, not water. The relation of mankind to the ambient air in which they live forms the most important chapter in the book of health." The air bath certainly provided a contrast to the industrialized, urban environment, and this immersion into the more natural landscape was designed to serve as a treatment for the patient's mental and physical health alike. The air itself became a commodity to be sold. A few resorts even sold their air in bottles, but generally it was so linked to the landscape that the patient, such as Heurich, had to travel to the location to get the full benefit. This blurred the boundary between medical treatment and tourism, which allowed busy men, such as Heurich, to take advantage of a vacation as a form of doctor-ordered medical treatment.[13]

As part of the cure, Heurich and his fellow patients were required to expose as much skin as possible to the air. "The skin is the organ by which vapours are given off by the body," Lahmann claimed. "These are indeed the most poisonous waste products of the body escaping through the skin." The cover of the second edition of his book shows a middle-aged man standing in the snowy woods wearing nothing but a pair of shorts and a set of cross-county skis. The fifty-nine-year-old Heurich visited in summer, so he escaped semi-naked cross-country skiing to go along with the sunbathing. An illustration

Postcard of Dr. Heinrich Lahmann's sanitarium (author collection).

in Lahmann's book shows summer sunbathers were separated by sex by a large fence. (Children's groups seemed to have mixed boys and girls.) Given Heurich's description of going out in "Adam's costume," it's likely the bathers were nude, at least some of the time.[14]

Heurich described the treatment as "successful" as his dizziness disappeared. However, he seemed more impressed by the diet regimen than the air baths. He remembered that after leaving Weiße Hirsch he went to Switzerland and enjoyed a beer with some Swiss cheese. His dizziness returned. Of course, in the good brewer's mind it could not have been the beer, so it must have been the cheese. "Since then," he remembered, "I have never eaten Swiss cheese." Heurich switched to a plain diet of "easily digestible food," which seemed to control his dizziness. He also continued enjoying water cures, and public baths both in Europe and in D.C., apparently unconcerned that his clothing was trapping the poisonous "vapours … given off by the body."[15]

Heurich's assorted medical treatments were not unusual for the time. He was outside the norm only in having the resources to try them on a regular basis. The nineteenth century witnessed a plethora of alternative medicines and efforts to understand health and illness. Some were more useful than others, and a few, such as vegetarianism, remain popular in the early twenty-first century, but their influence went beyond Heurich's "taking the cure," whether it be the waters at Karlsbad or the air bath at Weiße Hirsch. It's no accident that the industrial age, with its emphasis on machinery, also saw a change in views concerning health, as bodies were increasingly seen as systems that had to be kept clean to run properly. Poisons and impure material had to be expelled as quickly and efficiently as possible, and individuals had to carefully monitor what went into their bodies. Health was a matter of balance and moderation. By following a diet of moderation in food as well as in drink, Heurich was participating in a popular health practice of the day. Concerns about the healthfulness of alcohol, including beer, and the temperance movement that would shut down Heurich's brewery from 1917–1933, were part of this same trend, although the brewer would have been loath to admit it.[16]

The solutions to health issues could be either individualistic or communal. Heurich's treatments were individualistic. He was taking personal responsibility for his own health, even if it was in a communal setting. Individuals were responsible for avoiding inappropriate behavior that could injure their health instead of following healthy habits, such as watching their diet. However, there was also an increasing trend towards a communal solution, changing not only the behavior of individuals, but changing the environment in which individuals acted to help promote the health of the community as a whole. The WCTU's campaign to require anti-alcohol education discussed earlier was a part of this. So were community efforts to collect trash, vaccinate children, improve hygiene in the food industries, or to build public baths in urban areas. For Heurich these campaigns were both a help and a hindrance. The idea of the importance of environment in promoting moral and physical health alike influenced the sense of space and place that forced him to move his brewery. The press emphasis on the cleanliness of his new brewery in the 1890s, and his advertisements emphasizing the health benefits of his beer, were also part of this sense of a clean space, a healthy environment, in maintaining a healthy society. On the negative side, pressure was beginning to develop to make the entire city of D.C. "dry" because, prohibitionists would argue, as the capital of the United States, Washington should set itself aloft as a moral example to the nation, to be a moral "space."

After undergoing the airbath treatment, Heurich and his family visited his hometown, Römhild. Heurich had maintained contact after visiting in the 1880s. He had donated 10,000 marks in 1891 (approximately $2,500 in American dollars at the time, $66,000 in 2013[17]) after a fire destroyed much of the town. According to newspaper reports printed in the United States, the fire began in the town square, where the wealthiest families lived, and was spread through the rest of the town by an ongoing storm which "carried the flames to the adjacent streets." The "primitive fire brigade was inadequate to cope with the flames which left 1,500 out of 2,000 people homeless."[18] In 1902 he was there to dedicate a monument to his old schoolteacher, Rector Jung, "the simple dominie who had taught me reading, writing and arithmetic, and who had installed in me certain commonsense lines of procedure which, above all other things, had enabled me to make my fortune in my new land." Heurich paid for most of the memorial. The dedication ceremony was attended by "notables from all over the countryside." Heurich was gratified to see many of his old friends, but sadly noticed "the absence of what would have been many familiar face; time ... was marching on." "I was sorry for those absent ones," Heurich wrote, "but as for myself, I was young and healthy, only fifty nine years of age and the father of a baby son!" Heurich was greeted by Römhild's Mayor Griebel, and the dedication ceremony was followed by a "public banquet" which "revived memories of forgotten events." After Heurich returned home, he maintained contact with old friends, with whom he began to correspond. The ruling duke, Georg II, offered Heurich a knighthood, which he refused, apparently believing it was inappropriate for an American to accept a knighthood from another country, even if it was his homeland. Heurich loved his homeland, and always felt strong ties to Germany, but he had become a citizen of the United States as quickly as he could, and his loyalty was to his adopted nation.[19]

The offer of a knighthood, while doubtlessly a reflection of gratitude towards a generous benefactor and a hometown boy made good, also reflects the German attitude towards the *Heimat*. There is no exact English language equivalent, but it was the assumption that German émigrés would continue to feel not just a nostalgic affection, but a still vital connection towards their homeland. It was more of a regional bond than a sense of nationalism, although after 1871, German nationalists hoped that it would translate to a bond with the greater German state as well.[20] According to German law, emigrants who had lived abroad for ten years were considered to have forfeited their citizenship in the *Reich*.[21] Heurich certainly fit that criterion. However, he was greeted as something between the returning prodigal son and a hero. Part of this was likely because he was successful and shared the fruits of that success with his home town. There was also an additional factor. Heurich demonstrated this sense of *Heimat*. Not only did he donate money multiple times to help his home town, he maintained the cultural and emotional links to his homeland. Late in his life he was still bragging about the famous Germans who came from "my section of Germany," and named Rudolf Diesel, Johann Sebastian Bach, and Martin Luther as notables from his home region.[22] Evidence of an existing sense of *Heimat* among the D.C. German-American community could be seen in the *Sängerbund*, the German shooting clubs, and active charities such as the German Orphans' Home, in all of which Heurich actively participated. In November 1903 the German community in D.C., of which Heurich was a respected leader, held a five-day celebration commemorating the 220th anniversary of the first German settlers' landing in what would become the United States. President Theodore Roosevelt pressed an "electric button in the White House" to turn on the lights on the evening of November 23. Sponsored by the United German Societies, the festival featured Christmas trees decorated German style with toys, a German village, and a beer garden. While the brands of beer are not listed in the newspapers, Heurich's beers were likely among them. German and American flags and other national symbols decorated the Convention Hall. The young residents of the German Orphans' Home, of which Heurich was a director, were special guests. The local *Sängerbund* and *Turnverein* entertaining the crowds. Money from ticket sales went to various local German charities. A large banner hung over the festivities that read simply "*Ordnung*" (Order). The festival demonstrated how integrated the local German community had become in Washington society with the participation of President Roosevelt, who not only started the festival, but welcomed some of the young guests at a White House reception.[23]

Groups such as the Pan-German League and the Navy League promoted this sense of *Heimat* to promote German interests abroad, transforming groups of German émigrés into groups that would lobby local governments, represent German interests abroad, and, in some cases, act as *de facto* colonies. As historian Stefan Manz noted, the "notion of a multitude of Reich-oriented Little Germanies scattered around the globe tied in with Wilhelmine ideals of global expansion." Economically they could "act as promoters or customers of German industry." Culturally this diaspora could "disseminate a supposedly superior culture," and politically, "they could be used to legitimize territorial claims." This last factor clearly would not apply to German groups in nations such as the United States, Russia, or Britain, but applied in Africa and even, in some dreamers' views, in Latin America. In industrial nations, the first two, economic and social, played a larger part in the hopes, however exaggerated, of helping spread German influence abroad.[24] Ironically, the pan-Germans' hopes that *Heimat* would spread Berlin's influence often had the opposite effect. It emphasized the "otherness" of the local German populations, making them appear as aliens outside of their proper "place." When World War I began in 1914, local German populations in belligerent nations became targets for xenophobia. This was notably the case in the United States, especially after the country entered the war in 1917. Heurich and his family would fall victim to the xenophobic hysteria of the period, fueled in part by the fear that he was loyal not to the United States, but to his *Heimat*.

Back in D.C., Heurich dominated the local beer industry. Five area breweries— Heurich, Abner-Drury, Arlington Brewing, Capital Brewing, and Washington Brewing[25]—formed a Brewers Association during the local beer boycott of 1896 to cooperate in case there was labor trouble again in the future, so that none of them would individually be crippled by a strike. To prevent such a strike, the breweries signed a labor agreement with the local Central Labor Union. The Brewers Association also encouraged cooperation on other matters of mutual interest. For example, in 1901 all of the city's brewers agreed to get rid of the hated six- and eight-barrel packages that complicated taxes and sales. Rather than try to lobby Congress to modify the District's tax laws, they simply acted in unison to fix the problem by agreeing to no longer package their products in the unwanted sizes. Additionally, the Association set the total yearly output for all five breweries at 270,000 barrels. This was approximately 90 percent of the beer sold in D.C. About 20,000 barrels a year was shipped into the city from outside breweries, usually sold as bottled beer. Heurich sold about one-half of the beer sold in D.C., approximately 145,000 barrels. The brewers set a common price of $6.00 a barrel, with a 5 percent discount for paying in cash. That meant Heurich was grossing about $870,000 a year, not including sales made by his Baltimore and Norfolk branches.[26] However, the brewers' agreement expired in 1903, and Heurich decided that he was losing up to 10,000 barrels a year in market share to the Arlington Brewery. To regain the lost sales, he lowered the wholesale price of his beer to $4.00 with a 10 percent discount for cash payments. This sparked the D.C. Beer War. It lasted for four years, but when it ended, Heurich had solidified his position as the dominant local brewer.[27]

The Beer War began in the summer of 1904 when members of the local Central Labor Union (CLU), in cooperation with the D.C. Brewers' Association, attempted to force Heurich via a strike to negotiate with his fellow D.C. brewers. Not only would a strike disrupt Heurich's beer production, if local workingmen supported the strike and boycotted his beer, it would hurt his sales. The resulting labor battle revealed the fissures among the brewers, local labor organizations, and the liquor dealers. It also illustrated the economic influence Heurich wielded in the Washington brewing industry. When Heurich lowered his wholesale prices, Albert Carry of the National Capital Brewing Company called a meeting of the Brewers' Association to settle the matter. Heurich refused to cooperate by raising his prices. He told Carry, "You can stand it. Let us see what those fellows are doing." Heurich's strategy was dependent upon his status as the area's largest brewer. Beer is a perishable item once it reaches the consumer. Breweries could stockpile their product, but once it reached the saloons, it had a limited shelf life. Lowing the price of goods that can be stockpiled by consumers for a long period of time (such as soap or canned foods) can increase sales enough to make up for lost profits at a lower price. Price reductions on non-stockpileable goods, such as beer, must be maintained for a longer period of time, and may result in the consumer's expecting the lower price on a permanent basis. Heurich did not want to lose money, but with his volume of sales he could better afford to live with reduced profits over a long period of time than most of his local rivals. Meanwhile, Heurich's competitors' available responses were lim-

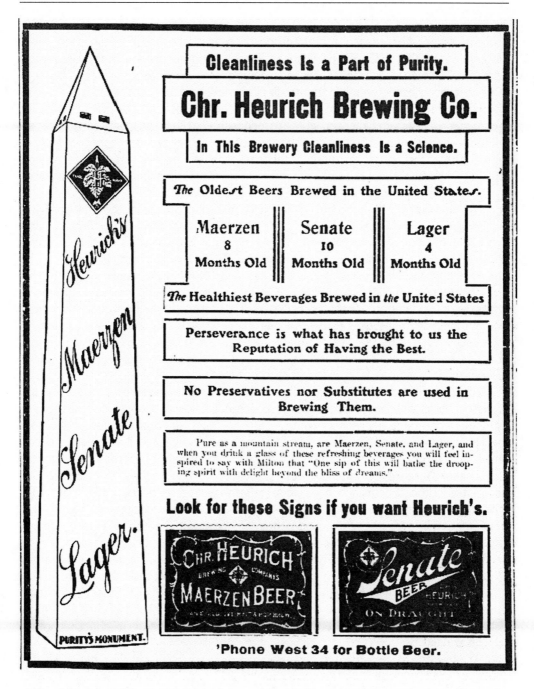

A Heurich ad from May 6, 1903. Note the use of the Washington Monument (author collection).

ited. They could ignore Heurich's price cut and lose business. They could match Heurich's prices and lose profits, which would hurt the smaller breweries before it would hurt Heurich. Finally, they could force a strike to interrupt his production and sales, forcing consumers to buy from his rivals at the higher price. This last strategy was the one Heurich's local competitors chose.[28]

News of the dispute spread, which meant that the existence of the purpose of the Brewers' Association attracted public notice. Carry denied that the Association was designed to set the price of beer, when in fact that was one of its primary functions. Given public concern over the trusts and monopolies at the time—President Theodore Roosevelt was winning popular support as a "trust-buster" in 1904—Carry's denial was understandable. However, the conflict was over the wholesale price of beer, which affected the breweries' profit and the cost of beer to consumers. That gave Heurich a boost in winning popular support, as he was acting not just in his own interests, but for those of local consumers as well. If the unions could get involved, however, the Brewers' Association could make the issue one of worker solidarity rather than consumer interests. For that they needed the cooperation of the local Central Labor Union.[29]

On Monday, July 18, 1904, the CLU held their weekly meeting at the Typographical Temple. Headquarters of the Columbia Typographical Union No. 101, the Temple was a popular meeting place for unions and local fraternal groups. They discussed a resolution calling for a strike against the Christian Heurich Brewery to be led by the firemen, the men who kept the boilers working, a necessary part of the brewing process. President Timothy Healey of the Stationary Engineers' Union came from Omaha, Nebraska, to ask for the strike declaration. He was backed by representatives of the Brewers' Association. The motion was opposed by representatives of the local retail liquor sellers' group. A press account noted that the discussion "waxed warm at times." Opponents argued that the CLU should not get involved in a dispute between different companies trying to force one of their competitors to raise their prices.[30]

Healey, however, had not waited for the CLU to act. He had arrived in D.C. earlier, probably about July 15, and asked to meet with Heurich. Heurich thought that the meeting was about continuing the existing contract with the men who ran his brewery's boilers, the "stationary firemen." The existing agreement, he thought, expired on July 1, 1905, but the union claimed it had run out on July 1, 1904. The brewer arrived at the Typographical Temple for his meeting, only to find that Healey had invited representatives of the Brewers' Association. Heurich refused to hold a discussion with the Association and left. Another meeting was arranged the next day at the St. James Hotel, where Healey was staying. This time Heurich's lawyer, Leon Tobriner, attended. When he arrived he found not only Healey, but several of the local brewers, including Albert Carry of National Capital Brewing, Bernard Catts from Arlington Brewing, and Abner Drury's Edward Abner and Peter Drury. Representatives from the CLU were also waiting. Tobriner was informed that unless Heurich agreed to match the others' price of $6.00 a barrel and rejoin the local Brewers' Association, the firemen would go on strike and Healey would fight "to a finish." Tobriner asked each of the brewers present if they agreed. Each did so. Heurich's lawyer refused and left.[31]

At a meeting of workers' and brewery association representatives on July 18, Healey presented the CLU with a *fait accompli*, noting that he had already presented his own ultimatum to Heurich, that unless the renegade brewer agreed by 6:30 p.m. that same day to meet the Brewers' Association's demands, all the engineers employed in his brewery would go on strike the next morning, and that "a sympathetic strike of all his brewers, drivers and others affiliated with organized labor might also result." Heurich refused.[32] Speaking to the press after the meeting, the brewers expressed their frustration that Heurich refused to join them. Heurich was an active member of the national brewers' association, they complained; why he "refuses to become a member of the local board has never be satisfactorily explained." They denied the accusation, made by Heurich and his lawyer, that the association was "organized to act as a trust or combine." Their purpose was only to cooperate in negotiating a fair labor agreement with all of the city's brewery workers at one time, a policy encouraged by the national association.[33]

Heurich was not the only one unimpressed with the association and their labor allies' argument. Even some officials of the CLU expressed their doubts to the press, albeit anonymously. It was not the union's job, they claimed, to try to force an industry to raise its prices. They were backing a butchers' strike against raising the price of beef. How could they then call a strike to demand a price hike from another group? In addition, the local liquor dealers were adamantly opposed to a price hike, which would, of course, impact their businesses. One member told the *Washington Times*, "If Heurich will have the nerve and stamina to maintain his right to put his own price on his own product, he will win the regard and respect of the local dealers." As for the firemen threatening to go on strike, Heurich announced that he already had replacements ready.[34]

Healey made an error when he failed to make certain of the CLU's support before launching the strike, and it quickly became apparent that it did not have the necessary backing to succeed. The single largest reason for this lack of support was almost certainly that it was taken not to improve workers' conditions, but to aid the other brewery owners. Healey tried to make the issue one of workers' interests by claiming that if Heurich did not join the other breweries and raise his prices, then some of his competitors would be forced to close. He warned, "Unless the price of beer in this city is raised within a short time," then three of the local breweries "will be forced against the wall." "This would," he noted, "throw a large number of employees out of work."[35]

This type of appeal might have worked in other industries, where industrial unions could muster support throughout an entire industry. The breweries, however, while they were moving towards industry-wide organization, still tended to act as craft unions, where workers at the same facility were divided by their skills and occupation. Healey might have been able to win support from the other workers in Heurich's brewery had he been able to make a better case that siding with the Brewers' Association would help the workers in some definite way, rather than a vague threat of possible lost jobs. Brewery workers were one of the groups most likely to conduct a boycott as a way to pressure brewery management. Heurich had been subjected to such a boycott in 1885 until he agreed to use only union workers. Healey's failure to garner such solidarity, which he needed to make the strike a success, illustrates the weakness of his attempt to argue that the workers' interests were at stake. Moreover, Healey was an outsider, not only because he came from outside D.C., but because he did not come from the ranks of brewery workers, which further weakened his appeal for solidarity.[36]

The strike was set to begin at noon on Thursday, July 21. Fifteen men, Heurich's entire staff of firemen, walked off the job, and were promptly replaced by fifteen new workers. Despite the fact that the new workers were reported to be non-union, the other employees did not join the strike in sympathy with the firemen. Even some of the firemen were not happy with the strike, according to one report, and participated only to maintain unity with their union—"They felt that they were striking without just reason ... in the interests of a trust."[37] Two saloonkeepers immediately filed for an injunction against the strike. In their request they targeted all of the D.C. brewers, plus the Arlington Brewing Company, and union president Timothy Healey. The suit asked that the Brewers' Association price agreement be declared "null and void" and that the Brewers' Association be forbidden from trying to force the Heurich Brewery to raise its prices. The saloonkeepers alleged that the four breweries—Abner-Drury, Washington, National Capital and Arlington Brewery—"conspired together" to "prevent competition in the business, to control the distribution of the product to the retail dealers, and to prevent competition in the price of the same." The plaintiffs alleged that if Heurich was forced to join the local monopoly and raise the price of his beer from $4.00 a barrel to $6.00 a barrel, it would cause them "loss and injury" as well as lead to the "deprivation of their customers." As for the strike, the saloonkeepers noted that there had been no dispute between Heurich and his firemen, that there had been no changes in hours, wages, or working conditions. The sole purpose of the walkout, they alleged, was to "embarrass the Heurich company in its business and compel it to abandon its competition in trade." Therefore the strike's purpose was to "stifle competition" and to "restrain the conduct of trade in violation of the rights of the complainants, of other retail dealers, of the general public, and in violation of the law of the land." Justice Wright of the Supreme Court of the District of Columbia announced that he would consider the suit on Monday, July 25, when all the parties were to have their lawyers present.[38]

The quick response of the saloonkeepers illustrates how great a threat to their business they believed this beer war to be. Saloonkeepers were under a great deal of economic pressure, and had to struggle to remain independent businessmen. Many failed and opened "tied" saloons, but even those who managed to stay independent could not avoid some financial ties to local breweries. Tied saloons were owned by the breweries themselves. This may be a direct ownership, or the saloonkeeper may have borrowed money from a brewery to pay for his furnishings, equipment and license. In either case, the saloon would be expected to sell only the products of the brewery to which they owed money.[39] One local saloonkeeper published an editorial in the *Washington Post* supporting Heurich:

> At most, it is but a transfer of profits from the rich brewer to the poor saloon-keeper, and why any labor organization should be engaged in battling on the side of the rich against the poor for the formation of trusts that grind the working man instead of battling to destroy them at every opportunity is something that will puzzle thoughtful people all over the country.[40]

The economic pressure came from several sources. The economic conditions of the country as a whole would, of course, play a role, but for saloonkeepers there was the extra pressure placed on them by the temperance campaign and various reform groups. Not only did the Drys work to convince people to stop drinking, thus cutting into the saloons' customer base, they also supported measures such as higher license fees which were designed specifically to drive saloons out of business. Washington's license fee went from $100 to $800 a year between 1893 and 1896,[41] the difference equivalent to approximately 14,000 glasses of beer at a nickel each. Reformers interested in political corruption also took an interest in saloons because they were so closely associated with the corrupt political machines that dominated politics in this period. Saloons were places where political organizations could meet, and where patronage such as jobs could be distributed. Under this increased economic pressure, some saloonkeepers began to allow illicit profit-making activities such as gambling or prostitution to operate in their businesses. This increased the ire of reformers, thus raising the pressure on saloons to close.[42]

Heurich was also able to take advantage of the "reciprocity culture" in which saloons operated. "Treating," where one bought beer for a group, was not a one-way street; each party was expected to give something to the other. The "treat" could be symbolic. For example, the bartender could accept a tiny glass of beer, a "snit" from a customer. The bartender could drink many snits, which were often mostly foam, without getting drunk while not offending customers by refusing treats. While the treat was often shared among equals, such as friends drinking together, it was also a business relationship between bartender and customers. Saloons provided rooms for local groups such as clubs or unions to meet for free, and in exchange those using the space were expected to buy drinks. This reciprocity could also extend upward. For example, by setting lower prices, Heurich helped the saloonkeepers who bought his beer. In exchange, they remained supportive of Heurich in his battle with his rivals. The barkeeps were most certainly not Heurich's equals in the relationship, but they did benefit from his actions, and because Heurich controlled half of the local beer business, he had more supporters among the saloons than did his rivals.[43]

Heurich also had an advantage in that the breweries operated in what tended to be a "price taking" rather than a "price setting" business. In the former, products are standardized and prices are set largely by supply and demand. If companies can differentiate their product from others on the market, however, they can become "price setters" with more freedom to control the prices they receive for their product. Heurich dominated the local beer industry, so he had the freedom to set the price at the level he wished. His local competitors had less leverage because they had smaller market shares, so they had less ability to set the prices they charged. Unless they could differentiate their beers from Heurich's in a significant manner, they would eventually be forced to meet his price levels. Beers and ales, however, were similar enough that such differentiation was difficult to establish in the minds of consumers. The most likely way to accomplish this would be by establishing their brands as "premium" brands worth the extra cost. Moreover, the local brewers' products were well-known and long-established, making it almost impossible to reposition their brands as now being "premium." The shipping brewers from outside D.C., such as Schlitz and Pabst, already filled that niche. Because Heurich dominated the local beer market, the walkout of Heurich's firemen had little real chance of succeeding in pressuring Heurich to meet the other brewers' demands. The *Washington Post* reported on the strike's second day that "it was the consensus of opinion among organized labor men that the strike would fail." One local union, the International Brotherhood of Teamsters, Soda, Mineral Water, and Bottle Beer Drivers Local No. 372, unanimously passed a resolution denouncing Healey's actions, "which could only result to the benefit of capital and reduce the earnings of labor."[44]

Heurich had supporters among the barkeeps and workers, but he was going against the industry's argument, as made by one of the leading brewers' journals, *The Western Brewer*. In an 1898 article the *Brewer* argued that retailers selling beer had sufficient profit even at the higher prices per barrel. They noted that the saloons bought their beer at a rate ranging from $4.00 to $9.00 a barrel, depending on location. The average was "not far from $6.00 a barrel," which is what the D.C. Brewers' Association wanted Heurich to charge. The article included a chart showing how much money the seller took in per serving size ranging from 16 oz (a pint) down to 8 oz while charging a nickel per glass. The profits per 31-gallon barrel ranged from $12.40 selling a pint glass for a nickel, to $24.80 for 8 oz glasses. The "average number of glasses which is considered as fair is 100 five-cent glasses to each quarter barrel, which means the receipt of $20 from the sale of a barrel of beer." That would give the saloonkeeper a profit of $14.00 per barrel at the average of $6.00 paid to the brewery. Even selling beer by the bucket, in quart growlers, would take in $15.12 per barrel, still more than double the cost of the beer for the seller.[45]

The Western Brewer dismissed other costs incurred by the saloons, claiming their "necessary expenses are comparatively slight." In contrast, the brewers' expenses, the Brewer contended, were "necessarily very large."

> In the first place, his investment, both in capital and skill, is enormously larger. Besides the interest upon his capital, he has to maintain wagons, horses, a small army of drivers and collectors; in very many cases he is obliged also to carry the retailer's equipment. He must supply the ingredients and the labor, machinery, etc., pay the internal revenue tax, and shoulder a heavy risk of loss both in the way of spoilage and bad accounts.

To make up the difference if they had to pay more, the Brewer suggested that the saloons serve slightly smaller amounts for the old price, "an almost imperceptible decrease in the amount given at each sale." This latter suggestion was not unique to The Western Brewer. The same suggestion was made that year by The Liquor Trades Review, which printed diagrams of beer glasses with slightly thicker glass so that while they were the same size as the glasses already in use, they would hold less beer.[46]

The Western Brewer was correct in its description of the costs incurred by the breweries, but the barkeepers could justifiably point out that they also had expenses which the brewery journal casually dismissed, including license fees, wages, food costs for the free lunches, insurance, rent, replacing broken glasses and equipment, as well as "spoilage and bad accounts." Moreover, the industry journal noted that the brewer had to "carry [purchase] the retailer's equipment" without noting that they would then demand the saloonkeeper repay or rent the equipment from the brewer. The journals' arguments succinctly illustrate the industry's position on relative costs and profits between the producer and the retailer. Heurich's attitude towards the price of his beer was going against the preferences of his fellow producers, even though he used tied saloons to sell his product.

While the local beer war continued in 1904, the local brewers faced another challenge, one that foreshadowed the successes of the Prohibition campaign in the 1910s, and which may have helped spark the Beer War. Across the Potomac River from D.C. is the area known as Rosslyn in what was then named Alexandria County.[47] Now a concentration of office buildings for government workers, lobbyists, and trade associations, in the early 1900s it was the downscale red-light district for the District of Columbia, filled with illegal gambling halls as well as disreputable brothels and saloons. A similar area known as Jackson City was not quite two miles downriver (near where the Pentagon now sits), and beyond that was St. Asaph's, a racetrack and betting parlor. Rosslyn was also the site of the Arlington Brewing Company, which stood a short distance from the illegal businesses that provided them so many thirsty customers. Rosslyn and Jackson City were frightening places, to be avoided by decent people if at all possible. Local farmers who had to pass through Rosslyn to get into D.C. to sell their produce in the city's markets would form armed caravans to pass through safely. Bodies were often dumped in a gully nicknamed "Dead Man's Hollow." Local law enforcement, on the take from the gamblers, did nothing to close the illegal establishments.[48] The area also provided an embarrassing example for the local brewers that the anti-alcohol Drys could use to good advantage to point out the relationship between crime, vice, corruption and alcohol, including beer.

For every brewery ad touting how pure and wholesome their product was, the Drys could point to a crime in the northern Virginian red-light district.

In 1903 a Good Citizens' League for Alexandria County met to pick a candidate for commonwealth's attorney to stand election in the fall elections. The existing attorney, Richard Johnson, was supported by the gambling interests because he allowed the illegal businesses to operate openly. Local businessman Randall Mackey garnered the support of those who wanted to clean up the county, for moral reasons as well as for business. Some owned land they wanted to develop into middle-class neighborhoods, but it would be impossible to attract enough buyers given the area's reputation. The election was described as "hard fought" as the existing political machine fought to keep its influence. Bribing voters was common at the time and no doubt added to Johnson's total. Johnson carried two of the three voting districts, those where the illegal establishments were located. Mackey carried the remaining district, but it was a largely residential area where he and his family lived, and his margin there was just barely enough to win the election, by a total of two votes. Johnson sued, claiming vote fraud, and produced eighteen witnesses who claimed they had been paid to vote for Mackey. Their stories fell apart in court, however, and Mackey took office in early 1904.[49]

The local sheriff, William Palmer, was a member of the political machine controlled by the gamblers, so after several months of fruitlessly demanding action to close the illegal establishments, Mackey took matters into his own hands. He recruited a half-dozen trustworthy men and met them in D.C. near the Long Bridge. They all boarded the local trolley line to Rosslyn. While on the car, Mackey issued axes, guns, and sledge-hammers to his new posse. On the attorney's signal, the conductor stopped outside one of the gambling halls and the men promptly jumped off to begin a series of raids. Inside the business, named Heath's Place, they found only a few gambling machines and few actual gamblers. Mackey later claimed that the sheriff had tipped them off, which the sheriff indignantly denied. They smashed what they found, arrested owner Eddie Heath, and continued south following the river, smashing saloons and gambling halls as they went. Heath may have been warned that the raid was coming, but not everyone was. Although they were only able to arrest six men, Mackey and his men shut down numerous saloons, pool halls and gambling dens, smashing equipment, furniture, "obscene" painting on the walls, and bottles of liquor.[50] The raid did not end all of the vice in Alexandria County all at once. Sheriff Palmer often refused to issue arrest warrants, so Mackey began serving them himself. St. Asaph's was a popular betting spot, with clientele who would never have dared to enter one of the area's brothels or saloons, but Mackey was eventually able to force its closure as well. The raids were a dramatic and effective beginning of the process that by the 1910s had significantly cleaned out the red-light districts in the county.

Mackey's raids began in May 1904, not long before the Central Labor Union attempted to force Heurich to negotiate with the local Brewers' Association. The timing of the CLU's actions is suggestive. Mackey's efforts had the backing of, among others, local temperance advocates, and Mackey would continually harass the Arlington Brewing Company, trying to drive it out of business. It's possible that Mackey's raid worried the local brewers as possibly marking the start of a more active, and more destructive, campaign by local Drys. By 1904 temperance activist Carrie Nation was in her fourth year of "hatchetations," smashing saloons regardless of the class of their clientele, and she was inspiring copycats. Mackey's raids, even though they were of illegal establishments, were likely a sobering reminder to the local brewers that not only was their business was under attack, but that such attacks might gain official sanction. While none of the local brewers advertised that they sold their product to the dives in Rosslyn and Jackson City, it's not likely that they would have refused the business either. If the local Drys were able to start driving saloons out of business, then it was even more imperative that they all be allowed to charge a higher rate for their product to make up for lost sales. That required cooperation from all the area brewers, including Heurich.

On July 26 the D.C. court threw out the liquor-dealers' suit, the judge ruling that the petitioners did not have the right to compel the brewers to sell at a particular price. With this victory for the Brewers' Association, it appeared that the strike would continue. The *Washington Times* reported on July 27 that the "firemen will remain out indefinitely." Money to support the strikers was being sent by supporters in New York. However, the walkout ended abruptly on the 28th as the fifteen firemen returned to their jobs. Timothy Healey, the Firemen's Union president, told the press that an arrangement had been made and that he believed that the dispute between the Brewers' Association and Heurich would soon be settled. Heurich's spokesmen, however, denied that any such agreement had been made. Some of the firemen told the press that the strike ended when Heurich agreed to conditions about overtime pay and "various matters relating to their work at the brewery would be adjusted to their satisfaction."[51]

While the Beer War carried on, family affairs continued to keep Heurich busy. In December 1903, Amelia gave birth to the Heurich's first daughter, Anna Marguerite. The following summer the Heuriches traveled to Europe on the SS *Bremen*, a large liner that traveled between New York and Hamburg for the Norddeutscher-Lloyd line. The ship had room for 392 passengers in first class, 273 in second class, and 1682 in third class/steerage. The Heuriches did not stay in Germany long, however. Anna Marguerite was ill, and they took the *Bremen* back to the United States. Once in Washington, the family hurriedly retired to their farm at Bellevue, probably to find a place with fresh air that was cooler than staying in their DuPont Circle home. Heurich, after all, as a believer in taking the cure in the spas of central Europe, which emphasized the benefits of fresh air.[52] The next day, September 9, Anna Marguerite died, only nine months old. The cause of death is unknown. Heurich said little about Anna Marguerite's death in his memoirs, other than "the day after we got back [from Europe] our little daughter died; the Lord giveth and the Lord taketh away; Blessed be the name of the Lord." The cause of death has never been clear. Family stories hint that a nanny may have dropped her. In 1923 the family added a fountain to their mansion's conservatory with two sculptures honoring their daughter. Crafted by Baltimore sculptor Hans Schuler, Sr. (1874–1951), the first is a bas relief of Anna Margarite's likeness. At the base is a small bronze statue of a child playing with a duck. Amelia always mourned her daughter's passing and wrote in her diary that the child's spirit sent her messages. Amelia believed in Spiritualism, then much in vogue in the United States as well as in Europe. In her diary she recorded "knockings" which she believed were Anna Marguerite. If the house creaked or a curtain moved in a breeze, she'd remark, "That was little Anna Marguerite." Nine months after the little girl's death, however, Heurich noted, "My wife and I were again restored in great measure to happiness by the arrival of another little girl." Anita Augusta was born at Bellevue Farm in June 1905.[53]

Heurich had more to celebrate in addition to his daughter Anita's birth in 1905 as he continued to enter his beers in international exhibitions. That year he entered his Maerzen and Senate beers at another World's Fair, the *Exposition Universelle et Interna-*

tionale de Liège in the industrial Belgian city. It was much smaller than the 1900 Paris exhibition. Originally the fair was to open in 1903, but when organizers found that this was an unrealistic construction schedule, it was moved back to 1905, which happened to be the seventy-fifth anniversary of Belgian independence. The fair's theme was focused on industrial and scientific advances made in that three-quarters of a century. Thirty-three countries participated, of which France was by far the largest contributor, while Germany declined to participate at Liège, a contrast to the 1900 fair in Paris, where they were the largest foreign exhibitor. When it was over, seven million visitors had attended, compared to over fifty million who attended the Paris 1900 Exposition. The Heuriches did not attend, but stayed in the United States that summer, visiting Atlantic City.[54]

The United States contributed its own exhibits, but not to the extent they had at other fairs. The

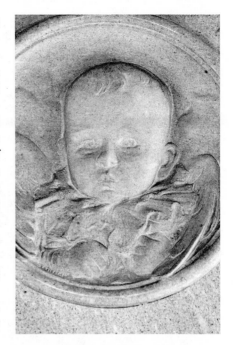

Top: **Detail on the fountain created by sculptor Hans Schuler to honor Anna Marguerite Heurich (1903–1904) (courtesy the Heurich House Museum).** *Bottom:* **A house in Atlantic City where the Heuriches stayed during summer vacation. The family visited Atlantic City in the summers of 1905 through 1908 rather than travel to Europe (courtesy Jan King Evans Houser).**

biggest problem for the American commissioners in finding participants was competition from the huge St. Louis Fair of 1904, officially "The Louisiana Purchase Exposition." The American commissioners' report to Congress after the exposition complained that companies that had been "unsuccessful in securing orders as the result of exhibiting at St. Louis" were "unwilling to incur the expense of taking part in another enterprise of like character." Those companies that had successfully drummed up new business in St. Louis "declared that their time would be completely taken up by filling new orders." The U.S. Congress did not approve American participation in the Liège fair until April 1904, and the commissioners were scrambling to organize themselves at the last minute, still trying to find companies to participate. One of the three American commissioners, James H. Gore, a professor of mathematics at the George Washington University in D.C., may have been the one to request Heurich's participation. Gore had studied in Germany and had authored several books on German science and politics, and he likely knew Heurich through Washington's German community.[55]

The most prominent part of the U.S. participation was the art exhibit, which included 120 different works, including two paintings by John S. Sargent, who was awarded the Grand Prize of Honor. There were also exhibits of American machinery, and the commissioners bragged that in "machine tools," the United States "received approximately half of the awards granted." American exhibitors won 178 awards ranging from twenty-one Grand Prizes to six honorable mentions. Fifty-six participants won a gold medal, including Heurich. The brewer boasted that he received a letter from the United States consul general at Liège in which the official noted "in view of the fact that there were several thousand beers competing and as foreign commissions are naturally averse to awarding the first prize to an American concern that Mr. Heurich's triumph is truly notable." He had a right to be proud. Only one other United States brewery won a gold medal, the Indianapolis Brewery, which had also won in Paris in 1900. No other American breweries won any awards, although a New York City bottler, the George Philippi Company, was awarded a silver medal in Category 62, the same group that included beers as well as sodas, water and ciders. Unfortunately, the official American commissioners' report copied the list of winners from a Belgian newspaper, and so Heurich was listed as the "Heurick Brewing Company, Indianapolis, Indiana." Despite this sloppy error, Heurich could brag about his accomplishment, and did so, adding the gold medal to his beer labels and proclaiming his beers' award-winning status not only in newspaper ads, but even on the bottle openers the brewery provided for customers.[56]

In addition to his medals, Heurich was proud of the purity of his beers. The fact that they contained no adulterants echoed a growing national campaign for laws protecting consumers from adulterated food and drink. Increasing public pressure built on state governments, as well as on the Roosevelt administration and Congress, to restrict what businesses could add to food and drinks, including beers and ales. Lobbying efforts that began in earnest in the 1890s resulted in the Pure Food and Drug Act of 1906. The brewing journals were somewhat dubious about the effort, referring more than once to the "Pure Beer Craze." The major objections, as expressed by the main trade journal, *The Western Brewer*, were:

Opposite, top: Heurich (center) and his son Christian Jr. on the beach in Atlantic City, circa 1905–1906. The woman looking down at the boy may be Amelia. The others are unidentified. *Bottom:* Heurich and his son, Christian, in Atlantic City, circa 1905–1906 (both photographs courtesy Jan King Evans Houser).

1. The laws should differentiate between "adulteration that is prejudicial to health and that which is not."
2. That the standards for "pure beer" would be written by a committee of politicians, "not one of whom is an expert brewer or chemist or acquainted with the practice or scientific manufacture of beer." One ludicrous example was a Missouri bill that specified a short list of what substances could be used in the brewing of beer. No other ingredients would be allowed. As the *Liquor Trade Review* gleefully noted, the law forgot to include water as one of the legal substances, suggesting that saloonkeepers would have to serve "beer in chunks."
3. That states setting different standards would be an impossible burden for brewers trying to sell their product across state lines. "The absurdity of having different standards of purity in different states is readily apparent."[57]

Not every business was opposed to this new form of regulation. There were numerous reasons why a brewery would want a national pure food act that applied to its products. Some of it was simple pride in their product and a desire to safeguard its integrity. Frederick Pabst, of the Pabst Brewing Company, wanted such a law because it would "go a long way in convincing the public that beer was a pure and safe beverage."

There were also significant reasons related to competition. Brewers who did not adulterate their products were at a disadvantage when competing against rivals who did so because adulteration was often used to lower production costs. A national law would level the playing field so that unscrupulous companies in states without pure food laws would not have an advantage over rivals in states with effective laws. The idea that such a law would prevent companies from "cheating" was a major selling point for the Pure Food and Drug Act. Indeed, even the Department of Agriculture's chief chemist and proponent of pure food laws, Harvey Wiley, did not object to adulterating foods with benign substances for health reasons, but because he believed it defrauded unsuspecting customers. Companies could add substances to some products, such as lard to stretch margarine, Wiley argued, if the products were so labeled. Customers, he claimed, had a right to buy cheaper goods of poorer quality if they wished, so long as they knew what they were getting. Of course, adding harmful adulterates, such as some preservatives or dyes, was objectionable for health and safety reasons.[58]

An additional business-related reason was the negative effect adulterated food had upon workers. Wiley's "Poison Squad" experiments noted, for example, that "daily doses of 4 or 5 grammes [of borax] usually bring about a loss of appetite and decreased efficiency for work." As author Donna Wood notes, this concern for the effect on workers was also found in the efficacy campaign of Frederick Winslow Taylor. His ideas about efficiency reflected a growing sense of the human body as a machine, requiring proper fuel. This emphasis on diet and efficiency would have struck a chord with Heurich, who had been taking various forms of the water cure in Europe for over two decades and ate a specific diet to avoid "dizziness." The pure food campaign's concern over workers' health and efficacy being affected by eating and drinking impure substances, of course, echoed the temperance forces' view of alcohol as a poison, even if Wiley did not agree with their inclusion of all alcoholic beverages as injurious to health.[59]

A series of pure food congresses were held in Washington starting in 1898 to promote various pure food laws then being considered in Congress. The meetings included representatives from academia, public advocacy groups, the Department of Agriculture, and industry representatives as well. At the first congress in 1898, the chair of the general committee and first vice-president of the congress was Frank Hume, a Washington grocer and liquor dealer, as well as a member of the board of directors of Heurich Brewing. One of the main issues debated at the meeting was who should judge whether a product was adulterated. Some industry representatives mistrusted Dr. Wiley, fearing perhaps that he was too stringent as to what made an adulterant. A compromise suggestion was that any group determining what made an adulterant should include chemists from universities and from industry, in addition to government chemists.[60]

Heurich did not specifically mention the final Pure Food and Drug Act, which passed in 1906, in his memoirs, but he had long bragged about the purity of his beer. However, even as the bill was being considered in Congress, Heurich was bragging about his connection with Dr. Wiley. In a full-page promotional story published in the *Washington Times* that January, he bragged that Wiley relied on the Heurich brewery for the pure yeast that he used in his labs. He quoted the chief chemist, "Whenever we have any fermenting work to do we send down to Mr. Heurich for yeast and we have stopped using the compressed yeast on the market because we find the yeast furnished us by Mr. Heurich is very superior in its action." Moreover, they also quoted Wiley as stating, "We use Mr. Heurich's malt in our experimental work in the conversion of starch into sugar and always find it fresh and active." Heurich was not the only brewery to quote Wiley, but he was the only one to brag, on multiple occasions, that the chemist used the brewer's materials in his lab work.[61]

The Pure Food and Drug campaign was not the only thing keeping Heurich busy at this time. He maintained his place as a prominent local business leader. When the San Francisco Earthquake devastated the California city in April 1906, Heurich was one of the District's civic representatives at a meeting to raise funds for relief. He pledged $250 to the fund (approximately $6,600 in 2015 dollars). He served on a committee to lobby Congress to provide for a new city auditorium. In July, Washington was hit by heat wave along with much of the rest of the United States. Heurich offered to run his ice plant extra hours to produce extra ice that the city could give out free to the needy. The District government, however, was unable to distribute the offered ice, as Congress had not appropriated any money to do so. Instead they announced that those who needed it could go directly to the brewery in order to get ice to preserve their food and drink.[62]

Heurich was also trying to improve Bellevue. In 1906 he purchased several dozen horse chestnut trees. The timing was unfortunate. The chestnut blight, *Cryphonectria parasitica*, had been discovered in the New York Zoological Garden (the Bronx Zoo) in 1904. As early as the autumn of 1905, the local press was reporting that "some blight has affected the chestnut trees, and many of them are dying near the city. What few leaves they possess are falling rapidly." Whether Heurich's 1906 order was an attempt to replace existing trees that had died is unknown, but in 1908 he reordered three dozen more to replace the dozens that died. It's likely they died as well.[63]

In 1907 Heurich participated in one more international exposition, the Jamestown Tercentennial Exposition held near Norfolk, Virginia. This was a fairly minor world's fair, so why did he bother to participate? Heurich did not enter his beers into every exposition of the era, despite the fact that they were numerous and popular. Heurich is not listed, for example, among the exhibitors in Chicago in 1893, Buffalo in 1901, or St. Louis in 1904, let alone in smaller fairs such as the one in Portland, Oregon, in 1905. Indeed, why even enter his beers in any fair? Participating in international expositions was one way to advertise a product to an international market as well as to earn recognition in competition: Heurich's beers had won a silver medal in Paris in 1900 and a gold medal in Liège in 1905. By doing so he had earned honors in international competition competing with European brewers, some of which he may have worked in as an apprentice.[64] As for finding new markets overseas, he did not seem to be especially interested in selling his beers internationally.[65] Why, then, did he enter his beers in competition in Norfolk in 1907?

Heurich left no records explaining his decision, but there were several likely factors that affected it. The most important factor may simply have been the fact that the Jamestown Exposition was in his local marketing area and would be the only chance Heurich would have to compete in a world's exposition locally. Washington, D.C., had failed to win the 1893 fair, which was held in Chicago,[66] and there were no other fairs held anywhere near the capital city during Heurich's lifetime. It made sense to promote his products in his own backyard. Both the Washington, D.C., Board of Trade (of which Heurich was a member) and the Chamber of Commerce promoted participation in the exposition. Local newspapers held contests to encourage group trips to Norfolk. Steamers carried visitors down the Potomac to the Chesapeake and Norfolk, and local railroads ran regular trains to and from the fair. The Norfolk and Washington Steamboat Company ran daily between the two cities. June 11 was declared "District Day" to host groups from the capital, one of a series of local "days" used by the fair organizers to promote attendance.[67]

In addition, the 1907 fair was going to be held in Virginia, and the state government encouraged the exposition as a way to promote Virginia's industry, while Norfolk's city government saw it as a chance to advertise and promote their city. The Christian Heurich Brewing Company was incorporated in Virginia. Moreover, Heurich had a branch office in Norfolk. The port had grown after the Civil War, one of the many "New South" cities that encouraged economic development through industrialization. The population had increased from 14,000 on the eve of the war to 46,000 in 1900, and would reach 67,000 in 1910.[68] Led by two local newspapers, Norfolk had begun pushing in 1901 for an international fair to celebrate the three-hundredth anniversary of the Jamestown settlement. Heurich joined other Norfolk businesses in what was a typical example of the "Southern Boosterism" of the period. They saw it as a chance to bring visitors to the city and to encourage investment and new businesses. Of course, it might also help his local sales, as he had opened his Norfolk branch in 1897 to expand his business into the populated areas of the Virginia coast.[69]

The Exposition's main theme was intended to be historic, but the organizers abandoned this idea when tight budgets prevented them from arranging shipping and displays for privately owned historic objects. Instead of a historic theme, the Jamestown Exposition took on a militaristic aspect that was generally lacking in this type of world exposition. Certainly it was the most military-centered of the three fairs in which Heurich participated. There were naval demonstrations by the U.S. North Atlantic Fleet, with additional representatives from the navies of Great Britain, France, the Netherlands, Germany, Japan, Austria, and Brazil. The fair also featured numerous encampments and military demonstrations and parades. Even the area set aside for purely recreational displays, as opposed to educational, was built on a street named "Warpath." As such, the fair fit the Zeitgeist of its period, with President Theodore Roosevelt's emphasis on naval strength and the increased popularity of naval powers exchanging "courtesy calls" from their latest warships. Roosevelt appeared twice at the Jamestown Exposition, once to attend a naval demonstration and once to review troops on "Georgia Day." Indeed, after the exposition

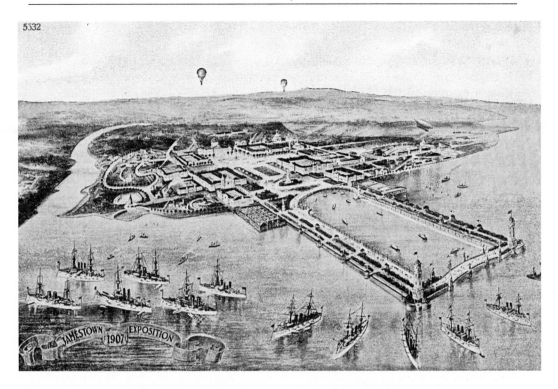

The Jamestown Exposition of 1907 (author collection).

closed, the fairgrounds became part of Norfolk Naval Base, and Roosevelt visited again at the end of 1907 to see off the "Great White Fleet," a force of sixteen U.S. warships that sailed around the world in a show of American naval power.[70]

Heurich participated in the Fair's Agricultural division, which included food and drink in the appropriately named "Food Products Building." Unofficially the exhibit was named "The Pure Food Show." The Pure Food and Drug Act had just been passed the year before, as discussed earlier, and there was a lot of public interest in the subject. Every entry had to meet the 1906 law's standards and had a label listing each ingredient and its amount. Such labeling was not required until the New Weight Amendment of 1913, but manufacturers were beginning to discover that it was helpful for their business. There was a great deal of consumer distrust towards packaged foods and beverages. As one historian noted, such packaged products were "synonymous with deception about quality." By following Food and Drug Administration (FDA) requirements, however, manufacturers could assure consumers that the products contained in the packaging met certain quality standards. Given the limited resources available to the FDA, and the tiny fines—usually under $200—available to punish those companies convicted of violating the laws, convincing producers of food and drink that following the law made good business sense as a sales tactic was the most effective approach available to the FDA. Certainly Heurich found that bragging about the purity of his product was effective, judging from the continued prominence of this theme in his ads in D.C. newspapers.[71]

The Food Products Building had over 60,000 square feet of space for almost one hundred displays. Several breweries besides Heurich's were represented, as were companies producing rum, whiskey and liquors, although teas and coffees were the products most represented. The other breweries included the Consumers' Brewing Company of Norfolk, Old Dominion Brewing and Ice Company of Newport News, and the Virginia Brewing Company of Roanoke. Each of these breweries won a single gold medal for its beer. There are no breweries listed among the silver or bronze medal winners in the "Department of Foods and Accessories."[72]

Heurich did not express any opinion of the fair in his memoirs, except to celebrate his joy at winning three gold medals, one each for Maerzen, Senate, and Heurich Lager. He could now brag that his beers had won medals in several international competitions. Heurich celebrated with his own parade. Thirty-three Heurich delivery wagons, "appropriately decorated with bunting and streamers," marched down Pennsylvania Avenue, led by a "band of music." Pennsylvania Avenue included D.C.'s newspaper row, and the parade participants "serenaded the local newspapers." It was, in its own way, Heurich's own version of the Great White Fleet, a show of strength to his rivals in the beer war, which was in its fourth year. Despite his competitors' best efforts, Heurich's company was still the largest in Washington. Moreover, as the only local medal winner, Heurich was able to position his own products as premium beers, further degrading his rivals' ability to answer Heurich's price-setting for beer in the D.C. market. The medals reinforced Heurich's ability to set his own beer prices locally.[73]

Heurich's memoirs barely touch on the end of the "Beer War." He simply noted that the "great four year beer war against all local and several out-of-town breweries ended in my favor." The economic panic of 1907–1908 may have played a role. The panic began in October 1907 when two speculators, Charles Morse and F. Augustus Heinze, failed in their efforts to buy out the United Copper Company. As historian Edmund Morris noted, they "succeeded only in bankrupting two brokerage houses, another mining concern, and a bank." There was a shortage of currency just then, and while this was normal in the autumn given the business cycle of the time, investors nonetheless were panicked by the speculators' failure and began withdrawing gold from the prominent Knickerbocker Trust. When the trust ran out of money and collapsed, Wall Street almost followed suit, until a consortium of bankers led by John Pierpont Morgan intervened. Because the panic occurred as the United States economy was already beginning a contraction, its effect was magnified. Bankruptcies increased, production of goods fell, and unemployment increased from slightly under 3 percent to 8 percent by the end of the year. Given rising unemployment, which hit 8.5 percent in 1908, the breweries in D.C., like other businesses, would have been under pressure to sell their product, so that lowering their prices would have made sense. On the other hand, brewery production in D.C. increased from 1907 to 1908 before dropping in 1909, suggesting that their market was not contracting. It's also possible that Heurich's local competitors simply grew tired and gave up after four years.[74]

In the summer of 1909, Heurich and his family continued their regular trips to Europe, which they had stopped briefly from 1905 through 1908, preferring instead to go to Atlantic City. Heurich gives no reason for this change, but it may well be out of concern for his wife's health. She gave birth to a daughter, Anita Augusta, in June 1905, so she would have been dealing with a newborn that summer. Their youngest daughter, Karla Luise Adolphine Henriette, was born in October 1907, so Amelia would have been late in her pregnancy in the summer of 1907, making travel difficult. Besides, Heurich was entering his beer in the Jamestown Fair that summer. The Beer War was also going on, and it's possible that he wanted to stay within easy communications and traveling range. For whatever reason, the Heuriches did not venture to cross the Atlantic for four years.[75]

When the family returned to Europe in the summer of 1909, the Heuriches took their three children, Amelia's mother, and her two sisters. They sailed on the *Blücher*, a ship of the Hamburg-Amerika Line. Launched in 1901, the *Blücher* could carry over 2,100 passengers, 333 in first class, including the Heuriches. Amelia recorded details of the trip in her diary. She forced her son, Christian Jr., to "show his feathers" by standing up to another boy in a fight. The family enjoyed "dancing in the evening on deck." Karla acted up and "got a good whipping" from Amelia. This came the day after the family was suffering from seasickness, so perhaps two-year-old Karla was still feeling sick and cranky. Amelia was clearly the disciplinarian of the family, which fits the family's later memories. Their granddaughter, Jan Evans, described her as "dominating" and "strong-willed." She was acutely family-minded and ran the household while Christian ran the family businesses, brewery, land holdings and the dairy farm.[76]

Once in Europe, the family went to Heurich's home town, then to Karlsbad to spend several weeks for the cure at Villa Mittgart. From there they traveled to Switzerland, then returned to Germany, staying several weeks in Wiesbaden. In September, having been away for three months, the family traveled from Hamburg to Cuxhaven, the port where the Hamburg-Amerika Line's ships left for New York. Four-year-old Anita saw a stork and asked, "Didn't the stork bring me? It seems to know me." Storks were already associated with babies, and in popular German folklore, storks found babies in caves or marshes and brought them to households. Families could attract storks, and therefore babies, by placing treats for the storks on their windowsills. The Heuriches' middle child apparently had heard this story, which had already spread from Germany to the United States by this time.[77]

Now well into his sixties, approaching seventy, Heurich had the life he had worked so hard to build. He had his family and his brewery was prospering. In 1912 an addition was added onto the north side of the house. There was an office with Heurich's Grant desk on the first floor. The family's pet parrots lived here in their cages. Upstairs was a playroom for the children. Along the high walls were painted portraits of fourteen great writers, leaders, and artists, presumably to act as inspiration for the children playing under their gazes. Five were Germans, including Johann Wolfgang von Goethe, Immanuel Kant, and Heurich's favorite, Richard Wagner. However, they were accompanied by five Americans: Abraham Lincoln, George Washington, Thomas Paine, Thomas Jefferson, and Henry Wadsworth Longfellow. None were major religious figures. There was no Martin Luther, for example. But Paine and Jefferson were famous for their unorthodox beliefs, which fit the Heurich family skepticism towards traditional religious faith.[78]

As was now the normal routine, the family sailed to Europe on one of the luxurious liners on the Hamburg-Amerika Line. In 1911 they again sailed on the *Blücher* and spent time at the Villa Mittgart in Karlsbad. They returned home on the *Cincinnati* after a three-month stay. In 1912 they sailed on the *Kaiserin Augusta Victoria*. Launched in 1905, it was the largest of the great Atlantic liners until the *Lusitania* launched the next year. *Kaiserin Augusta Victoria* carried 472 passengers in first class, 174 in second, 212 in third, and 1,608 in steerage, or fourth class.[79] The highlight of the Heuriches' 1911 trip was to be the dedication of new public baths at Römhild on July 7. The town was decorated with flags, as was the new baths building. The Heuriches inspected the facility, then enjoyed a banquet in "the rifle shooting hall" while the residents of Römhild and Haina had "pork sausages and beer" on the rifle range (probably at a Schützenverein). Römhild's Mayor Griebel welcomed and thanked the Heuriches, and Christian Heurich "told the story of his life." He proclaimed the baths to be a "Healtharium," as "a clean body requires much less medical care and that improves the working power." After Heurich's speech, the local fire brigade gave him an ovation, Haina's gymnastic club gave a demonstration, and "pretty Haina girls in local costume performed a round dance with flowers." The local orphans' home, to which Heurich also donated money, performed marches and games. In his memoirs Heurich noted that after leaving his home town they went to the Kissingen spa "so that I could get rid of whooping cough. It took me nine months to recover completely." Interestingly, he did not mention his contacts with local royalty, although his wife, Amelia, recorded an invitation to be breakfast guests with the Duke of Meiningen, Georg II, who had been duke since 1866, the year Heurich left for America.[80]

The breakfast required formal attire, Christian in a cutaway and Amelia in a mourning dress and hat. The duke ended up bowing out of the breakfast because of illness, but the next day the Heuriches received an invitation to breakfast with the Prince and Princess of Meiningen. The prince would later briefly rule as Duke Bernhard II from 1914 to 1918. The princess, his wife, was Princess Charlotte of Prussia, the younger sister of Kaiser Wilhelm II. Amelia liked both hosts. The prince was "a lovely man, so plain and so good," and after a walk through the palace gardens, the princess told Amelia to "call when I come to Meiningen again." The former orphaned apprentice who grew up in a tavern in a tiny town had found a place where, even if he did not regularly hobnob with royalty, he was wealthy and successful enough to warrant personal invitations. At some point on this trip the duke again offered a knighthood to Heurich, but again he refused. The Heuriches also visited another form of royalty as well. After visiting the family of the Duke of Meiningen, they visited Adolphus Busch, owner of the Anheuser Busch brewery, and his family at their villa in Schwalbach, where, Amelia told her diary, "they treated us like royalty." The family left for the United States onboard the *Kaiserin Augusta Victoria*, where the children found waiting for them their pet dachshund, Waldman.[81]

Heurich returned to find his brewery in good shape, and he was still the dominant local brewer. However, the temperance movement was gaining strength not just nationally, but in Heurich's marketing area as well. Maryland showed little evidence of going dry, but there was continued pressure for Congress to make D.C. alcohol-free. Most of Virginia had gone dry by 1910 via local option, and the state legislature was considering bills that would force the remainder of the state to follow suit. In a letter to a friend in March 1908, Heurich complained of the growing strength of the temperance forces, "a great wave for prohibition fostered by Protestant clergymen and other do-gooders." Heurich worried that the District would soon go dry, which he feared would ruin him financially, a fear repeated by Amelia. In a 1910 letter to Grace Hubbard Bell, Amelia Heurich donated one hundred dollars to an arts and crafts school in the District, but noted that her husband "does not see his way clear to commit himself for any subscription in the future." The reason given?[82] "There are nine bills before Congress, the passage of any one as introduced would legislate Mr. H main business out of existence and thereby confiscate the principal part of his accumulated wealth for which he worked so hard for nearly 40 years in this city." The comment may seem out of place in a letter to a young woman trying to raise money for a school. Miss Bell was, however, a member of a locally prominent family. Her father was cousin to Alexander Graham Bell. Her grandfather was the first president of Bell Telephone. Soon after receiving this letter, Miss Bell married

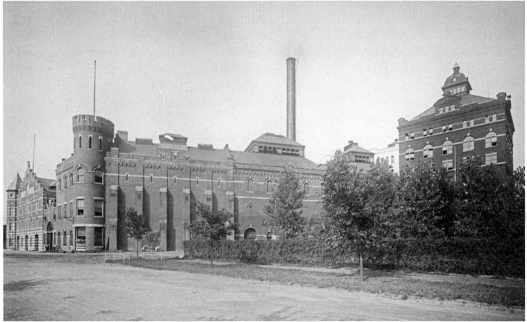

Top: Karla and one of the family's pet dachshunds at Bellevue, circa 1911. *Bottom:* The Heurich brewery in the 1910s (both photographs courtesy Jan King Evans Houser).

an Army major who was a member of his cousin Theodore Roosevelt's Rough Riders and served as a White House aide to President Taft. Heurich may well have hoped her complaint might reach someone with influence.[83]

Perhaps because he feared the economic effects of prohibition, Heurich made other investments aside from real estate. In late 1910 he invested in the Alaska Consolidated Copper Company in what is now the Wrangell-St. Elias National Park and Preserve. Copper had been discovered in the area in about 1899, including a two-ton copper nugget. Numerous copper mines sprung up in southeastern Alaska as more was discovered. To join in with this copper rush, Heurich purchased 1,500 shares at $2.50 a share, for a total of $3,750 paid in three installments to the First Mortgage Guarantee Trust Company in Philadelphia. The memoirs of a British adventurer, Alfred Bennett Iles, who managed the mine for a time, claimed that they raised $200,000 in Pennsylvania, Baltimore, and Washington, the latter apparently including Heurich. A new railroad in the area opened, allowing the ore to be shipped. Despite the presence of the huge copper nugget, which Iles claimed weight four and a half tons, the mine failed after several years of effort. It apparently produced only "two carloads of high-grade ore shipped prior to 1916, and 160 tons of hand-sorted ore shipped after." The mine closed in 1919, but not until one manager, who was reporting highly exaggerated production figures to justify his expenses, was found in the Philadelphia River "with a rock tied to his neck."[84]

Heurich seems not to have had high hopes for the investment even from the beginning, which seemed unusually risky compared to his normal careful money management. In November 1910, some of the mine owners wrote to Henry Brehm in Baltimore, which he forwarded to Heurich as a fellow investor. The mine principals, a pair of brothers named Stewart, harangued Brehm to pay his installment for purchasing stock. The letter writer noted that Brehm was required to pay only $2.50 a share, claiming that the stock was already selling for $6.00 a share. Stewart promised that the ore would start shipping in 1911 and berated Brehm: "If I had the means in the bank today I would purchase every share of this stock, and with a good bonus on top of $2.50 a share." Brehm forwarded the letter to Heurich for his opinion. Heurich's answer reflected his uncertainty. He told Brehm that he'd just paid the first installment of $1250, but "as a whole I do not know what to make of it and will trust for the best."[85]

In one of his scrapbooks Heurich pasted a cartoon of a sneering man wearing a top hat and dark suit, sharpening sheep shears on a grindstone. An accompanying editorial notes, "If you are one of the little lambs that grow the pretty wool and then go down to Wall Street to have it clipped, look at this old gentleman, sharpening the shears. This is old Mr. Wall Street, the Knife Grinder." In advice Heurich probably wished he had heeded before investing in the Alaska Consolidated Copper Company, the editorialist warned that investing in stocks was gambling, that the stockbrokers know more about it than the sheep, who know "as much about the inside of high finance as Mary's Little Lamb knew about geography." If someone offers you a stock tip, the author advised, tell him, "I know of something that will go up from 15 to 90 in less than eight months.... THE THERMOMETER." Whether Heurich invested in stock ventures other than the Alaska Consolidated Copper Company is unknown, but the fact that he saved this clipping strongly suggests he did not trust the stock market in the years after his poor investment.[86]

The copper investment was a bust, and Heurich's fears of local prohibition were not unfounded. Less than two years later, just before he turned over his office to incoming President Woodrow Wilson, President William Howard Taft signed an appropriations bill for the District that contained the "Jones-Works Amendment," which directly dealt with liquor sales in D.C. Amelia noted in her diary that her husband thought the bill "will work a great injustice on all the saloon business in the city.... Christian is greatly worried." The new law was scheduled to go into effect on November 1, 1914. Until then a liquor license would cost $500 a year, and $800 after that date. A barroom license cost $1,000 a year and would be raised to $1,500 a year after October 1914. That placed a genuine financial hardship on both liquor dealers and saloonkeepers. The bill also reduced the number of saloons that could legally operate to 300, down from the current number estimated by one congressman to be 580. Hotels could still serve liquor, and would be allowed Sunday sales, but the number of private clubs with a license would be limited to twenty-five. Saloons were limited to four on both sides of a street within a single block, and no more than three could operate on the same side of the street. Wholesale sales could only take place in business districts (as opposed to residential), and saloons could not operate near schools, universities or an "established house of worship." As a compromise for the saloons, closing hour was changed from midnight to 1:00 a.m., and existing saloons could operate until November 1, 1914, before some would have to close to meet the three-hundred-saloon ceiling.[87]

Clearly much of the temperance movement's energy was aimed at saloons, which accounted for at least 90 percent of brewery sales. As a result, brewers began looking for ways to expand into new markets. One result of this pressure was an effort by Heurich, as well as by many other brewers, to introduce low-alcohol beers. Heurich introduced his own entry into this market, named Home Brew, in late December 1913 with a newspaper campaign noting that "because of a tendency of a great many people to abstain from indulging in beverages containing a fair amount of alcohol, the CHR. HEURICH BREWING CO. has, after extended investigation and exhaustive experiments, made A DISCOVERY OF THE GREATEST IMPORTANCE, which will tend to revolutionize present conditions." Home Brew Beer "looks and tastes like other high-grade beers and has all their beneficial and nutritious qualities, yet comes entirely within the PURE FOOD LAW and **CONTAINS LESS THAN 2% ALCOHOL**" (emphasis in original). Reflecting the ongoing concern for purity in the production of food and drink, the Heurich ads emphasized the cleanliness and sanitary conditions of the production facility. Ads specifically mentioned the Pure Food law passed in 1906 and to show that it was it safe for family use, Heurich noted that his new brand, Home Brew, had less than 2 percent alcohol, so it was "exceptionally beneficial TO WOMEN and others with a weak stomach." Home Brew was "a beverage that was sure to prove highly acceptable to the greatest possible number of people," the latter remark echoing the brewers' complaints that the Drys were a small, fanatical minority.[88]

As part of the Home Brew promotional campaign, Heurich issued a cookbook, *Recipes of Quality*, in May 1914. Cookbooks issued by breweries were common after World War II, as was publishing recipes in advertising and packaging material. However, only a few issued cookbooks before Prohibition, and Heurich claimed that his edition was the first. However, it was actually one of several issued at about the same time, with the same recipes. They were apparently put together by Felix Mendelsohn, who later published some of the same recipes in 1920 on his own in *Sonia's Cookbook*. The 1912 edition was published by breweries in New York City; Buffalo, New York; Indianapolis, Indiana; Toledo, Ohio; and Oakland, California, among others. They had different covers, and listed different brands of beer inside, but the recipes were the same.[89]

Heurich begins promoting his low-alcohol Home Brew (*The Evening Star*, December 31, 1913).

The recipes in Heurich's edition did not use the brewery's own beer as an ingredient. Nonetheless, his beer was advertised. The back cover was an ad for Home Brew, described as "the ideal home beverage when thirsty" and "non-intoxicating." "You can," they promised, "drink HOME BREW yourself or serve it to your friends without restrictions." It is "appropriate at all times, and in all places." The cookbook was offered free with any order

Left: The cover of the cookbook offered by Heurich. *Right:* The back cover of the cookbook advertises Home Brew (both from author's collection).

of Home Brew.[90] As befitting a promotional item, the cookbook displayed "Presented by Chr. Heurich Brewing Co. Washington DC" proudly on the cover under a German-looking chef holding a platter with a large prepared turkey on it. The Heurich logo, an "H" superimposed over a hop leaf, also appears on the front cover. The prominence of the brewery name on the cover, however, was a small act of defiance, declaring that the housewife using the book had no reason to be ashamed of dealing with a brewery. This stood in contrast to some contemporaneous advertising, as will be noted later.

The recipes inside included both simple and complex dishes. The introduction flattered the "housewife" reading it, noting that too many cookbooks spent too much time on simple dishes, already "within the ken of every experienced housewife." The recipes included in this volume, it noted, were for the woman looking for something new to prepare, "the mistress of the home who is suddenly confronted with a houseful of company." Just in case, however, the first six pages were taken by basic instruction on measurements and cook times for different types of dishes. Broken down into the types of sections a reader would find in any cookbooks, including meats, fish, sauces, salads, and deserts, *Recipes of Quality* also included helpful menu suggestions for luncheons, dinners and suppers. The latter of which, being evening meals, included "Senate-Maerzen Beer" as the suggested beverage.[91]

In September, Heurich began a new campaign to promote Home Brew, a free forty-eight-piece set of porcelain dinnerware. Each case of Heurich's beer, including Home Brew, included a coupon. In exchange for sixteen of these coupons, the brewery would deliver, free of charge, a set of thirty-one plates. A second group of fourteen larger serving

48-piece Dinner Sets FREE!

To more generally introduce HEURICH'S BEERS and HOME BREW into HOMES using beer we are giving handsome Dinner Sets absolutely free to our family trade. Our QUALITY beverages have thrice been awarded medals for "Purity and excellence" at international exhibitions and are noted as America's oldest and best.

6-5½ IN. FRUITS.

6-6½ IN. PLATES.

6-9½ IN. PLATES

11¼ IN. PLATTER.

6-9½ IN SALAD.

6-IND. BUTTERS.

1-SUGAR   1-CREAM.   1-8½ IN. BAKER.   1-COV'D DISH   6-CUPS & SAUCERS

These Dinner Sets, comprising 48 pieces, are made of finest Porcelain China, fired to a high degree of heat, making them very durable, and are decorated with gold.

The cut, or picture, shown herewith is a reproduction of the beautiful design we have chosen.

SAVE THE COUPONS that come with every case of our noted beers delivered to your home. ONE coupon accompanies every case of 24 bottles. When 16 coupons have been saved, if you desire, we will deliver to you a Dinner Set of 31 pieces, the FIRST PART of the complete service. On presenting 14 more coupons, we will deliver to you 17 additional pieces of china, completing the entire Dinner Set of 48 pieces. ALL ABSOLUTELY FREE.

Case 24 bottles MAERZEN or SENATE Beer, $1.25
Case 24 bottles LAGER Beer, $1.00—24 bottles HOME BREW, $1.20
(NON-INTOXICATING)

☞50c DEPOSIT required to insure return of case and empty bottles. THIS DEPOSIT REFUNDED on delivery of case and bottles to drivers.

CHR. HEURICH BREWING CO.
Write or phone West 1600-1601-1602   **WASHINGTON, D. C.**

Heurich offers a dinner set in return for coupons that came with cases of his beer (*The Evening Star,* September 17, 1914).

pieces was available for an additional fourteen coupons. A free set then would require buying thirty cases of beer, or 720 bottles, at a cost of $30 to $36. The ads ran through the month of September, sometimes appearing on the women's page of the paper, and sometimes in the general news section. The ads emphasized the quality of the dish set, but did not expend much space extolling the virtues of the beer, although the earliest versions of the advertisements emphasized "Home Brew" over Heurich's other brands.[92] The advertisements even noted that out-of-town buyers could buy Heurich's products and have the dish set sent to them free of charge as well. This latter point was important, as most of Virginia was dry, but state law allowed residents to have alcoholic beverages shipped to them in limited quantities.[93]

Heurich's ads were not just aimed at a family market. They were directed at women as the specific target audience. The dinner-plate set made for entertaining show that the campaign was aimed at middle-class women. Upper-class and upper-middle-class women would already have a proper set of dishes, and the lower classes would not have been expected to entertain in such a fashion. Families in the lower ranks of the middle class would have been a prime audience for such an offer. Heurich was placing his products to appeal to those customers attempting to reach a particular level of middle-class respectability. The campaign's success is hard to measure. It did not last past 1914, although Heurich continued making the brand until he closed his brewery in 1917, and he brought it back briefly in the 1930s when Prohibition ended.[94]

Whatever their fears of a growing prohibitionist movement, Heurich and his family still continued taking their European trips. In 1913 they again sailed on the *Kaiserin Augusta Victoria* to Hamburg, then spent three weeks in Karlsbad. They visited Vienna, the city Heurich fell in love with as a young journeyman. On August 18 they attended the celebration for Austria-Hungarian Emperor Franz Josef's 83d birthday. He had taken the throne in late 1848, when Heurich was only six years old, and was in the 64th year of his reign. After celebrating the emperor's birthday, Christian and Amelia attended two concerts conducted by Johann Strauss, indulging Heurich's love of music and his love for Vienna simultaneously. A few days later, taking a car tour in Riederich, Germany, the Heuriches were passed by German Emperor Wilhelm II. "As he passed us," Amelia noted, "he saluted us and gave us a nice smile." From there they traveled to the Hague to attend the opening ceremonies of the "Peace Conference," and arrived as the Dutch were celebrating the 33d birthday of Queen Wilhelmina. To her diary Amelia sniffed, "It seemed as if the whole of Amsterdam was out. The people seemed to be like wild. I never heard anything like it. Would not be allowed in Wash[ington]." The Heuriches returned to the United States on the *Imperator* in September. Amelia noted that also on board sharing first class with the Heuriches were the Vanderbilts, the Tiffanys, and the steel baron Elbert Gary.[95] The *Imperator* was a brand-new ship for the Hamburg-Amerika Line. Launched in May 1912, just a month after the *Titanic* sank, she was a bit larger than that ill-fated vessel, and carried 5,500 passengers, an immense number. There was room for over 900 in first class alone, so the Heuriches had plenty of company. The ship seemed to be, if not jinxed, then somehow subject to unfortunate luck from the beginning. The bow was crowned by the Hamburg-Amerika Line's eagle with outstretched wings and talons grasping the globe. On its third voyage, a wave rudely ripped it off the prow. Moreover, the ship not only had a tendency to roll, but it would "'hang in the roll' so unendurably long that even her sea-hardened crew were almost as terrified as her passengers."

S. S. Imperator, Hamburg-American Line
Largest in the World.
50,000 Tons.   919 Feet Long

The *Imperator* (from a postcard in the author's collection).

Eventually 2,000 tons of concrete were poured into the bottom to stabilize her. Not every-body was enchanted with the *Imperator's* décor, either. Even one of the ship's own captains described her as "a ship of gloomy paneled majesty, hard to handle, clumsy and Teutonic, a creation of industry without pretensions to beauty."[96]

For the Heuriches, 1914 began normally. They visited the German orphanage, on whose board Christian served. On January 27 they attended a reception for the German emperor's birthday held at the German Embassy. Amelia hired a new cook, then fired her a month later. On February 12, Abraham Lincoln's birthday, Christian and his wife attended the ground-breaking for the Lincoln Memorial. It was bitterly cold, the tem-perature never rising above the teens, and so a smaller crowd than expected attended the ground-breaking. Senator Joseph Blackburn (D–KY), a former Confederate officer, gave a brief speech praising Lincoln. Such sentiments were common at ceremonies for the 50th anniversary of the war from 1911 to 1915. White veterans, at least, were more interested in making conciliation between the North and South than in rearguing the causes of the war, even though this left out the role of African American Union vets. For Heurich, the memorial would have an important long-term effect on his business. Placing the Lincoln Memorial at the far western end of the National Mall helped move develop-ment of the part of D.C. dedicated to memorials and for tourists further west, which meant they would move closer to Heurich's brewery. By the 1950s the brewery would no longer be in the solely industrial section of the city, but would be seen as an encroachment upon the scenic areas. The first hints of this appeared in the press in February 1914, noting that the new memorial was in line with the Capitol, the Washington Monument, and Arlington National Cemetery, and would be linked to the latter in the future by a memorial bridge.[97]

In the summer of 1914, the Heuriches were again visiting Europe. They had left New York for Europe on the *Imperator*, the second and last time they took the huge, gloomy ship. Heurich's travels between Europe and the United States illustrate how the relation-ship between immigrants and both their homeland and their new home extended beyond the traditional dichotomy of the assimilationist narrative. Heurich had become a citizen in 1872, but he maintained close connections to his homeland, not just with family ties, but emotionally and economically. For example, he gave money to both Haina and Römhild to build public works and to support those in need. He maintained a presence in both places, even as his own role in each of his two hometowns evolved over time. He was an active agent defining the boundaries of his proper place, creating a space that he felt comfortable occupying. He refused to accept a knighthood from his hometown on multiple occasions, because he believed it was not proper to do so, at least within his proper space as he defined it. There must have been a sense of obligation as well. Heurich loved Vienna and regarded his time there as one of the happiest times of his life. However, he did not act as the benevolent philanthropist for that great city. Of course, it was wealthy compared to Heurich's small hometowns, but no doubt there were plenty of charities there that would have loved to receive a gift from a wealthy American expatriate. Heurich felt the sense of *Heimat*, that tie to his homeland defined on a smaller scale, that was such a common theme among German migrants. Despite Heurich's redefinition of his place in society, from poor tavern-keeper's son to wealthy industrialist, that tie remained strong. He was not, therefore, a completely independent agent, as he and his family would discover in 1914. The outbreak of World War I illustrated how governments could enforce their own expectations for acceptable behavior within their own national spaces, and how those who tried to cross these boundaries could find themselves, as the Heuriches would, subject to the authority of multiple nations. The Heuriches would find themselves in conflict between their roles as Germans and as Americans, between being wealthy tourists and foreign nationals in nations at war, and between the claims of the *Heimat* and the claims made by citizenship.

6

War and Prohibition: 1914–1920

The year 1914 would be marked by a series of challenges to Heurich that would continue for the rest of the decade, both professional and personal. In the next few years he and his family would be trapped in Europe by World War I, his loyalty to the United States would be publicly questioned, and the prohibition campaign would win one victory after another, eventually forcing Heurich to close his beloved brewery even before the Eighteenth Amendment forced the rest of the nation to go dry. By decade's end he would be living in a sort of exile at his Maryland farm, permanently retired, so it seemed, from his life's work. He had invested wisely in real estate, so he was still wealthy, and his family need not fear poverty, but Heurich had identified himself as a brewer for most of his life, and to have to leave that life (it was far more than just a job) must have severely injured his pride and his sense of self.

The trials of the nineteen-teens began in 1914 in Virginia. When the 1914 legislative session began, the Anti-Saloon League (ASL) and the Woman's Christian Temperance Union (WCTU) both believed that the time was right to push a bill through both houses of the Virginia legislature to schedule a referendum on state-wide prohibition. In the 1913 election, temperance supporter Henry C. Stuart had been elected governor with no opposition, and he promised that he would sign any bill providing for a state-wide referendum on prohibition. The only remaining obstacle was a handful of senators who answered to U.S. Senator Thomas S. Martin and his supporters, known as "The Ring." Prohibition opponents, they had successfully killed referendum bills in 1910 and 1912.[1]

In January 1914 the "Williams Enabling Act," calling for a state-wide referendum on prohibition, passed the House by a vote of 75–19. If the referendum was approved by a majority of voters, the bill stated that during the "regular session held next after the date of such election" (the 1916 session), the legislature would pass a bill establishing state-wide prohibition beginning November 1, 1916. The Senate vote was expected to be close, and if Martin again instructed his men to vote against it, the bill would undoubtedly fail. Unlike in 1910 and 1912, however, this time there was a prospective third party—the Virginia Progressive Democratic League—which competed for ASL leader Bishop Cannon's support against Martin's political machine. Faced with the possibility of Cannon's siding with reformers against the senator's organization, Martin decided to give Cannon and the ASL what they wanted. He instructed his allies to support the bill.[2] Despite Martin's capitulation, however, the vote was still close. Facing defeat, the night before the vote, a group of Wets took a senator who voted Dry but drank alcohol nonetheless, out for an evening's entertainment at a local hot spot. Early the next morning, the day of the final

158

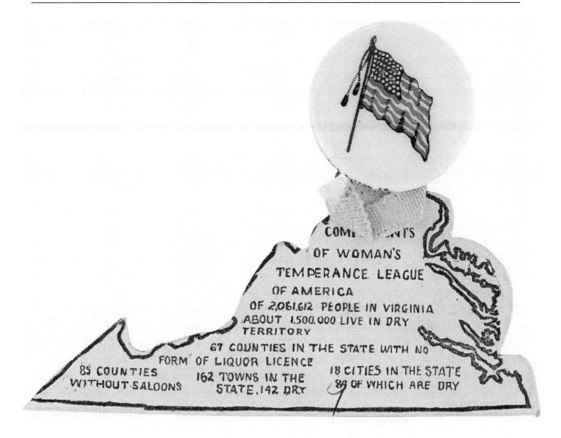

A pro-dry campaign button from Virginia (author collection).

vote, several of Cannon's men found the senator woozy from a night of heavy drinking and carousing, and helped him stumble back to the Senate chambers to cast his vote. Some sources hint that the partying senator was found in a brothel. The observer can look back with amusement at the thought of several loyal ASL members, probably good Methodists or Baptists, searching through Richmond's houses of prostitution looking for the senator. The drunken senator's vote created a 20–20 tie. As promised, Lieutenant Governor James Taylor Ellyson cast his vote in favor of the bill and it passed.[3]

Governor Henry Carter Stuart signed the bill on February 18. The bill called for a state-wide referendum on full prohibition for all of Virginia. The election was to be held on September 22, 1914, provided the governor received a petition requesting the election with the signatures of qualified voters representing at least one-quarter of the total votes cast in the November 1913 election for governor. Stuart had run largely unopposed in 1913, but 72,000 votes had been cast, so 18,000 signatures were required. On July 11, Dry supporters presented their petition with over 69,000 signatures, almost four times more than required. Prohibition opponents tried to have the petition declared invalid, claiming that it had been padded with illegitimate signatures, but their efforts were rebuffed. Despite Wet protests, the ballot would present the voter with two simple choices, "For State-Wide Prohibition" and "Against State-Wide Prohibition." The referendum opponents had wanted the opposing choice to read "For Local Option," which would allow moderate Drys to vote against the state-wide option while still technically voting dry. By starkly wording the ballot as a straight up-or-down vote on prohibition, proponents hoped to capture more of the moderate Drys' votes.[4]

During the seven months between the bill's passage and the referendum, Virginia's voters were inundated with campaign propaganda both for and against prohibition. Most of the state's major newspapers were Wet, while many small-town and county papers, including Cannon's *Virginian*, called for a Dry vote. Cannon spoke at rallies and meetings throughout the state and published a stream of editorials. In one typical example, he proclaimed that alcohol produced only "pauperism and insanity and crime and shame and misery and broken hearts and ruined homes and shortened, wasted lives." The Dry campaign put on parades and rallies. Speakers and printed material alike emphasized the cost to home life from liquor, using women and children to emphasize their "protect the home" theme. Get rid of the liquor trade, they promised, and the levels of crime, poverty, broken homes, and mental illness would all drastically decrease.[5]

The Wets did not have the same level of local organization as the Dry cause, but they were represented by the Association for Local Self-Government (ALSG). The ALSG was based in the Richmond Chamber of Commerce building and included numerous influential businessmen from around the state, as well as judges and lawyers from the state bar association. The ALSG started its campaign with a rally at Richmond's Academy of Music on May 14. ALSG leaders spoke to a crowd of 2,000, claiming that prohibition "violates the fundamental principle of local self-government, and has invariably caused social and political unrest, bitterness and hypocrisy, and has brought the law into contempt." They published a newspaper called the *Trumpeter*, which ran anti-prohibition editorials and news articles. They also printed broadsides, pamphlets, and booklets, carrying the message that prohibition would only create more problems than it would solve. Their message was also carried by most of the state's major newspapers, a majority of which were wet.[6]

The Wet Virginia campaign followed a pattern similar to that used in other states. Prohibition, they argued, would violate local self-rule and it would also deprive the state of over $600,000 a year in tax revenue. This would require an increase in other taxes to make up the difference. Drunkenness and other abuses would only be driven underground, and Dry campaign claims that crime and poverty would fall were false. They also warned that once alcohol was outlawed, tobacco would be next, threatening one of the state's most important crops. Moreover, according to the Wet campaign, prohibition would increase popular disrespect for the law because average citizens would ignore and violate it. In short, the Wets argued, prohibition would be an unpopular law and would be unworkable.[7]

The Wets were handicapped by not being able to openly argue that drinking was a good thing in and of itself. Dry educational campaigns had been too successful in pressing the idea that alcohol was a poison to argue against prohibition on any grounds except personal liberty. This also meant that those businesses that were most obviously affected by prohibition—breweries, wineries, distillers, liquor dealers, and saloons—had to keep a low profile. They had to find ways to launder their campaign donations through front groups. Any group opposed to prohibition that openly took money from the alcohol industry faced charges of allying with, in Cannon's words, "the most unscrupulous organization of capital in the world." Despite this handicap, the Wets outspent Dry proponents by a factor of at least four to one.[8]

Before the election, both sides predicted victory. The Wet press expressed confidence that the "zealots" would be rebuffed by the voters. A headline in the *Alexandria Gazette* the day before the election forecast, "Prohibition will be defeated by no less than 10,000 majority." The *Richmond Times-Dispatch*, one of Bishop Cannon's main antagonists, was more cautious, noting that both sides were predicting a large victory. The *Times-Dispatch* editorial page, however, clearly took sides, noting on the morning of election day:

> Left to themselves the vast majority of the people of the State, upon whom Virginia's prosperity and progress depend, would not have dreamed of attacking local self-government in order to agitate state-wide prohibition, a system which makes the liquor traffic immensely more complex and menacing than it can be and is under local option. The agitation has come from without.[9]

On election day the Drys won easily with almost 60 percent of the vote. The referendum passed by a vote of 94,251 in favor to 63,886 opposed. Of Virginia's 100 counties, 71 voted in favor of prohibition. Eight of the state's ten congressional districts voted dry, and one of the remaining two voted against prohibition by only ten ballots. Surprisingly, sixteen of the state's twenty cities also voted in favor of going dry. Traditionally cities were strongholds of Wet votes. However, only Alexandria, Norfolk, Williamsburg and Richmond stayed Wet. The turnout was also remarkably high, with over 158,000 total votes cast. For comparison, during the 1912 presidential election, there were 136,900 votes cast in Virginia even though the Democratic nominee, Woodrow Wilson, had been born in the state.[10]

What impact did the presence of breweries have, providing jobs as well as anti–Dry campaign funds? Of the six breweries active in Virginia in 1914, five were based in or near the few towns that voted against prohibition. Robert Portner's brewery was in Alexandria City and Arlington Brewing Company was in neighboring Rosslyn, in Alexandria County. Richmond and Home Brewing companies were in Richmond and Consumer Brewing was in Norfolk. Norfolk and Richmond were also home to several bottling companies that bottled and sold the products of large regional and national breweries, including Heurich, St. Louis's Anheuser-Busch, and Milwaukee's Pabst Brewing. Of the cities that hosted a brewery, only Roanoke, home to Virginia Brewing, as well as bottling companies and whiskey mail-order businesses, voted dry.[11]

Heurich was in Europe as the Virginia referendum campaign was ongoing. For him Virginia's going Dry meant that he was losing a part of his customer base. He would have to close his Norfolk branch, and any saloons in northern Virginia that sold his product would be closing. He could still ship beer to customers in Virginia, but this would not make up for lost sales from other venues, especially as shippers were limited to carrying the same amount allowed to individual heads of households in the state. This meant that potential customers could buy Heurich's products, but only carry a limited amount back home. As for Arlington and Alexandria, according to the *American Brewers' Review*, the last unsold stocks of liquor were hurried across the Potomac into (still-wet) D.C. just before midnight.[12]

Heurich also lost a longtime employee and friend, Charles Meyer. A Baltimore native, Meyer began working for Heurich in 1883 as his bookkeeper and secretary.[13] In April 1912, a recently fired teamster, who blamed Meyer for the loss of his job, tried to kill Heurich's secretary in his office at the brewery. The man shot Meyer once, wounding the victim in the left hand, but was subdued before he could fire again. Meyer died in March 1914—the cause of death was not mentioned in his obituaries.[14] Heurich promoted William Dismer to replace Meyer. A Washington native, Dismer had started working for Heurich in 1896, when he was eighteen.[15]

Dismer's promotion, however, caused a serious, if temporary, rift in Heurich's marriage. Amelia had wanted her husband to give her brother Dolph the position instead, and Heurich's refusal set off several weeks of crisis. Amelia's diary at that point is full of *Sturm und Drang* over the perceived slight to her brother. On March 11, she filled seven pages of her diary with her anger and disappointment. She apparently hated and distrusted Dismer, for what reason is unknown, but Heurich steadfastly refused to follow his wife's recommendation. Amelia complained that this "has been our first unpleasantness since we were married." All she wanted, she noted, "was justice." On the 16th she was still distraught. "O how happy we were together until this came into our lives. I hope the children will read these lines very carefully, & will always know how to treat this Willie Dismer, the hypocrite, this lover of money, this mean contemptible man." On April 7 she sniffed that she "will not write any more of the unpleasantness we had—My heart still aches when I think of it."[16] This episode illustrated several aspects of the Heuriches' married life. The family remembers Amelia as, among other things, a worrier and somewhat thin-skinned. These traits show up repeatedly in her diary. This is but one instance. The episode also shows how Heurich kept a strict division of labor between husband and wife in his life. Amelia ran the house, but when it came to the brewery, Heurich acted as he saw fit, even if it made things tense at home.

The Heuriches traveled to Europe again in June 1914. This time they traveled aboard the *Imperator*. Launched in 1912, it was for a short time the largest of the great Atlantic liners, but the Heuriches liked to take the newest, more luxurious of the German ships on their annual trips. Amelia noted in her diary that they had three staterooms. The nanny, Fraulein Inge Schurengeis, and "Aunt Gussie" had one, Christian Jr., and Anita had the second, and the youngest child, Karla, stayed with her parents in the third. The *Imperator* landed on July 4, 1914, delayed by a few hours because of heavy fog. The entire party stayed overnight in Hamburg. Amelia failed to note the most important event in her diary, however. The day after they set sail to Europe, a Serbian assassin had shot and killed the heir to the Austro-Hungarian throne, Archduke Franz Ferdinand, and his wife, Sophie, while the couple was visiting Sarajevo. There is no hint in her diary of the gathering storm as the family traveled to Haina, where the people "stood and looked at us as if we were something to look at." They visited Heurich's sister in Jüchsen, and then traveled to Karlsbad for Heurich to spend time at the spa.[17]

Amelia first noted the European crisis on July 25, when Austria-Hungary declared war on Serbia. She wanted to return home quickly, but Heurich refused: "I wanted Christian to pack up and leave Carlsbad—but no he wants to finish his cure." Amelia drew a heavy purple line through her diary at this point with the words "from here on" setting apart her remarks as she watched World War I begin. She wrote entries every day from July 25 until September 22, after they had safely returned to the family farm in Maryland. Her entries record the growing sense of escalating crisis and the awkward position of Americans stranded in Germany. She credulously recorded the rumors that she heard about foreign spies and saboteurs, cheered news releases about German victories, and complained that British papers were reporting lies.[18]

As soon as Austria's declaration of war against Serbia came on July 28, 1914, the confusion began. Men eligible for duty had to report to their units, and visitors and tourists began trying to find their way home. In Karlsbad, Amelia reported that the railway station was packed with people, and that it was "difficult to get near the telegraph office," probably because of crowds there as well. The next day, Monday, she noted that people were "fast leaving the city," but she could still not get her husband to leave. Christian was determined to finish his "cure." Amelia feared that he war would spread to all the "civilized nations of Europe."[19] By the thirty-first, even Christian was willing to leave. He wanted to go across the Swiss border and made reservations in Sonnenberg, near Lucerne. Amelia told her diary that she did not want to go: "I wish we can move on towards Holland or Belgium or even England." She may have been worried that they'd be stranded in landlocked Switzerland if the surrounding nations were all at war. The next day they were still debating which direction to go when they found that civilians could no longer use the telegraph system.[20] It was now limited to German military and government use. Even Christian now saw the need to leave quickly, and the family packed their trunks and made arrangements to go to Nuremberg. Their last dinner at the West End Hotel in Karlsbad must have been disturbing and lonely as few people were left; "nearly everybody was gone."[21]

Railroads were being used to mobilize troops, making civilian traffic increasingly difficult, not just in Germany but across Europe. The Heuriches' train left Karlsbad for Nuremberg slightly late. It made several stops along the way, and at least once the family's baggage was searched by authorities. When they reached Nuremberg the evening of August 2, the Heuriches learned that Germany was now at war with Russia. That same day German troops occupied Luxembourg and issued an ultimatum to France. The Heuriches settled into their rooms at the Grand Hotel and then called on the American Consul, Charles S. Winans, who had just started in that position in late June. Winans was an experienced, professional diplomat, but had served in Spain until mid–June, did not speak German, and quickly found himself swamped by Americans wanting information and needing help.[22] The situation was similar all over Europe. As nations went to war, foreigners frantically tried to get back home only to find both communications and transportation increasingly unavailable to civilians.

On August 3, Germany declared war on France and invaded Belgium. Amelia noted it in her diary and wrote that it was "doubtful" when the Americans in Nuremberg could leave for home. She included a short prayer, but because she was not a devout Christian, it was directed in a more general direction:

> May the good spirits be with us, guide us the right direction. That we will not make a false move about us leaving for our dear home and parents & relatives in America. May the good sweet spirits be with us in this hour of great trouble. And may this war not last long.

The next day Britain issued an ultimatum to Germany to withdraw from Belgium. Germany refused and London declared war. Amelia sniffed that the real reason was British "jealousy over the progress Germany has made in every direction over all other bordering countries." France, she declared, had sided with Russia because Paris wanted to regain "Elas-Loraine [*sic*]." Germany was united, she proudly proclaimed; "they are like one man, no creed, no religion, no socialism prevails here. All are one."[23]

The German military controlled the railroads, the mail system, the telegraph, and the telephones. German civilians could use the train to get home if they were stranded elsewhere, but foreigners had to remain where they were. Amelia began recording rumors of spies and saboteurs being caught and killed, which she apparently believed:

> [A]t present marshal [*sic*] law prevails everywhere in Germany. Many Russian spies are caught and shot. There seems to be very few French spies—few if any English spies that we have heard about. The Russian spies outnumbers any other by hundreds in Germany for many months. They wear wigs & dress like women. A young officer told me himself that he saw three Russian spies riding "bravely," in

an open auto near Erlangen a short distance from Nuremberg who were shot then and there on the road. No trial is given a spy here—which is very good.[24]

Ironically, the Heuriches would be victims of a similar spy mania in the U.S., but Amelia was not alone in fearing foreign espionage, nor was it unique to Germany. The late nineteenth and early twentieth centuries in Europe were marked by fewer controls on peoples' movements over borders and a corresponding increase in travel and tourism. Heurich's annual trips to the health spas of central Europe were part of a larger trend, as was his trip to see the Paris World's Fair. When war began in the summer of 1914, there were hundreds of thousands of tourists and other travelers who suddenly found themselves in a foreign land, often in a country with which their own nation was at war. For example, there were 150,000 Germans in France and tens of thousands in Britain.[25] With so many foreigners from now-hostile states scattered all over Europe, suspicion that they included spies and saboteurs was a natural outgrowth of the fears born of uncertainty. The nature of each nation's space had been suddenly redefined so that groups that had been welcome were now "others" who did not belong in the redefined space. The leap from "you do not belong here" to "you must be up to no good" was a remarkably small one.

Of course, many Americans were caught in the panic to return home, as were other neutrals. The American embassy in Berlin and the consulates were swamped with Americans needing money, train and ship tickets, and even passports, which suddenly became necessary to prove one's identity and citizenship. Like other Americans, Heurich found himself strapped for cash as banks refused to cash checks from foreigners, and Heurich was no longer a German citizen. Amelia complained that they had to borrow some money from a friend to tide them over. She also noted that people were only allowed to have a certain amount of money (she does not specify how much) and that this "is an excellent thing." However, they were unable to communicate with the United States, as all cable traffic had been cut off: the British had cut the five German cables in the North Sea on August 5. The American women in the Nuremberg Grand Hotel, now renamed the Fürstenhof, worked making bandages for the Red Cross, and Heurich contributed to a collection to furnish a hospital train for them as well.[26]

Heurich was, however, still a favorite son of Römhild, and the city government guaranteed any money Heurich needed. Friends in Berlin promised to help, and he was able to book passage on a Dutch ship leaving Amsterdam. Other Americans also trapped in Nuremberg formed committees to deal with the German government and often relied on Heurich to use whatever influence he might have as a German native. Finally, he managed to arrange for a train to take the Americans from Munich to Rotterdam.[27] The special train, full of Americans trying to get home, left Nuremberg for Amsterdam at 6:46 Monday evening, August 17. Amelia recorded the "Bahnhof was crowded with people who came to see us Americans off. We were given a great ovation and everyone asked us to carry the truth back to America." The train ran slowly, about twenty-five miles an hour. It stopped at every station, and each station had dimmed its lights, probably for fear of bombing by French aircraft. Amelia smugly told her diary that "those who were opposed to our getting up this train are now left in the lurch. They have to travel the best they can." She did not, however, note just who these people in opposition were or why they were opposed to getting the train. Their train arrived in Amsterdam at 9:00 a.m. Wednesday.[28]

Once in Amsterdam, expecting to take passage on the liner *Rotterdam*, Heurich found that "we had no reservations although we had been given reservations." He later indicated that someone had passed bribes to take the Heuriches' place—supposedly, according to notes in Amelia's dairy, the Guggenheims. Once again stranded, the Heuriches began trying to find passage on another ship. The Holland-America Line offered them junior officers' quarters on the *New Amsterdam* for $2,850, an extremely high price, in Heurich's words, "out of all proportion to prevailing steamship passage costs." The Heuriches also tried to book passage on the *Lusitania*, although Amelia did not record the price, if one were even quoted. They also had access to non–German newspapers for the first time since the war began, and learned that Ellen Wilson, President Woodrow Wilson's wife, had died earlier in August, and that Pope Pius X had passed away as well. What really upset Amelia was the British press's war news. Reporting was censored in every belligerent nation, but she accepted the German version of the war as true, and condemned the British press as being "full of untruths." She could not even force herself to finish the sentence "cannot understand how the English paper can be as...." While Amelia fumed, Heurich unsuccessfully continued to try to regain the promised reserved spots on the *Rotterdam*.[29]

The *Rotterdam* sailed without the Heuriches on August 29. It had been over a month since Austria-Hungry declared war on Serbia and the Heuriches were not much closer to being home. They settled into a routine, enjoying the fresh air and sunshine along the sea. It was difficult to get money even with a lien of credit, so they did little shopping. Amelia continued to report good war news from Germany while disparaging the British press. "It seems," she sneered, "according to the papers that the English is [*sic*] a nation of liars. It is simply disgusting." The good news was that the cruisers USS *Tennessee* and *North Carolina* arrived from New York with almost eight million dollars in gold appropriated by Congress to aid Americans stranded in Europe. This made getting cash easier as American citizens were able to cash letters of credit at European banks, or get loans to pay for tickets home. An American Relief Commission in Europe was organized by the American diplomats in Europe, and they assisted those trying to book passage back to the United States. The Relief Commission loaned money to American citizens; they were expected to repay the money once they reached home. Tasked with aiding American citizens, their mission left American residents who were not citizens, i.e., non-naturalized émigrés, in a state of limbo.[30]

The Heuriches traveled to Rotterdam and boarded the *New Amsterdam* on September 11. They were lucky to have gotten passage when they did, as according to the official report of the American Relief Commission, the Holland-America Line was completely booked well into October. The relief agents also had problems with Americans who "apparently have strong anti–English feelings" and objected to taking passage on any ship that stopped in Britain, a regular stop on many routes from Europe to the United States. Amelia did not indicate in her diary that she so objected, although she did complain that the ship was stopped several times by the British Navy, and the *New Amsterdam* was ordered at least once to disconnect its wireless, presumably so the crew could not report sighting the British warships. When the British boarded, Heurich recalled, "I came in for their particular attention as my passport showed plainly that though an American citizen in good standing, I was nevertheless a native of the country with which their country was at war."[31] Heurich was lucky he had a United States passport and was a citizen. British officials seized German non-naturalized American residents and interned them in camps throughout Britain, most for the duration of the war.

The British were not the worst the Heuriches had to endure. They occupied the junior officers' quarters, which Heurich remembered as an "evil smelling little cabin." The rooms were across from the engine room; they could hear the signals from the bridge and "have learned," Amelia wrote, "to know the signals." They stayed on deck as much as they could, avoiding spending time in their cabins. The food was apparently not what they were used to enjoying in first class. Amelia remembered that they ate almost nothing but potatoes: "We get so little to eat—and when we get it is after very long waiting." She also remembered seeing an "immense rat" running around below decks. Certainly the ships they normally traveled on must have had some rats in the hold, but the Heuriches would not have seen them while staying in first class. To add to the misery, the seas were especially rough: "The ship is rolling and pitching—never did see the waves so high and so beautiful when they rolled toward us they looked like the mountains of Switzerland." They even spotted an iceberg. Still, Heurich later noted, "I would have chartered a ship for myself and my family if necessary—and would have told them to take the brewery in exchange if I had to." "I was going," he remembered, "to get away from here and get home." Finally the seas calmed, and they enjoyed watching the waves breaking on the rocky coastline as they sailed past Cape Race at the far southeastern tip of Newfoundland. Their spirits improved as they got closer to New York, finally landing the morning of September 21. After a short quarantine and inspection they caught the 1:08 afternoon train for Washington and arrived at Union Station at 6:00 p.m. They immediately headed for their farm to enjoy the peace of home. In her diary Amelia noted "The End" in purple. It had been fifty-eight days since news of the war interrupted their vacation. It would be Heurich's last trip to Europe until 1922.[32]

Heurich's trials created by World War I were just beginning. When war broke out in Europe in August 1914, President Woodrow Wilson asked Americans to "be neutral in thought as well as in action." The sentiment was well-intentioned, but it was largely unheeded as many Americans favored the Allies, particularly Britain, or the Central Powers, especially Germany and Austria-Hungary. An individual's own ethnicity often decided his preference. In Washington, the local German and Austrian communities tended to favor the Central Powers and participated in fund-raising to support such causes as providing aid to the wives and children of fallen German and Austrian soldiers. These fund-raisers were reported in a matter-of-fact tone by the local press on the society pages, along with other charity events. For example, in February 1916 the *Washington Post* reported that "much interest is manifested in the charity bazaar in aid of German and Austrian war widows and orphans to be held in the Odd Fellows Hall … under the patronage of the German Ambassador."[33]

One of the biggest frustrations for the German-American community in the United States[34] was the issue of arms shipments to the Allies. Under international law, the United States as a neutral nation had the right to sell weapons and munitions to belligerent nations. However, the British navy controlled the Atlantic Ocean, bottling up the German fleet in its home ports. German civilian vessels were forced to find refuge in neutral ports, or risk being captured by Allied warships. As a result, Germany and its allies could not reach the United States to buy any arms or raw supplies. They made some attempts, such as those of the submarine cargo ship *Deutschland*, which made two trips to the United States in 1916. Such efforts had no real effect, except for propaganda purposes. Germany was shut out of the American market, and so the United States was arming only the Allies, a seeming contradiction with Washington's official policy of neutrality. The

German-American community began demanding that the United States cut off all arms shipments to any nation at war, a policy with which the Heuriches agreed. Neutrality Leagues began to spring to life in cities around the country, gaining support not only from Germans and their allies, but from some Irish-Americans as well.[35]

D.C.'s German-American community took advantage of their proximity to Congress, organizing mass meetings to express their anger at American sales to the Allies. One such gathering was held at the Polis Theater on Sunday evening, January 24. Advertised in the weekly German-language *Washington Journal*, the rally was organized to promote the "proposed Hitchcock-Bartholdt-Vollmer Bill which aims to stop the export of war materials; to prevent that American missiles are deployed whose victims will be our relatives in the old fatherland." The rally noticed continued, "Please attend en masse, including women, bring your American friends ... some Members of Congress and other speakers of national importance will speak."[36]

On January 30, 1915, Congressman Richard Bartholdt (R–MO) a native of Germany, hosted a meeting of embargo supporters at the New Willard Hotel in D.C. Fifty-eight delegates attended, representing all of the major German-American organizations in the United States, as did several local leaders including Heurich.[37] Their complaints went beyond the arms sales. While not mentioning Britain specifically, they noted the Allies' violations of neutral rights. The British, they protested, had seized Americans off American-flagged ships. They complained that goods normally allowed to be shipped in wartime had been declared contraband, and that there existed "foreign control of our news service and of our communications by sea." This latter point referred to British control of the cables crossing the Atlantic after they had severed the German cables. As a result of British and French censorship, American news services were receiving largely news that favored the Allies over Germany. The meeting's complaint about control of the news reflects the complaints Amelia Heurich made in her diary about how the British press "lied" to make Germany look bad. The attendees decided to form a new organization the American Independence Union, to lobby for an arms embargo. They considered electing an "Anglo-Saxon" to head it, to make it appear as if it were not a pro–German organization, but instead at their next meeting, held later in February in New York City, chose Representative Bartholdt as president. The Union issued a statement of principles, requiring that members be citizens of the United States declaring that their loyalty was to their country; and they declared that the United States should be truly neutral, and should discontinue current policy that favored the Allies.[38]

Bartholdt was also the featured speaker at the D.C. *Sängerbund's* annual carnival a week after the initial meeting at the New Willard. In his speech he repeated the same themes: freedom of the seas, a "cessation of the shipment of arms and ammunition to the warring states," and the American-owned cable "from a neutral country for transmitting news of the conflict abroad," bypassing the British-controlled lines. The Congressman also claimed that the British liner *Lusitania* had been flying the American flag, a violation of international law. The *Washington Post* article describing the *Sängerbund* added the headline "Lusitania Incident Alarms," a phrase that would have ever more impact a mere three months later when a German submarine sank the liner, killing over 1,200 people. Not everything at the event was so solemn. It was, after all, a carnival as part of the pre–Lenten celebrations. According to the *Post*, "songs and jollity were rampant." Guests wore costumes, and the *Sängerbund* performed, as did a band. The decorations were timely—"a model of a formidable submarine hung above the entertainer's platform." The "speaker's rostrum was modeled in the shape of a 42-centimeter shell and so designated." Among the speakers from the local German community was Christian Heurich. Although the topic of his speech was not noted, he strongly supported Germany over Britain: "Naturally, my sympathies were with Germany," he remembered, although "I was against the first world war [sic]."[39]

The submarine display was timely. Just a few days before, on February 4, the German government announced that they has established a "war zone" around the British Isles. Any enemy merchant vessel that entered this zone was liable to be attacked and sunk. Complicating the situation, ships belonging to belligerent nations sometimes flew the flags of neutral states to avoid destruction. At the *Sängerbund* meeting, Representative Bartholdt complained that the *Lusitania* did just that. Berlin disavowed any responsibility for the safety of neutral vessels in the war zone because it was often impossible to determine if a ship were truly neutral or not. Moreover, submarines could not follow international convention by stopping suspect vessels on the seas, searching them, and then guaranteeing the safety of the crew and passengers before sinking the ship. Submarines were too vulnerable to risk such exposure, especially as some Allied merchantmen were armed. The only recourse was for the submarine to attack by stealth, which often resulted in civilian casualties. The German justification for their decision to expand submarine warfare echoed the charges made by the German-American neutrality group. Britain was violating international law regarding neutral shipping rights, and the United States was not maintaining a strict neutrality between Germany and its enemies. Reaction to the German decision in the United States German-language press was mixed. Some papers hailed it—the German U-Boats were "liberators of the world from British tyranny over the highs seas." However, others were more concerned how the decision might affect American relations with Germany. It could easily, after all, reinforce the idea that Germans in the United States were loyal to Germany first.[40]

A few days after the initial Washington meeting, but before the German declaration, President Woodrow Wilson was asked if he had given consideration to Representative Bartholdt's "plans" for neutrality. Wilson brushed it aside with, "He hasn't presented them to me." A week later Wilson was asked about the *Lusitania*'s using the American flag, and what he thought of the German declaration of a war zone around Britain. He dismissed the flag issue, noting that the *Lusitania* was a "privately owned ship" and that flying another nation's flag did not violate international law. But while he dismissed the *Lusitania* issue, which so angered many German-Americans, he also reserved judgment on the German declaration, noting that he was still waiting for clarification from James Gerard, the American ambassador in Berlin.

The ambassador had, however, already sent a message to Wilson that would have undermined the German societies' influence over the administration. When Gerard spoke to German Undersecretary of Foreign Affairs Arthur Zimmermann, the latter noted that "in case of trouble" between the United States and Germany, there "were five hundred thousand trained Germans in America who would join the Irish and start a revolution." Gerard noted that at first he thought Zimmermann was joking, "but he was actually serious." Wilson highlighted Zimmermann's quote in the message and marked the paragraph, something he did if he thought the information was especially important. In a cover note Wilson wrote, "Is not the last paragraph [the one with Zimmermann's threat] amazing?"[41] Wilson certainly did not take the threat of a revolution by half a million Germans in the United States seriously, but he was suspicious that Berlin (and Vienna) would use some of their supporters in America to act in their homelands' interests and against the interests of the United States. This information was still fresh in Wilson's mind when the first German-American meeting was held in D.C. with Heurich in attendance.

The war was not the only issue disturbing D.C. in 1915. The local breweries went through more labor problems, when once again the unionized workers tried to win concessions in a new contract. The local breweries, excepting Robert Portner's, all signed a common contract with their workers so that the unions could not pressure individual breweries one at a time. The current contract expired on April 2, and rumblings of a strike began in March. Despite the relative peace between the D.C. breweries and the union, this was an especially tense time in which to negotiate a new contract. The American economy had been sliding into a recession in 1914, but the growing wave of munitions orders from the Allies was spurring an industrial boom. There were twenty-eight strikes against breweries in 1915, often caused by disagreements over issues in the workplace. Only four of these, including the Washington strike, came when workers and owners disagreed over a new contract once an old one expired.[42] The main point of contention was how to handle layoffs when business was slow and production cut. The brewery managers wanted to lay off workers. The unions wanted workers to rotate through times without work, so that no workers were laid off entirely. The D.C. breweries' representative, Leon Tobriner, who was also Heurich's lawyer, argued that cuts were necessary, as production for D.C.'s breweries had decreased by 40 percent. Tobriner blamed the 1913 Jones-Works excise law, which cut the number of saloons allowed in the District to 300, down from 497.[43]

The strike followed what must have seemed a familiar pattern to Heurich, as it matched the one in 1904. The union employees for the D.C. breweries and Arlington Brewing all walked out. (Portner's had its own, separate strike.) The breweries hired new workers to take their place. The union declared a boycott of beer made by the D.C. breweries, and of any saloons that still sold "local" beer. Out-of-town union shops had shipped in non-local beer for saloons that supported the strike. The saloonkeepers and liquor dealers were caught in the middle and went to court to try to prevent union pickets. The breweries held together and some workers began coming back, abandoning the strike. Predictions that the strike was about to end proved to be false, and it continued for eleven months. Finally, in March 1916, an agreement was reached, assisted by mediators appointed by the new United States Department of Labor. The Department of Labor became involved upon a request in January 1916 by the local liquor dealers' association.[44] The agreement satisfied both sides, and neither admitted to making any substantial concessions.

A considerably larger cloud than union troubles was gathering for the D.C.-area brewers. Their entire remaining customer base was about to go dry. Virginia's prohibitionists had been slowly drying up the state, county by county, town by town, until by 1914 only a few small areas were still considered Wet, notably Norfolk and Alexandria. The 1914 referendum had voted overwhelmingly to make the entire state dry, details to be decided by the state legislature when it met again in 1916. Indeed, when the Virginia legislature met in March 1916 it quickly passed a prohibition law. The Mapp Law, named after state Senator Walter Mapp of Accomack County, made the entire state Dry as of midnight, the morning of November 1, 1916. The new law closed hundreds of saloons and deprived bottling companies and distributors of business. Breweries and distillers were allowed to stay in business as long as they sold their product out of state. Five of the six Virginia breweries stayed open at least temporarily. Only Robert Portner's in Alexandria, then one of the largest breweries in the South, closed immediately. Several breweries also turned to making soft drinks or bottled water. The others tried to survive by making near-beers or beer solely for the D.C. market. None of these efforts lasted.[45]

Virginia was followed a few months later by the District, the final act that would close Heurich's brewery after forty-five years. The lame-duck 64th Congress (1915–1917) actually started the movement towards passing Dry legislation for D.C. The election results had emboldened the Dry members and disheartened the Wets, so when the 64th Congress met for a final time at the end of 1916 and early 1917, it began considering several prohibition laws. One of the first to pass was the Sheppard Act—named after Dry Senator John Morris Sheppard of Texas—which made Washington, D.C., totally dry, banning any alcoholic beverage outside of the home. The Wets tried to derail the law by asking for a referendum to allow the citizens of Washington to vote for or against the law. Congress refused to allow such a referendum and Wilson sided with Congress, noting that there was no mechanism for such a vote. In his January 15, 1917, press conference he told a reporter, "You see, there is no voting machinery in the District of Columbia. It would have to be created. There are some practical difficulties about it." The Drys continued their efforts, however, and the bill finally passed.[46]

The Drys had been trying to make Washington alcohol-free for years. Why did they succeed in early 1917? The political situation had gradually changed so that after the 1916 election neither Democrats nor Republicans would be willing to alienate the increasingly powerful Dry wings of their own parties. President Woodrow Wilson, narrowly reelected in 1916, was not especially sympathetic to the Drys, but he knew he needed their support. The election put Wilson in a difficult spot. While the Democratic Party was split between Wets and Drys, 17 of the 30 states Wilson carried in 1916 were dry. The Republican opponent, Charles Evans Hughes, only carried six Dry states. Wilson knew that the Drys had carried him to reelection. Progressive writer and Prohibitionist John Palmer Gavit made this clear to Wilson when he wrote that he should not forget that he had "been elected by the vote of 'dry' states."[47]

Wilson's attitude towards alcohol came from his father—a Southern Presbyterian minister—and it fit the model of temperance rather than of prohibition. His father, Joseph Ruggles Wilson, considered issues such as tobacco use and drinking as habits of personal choice rather than sins. Wilson had the same view, occasionally enjoying a social drink, condemning not the use of alcohol but drunkenness. When he was president of Princeton, Wilson allowed undergraduates to drink beer and he allowed student organizations to serve wine at yearly dinners. However, students were disciplined for becoming drunk or for frequenting disreputable saloons in town.[48] As governor of New Jersey, Wilson came down firmly on the side of local option, allowing local communities to vote on whether or not to implement local prohibition. When asked by the Democratic Party bosses what his position was on alcohol, Wilson noted, "I am not a prohibitionist. I believe that the question is outside of politics. I believe in home rule, and that the issue should be settled by local opinion in each community." In 1911 he publicly restated his position in a letter to the Rev. Thomas Shannon, the head of the New Jersey Anti-Saloon League. Wilson wrote:

> But the questions involved are social and moral and are not susceptible of being made parts of a party programme [sic]. Whenever they have been made the subject matter of party contests, they have cut the lines of party organization and party action athwart to the utter confusion of political action in

every other field. They have thrown every other question, however important, into the background and have made constructive party action impossible for long years together. So far as I am concerned, therefore, I can never consent to have the question of local option made an issue between political parties in this State. My judgment is very clear in this matter. I do not believe … [in] making a political issue of a great question which is essentially nonpolitical, non-partisan, moral and social in its nature.[49]

In the 1916 presidential election, both Wilson and Republican candidate Hughes did their best to ignore the Prohibition issue, as did both partys' political platforms. Dry organizations, including the Anti-Saloon League, concentrated on electing Dry candidates to Congress. Their success surprised both sides. The Republicans made large gains in Congress and added 65 new Dry representatives to the House. The Democrats lost seats but maintained control of Congress, and added 20 new Dry members despite their overall losses. When the 65th Congress first met in 1917, the Democratic Drys outnumbered the Wets by 140 to 64, while Dry Republicans outnumbered their Wet companions by 138 to 62. Split between factions, both parties were caught in a dilemma. The best way to deal with the problem, it seemed, was to allow the Drys to pass a prohibition amendment to the Constitution. That way it would be out of Washington's hands and responsibility would shift to the states.[50]

As for the District of Columbia, the Sheppard Act would make the entire district Dry. The Washington press was divided over the bill. The *Evening Star* and the *Herald* supported the measure, while the *Post*, the *Times*, and the *Bee* opposed it. All the local press was united, however, in denouncing Congress's making the decision for the capital city without the locals' being able to voice their opinion. The *Herald* called Congress "high-handed," while the *Times* reran an editorial from the *New York World* titled "Washington Despotically Dry."[51]

The African American *Bee* was perhaps the most vehemently opposed to the Sheppard Act. They attacked Prohibition not just for D.C. but for the entire country as being a hypocritical "sham." Throughout the debate, the *Bee* attacked the Drys' priorities, noting that prohibitionists who were so concerned about the effects of alcohol on individuals and communities seemed to have no problem with the worse crime of lynching. "Which is more evil to society," the *Bee*'s editor Calvin Chase wrote, "lynching or the sale of liquor? This is a good question for the prohibitionists to discuss. Many of these Prohibitionists ought to be caged." Moreover, Chase claimed, Prohibition was an example of the violation of minority rights, in this case, violating the rights of those who enjoyed drinking.[52]

The *Star* was almost as strident in their support of the bill as the *Bee* was in its opposition. On March 1, 1917, as the bill sat on Wilson's desk, a news story in the *Star* noted that "the 'wets' built a fortress of deliberate parliamentary moves and the 'drys' sharpened an axe which cut it down." The Wets' efforts to stop the bill, sniffed the *Star*, were merely "moves to waste time." The paper was confident that Wilson would ignore the Wets and sign the bill.[53] If Heurich was looking for a sign of what was to come, the news was not good. That same day the horses of one of Heurich's delivery wagons ran away and crashed into a wagon belonging to the G.W. Bamgartner and Company, a local rubber firm. The wagons then crashed into an electrical pole. "Both wagons were damaged and the pole was demolished. No one was injured."[54] Heurich's business was about to get as rude a jolt as his delivery wagon.

Once the Sheppard Bill passed, the Wets began lobbying Wilson to veto the law. American Federation of Labor President (and Wilson political ally) Samuel Gompers visited Wilson and pressed him to kill the bill, noting that beer was the working man's beverage. Caught between the two factions, Wilson told his secretary, Joseph Tumulty, "how impossible this is for me, especially at present." However, on March 3, 1917, Wilson signed the bill, noting that Congress had been given police power for the District, so the law fell within Congress's responsibilities. Traditionally, presidents had rarely interfered with Congress when it came to governing the District. Wilson was no doubt aware of the precedent, and so his signature was the result of respect for precedent rather than support for local prohibition.[55]

Disappointed Wets did not give up, however, and seven saloonkeepers filed suit with the District Supreme Court. The plaintiffs claimed that by selling them licenses, the District government had recognized the saloonkeepers' right to sell liquor, and that the Sheppard Act therefore violated their property rights. The District of Columbia Supreme Court, however, refused the claim, noting that the internal revenue license was in fact a tax, and did not actually guarantee the right to sell intoxicants. The ruling judge noted that the U.S. Supreme Court had earlier ruled that there was no right to property in selling liquor, as there were important public health and safety rights which took precedence.[56]

The *Star* applauded Wilson's signing the bill, noting that while there would be a temporary loss of jobs for those who made or sold liquor, more jobs would be created by the economic benefits of prohibition. With this argument, the *Star* espoused the same political reasoning used by the Anti-Saloon League and other Dry groups, that alcohol was an economic drain on society and money spent on alcohol would be better spent on clothes, food, and rent, or placed in a bank account. In contrast, the *Bee* grumbled that "the southern Democrats have played the devil with the property rights of the people." In reality, prohibition sentiment spread far beyond the South, and was as strong in the West and Midwest as in the South. However, the *Bee*'s editorial focus was normally on the segregationist Southern Democrats, and in this case the editor's ire blamed them for prohibition as well.[57]

The other Wet papers were more resigned than angry, simply noting that appeals to Wilson to veto the bill had failed. Why did not they care more? Opponents of prohibition, not just in Washington but nationwide, were in an awkward position. They needed to somehow strike a balance between opposing bans on alcoholic beverages while not seeming to defend alcohol abuse. One common tactic to avoid the appearance of defending drunkenness was to emphasize legal procedure rather than individual rights: had the Drys followed a proper legal and constitutional course? In the case of the Sheppard Act, there was little legal ground for the Wets to defend. Congress had the responsibility to legislate for the capital, and there were no mechanisms established for a popular referendum. This left the Wets with little realistic means to stop Washington from going Dry at Congress's whim.

At midnight, October 31, 1917, Washington, D.C., joined the Dry ranks without a great deal of fanfare. Heurich noted that "my brewery business was wiped out in that single gesture ... an investment of over a million dollars was hamstrung."[58] Many restaurants had already run out of liquor and were serving ice water. Private clubs had sold their remaining stock to their members because private stocks of liquor were still allowed. A few areas remained crowded with drinkers as midnight approached. Ninth Street from Pennsylvania to K Street, which includes Washington's tiny Chinatown, was crowded until after 1 a.m. with people celebrating, or mourning, the end of John Barleycorn (the personification of alcoholic beverages). M Street between Rock Creek and the Aqueduct Bridge, another saloon-heavy area, ended up closing before midnight as stocks of alcohol were exhausted. The same was true along H Street NW, another area well-populated by saloons.[59]

The Washington press gave heavy coverage to the transformation from Wet territory to Dry. The *Times*, perhaps the most "wet" of the Washington papers, bemoaned the closing of historic bars where past greats such as Henry Clay and Daniel Webster had discussed the issues of their day over a drink. The *Times* also warned that prohibition meant that legal products such as beer with low alcoholic contents would be replaced by high-alcohol illegally bootlegged distilled beverages. The *Bee* predicted that Washington would suffer economically, and would in essence become a "Middle West dreary prohibition example ruled by well-meaning and ignorant prohibitionists." If the District of Columbia was freed from Dry fanaticism, it would grow and be prosperous. However, wrote the *Bee*'s editor, "Ice water is not the beverage of the successful man."[60]

The *Star*, as the leading Dry paper in the city, was jubilant. It editorialized that a full, vigorous and unceasing enforcement of the new law would undoubtedly make Washington a better, happier, more prosperous city. As for the warning about bootlegging sounded by the *Times*, the *Star* noted that "it will be impossible, save through a violation of the law, to buy intoxicating beverage within the price range of the average person." The *Star* also gave favorable coverage to the Anti-Saloon League's meeting in Washington to observe the move of the capital city into the Dry column.[61]

The *Herald* joined in the *Star*'s triumphant attitude, even though it earlier tried to straddle the issue. The day before the District of Columbia went Dry, the *Herald* printed a cartoon by Dry cartoonist "Ding" Darling titled "The Kaiser's Submarines Haven't Begun to Wreck as Many Lives." The cartoon showed ruined families exiting from a whiskey bottle while a bartender "dealer" watches. The next day, the *Herald* ran a cartoon showing a bedraggled whiskey bottle being driven over the state line into Maryland at bayonet point. An accompanying editorial, titled "Good-by John," noted:

> But old whimsical, alluring, though deadly John lapsed into a state of coma…. What will the passing of liquor mean to Washington? Will it be beneficial or otherwise? It's up to the reader. With the conflicting views of equally prominent parties on both sides, we hesitate to hazard a guess. We believe, however, that on the whole, the city will derive blessings from the new order of things. Whether we are right or wrong, time only will tell. In any event let there be no moaning. Good-by John.[62]

Not one to wait for events to overtake him, Heurich attempted to prepare for the coming of Prohibition, and kept his business running and his workers employed as long as he could. In August 1917, a few months before the law took effect, he tried making a non-alcoholic fruit drink. He purchased $100,000 worth of apples (approximately $1,700,000 in 2010) and stored the mash in sterilized beer barrels. After the addition of some hops, the drink was ready for sale. Like many Americans, Heurich was eager to show support for the wartime effort and gave his product an "American" name, as opposed to a German one. Just as sauerkraut became "liberty cabbage," Heurich's new drink was named "Liberty Apple Champagne." To the brewer's chagrin, however, his new beverage fermented and he was unable to keep it on the market as a nonalcoholic beverage. He placed it in storage in the hopes that someday he could sell it.[63] In January 1920, shortly before national prohibition started, Heurich was given permission to sell as much of his stock of Liberty Apple Champagne as he could. He sold about one-third of his supply, even though customers had to come to the brewery to pick it up. Some of it went to the White House.[64]

Washington's German community opposed the measure, but it came at a time when they had little political influence and larger problems due to the impending American entry into World War I. Heurich noted that when the war began, his "sympathies were with Germany, as were the sympathies of thousands of German-born people in this country who were loyal Americans, but who could never forget that Germany was the land of their birth." As early as 1915, well before the United States entered the war, Heurich was the subject of investigations by the Bureau of Investigation (forerunner to the FBI). In September 1915 a Washington resident sent a letter to the Bureau claiming Heurich was building concrete gun emplacements at his Maryland farm, which had an unobstructed view of Washington. The Bureau sent local agent George W. Lillard to investigate. The agent submitted his detailed report in mid–September 1915. Lillard examined the farm at length and was most concerned with the amount of concrete. Heurich was a pioneer in building fireproof structures out of concrete after his brewery on 20th Street NW suffered numerous fires. Lillard found the number of such buildings suspicious. He found several "lakes" of special concern, noting in his report that one had a small island in the middle, "a suitable base for a large gun," and "the other parts of the lake would be suitable for intrenchments." The "lakes" were actually ponds used for drainage. One was a fish pond that provided different types of fish for dinners. There were also two deep cisterns. One was six feet deep and eight feet wide. It caught the water and urine from the cow barns, and the waste was then sprayed onto the farm's cornfields.[65] In addition, Heurich had placed old beer vats on the property for his kids to use as swimming pools. Lillard was also suspicious of metal posts set in concrete that were used to make a fence around

One of the old beer vats used as a pool at Bellevue. Karla and Anita are enjoying some warm weather (courtesy Jan King Evans Houser).

the property: "These posts are suitable for barbed wire entanglements." Lillard took photos of some of the structures and concluded, "The general idea as it appears to me is that these buildings, etc., are for some purpose other than for which it is claimed they are to be used."[66]

Lillard was not the most discerning judge. In 1917 he investigated a native-born Anton Dilger, American physician of German descent living in Virginia.[67] The doctor had just returned from Germany and the Bureau suspected his loyalty. Lillard was friends with Dilger's brother, and his report cleared the man of any wrongdoing, accepting Dilger's claim that he was going to operate a manganese mine on his farm in western Virginia. (Such mines did exist in the area.) In reality, Dilger was a German agent, working to infect horses sold to the Allies in America with infectious diseases. He fled to Mexico and then Spain before he could be arrested. So much for Lillard's judgment. Ironically, the Dilgers were related by marriage to Christian Heurich, although there is no evidence he had anything to do with his in-law's actions.[68]

The Bureau took no action against Heurich after Lillard submitted his report. Perhaps one of the agent's superiors realized that farms normally held ponds and wire fencing. Nonetheless, the rumors continued. In September 1916 one of Heurich's friends told him that he had heard the same "gun emplacement" tale while at Mountain Lake Park, a summer resort town in western Maryland. A reporter from the *Evening Star* told Heurich he had heard that the Navy Department had taken over the brewery. Heurich's secretary, Charles Meyer, reported that the barber at the Raleigh Hotel told him that Heurich had "carloads of munitions and dynamite" at his farm. Finally, Heurich was informed that a "temperance woman" was telling people at the city's central market that Heurich was a spy.[69]

Given the number of rumors and their persistence, it perhaps should have been expected that Heurich would be the subject of still more investigations. In early March 1917 another informant told the Bureau that Heurich was having concrete work done on his farm. Agent E.S. Underhill went to meet Heurich at his home, and rode with the Heuriches in their limousine to the farm. Underhill's report indicated that there were concrete structures that could be used as gun emplacements, but that "I found nothing to indicate that they were constructed for that purpose." For example, he found that the concrete barn had been built over twenty years before, and his report noted that Heurich was a "pioneer in concrete construction in this country." There were ten men who worked on the farm, Underhill found, but only one was German.[70]

Underhill also visited the Heuriches' home. The family had received a postcard from Philadelphia telling the elderly brewer that he should go to the Department of Justice "and confess about his pro–German activities." To clear his name, Heurich asked that the department interview him. Agent Underhill went to the Heurich mansion on New Hampshire Avenue and was allowed to go through the house. Heurich and Amelia admitted that they favored Germany over Britain, but that allegiance to the United States "stood ahead of everything else." Heurich noted that he'd lived in America for over fifty years, showed the agent his naturalization papers from 1872,[71] and claimed to be the biggest taxpayer in the District, having paid $37,000 in taxes in 1916, aside from the excise taxes his brewery paid. Underhill did find a wireless set, but noted it had already been inspected. The Heuriches' cook was English, and there was a "Colored" male servant who had previously worked at the British embassy. "The attitude of the whole establishment," noted the agent, "was such as to disarm suspicion."[72]

This did not end the rumors, which would last for the length of the war. Heurich also had to deal with the credulous Agent Lillard again at the beginning of April 1917 when the agent inspected the brewery. He did not report anything suspicious, despite the plethora of concrete in the facility, but did note that "it is impossible to state that there is nothing concealed there which should not be." There were, he warned, "many places in the brewery where arms and ammunition might be stored." However, it would take "several men four or five days" to completely inspect the facility.[73]

In early 1917, as the United States drew closer to war with Germany, Heurich became the target of more frequent, and often ludicrous rumors. They even began to appear not just in letters from suspicious neighbors, but in the press. The *New York Times* reported that Heurich was involved, along with other prominent members of Washington's German immigrant community, in treasonous activities. In a front-page story, the *Times* noted:

> According to report around Washington, it was found that the principal man concerned [Heurich] had built concrete foundations for German siege guns on his country estate outside the city, placed to enable them to demolish the Capitol and disguised as fish ponds or similar landscape gardening, and that a secret wireless outfit was found on the estate, with which he had secured valuable information and conveyed it to the enemy.

The *Times* article continued, noting that an "officer of the Secret Service" said he "paid no attention" to this and similar reports. In reality, the "concrete foundations" on Heurich's farm in suburban Maryland were the burial vault for Heurich's second wife, Mathilde, who had died in 1895,[74] as well as the chicken house and ponds. Such rumors were not uncommon, and centered on the entire D.C. German community, not just on Heurich. One congressional wife noted in her diary in February 1917, "*The Washington Post* is … full of silly gossip." The rumors were part of a growing fear that led to increasingly greater restrictions placed on German-Americans in Washington during the First World War.[75]

Why did these stories suddenly proliferate? On January 31, 1917, Berlin announced it would begin unrestricted submarine warfare the next day, and in response, on February 3, the United States broke diplomatic relations with Germany. On February 24, Britain passed the text of the Zimmermann telegram to the Wilson administration. In the telegram, the German foreign secretary told the German ambassador in Mexico to propose an alliance. Mexico and Germany would ally with Japan in a war against the United States. Germany promised to return the American southwest to Mexico when the war was over. The Wilson administration released the text to the public on March 1 to general shock and outrage. The evening of April 2, the day Lillard wrote his report on Heurich's brewery, President Wilson asked Congress to declare war on Germany. It did so on April 6.

As events escalated from January into April 1917, the tone of the press in Washington markedly changed. War news had been understandably prominent since the summer of 1914, but it now took on urgency and, in many cases, a militant tone warning of a German threat to the United States as it joined World War I. Rumors began to appear in the press along with more reliable news. On March 26, 1917, the *Evening Star* reported a sermon given at the Washington Soldiers Home by a local Methodist minister. Abandoning his original text, the minister warned the old soldiers that "Washington is filled with German spies." On the same day, the *Star* reported that "large communities" around the United States were preparing for a possible "uprising on part of Teuton [sic] sympathizers." On March 29 the *Star* and the *Washington Times* claimed that the head of the American Red

Cross's Atlantic division confirmed that while ground glass had been found in "one or two instances" in bandages, it was not true that "medical supplies ... had been found tampered with by spies and that bandages had been discovered soaked with poisonous chemicals." The next day the *Star* reported that information obtained in New Orleans indicated that Germany was plotting to overthrow the governments of all the Central American states and unite them against the United States. Meanwhile, the paper stated that "officials at the Department of Justice" would "neither confirm nor deny" the reports that they were searching for German spies working in parts of the executive branch.[76]

Provocative stories continued in April as the United States declared war on Germany, and although authorities sometimes denied rumors were accurate, the stories became more frightening. The *Star* reported that Germans were trying to "incite Negroes" in Alabama and North Carolina against the United States, but that the "agents of the Imperial German government" were unsuccessful. The Justice Department reported that "tens of thousands of 'tips'" had been sent to them in just a few days and the superintendent of police in D.C. was quoted as denying "that men were sent to the Capitol grounds ... because of a reported plot to destroy the building." In a clear case of panic, a minister in Fairfax County, Virginia, just across the Potomac River to the west from Washington, called the police to report that several men were taking photographs of the Great Falls, a local scenic tourist site. Police noted that "pictures of Great Falls have been taken by hundreds of residents of this city," and that "they are at a loss to understand what is expected to be accomplished with photographs of the river at that point."[77]

The William Randolph Hearst–owned *Times* made the most of the growing patriotic fervor. They ran a loyalty pledge on their front page on March 20, 1917, launching a campaign that lasted for several weeks. The "Pledge of Loyalty" was addressed to "The President" and swore "absolute and unconditional loyalty to the Government of the United States." The *Times* asked its readers to cut out the oath, paste it onto a sheet of paper, and collect signatures from neighbors and friends. After getting the signatures, readers were supposed to send it to the *Times*, which would collect them and pass them to the president. For the next three weeks the *Times* ran stores praising those, especially children, who collected signatures. They bragged when prominent local citizens signed the pledge, including sixteen-year-old Christian Heurich, Jr.[78]

The day after war was declared, April 7, the *Times* ran an editorial titled "In Words of One Syllable." The editors noted that those "who were technically alien enemies of the United States resident therein should follow a simple rule, 'Obey the law; keep your mouth shut.'" Insinuating that many German-Americans did not know English, further labeling them as outsiders, the paper concluded that family members who did know English should "translate that into German." Perhaps, the editor suggested, "school children can be requisitioned for the task." Finally the *Times* noted that the German-language press should "print it in box-car type."[79]

In the face of the rumors of disloyalty and growing fears, on March 28 several prominent members of D.C.'s German community issued "formal statements pledging their allegiance to the Stars and Stripes." Martin Wiegand, head of the city's United German Societies, noted that he came to America as a child, that members of his family had fought in the Civil War, and that a stepbrother had died in the war. A local German-American hotel owner declared, "Now that this country seems to be on the verge of war, I want it plainly understood that my sympathies are with the land of my adoption, and that my loyalty knows no conditions and no reservations."[80]

Heurich noted in his statement to the press that "[h]is loyalty as a citizen was so far beyond question that he regarded the sensational rumors as being beneath his notice." This did not quell the stories. In his memoirs Heurich noted that rumors of his disloyalty were rife throughout much of the war. "I was," he wrote, "in the opinion of these people, a master spy, an intriguer, a German propagandist, a fearful and dangerous person." Besides the rumor of the gun emplacements, Heurich recounted inviting the newspaper that claimed he had built a wireless station to send secret messages to Germany to inspect his property for such a facility, an offer they failed to accept. The same paper later reported erroneously that the brewer had committed suicide. The editor offered to print a retraction, but Heurich told him to "let me remain dead. Leave me in my grave where you have got me for the remainder of the war, and I won't sue you."[81]

Heurich's experiences were not unique, but they are an instructive example of how rumors spread during wartime. So let us examine the phenomenon of rumors themselves. What is a rumor? Nicholas DiFonzo and Prashant Bordia, two psychologists who study the phenomenon of rumor, define it as "unverifiable and instrumentally relevant information statements in circulation that arise in contexts of ambiguity, danger or potential threat, and that function to help people make sense and manage risk." Rumors may be about activity by an individual, such as Heurich, but they are designed to deal with an ongoing community-wide threat. Rumors are particularly strong in certain contexts, when "people feel an acute need for security." Passing on such rumors might make those spreading them feel as if they are not helpless, but are taking action against a perceived threat, by spreading awareness of that threat. Similarly, in *Rumors and Gossip*, Ralph Rosnow and Gary Fine note that rumors are an attempt at problem-solving to fit new information into an existing belief system.[82]

Rumors thrive as a way for society to "make collective sense in an ambiguous situation." DiFonzo and Bordia argue that when individuals are unable to make sense of a situation on their own, they may then participate in collective efforts—to listen to, evaluate, and spread rumors. Rumors that are judged to add to the community's understanding of events survive and spread, while those that are not believed, or do not seem useful, are ignored. In uncertain times, such as when wars begin, societies are especially prone to rumors as people try to understand a potential threat to their well-being, most commonly negative or "dread rumors." Such rumors "forecast unpleasant consequences" and are passed with greater speed than "wish rumors," those "that predict pleasant consequences." Dread rumors may be passed more quickly because they arouse strong emotions, and "to reduce their anxiety," people quickly pass them to others. Spreading dread rumors helps establish "social support" among a community that feels threatened as members of the community unify against the perceived threat.[83]

Rumors then act as a coping mechanism and as a form of threat management. Simply gaining an understanding of events is, in itself, a form of exerting a small measure of control. Uncertainty in March 1917 gave rise to fears that Germany was planning to attack the United States directly. These fears were not totally unreasonable, given the Zimmermann telegram and events such as the 1916 explosion at Black Tom Island in New York Harbor, where a large depot of ammunition destined for the Allies was destroyed by sabotage. In wartime, people correctly assume that governments do not publicly report everything, including the possibility of such attacks. Even those who support an administration may accept that security requires some things be kept secret. Those who do not support the administration may be predisposed to believe rumors that reflect badly on the government's ability to cope with the threat. For example, Ellen Slayden, wife of Congressman James Slayden (D–TX), did not like or trust the Wilson administration and noted in her diary that one of her friends, who also was not a Wilson supporter, worried that the Germans would simply cross the Atlantic and America would be "annihilated" because the administration had left the country unprepared. In either case, both groups could assume that those in charge were hiding information from the public.[84]

Because they are a coping mechanism for dealing with uncertainty, rumors ideally are also declarative. Sometimes rumors may be prefaced with some cautionary note such as "I am not certain if this is true," but the rumor is still phrased as a fact even if the evidential base is weak or absent. Often no evidence is presented or it is second- or even third-hand, i.e., "a friend told me that he heard." However, some form of source description, even if vague, helps the rumor appear reliable. Likewise, attributing the rumor to someone "in the know" gives the story enough believability to encourage belief, such as the *Star*'s "source in New Orleans" that reported on supposed German plotting in Central America. The story about Heurich's building gun emplacements at his Maryland farm is a good example of stating a rumor as fact. The reporter who said there were gun emplacements at Heurich's farm did not ask why there were concrete structures, but simply stated that they were evidence Heurich was working for the enemy. Agent Lillard could not seem to imagine why a farm would use metal fencing or multiple ponds. Posing it as a question would have added to uncertainty, while stating it as a fact, even a threatening one—German guns can bombard Washington!—help to make sense of ambiguity.[85]

A rumor's believability depends on the perceptions and biases of both the storyteller and the audience. Rumors that fit existing negative stereotypes are more likely to be spread than rumors that contradict existing stereotypes. By 1917 in the United States, the popular stereotyped image of Germany was centered on that nation's alleged treachery and untrustworthiness, the infamous "Hun" that Allied propaganda had been warning against since August 1914. In Washington, for example, there was a rumor that Heurich had plotted to assassinate President Wilson by planting explosives under his fiancée Edith Bolling's house on 20th Street, across the street from Heurich's own home on New Hampshire Avenue. Since Wilson walked to Miss Bolling's house accompanied by only a single Secret Service agent, this was a convoluted and unnecessarily complicated way to carry out an assassination. But the secretive nature of the plot—hidden explosives killing the unsuspecting president—better fit the stereotypes of the Germans as engaging in underhanded attacks. It's no accident that this particular rumor spread around Washington at the same time as the *Lusitania* crisis, after a German submarine torpedoed a passenger ship, killing women and children.[86]

One of the original and influential studies of rumors, Gordon Allport and Leo Postman's *The Psychology of Rumor*, labeled stories about feared enemies "wedge drivers." In their judgment the largest class of rumors, wedge drivers, in their words, "reflect hate and hostility,"[87] focusing on groups viewed as either powerful enough or numerous enough to be a threat. Wedge rumors focus on outsiders judged to be in the strongest position to threaten the status quo either through numbers, or because they were perceived to control powerful local financial or other resources.[88] Did the German population in Washington in 1917 fit the criteria as a threatening minority? Certainly while Germany had a powerful military, they did not have the capacity to, as Ellen Slayden's friend feared, "just come over in their ships and submarines and do it!" According to the 1910 Census, the native German population was the second-largest foreign-born population in the

District, just behind the Irish. There were 5,179 German-born residents in the city, compared to 5,347 Irish. The Russians were a distant third with fewer than 4,000. Moreover, the city's population was over 330,000, of which only 25,000 were foreign-born. Even if you include spouses and first-generation German-Americans, the German population of Washington was small enough that they would seem not to be a threat. One must consider, however, the community's visibility in the community as a whole, and the German-American community was one of the most visible the area. Unlike other major cities, Washington had no distinctive immigrant neighborhoods of any consequence. There was a tiny Chinatown, no *Kleindeutschland*, and "Little Italy" was a minuscule shantytown by the quarries on the Virginia side of the river. The Germans of Washington, however, had their own language newspaper, the only foreign-language newspaper in the city, their own clubs such as the *Turn Verein*, and so were more visible than other groups. Their presence in the larger community was greater than might be guessed from their numbers alone. The District's status as the nation's capital also added to the sense of unease, as it magnified the importance of local possible military targets. The sense of increased vulnerability magnified the sense of an existing threat.[89]

Wedge rumors spread easily and serve to crystallize a community's unease. Terry Ann Knopf's study of race riots in the United States led her to conclude that animosity is crucial to wedge rumors. They confirm prejudices as "fact" and help focus a community's hostility. In the case of the German community in Washington, the rumors helped reassure those spreading them that Germany was a real threat to the United States. The Wilson administration's loyalty campaigns, and the unofficial loyalty efforts that were tolerated and sometimes supported by the Wilson administration, only served to exacerbate the problem because they gave official confirmation to the idea that there were those who were actively disloyal.[90]

The local press helped stir these fears, including the staid establishment *Evening Star*, as well as the sensationalistic William Randolph Hearst–owned *Times*. The *Star*, while a bit less alarmist as befitting its role as the voice of the city's elite, still ran stories such as "Another German 'Plot' Comes to the Surface." The *Times*'s penchant for scare headlines such as "Capital Spies to be Arrested at Once" has already been noted. The *Washington Post* switched from an antiwar to a pro-war position, and attacked those it felt were disloyal, including opponents of the war, whom they labeled as "slackers" and accused of "skulking behind skirts and taking to the bush, with a cowardice that is worse than sudden panic." The *Herald* likewise warned of German spies.[91]

Preparation for war was not the only factor contributing to unease in Washington during March and April of 1917. There was a railway strike against a local transit company in which a mob attacked and burned one of the railroad's cars. The strike disrupted life for the average worker in D.C. and raised fears of further violence. On March 28 the *Star* ran a story on page two about German residents in D.C. swearing their "allegiance to [the] United States." Next to it was a photo of a streetcar wrecked when a "mob" ejected the crew and three passengers, then sent the car driverless hurtling downhill to be wrecked when it jumped the track at a curb. The mob, made up of "strikers or their sympathizers," forced the crew off at gunpoint, according to the *Star*. The paper did not blame the streetcar incident on "enemy aliens," but the juxtaposition of stories linked the threats with one another.[92]

The rumors about the German community and Heurich fit the model of how rumors spread. Local German-Americans were singled out as a threat despite the lack of any

A cartoon by W.A. Rogers showing Uncle Sam finding himself surrounded by weeds in the form of German spies and saboteurs (Library of Congress).

tangible evidence of acts of disloyalty. Nevertheless, the unsubstantiated stories were often stated as fact and used to "prove" that Germany posed a danger to the United States. Moreover, the stories reached a peak during the time of most uncertainty, in early 1917. In contrast, the rumors appear to have decreased beginning in the summer of 1917 when Washington seemed less vulnerable as the government took actions that reduced the perceived threat from disloyal German-Americans. The Army was expanding via conscription and soldiers guarded the city. However, even as the perceived threat decreased and rumors diminished, they did not entirely stop. During the exceptionally hot summer of 1918, a rumor spread that Heurich was hoarding ice produced by his brewery. The *Washington Post* worked to quell the story by reporting that Heurich was working with the local food administration office. The paper stated, "The report that Mr. Heurich is hoarding ice is unfounded."[93]

Rumors also spread throughout the German-American community itself, which also felt vulnerable and uncertain about what might happen to them during the war. In early February 1917, the Wilson administration was informed that German-Americans were withdrawing their money from banks around the country. The story had spread that German-American assets would be seized by the government. At the request of Treasury Secretary William McAdoo, Wilson issued a statement on February 8, 1917, that the fears were "unfounded" even though, in truth, the government could seize assets if they could be shown to be aiding Germany during the war.[94]

The District's German community, however, had far more serious thing to worry about than rumors, as hateful as they could be. Although they did not suffer through some of the violence seen in other parts of the country during the war, they found their activities increasingly restricted. Congress declared war on April 6. Immediately President Wilson issued a proclamation designating German citizens living in the United States as "enemy aliens." The proclamation forbade them from possessing weapons or wireless sets as well as more obvious items such as code books. Germans in the District had until April 23 to turn in any weapons to the local police. They were also forbidden from going within one-half mile of government military and other sensitive facilities. Within Washington this would have included the Navy Yard as well as numerous other facilities.[95]

These restrictions were only the start. On November 16, 1917, Wilson issued a second, more far-reaching proclamation regarding "enemy aliens," defined as German males at least fourteen years old who were not American citizens. They were banned from being in either the District of Columbia or the Panama Canal Zone, and they were forbidden from being within 100 yards of any canal, dock or pier used for shipping. No enemy alien "shall ascend into the air in any airplane, balloon, airship or flying machine." Enemy aliens had to register with the United States Attorney General and receive permission to move or to travel. As Washington had not yet declared war on Austria-Hungary, these restrictions still only applied to Germans within the United States.[96] German men who had been living in Washington before declaration of war had until December 15 to leave the city. Those who had come to Washington after April 6, labeled "Teuton [*sic*] Transients" by the *Washington Post,* had to leave before November 22 or be arrested.[97]

While the spouses of German nationals were affected by these proclamations even if they were citizens, German-born naturalized citizens of the United States were not, so some of the German-American community in Washington remained. However, their lives were disrupted as well, in matters both large and small. Several local churches stopped giving sermons in German and a newly arrived German Catholic priest transferred from D.C. to a parish in Maryland. The local German singing club, the *Sängerbund*, first substituted English titles for German and then suspended all its activities in 1918. Washington schools eliminated German courses in 1918 after enrollment dropped. Heurich's school-aged daughter noted that her playmates claimed they couldn't play with her, taunting her with cries of "She's a Hun!" The German-language newspaper, the *Journal*, self-censored to avoid printing any "pro–German" news.[98] Heurich later wrote that, being of German birth, he had to beware of "people intent on witch-burning." He was careful not to "express opinions of any sort" and was mindful of how he spoke.[99] Like other local German-Americans, brewer Christian Heurich was angry over the rumors of his disloyalty, but continued living and working in D.C. although his brewery closed. Heurich was already seventy-five years old, and owned enough real estate investments that he did not need to continue working. He retired from public view for the remainder of the war, although his company continued making ice so that he did not have to lay off his workers.[100]

Washington in 1917 demonstrated how a local minority, even a well-established and seemingly integrated community like Washington's Germans, could be the subject of hostile rumors. The media played a decidedly mixed role, both spreading and quelling them, although with a decided emphasis on the former. Heurich's memoirs, written in the 1930s, discussed the rumors with a somewhat bitter tone towards the press that published them, and his third wife's diaries remained bitter towards Woodrow Wilson. The German-American community in D.C. never did restore the status they held before the war, and even though the hysteria of the spring of 1917 was not repeated in the Second World War, the rumors of 1917 remained an unpleasant memory of a local community whose institutions' role in the larger community remained permanently diminished.

What seemed to be yet one more blow to Heurich's pride came in 1919 with the Eighteenth Amendment to the Constitution, which banned "the manufacture, sale, or transportation of intoxicating liquors within, the importation thereof into, or the exportation thereof from the United States." It passed Congress in 1918, was ratified in January 1919, and went into effect a year after ratification. Even before the amendment passed, however, wartime prohibition limited the amount of material available to brewers, and made much of the country Dry before 1921. Heurich, now in his mid-seventies, remained in semi-retirement, but his real estate investments more than sufficed to provide a comfortable living.[101] He did have other alternatives. Heurich noted that another brewer asked his advice. He'd been offered a job in a bootleg brewery at a decent wage. Should he accept the job? Heurich noted that he advised him not to do so: Prohibition was now the law, and while it was "an iniquitous law," it existed. Heurich had "no hope" they'd ever be able to practice their trade again. "That is the sad part" he said, "but you have no alternative."[102]

Even though Heurich was wealthy and could have retired comfortably, the brewery continued making ice, which Heurich sold to both Congress and the Supreme Court. The ice business was not a big moneymaker, but it did allow Heurich to continue providing employment to his workers. Moreover, Heurich had been active his entire life, and he preferred work to a leisurely retirement. It appeared that he had made the last batch of Senate beer ever and that Heurich was permanently retired as one of the senior businessmen of the city. Given the hostility shown to him during the First World War, this was a remarkable turnaround. Heurich had, however, had spent several decades building a solid reputation as a local businessman in Washington, and once the hysteria

One of the huge sheets of ice produced in the brewery's ice plant (Library of Congress)

of 1917–18 had subsided, he would reclaim his place among the leading businessmen of the community. Of course, there was no longer any advantage for the local press in stirring up hostility against Heurich to sell papers. By 1919, anti–Communist panic had taken the place of anti–German hysteria when it came to selling papers and winning votes, and as a longtime large business owner, Heurich was a remarkably unconvincing "red."

Once the 18th Amendment was part of the Constitution, then what? Note that the 18th Amendment refers to "intoxicating liquors." What, legally, is an "intoxicating liquor"? That is where the Volstead Act comes in. There was hope, especially on the part of brewers and wine makers, that Congress would define "intoxicating" as 3.2 percent alcohol by weight. This would allow some beer and wine. Andrew Volstead (R–MN) had other ideas. A dedicated Prohibitionist, Volstead was chair of the House Judiciary Committee. His bill, the Volstead Act, defined "intoxicating" as ½ of 1 percent alcohol by weight. Congress passed his bill by large majorities. It was vetoed by Wilson, largely on technical grounds, but Congress overrode the veto. The main part of Volstead's law read "no person shall manufacture, sell, barter, transport, import, export, deliver, or furnish any intoxicating liquor except as authorized by this act." Note that it did not ban consumption. There were provisions for alcohol use for religious ceremonies, including Christian communion and Jewish ceremonies. Alcohol could also be obtained by prescription from a doctor or dentist. The country went "dry" officially on January 16, 1920. Amelia vented to her diary, "This is the last day before prohibition goes into effect and my blood boils to think that we have to suffer such treatment in our own country." Heurich waited, hoping that some-day Prohibition would end and he'd be able to sell his beers again. In the meantime, his brewery continued making ice, and his alcoholic apple drink remained aging in the cellars.[103]

7

Rebirth and the Final Act: 1921–1945

Heurich's brewery closed, but the equipment remained intact, just in case Prohibition ended. The ice plant remained open, selling to local customers, including the Supreme Court, and Heurich still went to work in his office at the brewery to take care of his other businesses. Meanwhile, the Heuriches' children were entering adulthood. Christian Jr. who went by Chris, was attending college. Anita and Karla were both in their teens. Amelia's diary is filled with entries worrying about them, not always with good reason, although some issues did arise. Chris graduated from high school and began attending Wharton in Philadelphia. It had been common for the sons of brewers to train to work in their fathers' businesses, but with the coming of Prohibition, the Heuriches instead sent their son to a business school. Wharton was the first business school in the United States, founded with a donation from Joseph Wharton in 1881. Ironically, it was created to teach the skills needed to run a business in a college setting, replacing the traditional apprentice system of the type in which Heurich Senior had experienced.

Chris struggled at school. He had really wanted to attend the Naval Academy, but was sent to Wharton instead, and the curriculum did not fit his natural interests, which bent more toward science than business.[1] Amelia's diary records getting notices from the school that their son was not doing well in all his classes. Amelia tried to keep a tight rein on her son. She complained when he did not write regularly, normal enough for the parent of a college student, but in April 1920 she noted that she received Chris's seventy-second letter. She was not only counting his letters, but apparently expected several a week.[2] Still, Amelia sent him "a good strong letter for not sending his laundry and for not writing to me as he should." She even tried to call him, noting that she "tried to get him on the phone, tried from 5 until 9—could not get him." She had Christian Senior write their son to tell him to write to his mother more often. "Am so worried about him," Amelia wrote. "O, if the good spirits would stand by him—I have asked them."[3] Chris failed some classes but returned the next fall nonetheless. Always interested in sports, he joined the football team. When he helped his father run the brewery after Prohibition, the younger Heurich made sure that they had successful company teams to represent them, especially in baseball and basketball. He joined a fraternity, Alpha Sigma Phi, and the Capital City Club for students from Washington.[4] When he came down with the "grippe" (the flu), Amelia drove to Philadelphia with meals made by the family cook.[5]

In early 1921, Chris became engaged to Dorothy Ake, a student at Drexel Institute. This caused a family crisis, as neither of his parents was happy with his decision. Amelia was beside herself: "[I] am so down cast & hurts me to think my boy whom I had placed

The Heurich family, circa 1920. From left to right: Anita, Chris, Karla, Christian, Amelia. They are in front of the Grant desk (courtesy Jan King Evans Houser).

such high confidence in should do anything against my wishes." She continued, "What does that idiot of a boy think only 19 years & two months old. Why Christian is only a baby. He has no experience what so ever—does not know the girls their intrigues—shams, etc." Amelia and her brother wrote letters to the young man, apparently to dissuade him. It must have worked. Heurich was engaged to another young woman the next year.[6]

Worries about Chris were not limited to his mother. In one of his scrapbooks, Heurich pasted a clipping of a 1922 article written by Bertie Charles Forbes, founder of *Forbes* magazine. Titled "Sons of Rich Men Carry On: Instances Pointed by Forbes," the article reassured readers that the popular conception that wealthy men's sons "rarely amount to much" was false: "I do not doubt whether the sons of rich men as a whole do not make quite as credible a business record as the majority of nonrich sons." Perhaps Heurich kept the clipping to reassure himself as Chris struggled with his coursework at Wharton.[7]

Amelia's diary is a mixture of treating her growing family as children, yet sometimes writing proudly of their growing up. In the midst of the turmoil over Chris's engagement, she noted that thirteen-year-old Karla and some friends had a dance in the mansion's conservatory: "It was a beautiful sight to see the boys and girls dance." She let the girls go to the movies, although she complained bitterly to her diary, "I do not like the 'movies' as they are often called because the pictures are often very immoral."[8] The children could have parties and dances in the conservatory, an airy large room with walls designed to look like bark. The conservatory had a glass roof until 1922. After the Knickerbocker

Above: The Conservatory as it looks today (courtesy the Heurich House Museum). *Below:* The doll named Michael, which was used to provide a fourteenth person at the table so that thirteen would not be seated for dinner. Photograph by Mark Benbow (courtesy the Heurich House Museum).

Theater disaster in January 1922—following a record twenty-two-inch snowfall, the theater roof collapsed, killing ninety-eight people—a stronger roof replaced the old glass one. Amelia was, as her family remembered, a worrier.[9]

Amelia picked her children's clothes when they went shopping, but then complained how much she hated all the shopping she had to do. She ran the Heurich household, which is clear not only from her diary entries, but from the oral histories collected from the family. The family sat at the dinner table in specific spots, Christian at one end, Amelia at the other where she could keep an eye on the servants. The children sat in the order of their ages, the youngest nearest Amelia. The dining room had a doll, named Michael, that was used as the fourteenth "person" for dinner if there were an unlucky thirteen people seated. While Amelia managed her children and the servants, and fussed over them (a nephew later wrote that "she had the best of intentions but could come on too strong without realizing it"[10]), she had little control over the physical aspects of the house. Christian forbad her to change anything in the house, which had been decorated by his late second wife, Matilda. The home at the farm in Maryland, however, was Amelia's to do with as she wished.[11]

Amelia and her husband both found some comfort in Spiritualism, still highly popular in the United States. Amelia, as already noted, expressed her belief in spirits numerous times in her diary, and repeatedly reported hearing "knocks" that she often interpreted as messages from Anna Marguerite, her infant daughter who died in 1904. In 1922 Amelia went to see Arthur Conan Doyle appear at the National Theater, where he gave a presentation titled "The Proofs of Immortality." Doyle was not only a famous author, but a firm believer in Spiritualism. The proceeds from his talks went to sponsor "psychical research." Amelia may have found comfort in his talk, especially as she still mourned Anna Marguerite. To a full house, Doyle declared that in the next world after death, every person has an "ethereal body, the exact duplicate of the earthly body." "The passage from life to death" is without pain, and rather pleasant, being followed by a three-day coma, from which the dead awakens in the life beyond. Life after death was, he reassured Amelia and the rest of his audience, "strangely like this life on earth, except much happier."[12] The next year the Heuriches commissioned Baltimore sculptor and German-American Hans Schuler to build a bronze and marble fountain in the mansion's conservatory in Anna Marguerite's memory.[13]

Amelia was not the only member of the family to need such comfort. In late 1918 she recorded in her diary: "Christian went to see Mrs. Warneke, a medium. Christian came home very much pleased. Papa came and did most of the talking. Papa, Marguerite, Tante, Tante Jacobsen, Capt. Jacobsen, 2d Mrs. Heurich and many others came. They all told him that beer will soon be brewed again which we sincerely hope."[14] "Mrs. Warneke" was for years a popular medium in Washington, with a list of clientele that included the powerful (she was Clara Barton's favorite) as well as the average local resident. She set up her practice in 1899 under the aegis of "The Educational and Religious Society of Spiritualists," which met at Schmidt's Hall, a popular meeting spot for local organizations.[15] In early 1900 she was the subject of one of a series of exposes published by the *Evening Star* revealing local mediums as frauds. She worked in partnership with a "Professor J. Emmer, Jr.," in producing "Spirit Photographs." The customer, or the mark depending upon your perspective, could have his photograph taken with the spirits of his deceased loved ones surrounding him. As Emmer told a reporter, "Spirits are like mortals, they love to have their pictures taken." Mrs. Warneke would contact those on the "other side" so they would know when and where to show up for the photo in Emmer's studio. Mrs. Warneke also held regular séances for a small fee in the evenings. While the description of her holding a séance was written in 1900, Heurich probably experienced much the same thing when he visited later:

> The price is 25 cents, and I contributed a shining quarter, which fell with a ring among the many others that had gone before. It was 7:45 exactly when the door was closed and the medium, who had been flirting with the spirits now for some fifteen or twenty minutes and had made all sorts of conversation for the benefit of a gentleman near her, arose and left the room. "She is going out into the cold air for the purpose of getting a rapid change of temperature before going into a trance," said a lady nearby in explanation of her disappearance. This was the signal for the medium's daughter to hand around the little wicker basket which does duty as an ornament when not pressed into service

as a collection basket. Everybody responded willingly, and I counted $7.25 in the treasury. Ten minutes perhaps elapsed before the medium reappeared. She carried a long red silk handkerchief In her hand and took her seat in the corner opposite me. This red silk handkerchief was the open sesame to Spiritville. She drew the silk handkerchief, with a Delsarte movement, through her fingers and closed her eyes.... The exercises opened with a hymn. It was "Rock of Ages." ... The medium closed her eyes a moment, snapped her fingers, threw her head to one side and then commenced. She selected the female representative of *The Star* to begin with, and said she saw a woman standing over her. It was the form of her mother, and she was reaching for the little bundle she held in her hand and was saying: "Child, that is your mother's picture in the lower left-hand corner [of a "spirit photograph"]? It is not very clear, I know, but I am not a strong spirit yet, and cannot come to you in the form that I will be able to after a while. I have brought baby with me, too, but he has run away, and you will recognize his dear little face in the upper part of the picture. I am very happy, child." She said that "child" much as the heroine does on the stage when she exclaims, "Me che-Ild!" Then she went on to tell about how another woman with gray hair was also present and talking, and she wanted to tell her to continue her work, that everything would go right. It was Mrs. Southworth,[16] for she was her guiding spirit. She was to finish Mrs. Southworth's life work on this earth.

The young woman, one of the two *Star* reporters at the séance working undercover, reported afterwards that her mother was still alive, and that, being unmarried, she had no children.[17]

The Heuriches' interest in spiritualism was not uncommon for the period. The Victorian Age was fascinated by the supernatural and a search for answers that went beyond established religious channels. This interest continued into the twentieth century and experienced a rebirth after the First World War, at least in part because of the trauma of so many deaths from the war. For example, Sir Arthur Conan Doyle had been interested in Spiritualism since the 1880s. But it was his son Kingsley's death in 1918 that seems to have "solidified his belief." Within two weeks of his son's death, Doyle had "contacted [him] through a medium."[18] The famous writer found solace through Spiritualism, contacting his son, his late wife, and other loved ones. No doubt Amelia and Christian felt the same way contacting their late family members, especially their lost infant daughter.

Beginning in 1922 the Heuriches returned to their prewar habit of traveling to Europe most summers. That year they sailed on the *Rotterdam*, the Holland-America Line ship on which they were originally supposed to return home in late August 1914. Before the war the Heuriches always took one of the big luxurious German liners. However, Germany had been forced to give up its famed ocean liners to the Allies after the war as reparations. For example, the *Imperator*, which the Heuriches had taken to Europe in 1914, had been given to Britain and was renamed RMS *Berengaria*. The *Kaiserin Augusta Victoria*, on which the Heuriches traveled in 1912 and 1913, went to Canada and became the RMS *Empress of Scotland*. The German shipping lines HAPAG and Norddeutscher-Lloyd were left with but a handful of small, slow ships. They began rebuilding their fleets, and in 1922 they were readmitted into the North Atlantic Passenger Conference, which controlled Atlantic shipping including the routes and rates. Without membership in the conference, the German lines had a difficult time operating. Once they were readmitted they could again begin to compete, but it would take time to rebuild their fleets. In the meantime, rather than travel on one of the other British lines, the Heuriches took Dutch liners, although the 1922 trip, in Heurich's words, "brought back painful memories ... of the fearful, anxious trip we had made away from war-torn Europe with the same line in 1914." The painful memories came flooding back, despite the better conditions in 1922. Happily there were no giant rats skulking about outside their cabin this trip.[19]

The family landed in Rotterdam and took a train to Bremen. Their experiences in Europe that summer made the 1922 trip one of their most memorable, but also one of the most disturbing. In July 1922 when the Heuriches arrived, Germany was in crisis. Switching from a wartime to a peacetime economy was difficult for all the belligerents. The United States had a short but sharp depression in 1919–1920. Britain went through a boom in 1919–1920, then unemployment rose to over 10 percent and remained there. Germany, however, because it had lost the war, had even less room to make policy decisions than the victors. The German government could not choose to demobilize its military slowly, nor could they phase out military spending on weapons contracts. Without job prospects, the veterans were returned to the civilian life in large numbers. Paramilitary groups of disillusioned veterans fought each other in the streets of Germany's major cities. In 1922, the left-wing parties that controlled the government began to lose control as the German right began its ascension. The German foreign minister, Walter Rathenau, was assassinated in late June by young reactionaries. Allied forces, including French, British, Belgian, and American troops, still occupied parts of western Germany. Finally, the 1921 London Schedule of Payments required Germany to pay 132 billion gold marks (approximately $33,000,000) in war reparations.[20] The combination of the sick economy, the reparations, and the political crisis led to the hyperinflation of 1921–1923. When the Heuriches arrived in July 1922, Amelia noted that a dollar was worth 433 marks, compared to 90 in 1921. It quickly got much worse. By the end of July 1922, 670 marks equaled one U.S. dollar. By August one dollar was equal to 2,000 marks. By November of that year a dollar could buy 100,000 marks. A new form of currency, the *Notgeld*, was introduced, and the hyperinflation only accelerated. By the autumn of 1923, one dollar would was worth well over four billion paper marks. The Heuriches discovered just what it was like to come visit a nation in such a state of crisis. It must have made an impression on Heurich. A copy of a chart marking the inflation of 1923 is pasted in one of his scrapbooks. It records that as of November 30, 1923, one American dollar was worth 6,666,666,666,667 marks.[21]

Heurich remembered that as they traveled to Meiningen they saw "many undernourished people—consequences of the war." They rented a car and traveled all over southern Germany—Schmalkalden, Oberhof, Nuremberg, and Munich. They canceled the planned visit to Karlsbad, in Heurich's words, because of "extraordinary regulations; for example in making a trip from Karlsbad to Nuernburg [*sic*] we were told that we must be back in Karlsbad within twenty four hours—otherwise we could not reenter the city." The resort town was now part of the new nation of Czechoslovakia, and there were already tensions between Germany and the Czechs over the treatment of the German-speaking population in Czech territory. In her diary Amelia complained, "It was not homelike in Carlsbad [*sic*] as in former years things have changed so much. The Czechs are terrible, rough people." Back in Germany, they saw the Oberammergau Passion Play again, the third time for Heurich. It was supposed to be held in 1920, but was delayed because of the lingering effects of the war. The official greetings were warm. Amelia noted in her diary that they drove to Jüchsen, Hain, and Römhild, where "we were showered with flowers and everywhere we had to have coffee and cake." Part of this was no doubt because Heurich was a favored native son. But his being an American was probably not unwelcome either. American businesses were finding opportunity in Germany at that point, and investment was increasing. However, more than once while they traveled, they ran into angry crowds, even in Heurich's home territory. First, while driving to

Murnau vor Oberammergau   LEONHARD NODER 1922

A postcard from Oberammergau shows the town (courtesy Jan King Evans Houser).

Heidelberg, and then on a trip to Meiningen in Thuringia, "we were greeted by a number of workers shaking their fists with cries of 'You robbers, you racketeers.'" On a trip to Coblenz they escaped being physically attacked as well as verbally. Their chauffeur tried to pass a stuck hay cart in a narrow village street. There wasn't enough room, and the car tore a shutter off a house and damaged the hay cart. Bystanders began to yell at the car's occupants, including 79-year-old Heurich and his wife. "Within minutes there were hundreds of people gathered around with the same threatening attitude." Heurich and his wife got out of the car to try to calm the crowd. A man from the crowd convinced them to get back in, then told the chauffeur to start the car and get out of there.[22] Heurich also saw foreign troops in Germany, Allied occupation forces. In Wiesbaden was "full of French military, so the stay there," Heurich wrote, "was not especially pleasant. Amelia was blunt: "We do not like the French," she wrote in her diary entry for August 20. "They are certainly treating the Germans miserably. We are sure they will get their just dues someday."[23]

Anger against German industrialists was rapidly growing all though the country, and anyone who looked like a wealthy manufacturer, such as Heurich, could be a target of that anger. Workers' wages were rising, but not as fast as inflation. Meanwhile corporations' profits also continued to rise, and many workers began to believe that their employers were using the inflation to shift their tax burden downward. Companies made profits, but because of the high inflation, paid the taxes with much depreciated money. German Minister of Commerce and Industry Eduard Hamm sent "a confidential memorandum to the leading trade associations and business organizations of Bavaria sharply critical of what he considered to be excess industrial profits." Stockholders were benefiting because they could buy additional stocks at much reduced prices. Hamm criticized the businessmen for taking care of their stockholders while ignoring the plight of their own employees. Hamm's letter was not well received. Businessmen responded that it was the merchants who were causing inflation and profiting from it, and that businessmen were supposed to take care of their stockholders first.[24] Heurich was the victim of popular outrage over such high-handed attitudes towards the suffering of the average German. Traveling in a limousine, undoubtedly dressed well, he looked like a wealthy industrialist. Of course, he was a wealthy industrialist, just not one operating in Germany.

While in Germany the family received word that Christian Jr., now twenty-one years old, did not pass his exams at Wharton. His father wrote to the dean asking that Chris be allowed to continue his studies. The dean apparently accepted, because on August 29 the young man sailed from Rotterdam on the *Nieuw Amsterdam* by himself, returning to the United States to retake his exams. He may not have been too upset to have to leave. The Heurich children, Chris, seventeen-year-old Anita and fifteen-year-old Karla, were apparently not enjoying their trip. Amelia told her diary, "The children are not satisfied, they would rather have remained home."[25]

While the family did get to visit relatives, it was perhaps the most unpleasant trip the family took to date, aside from their traumatic 1914 journey. They returned home, setting sail on the *Rotterdam* on September 12, Heurich's eightieth birthday. Arriving in New York ten days later, they took the train to D.C., then returned to their farm. A few days later Anita went to Baltimore to begin her studies at Goucher, a women's college in downtown Baltimore. Chris passed his exams and graduated with a bachelor's in economics from Wharton School of Finance and Commerce at the University of Pennsylvania. He then began to work for his father at the brewery, which was then essentially an ice plant.[26]

Now entering his eighties, Heurich seemed to be retired from brewing. When Heurich was about to turn 84, his ice business and land investments still gave him a stable financial base, and the American economy was booming, so the Heuriches splurged and explored. The 1922 trip to Germany had been a disturbing reminder of how badly Germany had suffered during and after the war. The Heuriches returned to making their yearly European trips in 1925, traveling every year through 1932. Having taken Hamburg-Amerika ships for decades, they switched to Norddeutscher-Lloyd. The 1925 voyage was also the first trip in which all three of their children did not accompany them, although Chris joined them at Southampton for the trip home. Chris and Anita were in their twenties, and Karla turned eighteen. The daughters were going off to school and Chris was engaged. His fiancée, Connie Young, accompanied them on the 1925 trip. They took the *Columbus* to Bremen. Laid down before the war, the ship was not finished until 1924, when she was the pride of the German passenger fleet. Christian remembered the trip as "the most beautiful we ever had." Once in Europe, Christian, who was still in the habit of "taking the cure," returned to Wiesbaden. The family visited Haina to see where Christian had been born and to visit the children's home he had provided his hometown. They also visited Paris and went to see some of the battlefields from the recent war. Heurich did not note his feelings in his memoirs, but Amelia recorded in her diary that they visited the Belleau Woods American cemetery and a German cemetery with "black crosses on graves. Heurich noted when someone said that the Germans were rascals, 'yes, clever rascals.'" Amelia said that "seeing this makes me feel like forming an organization of mothers to oppose war at all times."[27] On December 5, Chris married Connie Young at the Baptist Church of Evangelism in Narberth, near Philadelphia. As a wedding present, Christian gave his son and his bride a home near Massachusetts Avenue, not too far from the Heurich mansion. After a honeymoon in Florida, they returned to Washington, where Chris continued working for his father.[28]

Enjoying an active retirement, Heurich continued making his yearly European trips throughout the rest of the 1920s, but the family group accompanying him grew ever smaller as his children married and began lives and families of their own. The family's 1926 trip proved to be the most memorable as an enjoyable vacation. They sailed on the *Columbus* again, the second of four round trips they'd make on this luxurious liner. What made the 1926 trip so unforgettable was a side trip from Germany to the north to see Iceland, Norway, and Sweden. Their "Polar Trip" was the only such elaborate trip the Heuriches took, as opposed to their regular visits to Europe. In 1927 they made the first trip to Europe without any of their children. They took the *Columbus* for the third straight year, and this trip they visited Haina to see the inn where Heurich was born, and to see his sister Emilie Heurich Rust, who lived nearby. They also took side trips into Switzerland and into northern Italy. They went to Domodossola, Milano, Verona, and Venice, and traveled through the Brenner Pass to Innsbruck. Increasingly Heurich spent these trips reminiscing. This time he told his traveling companions that in 1862 he had walked "from Vienna to Graz. Through northern Italy to Milano, and then through the Brenner Pass to Innsbruck."[29]

On June 21, 1928, the Heuriches' middle child, Anita, married Charles Eckles shortly before her twenty-third birthday. Eckles worked for the Department of Agriculture. The wedding took place in the front parlor of the Heurich mansion, and, as he had with his

Heurich visits his sister Emilie Heurich Rust in Germany in 1927. Heurich is at the far left, next to Amelia, and then his sister. The others are unidentified. Emilie died in 1928 (courtesy Jan King Evans Houser).

son earlier, Heurich gave the newlyweds a new home in the expensive neighborhoods of northwest Washington. That summer Heurich left for Europe with his wife and her sister Anna. This was the smallest group Heurich had traveled to Europe with since he and Amelia had begun having children in 1901. Once again they traveled on the *Columbus* to Bremen. They stopped in Wiesbaden so the eighty-five-year-old Heurich could take the cure. While there he climbed the Neroberg, a popular site for climbing. He "made a false step" on the descent and injured his leg. In his 1934 memoirs he lamented that his leg was never the same again. He also grieved that the Vienna he knew as a young man was gone. Heurich remembered that "the conditions we found there affected us deeply." While the Great Depression had not yet hit, the Austrian First Republic (1919–1934) was unstable, with both right-wing and left-wing paramilitary forces fighting in the streets, including the July Revolt of 1927. When the Heuriches visited the next summer, the city was still the center of unrest and political violence.[30]

The Heuriches continued their annual trips even as the Depression hit, traveling on the brand-new *Bremen* in 1929 and the *Bremen*'s sister ship *Europa* in 1930, both of which captured the coveted Blue Riband for the fastest trip west to New York. Each trip they visited Heurich's childhood hometowns, where he was always honored. In 1929 he inaugurated the local Steinburg Museum, which focuses on the region's prehistoric inhabitants.[31] In 1930 Heurich was invited by Römhild's Mayor Griebel to come see the German army maneuvers. President Hindenburg would be there as well, and Heurich and Amelia were introduced to the German leader.

The 1930 maneuvers in Römhild were notable because by 1930 the German Army was dominated by younger officers who were sympathetic to the Nazis. Several young officers went on trial in September 1930 for spreading Nazi propaganda against the existing Weimar government. They were found guilty of treason and sentenced to eighteen months in prison. They were not alone in their dissatisfaction. A British military attaché reported in September that the officers "tolerate the Weimar Constitution and all that it stands for only so long as the field-marshal [Hindenburg] remains as the … Head of State."[32] This was just one sign of the storm that was coming. Germany held elections on September 14, 1930. The Nazi Party polled over six million votes, 18 percent of the total, an increase from 2½ percent in 1928. Nazi Party representation in the Reichstag jumped from twelve seats to one hundred and seven. This made them the second-largest party after the Social Democrats.[33]

In the midst of this increased support for the German right wing, Heurich was presented to the German president, who remarked that they were both "honorary citizens of this town." Hindenburg said to the elderly brewer, "You are a loyal German. In your fidelity you are an example for Germans." "Hundreds of people looked on from the rooftops" to witness the reception as the mayor toasted Hindenburg: "To His Excellency, the President of the Republic and Field Marshall von Hindenburg, the first in war, the first in peace, and the first in the hearts of all Germans, three cheers!" It's perhaps not too cynical to wonder if the mayor based his toast on the famous toast for George Washington in part because of his famous German-American guest. From 1:00 until 4:00 they watched as the army went through its paces. Afterwards the Heuriches drove to Haina to see the inn where Heurich was born almost ninety years before. It was "exceptionally busy," he remembered, and they met some U.S. Army officers who were there as well to observe the maneuvers.[34]

In March 1931 the Heuriches' youngest daughter, Karla, married Charles King, a

Heurich (at left in back of the group) waits with other dignitaries to greet President Hindenburg. Amelia stands to Heurich's left. The others are unidentified. Römhild, Hindenburg Parade (9.09.1930 Bildnr.: a334666 arkivi.de. Used with permission).

1928 graduate of the U.S. Military Academy (West Point). They were married in the mansion's front parlor. The Kings would live first in Hawaii, at Schofield Barracks where Charles was posted. The Heuriches' three children were now all married, with homes of their own, and starting their own families. Once again that year the Heuriches traveled to Europe in the summer, and as before, they visited Römhild. Once again they traveled on the finest liner in the Norddeutscher-Lloyd, now the *Europa*. Despite this luxury, even the Heuriches could tell that the Depression was getting worse and worse. Heurich noted that some of his tenants were having trouble paying their rent.[35]

In 1932 Heurich celebrated his ninetieth birthday, not in Römhild, but at the spa in Wiesbaden. The spa wanted to make the most of the celebration, promoting the man who had taken the cure for forty years and, while ninety, looked as if he were only fifty. There would be a big public ceremony with speeches by local dignitaries. Heurich refused, but there was a ceremony anyway. He noted that the book "would become too lengthy if I report all the details, but I must include the pretty young ladies who kissed the young ninety-year-old!" Hindenburg sent Heurich a telegram including "best greetings in grateful appreciation of your loyal fidelity to the old homeland." The phrasing must have bothered Heurich as he responded graciously, but noted, "Indeed, my heart beats for the old homeland, but my duty belongs to the United States."[36]

Even with the Depression getting worse and worse, Heurich had enough real estate investments to live comfortably. His health was generally good, but with a few issues to be expected in a ninety-year-old. In 1927 Heurich had his teeth removed and replaced by dentures. He was still walking, using the stairs in his mansion instead of an elevator,

Wedding of Karla Heurich and Charles King, March 1931 (courtesy Jan King Evans Houser).

Das junge Jahr und das Ableben depicts the Old Year welcoming the New Year. The artist, Detlef Sammann (1857–1938), was a German immigrant who also painted murals at the White House for the Harrison administration (courtesy the Heurich House Museum).

and only being driven to his office rather than walking because Amelia insisted. He was somewhat hard of hearing, and found that he sometimes understood spoken German better than English. Because of Prohibition, he had to give up drinking a couple bottles of Senate Beer during his weekly game of skat with friends (the beer slightly warmed on a handy radiator), so he switched to Valley Forge near-beer, made by Adam Scheidt in Pennsylvania.[37] He maintained a lively interest in other matters as well. The ceiling of the mansion's parlor featured a fresco with several cavorting young women in various stages of undress. Titled *Das junge Jahr und das Ableben*, it depicts the Old Year welcoming the New Year. According to one family story, he would sometimes lie on the floor, looking up to enjoy the view with the pretty girls.[38] In short, he was in good enough health to continue enjoying retirement, even one forced on him by Prohibition. In 1932, however, Prohibition was increasingly unpopular, and the movement to find a way to end it was growing in strength. In the 1932 presidential election, incumbent Republican Herbert Hoover supported attempting to make Prohibition permanent, while the Democratic nominee, New York Governor Franklin Delano Roosevelt, promised to support efforts to end it. With Hoover catching the brunt of the blame for the Depression and Roosevelt's promise for a New Deal, the latter won in a landslide. When Prohibition began in 1920, Amelia raged in her diary that she hoped the Democrats never again regained office. Now they were back in office with a promise to repeal the so-called Noble Experiment.[39]

The problem for repeal advocates was that the 18th Amendment established Prohibition as the law of the United States and no amendment had ever been repealed. However, there was an opening for some reform even without changing the Constitution. The 18th Amendment concerned "intoxicating" beverages, but it took the Volstead Act to define the term "intoxicating" and otherwise set restrictions on what was allowed and what was illegal. Throughout the 1920s there were suggestions not to repeal the 18th Amendment, but to modify the Volstead Act, increasing the definition of intoxicating from .5 percent ABV to 3.2 percent ABV in the hopes of allowing low-alcohol beer and wine. This seemed to some to be the only workable solution. After all, overturning the 18th Amendment seemed to be impossible. Thirty-six states would have to ratify a new amendment, which meant that if just one legislative house in each of just thirteen states rejected a new amendment, it would fail. To put that into perspective, there were 95 state legislative houses (Nebraska has a unicameral legislature). If only thirteen of those ninety-five bodies voted "no"—merely 14 percent of the total—then an amendment would not be ratified. A small Dry minority could, theoretically, vote to keep the entire country dry.

Heurich had not given up hope that Prohibition would be at least modified. On March 4, 1929, the day before Herbert Hoover was inaugurated as president, Heurich took out a full-page advertisement in DC's newspaper to decry the dry regime. He did not hold back; his strong feelings were made abundantly clear:

> There is no such thing as prohibition, except in name; it is a theory—not a fact; it is a grim farce … a tragedy as complete as was ever conceived in distorted imaginations and as poisonous as the vile stuff it has thrust upon a normal, healthy people.

Heurich decried the loss of billions in tax revenue to the government, as well as the wasted money spent on enforcement. In 1927 General Motors co-founder William C. Durant had offered a $25,000 prize for the best way to enforce the 18th Amendment. Heurich noted that many of the entries were excessive, including the use of torture, abandoning juries, allowing only Protestants to enforce the law, and using the Army and Navy to enforce it. Other entries suggested that churches should promote the law, a suggestion which must have amazed Heurich; one reason he was not fond of many Protestant churches was their support of Prohibition. Heurich offered no specific solutions, but noted the failure of Prohibition to reduce crime and to keep people from drinking hard liquors. He called for "Temperance" and held up the old German beer garden as a model.[40]

By 1932, however, the anti-Prohibition forces had a new strategy. The Constitution allows the states to each call a state convention to consider constitutional amendments. Those conventions would be chosen by state-wide vote. In other words, it was possible to bypass the state legislatures. The 21st Amendment, which repealed the 18th, passed Congress in February 1933 and went to the states, which began holding elections to determine whether to hold a state convention. Eight states took no action.[41] North Carolina rejected calling a convention. This left thirty-nine states to consider the amendment, thirty-six of which would have ratify it.[42]

The 21st Amendment has two main parts:

> Section 1. The eighteenth article of amendment to the Constitution of the United States is hereby repealed.
> Section 2. The transportation or importation into any State, Territory, or possession of the United States for delivery or use therein of intoxicating liquors, in violation of the laws thereof, is hereby prohibited.

The second section allowed those states that wished to continue Prohibition to do so, thus undercutting a potential Dry argument against this amendment.

While the states were considering the 21st Amendment, Congress finally got rid of Volstead's handiwork. In March 1933, the Volstead Act was replaced by the Cullen-Harrison Act, which redefined "intoxicating" as 3.2 percent ABV. This made light beer and wine legal. Heurich, then ninety years old, was welcomed at the White House, where he thanked President Franklin Roosevelt for signing the bill, a far cry from the elderly man's treatment as an enemy alien in 1917. However, the law still left D.C. dry, at least until the 1917 Sheppard Act was repealed. The District Wine and Beer Law was signed by President Roosevelt on April 5, 1933, just a bit over twenty-four hours before the midnight, April 7, start of "New Beers' Day." The law was passed and signed quickly. The Senate passed it on Tuesday, April 4, by a vote of 42–34. The House passed it 131–65 on Wednesday, and Roosevelt signed it two hours later. Thirty-two hours later, District residents started buying legal 3.2 percent beer, as did residents in Maryland and eighteen other states. None of it was Heurich's. His beer was not yet ready to drink. Baltimore breweries filled the gap as beer began arriving by truck at 2:00 a.m. It was served first in the White House, then around the city.[43]

In December 1933, the 21st Amendment to the Constitution was ratified. Maryland ratified it on October 28, and Virginia on October 25. Of the thirty-nine states holding conventions, the amendment was approved by all but one—South Carolina. The 18th Amendment was repealed and it became legal to make and sell higher-alcohol content beverages again in most states. Both Maryland and Virginia allowed retail outlets as well as licensed bars and restaurants to sell beer and wine (Virginia set up state liquor stores to sell hard liquors), thus restoring much of Heurich's pre–1917 market.

Heurich originally planned not to return to the beer business, but anticipation of a tremendous demand for beer and the desire to remain active convinced him otherwise. Besides, by reopening he could claim that the Prohibitionists had only closed his brewery temporarily. Heurich refused to rush his product to market. It would have to be aged properly, so customers would have to wait. The huge brewery on Water Street once again began to hum with activity and employees began to work the enormous vats.[44]

First, however, Heurich had to deal with the sixty thousand gallons he still had of Liberty Apple Champagne, the originally nonalcoholic drink he had made in 1917 that had fermented. Its alcohol content was 6 percent ABV, too high to sell in 1933, but it took up a lot of space in his lagering cellars. He tried to find a buyer, but the only offers he had received were from vinegar companies, and Heurich had too much pride to see some of his product turned into vinegar. He could hold onto it and wait for the 21st Amendment to pass, allowing him to sell products with a higher alcohol content, but the passage of the amendment was still uncertain. In the meantime, there was a market for beer that he could meet. Reluctantly, he dumped the rest of the Liberty Apple Champagne into the D.C. sewer system, sighing, "It was an enormous loss."[45]

While Heurich lagered his beer, breweries around the nation began to reopen, many rushing their products to market. Parties were held at breweries waiting for 12:01 a.m., April 7, "New Beers' Day." Police escorts accompanied brewery delivery trucks making their first legal deliveries in twelve years. About 750 breweries opened, most of which had been in business before Prohibition, although a few were new. This was still significantly fewer than the 1,200 that had been closed by Prohibition. Five breweries had been in operation in Washington when Prohibition began, but only the Abner-Drury Brewery

Top: The west end of the National Mall in 1934. The Heurich Brewery is visible at the upper right. By this time government buildings (including the "temporary" buildings along the right side) and memorials are getting ever closer to the brewery and the industrial area is being slowly squeezed out (Library of Congress). *Bottom:* The Heurich brewery in the mid–1930s. From the brewery tour pamphlet, "A See Trip through a Great Brewery," circa 1937 (author collection).

Above: The fermenting vats. When they were replaced, some of these vats were used at Heurich's Bellevue farm as swimming pools. From the brewery tour pamphlet, "A See Trip through a Great Brewery," circa 1937. *Left:* The beer kettles in the Heurich Brewery. From the brewery tour pamphlet, "A See Trip through a Great Brewery," circa 1937 (both photographs, author collection).

immediately reopened. They lasted only a few years, however. Apparently, they rushed their beer to market while it was still "green" and acquired a reputation for selling bad beer. John Fowler owned the old Arlington Brewery across the Potomac in Rosslyn and had been using the facility to make Cherry Smash soda. He placed advertisements in local papers offering stock in a new Dixie Brewing Company, which would use the old brewery. Apparently the plans fell through, and Fowler continued making his sweet red soda instead. Heurich began selling his beer again on August 2, 1933, the sixtieth anniversary of his first brewery opening in D.C. back on 20th Street. He began by selling Heurich Lager, but soon began introducing more brands, including, at some point, Home Brew.[46]

Not everything went smoothly on Water Street. On August 18, 1933, only a couple of weeks after Heurich began reselling his beer, a fire broke out in the brewery. Since he had lost his 20th Street brewery to fire, this blaze must have given Heurich a horrible sense of *déjà vu*. The three-alarm fire began with an oil leak, and a spark from a workman's torch may have set the resulting oil pool alight. An engineer, no doubt seeing his job about to go up in flames at a time of 24 percent unemployment, saved the day by rushing into the smoke to turn off the leaking oil. There was little damage and the brewery continued to operate.[47]

More excitement fol-lowed. On October 5, 1933,

The aging vats, also made of wood. From the brewery tour pamphlet, "A See Trip through a Great Brewery," circa 1937 (author collection).

three armed men entered the brewery offices while a fourth waited in their car outside. With guns drawn (probably including some Tommy guns, given their habits at other robberies), one of the robbers grabbed the switchboard operator, throwing a coat over his head, and forcing him under a desk. They then forced the other brewery employees in the office to lie on the floor. The group's leader, Arthur "Big Dutch" Misunas, later testified, "I went up to the guy who had the money bag and told him to reach for the sky. I

The bottling line in the 1930s. From the brewery tour pamphlet, "A See Trip through a Great Brewery," circa 1937 (author collection).

had to tell him three times. But he reached." Misunas grabbed the bank bag containing a bit over $1600 and the gang fled. The thieves knew many of the city's police would be at Griffith Stadium for crowd control at the third game of the 1933 World Series between the Washington Senators and New York Giants, and used this to their advantage, escaping the city with the cash. Chris just missed the raid. As he approached the brewery, an engineer ran out shouting that there had been a robbery. He had been at Griffith Stadium watching the Senators defeat the Giants 4–0.[48]

The robbers were caught and convicted in late 1934. Members of the Tri-State gang operating between Philadelphia, Baltimore, and Richmond, they were, regionally at least, as infamous as John Dillinger. They had robbed Baltimore's Globe Brewery earlier in 1933 and, closer to Heurich, held up a U.S. Post Office truck at Union Station in December 1933. In the latter they shot and wounded a guard, but only managed to get away with a bag of useless canceled revenue stamps. They had also robbed a Federal Reserve truck in Richmond, killing a courier, but escaped with only worthless canceled checks. The two gang leaders were convicted and sentenced to death for this last crime, but escaped from jail and were on the run while the trial of their fellow gang members was held in D.C. for the Heurich robbery. Gang member Arthur "Big Dutch" Misunas, who led the Heurich raid, turned state's evidence in order to avoid the electric chair for his part in other robberies. After the trial, in which his two confederates were convicted, he visited the brewery, explained how he had planned the robbery, signed the brewery's guest book, and enjoyed a glass of beer.[49]

Not everything for Heurich in 1933 and 1934 was quite as exciting or disturbing. In September 1933, brewery employees presented Heurich with a silver cup for his 91st birthday. He was not shy about using his age to promote his product. Display ads in local newspapers noted, "To brew THE BEST has been the aim and achievement, for over 60 years, of Christian Heurich ... the 91-year-old manufacturer ... who has received the HIGHEST AWARDS, for Purity and Excellence, from the foremost authorities at home and abroad."[50] In May 1934, President Franklin Roosevelt dedicated a statue to William Jennings Bryan near the brewery. Sculpted by Gutzon Borglum, who created the faces on Mt. Rushmore, the statue of the famous prohibitionist stood with his back to the brewery, a position that may have made both the Dry three-time Democratic presidential nominee and the anti–Prohibition Republican brewer a bit more comfortable. The Bryan statue was taken down in 1961 to build the Theodore Roosevelt Bridge, the same project that doomed Heurich's brewery.[51]

Left: **Stacks of Heurich crates in the brewery in the mid–1930s. From the brewery tour pamphlet, "A See Trip through a Great Brewery," circa 1937 (author collection).**

Despite Heurich's high hopes, however, the market was not what the nation's brewers had expected. Demand for beer was far lower than before Prohibition. Many customers had gotten out of the habit of drinking beer, which was often dreadful during the dry years. Many former customers had switched to soft drinks and others had developed a taste for hard liquors in cocktails. Companies like Coca-Cola had no intention of giving up any market share to the brewers. Sales of soft drinks had tripled between 1911 and 1934. Moreover, between 1920 and 1933, soda manufacturers had access to the eyes and ears of consumers that was denied to brewers, distillers, and wineries. Radio had become a mass market, magazines were increasingly speaking to a national rather than regional audience, and billboards were popping up all along the new road systems, and they all carried advertisements for colas, ginger ale, root beer, and a wide variety of other soda pops. They would battle the brewers for every consumer dollar. Soft drinks also had an advantage with woman customers, as beer was associated with heavy-set men. Moreover, women's fashions had changed since the 1910s, and the new styles and cuts made it harder to hide a larger figure. Slim figures were popular, and all the pre-Prohibition advertisements about beer being "liquid bread" now came back to haunt the brewers. Beer was almost irrevocably associated with weight gain, an image problem sodas did not yet have. A few brewers tried to position their product as "non-fattening," but with little success.[52]

Moreover, improvements in bottling and shipping made between 1920 and 1933 meant that there was more competition for local brewers from out-of-town breweries. A few attempted early on to repeat the methods used by shipping breweries before 1919— shipping barrels of beer to be bottled at the destination—but most were able to ship bottles more efficiently and cheaply. The successful development of the beer can—first tested in Richmond, Virginia, by Krueger Brewing in January 1935—allowed beers to be shipped greater distances. The disposable bottle was introduced at about the same time. These new packages eliminated the need to return bottles for a deposit, making shipping longer distances from the brewery even easier, as well as making home consumption more convenient.

Locally, most of Heurich's Washington-area pre–1917 competitors never reopened, and the one that did, Abner-Drury, closed after only a few years. But the changed market meant that Heurich had far more breweries competing with him for the Washington market than before. Newspaper ads from the 1930s show breweries from Baltimore as well as Norristown, Northampton, and Philadelphia, Pennsylvania; from New Jersey; and from New York City entering the D.C. market, along with nationals like Schlitz and Pabst from Milwaukee and Anheuser-Busch from St. Louis. As a result, more breweries were competing for a shrunken market. One year into the era of legal beer, total national brewery capacity stood at 80,000,000 barrels annually, but sales were half that at best. Moreover, beer was increasingly becoming a product consumed at home, or at least in restaurants. Bars opened, but the old tied saloon was gone as new liquor laws now required an extra layer, the distributor, be inserted between brewer and customer. Distributors now bought the beer from the brewery and provided it to stores and retail outlets. That meant bars could switch between brands, or even sell multiple brands. It also meant if a brewer could not find a distributor to carry its beer, it couldn't get its product on the shelves to sell, and distributors were often under pressure from the large breweries to stop carrying the products of smaller rivals.[53]

To counter this changed environment, Heurich's ads emphasized his long ties to the city, an appeal to local pride in the face of so much new competition from outsiders. Finally, Washington was also growing quickly in the 1930s, driven by the many New Deal agencies, and then by the expansion of the U.S. government right before the Second World War. From 1930 to 1940 the city's population surged from 486,869 to 663,091, an increase of more than a third. Newcomers would not have any sentimental memories of Heurich's beers and may have wanted to consume products they remembered drinking back home. As a result of all these changes, Heurich, as did other brewers, had to try to simultaneously appeal to their old customers to return while winning new customers in a changed market. It was not intuitively obvious how to do that, and Heurich would try a plethora of new tactics, and new brands, in his quest for customers.

Of course the brewery's initial 1933 offerings were limited by the still-existing restrictions on alcohol content. The first product back on the market was a 3.2 percent ABV Heurich's Lager. Heurich followed by reintroducing additional brands. In early 1934 Heurich began to advertise his beer was at "pre-war strength," so it had more than 3.2 percent ABV. In December 1934, Heurich reintroduced his dark Maerzen beer, and in March 1934, Heurich Bock Beer was available. Finally, in December 1934, Heurich announced that his old flagship brand, Senate Beer, would be back on the market.[54] Senate Beer would remain the brewery's flagship brand until 1949. More brands and different forms and sizes of packaging would soon follow.

Heurich's newspaper advertisements emphasized Heurich Brewing's long history in the city. Their illustrations not only showed people in 1880s and 1890s attire, they were often set in historic D.C. locales. For example, one October 1934 copy showed early government "typists" sitting on the steps of the State, War, and Navy Building (now the Eisenhower Executive Office Building) enjoying Maerzen Beer. Others reminded readers

One of the "For Old Times' Sake" advertisements from October 25, 1934 (author collection).

Heurich advertisement from their "For Old Times' Sake" campaign, May 21, 1934. Note the dachshund in front (author collection).

of the old steam railway, a watering trough at 16th and Q Streets, local fire horses "Barney, Gene, and Tom," and the old Schuetzen Park. The latter choice was an interesting one, as it emphasized the former prominence of the local German community. Many of the ads also featured a dachshund, a hat-tip to Heurich's German heritage. The Heuriches owned numerous dachshunds over the years—Amelia leashed them to the railing at the top of the stairs on the second floor where they could bark at intruders—so perhaps their inclusion was simply because Heurich liked them.[55]

For the first few years after Prohibition's end, Heurich's ads often emphasized some familiar pre–Prohibition themes. Heurich's beers were a "tonic for health" and unmatched for "purity." In 1937 they used the slogan "Senate, The Beer That's Good For You." Other advertising themes were not particularly original. They showed a bottle or glass of Heurich's beer next to a lunch box, or next to food. They emphasized that Heurich was good to serve in the home, a return to the brewery's efforts from the 1910s with the short-lived "Home Brew," but one that was being copied by many breweries across the country. Companies like Heurich were aggressively marketing beer as appropriate for home consumption as opposed to at a bar, let alone, God forbid, a saloon. In 1936 Heurich was one of the few brewers to experiment with a half-gallon bottle of draft beer. Marketing it as something to take on a picnic, the advertisements called it "the modern growler" and noted that it sold for only forty cents. A twelve-ounce bottle of beer cost about fifteen cents (or two for a quarter), so this was a saving of about twenty-five cents, a nice cut in price during the Depression. This giant bottle seems not to have lasted long, but Heurich was clearly trying to locate any new market niche he could.[56]

In December 1938 Heurich introduced Senate Ale in a series of advertisements with an Olde English Christmas theme. Jolly men with top hats and scarves straight out of a production of *A Christmas Carol* were shown carrying large bottles of Senate Ale. "Ale Ale The Gangs All Here," the advertisements read, "It's Arrived to lead Them All." The ads included "Points by which to judge ale" for those consumers who were normally lager drinkers. The latter style had replaced ales as the most popular form of beer in most of the United States, although New England still drank more ales than beers, and there were other ales on the market in D.C., including Rams Head and Ballantine. Heurich's introduction of an ale, a type of beer his brewery had not produced before, reflects his efforts to hold on to the rapidly growing D.C. market. Expanding his line of products would help him find a market among new residents who came from areas where ales were still highly popular.[57]

The American Brewer reported on Heurich's efforts in 1938, noting that Heurich had to deal with a local transient population and compete with the big national breweries and "strong nearby competition from Baltimore, only forty miles away on an excellent highway." Heurich, they reported, concentrates on selling in D.C. and in the surrounding area for a radius of only twenty miles. The author contends that for Heurich, "introductory" advertising was "comparatively unnecessary." Actually, Heurich did use his ads to educate consumers about his product, but they focused on telling people about his brewery's long association with Washington. Most ads were "reminder" advertising, in Heurich's case explaining why his product was so good. The ale advertisements' "points by which to judge ales" would fall into this category. About one-fifth of the brewery's promotional budget went to radio, and they sponsored various programs at a time when most shows were still sponsored by a single advertiser. One-third of the budget went to billboards in D.C. and the immediate area. Newspapers took up one-quarter of the advertising dollars, and point-of-sale miscellaneous items used the remainder.[58]

One local population Heurich had traditionally sold to was D.C.'s African American population. Heurich had hired black workers as far back as his original 20th Street brewery. Some black construction workers worked on building his Water Street Brewery. But inside the brewery itself, they were limited to low-paying menial jobs, which in the 1930s was becoming a point of contention as civil rights organizations lobbied for new, better-paying opportunities. Moreover, D.C.'s African American community was making up a

Heurich advertisement promoting their ale, December 22, 1938 (author collection).

great percentage of the city's population, even as the city and the suburbs both grew. In an early example of "white flight," while the populations grew in surrounding areas—such as Arlington County, Virginia, and Montgomery County, Maryland—the percent of non-white population shrank. In contrast, the non-white population of the District of Columbia increased to 28.2 percent by 1940 as the city itself grew from 486,000 to 663,000 in that same period.[59]

Heurich advertisement promoting the *Old-Time Minstrel Show* (*The Evening Star*, November 1, 1934).

Heurich was well within the mainstream in terms in racial attitude at the times. For example, on Washington's WRC, part of the NBC Red Network, he sponsored the *Minstrel Show of the Air*, an "old time minstrel show," on Monday nights. An advertisement promoting the show, complete with performers in blackface, appeared in November 1934. A local radio column reported that *Minstrel Show* would "recreate all the old formulas of minstrelsy with 'end men,' 'Mistah Interlucutor,' medleys of song hits and a spectacular 'closing chorus by the entire company.'" It featured local talent, including a "'bones' rattler," Harry Plattner, a "press man of a local newspaper who has played his 'clappers' to the rhythm of the presses."[60] This was not the only such show on the radio. Minstrel shows were a popular format, and *Amos 'n' Andy*, with its stereotyped African American characters, was a popular radio show for almost thirty years.[61] But it was not the type of programming that would make the local African American population look especially kindly upon the brewery.

Jobs, however, not embarrassing radio shows, were the key issue. The Depression hit African American workers even harder than it had white workers. In some cities African American unemployment hit 75 percent. In 1939 a local civil rights organization, the New Negro Alliance, began looking at Heurich's hiring policy. Formed in 1933, the Alliance already had a successful history of picketing and organizing consumer boycotts of local businesses that discriminated against African Americans in employment. They simply asked local black consumers to not buy where they could not work. Between 1933 and 1936, these tactics created about 300 new jobs that had previously been whites-only.[62] This looked as if it could be a successful tactic against Heurich as well, should they choose to use it. There were a lot of African American bars and restaurants in D.C. that served Heurich's beer. In November 1939, one local African American business owner told one of Heurich's salesmen that he'd buy more beer if the company hired black men as truck drivers. He then alerted the Alliance, which contacted the brewery and noted that while Heurich enjoyed "the patronage of many colored people and colored places of business, colored men are not employed by you as drivers." "We are certain," the letter from the Alliance continued, "that this fact has been over-looked by you and that your employment policy is fundamentally fair." The problem for Heurich was that many unions were for whites only and hiring black drivers might prompt a strike. The Alliance kept the pressure on Heurich as over a dozen "colored" customers "withdrew their patronage" of the brewery. Fortunately, Brewery Workers' Union Local #48 agreed to issue work permits to black drivers. However, they would not be made full members of the union. While this latter condition did not satisfy the Alliance, they did not boycott the brewery, and 140 new jobs as drivers among seven different distributing companies were opened up to black men.[63]

Heurich did advertise in the black press, including the *Baltimore Afro-American*. He participated in local events among the African American community, including a cooking exposition in Baltimore. He donated silver dollars for a local black beauty contest. Finally, the brewery did put out some advertising showing African Americans enjoying Heurich's beer. This last point should not be taken for granted. Being known as the "negro beer" at the time could kill a brand's reputation among white consumers. Breweries often used much more generic ads in the black press, ones not showing any consumers, only featuring the product itself. Even fewer brewers used black models in point-of-sale advertising unless they sold in largely African American neighborhoods. Heurich's rival, Adam Scheidt, issued multiple examples of such pieces. It may be no coincidence, then, that Adam Scheidt's products eventually outsold Heurich's even in D.C.[64]

In September 1939, Heurich was again in Germany on what would prove to be his final trip. He traveled for one last time to Europe, probably on the *Europa*, the luxurious ship had been his vessel of choice since 1930. Heurich and Amelia, along with her brother and sister-in-law, and two (unnamed) friends from California, left on August 2, 1939. Once again Heurich visited Wiesbaden to take the cure, his habit for over forty years. On August 27, the Heuriches were warned to get out of Germany, though Heurich did not note who warned him. On the 24th, Germany and the Soviet Union had signed a nonaggression pact, clearing the way for Germany to attack Poland. On the 27th, Germany demanded Poland turn over the free city of Danzig and the Polish Corridor. European nations began mobilizing. On September 1, Germany invaded Poland. On September 3, Britain and France declared war on Germany. That night the Heuriches were in Bremen, and they had their first "encounter with war conditions." Heurich was asleep and the city went into a blackout for a British air raid. Heurich woke up and asked Amelia why she was burning a candle. Amelia told him there was a blackout and Heurich went back to sleep, ignoring the air raid sirens. Heurich claimed he slept through them because had a good conscience, but his increasingly poor hearing probably had something to do with it. Fortunately for the Heuriches, the air raid was small. Ten British bombers dropped millions of propaganda leaflets over Bremen, Hamburg, and the Ruhr. The leaflets warned the Germans, "You cannot win this war. Against you are arrayed resources and materials far greater than your own." They further warned that the Nazi government was lying to them. The leaflets were most certainly ignored. Heurich laughed when he recalled the raid.[65]

The Heuriches and their party drove into Denmark, where Heurich celebrated his ninety-seventh birthday, and from there they traveled to Sweden. As they had in 1914, the Heuriches found themselves working with an American consul to aid other stranded Americans. In this case it was the American Consul in Gothenburg, William Corcoran, a Washington native. He had his hands full trying to deal with Americans fleeing Europe, and, Heurich noted, "precious little money to do it with, general funds being low." Heurich

The Heurichs in Copenhagen in September 1939. Having left Germany for neutral Denmark, they are on their way to Sweden to catch a ship back to the United States. From the collection of Jan King Evans Houser. Used with permission.

provided money, as he had in 1914, to create a fund to "shelter, clothe and feed stranded Americans." After a few weeks waiting for available space, the Heuriches took the MS *Kungsholm* to New York. Unlike their awful trip on a Dutch liner in the fall of 1914, this trip was probably more pleasant. The *Kungsholm* was the flagship of the Swedish-American Line and had carried members of the Swedish royal family on an official trip to the United States in 1938. The *Kungsholm* made multiple trips carrying Americans home in the fall of 1939, and the Heuriches had to wait until October 5 to leave Sweden. The ship took the "far northern route," presumably thinking it was safer. Already this early in the war, neutral ships had been torpedoed by German submarines, and both the Germans and British had stopped neutral ships at sea to be searched. The *Kungsholm* was stopped twice near Iceland by the latter, and delayed briefly while the Royal Navy determined its identity. On Saturday, October 14, the *Kungsholm* reached New York with 1,116 probably exceptionally relieved passengers. It was Heurich's seventy-third trip across the Atlantic, and his last.[66]

By this time Heurich was the only brewer left in Washington, D.C. He sold his beer in Maryland, the District, and northern Virginia, although Washington and its suburbs accounted for most of his business. In December 1939 he began canning his beer. The decision was apparently a reluctant one, but it was made necessary by the changing market in which canned beer was becoming more popular.[67] Canning their beer allowed

Christian Heurich (courtesy Jan King Evans Houser).

Heurich's products to be cheaply shipped further than before. Heurich still concentrated on the area around D.C., however.

Heurich's marketing emphasized the traditional skill that went into making his beer as well as local pride. His promotional material featured both beer and ale, generally in bottles. The bock was a seasonal product, so it had its own advertising when it was released in March. Heurich also used his age as a marketing hook, as he was now the oldest brewer in the U.S., perhaps the oldest in the world, and this meant he could emphasize his experience. In June 1940, the ninety-seven-year-old Heurich celebrated his 75th anniversary as a brewer in the United States (this included his time working in Baltimore). Even though Germany was increasingly unpopular in the U.S.,[68] Heurich was treated as one of the grand old men of D.C. Over 4,000 people came to the brewery for the celebration, which featured Senate Beer. Newspapers ran congratulatory messages on his anniversary, and the *Times-Herald*, one of the city's major newspapers, printed a special section on Heurich's history. It was filled with well wishes from local businesses and civic leaders.[69]

Autumn 1940 was busy for the brewery. In September, over fifty rhesus monkeys escaped from a medical lab in the National Institute of Health by the Navy building across the street from the brewery. Several made their way to the brewery, and while firemen knocked their brethren from trees with fire hoses into the waiting arms of doctors and Marines below, a few of the monkeys enjoyed swinging around the inside of the huge brewery buildings before being caught.[70] On the more somber side, Heurich also made certain that his brewery was overt in its patriotism. The brewery closed on October 16, 1940, to allow its employees to participate in National Registration Day for the first peacetime draft in American history. During the war, Heurich made the brewery's gymnasium available for volunteer work, such as mailing ration books. His wartime ads featured symbols of American democracy, such as the Lincoln Memorial. Heurich was not hounded by rumors disparaging his patriotism as he had been during the First World War, since anti–German paranoia was not as evident as it had been in 1917–18. Of course, remembering how Prohibitionists had used the First World War to win support, the brewing industry as a whole was careful to emphasize its patriotism and support of the war.[71]

Heurich's support for the war effort went beyond bond sales and patriotic advertising. Across the street from the brewery, several gray office buildings were used by the Office of Strategic Services (OSS). The American wartime intelligence agency during World War II, it was the predecessor of the modern Central Intelligence Agency. According to some stories, the OSS employees, who included both men and women (famed chef Julia Child served in the OSS), would gather to relax after work in the brewery's rathskeller. They also apparently used the brewery for more official, if unacknowledged, meetings. One OSS veteran recalled being told to report to the brewery one night for training. Once he was there, "a dozen green volunteers were loaded aboard a shrouded military transport and taken on a long drive to a secret training facility—a farmhouse in the middle of nowhere—called Area E," where they underwent testing.[72]

Heurich's autumn 1941 advertising campaign illustrates how he tried to appeal to local pride in an area where there were so many people from other parts of the country. Beginning around Labor Day and continuing well into November, the ads all featured someone announcing that he was from elsewhere in the United States, but exclaiming, "I'm a real Washingtonian Now!" Why was he now a "real Washingtonian"? Because he now drank Senate beer and ale: "Drink Senate—Washington's favorite brew." Each week the ad featured someone, usually male, from another part of the country: the Far West, Dixie, the Middle West, New England, the Coal Belt, etc. Sometimes the text tried to add a little authentic flavor, such as the man from the Far West claiming Senate had "more 'pep' than a buckaroo!" Each ad also included a small figure, sometimes multiple figures, representing some stereotypical occupation from the region, such as a Midwestern farmer. All were white, except for the figures from the "Cotton Country" ad, which showed a white man overseeing an African American couple picking cotton. Almost all were men, except for Dixie, which featured a Southern belle: "What peaches are to Georgia, Senate Beer and Ale are to this part of the country."[73] The campaign ran as America began to rearm in preparation for the war that seemed to be coming. Military spending increased and construction began on the Pentagon on September 11, 1941. The people flooding in

One of Heurich's "Real Washingtonian" advertisements (*The Evening Star*, November 21, 1941).

to staff the growing War and Navy departments joined all the newcomers who came to Washington for Roosevelt's New Deal. Newcomers from the mid–Atlantic might well find their favorite beer sold in D.C., and large national brands such as Budweiser were sold locally. However, many arrivals, unable to find the beers they liked at home, would have found themselves looking for a new favorite brand, and Heurich worked to convince them that drinking his beers was part of settling into their new home. Heurich's efforts showed some success. In 1945, sales reached a peak of 200,000 barrels, produced by about two hundred employees.[74]

This peak sales figure was especially impressive given the restraints under which the American brewing industry operated between 1942 and 1945. One critical difference between the world wars was in how beer was treated by the federal government. During World War I, the Wilson administration, under heavy pressure from the Drys, refused to ban the brewing of beer, but did cut back on the amount of grain that breweries could use. Wide areas around military bases and training camps were made officially dry and red-light districts were closed. "Wartime prohibition" made many areas dry even before national Prohibition officially started. In Europe, the commander of the American Expeditionary Force, General John Pershing, allowed American servicemen to consume light beers and wines with low alcohol content. Of course, many found stronger beverages to consume, but risked official sanctions by doing so. The 19th Amendment, passed by Congress during the war, was ratified not long after the war ended, and many soldiers, sailors, and Marines came back to find a beer-less American waiting for them.

As a new war began to loom in the distance in 1941, Prohibitionists in the United States saw an opportunity. Insisting that repeal was only a temporary setback, groups such as the Woman's Christian Temperance Union (WCTU) began a new campaign hoping to repeat their successes of 1917–1919. They petitioned Congress to reenact wartime prohibition, to ban brewers and distillers from using grain, to reinstate the dry areas around bases and camps, and to forbid American servicemen (and women) from drinking alcoholic beverages. Moreover, one of their old champions was still in the Senate and still fighting the good fight. A dedicated Dry, Senator Morris Sheppard (D–TX) had sponsored the 1917 law that made D.C. dry and closed Heurich's brewery for sixteen years. In 1933 he filibustered the proposed 21st Amendment for over eight hours. In February 1941, blaming alcohol for the defeat of France the previous year, Sheppard put forward Senate Bill 860, which would have made not only American military facilities dry, but the area around each one. Because there were military facilities in most major American cities, the bill, had it become law, would have made most urban areas in the United States dry. Prohibition had little support in 1941, however, and the bill died in committee. Instead, the Army allowed beer with only 3.2 percent alcohol to be sold in Army Post Exchanges (PXs). Each twelve-ounce bottle sold for either a dime or fifteen cents and was sold only between 4:00 and 11:00 p.m. Most enlisted men had about $14.00 a month in spending money, which went for other items such as tobacco and candy, so the amount of beer each soldier could buy was limited. The brewing industry as a whole was pleased with this policy, but with caveats. An article in *Modern Brewery Age* noted that this market was not a new one, but rather "transplanted ones." Soldiers were not expected to drink more than they did as civilians, and the article warned brewers against "becoming overly enthusiastic about the importance of their 'new' customer, who may be just the same fellow in a new suit." Not every brewery could afford to make separate batches of 3.2 percent beer, which had a limited market, but the Army regulations eliminated much of the prohibitionist threat, and exposed millions of young men to beer drinking as an approved activity.[75]

Restrictions were placed upon the brewing industry, but they avoided the wartime prohibition of World War I. As of May 1942, because of the military's need for metals, beer cans were no longer available for civilian use, although breweries would can beer for the Army. Cans were lighter to haul than bottles and far less likely to break. With shipping space at a premium in the war, overseas shipments of beer and ale had to be canned. (Domestic shipments, such as to the PXs, could be in bottles.) In mid–1943, brewers were required to set aside 15 percent of their production for the military, which could take the form of canned beer. Servicemen and women in the field were sent cases of canned beers, often painted in official U.S. Army olive-drab, along with their other rations.[76] Shipments of grains and hops were rationed, and many breweries began trying to stretch their production using cheaper grains. Bottle caps and bottles were also rationed, and many brewers, including Heurich, encouraged their customers to buy their beer in quart bottles. Buying one quart bottle instead of three 12-oz ones used only one precious crown instead of three. Long-range shipping of beer also decreased dramatically, which helped smaller brewers far away from St. Louis and Milwaukee who no longer had to compete against those cities' big nationals such as Anheuser-Busch and Pabst, at least for the duration.

Heurich advertises their new throwaway bottle as beer cans for civilian use disappear for the duration of the war. April 3, 1942 (author collection).

Heurich was as affected by the restrictions as any other brewer, but still prospered. There are no surviving records indicating whether or not he used cheaper substitute grains, but it would have been notably implausible for him to do so, given his pride in his product. Nor was it economically necessary, as his local market grew in size. He did have to eliminate canning, which his ads noted in early 1942, as a contribution to the war effort. None of his cans have ever shown up in Army olive-drab, and it's unlikely

Top: A Senate billboard on 14th Street NW in D.C. in 1943. Note the "Buy War Bonds" addition (Library of Congress). *Bottom:* A panoramic photographs of all the Heurich Brewery employees in 1943. Chris Heurich is at left. Note the distinctive beer trucks Heurich used (courtesy Jan King Evans Houser).

Heurich with his children and grandchildren, circa 1937. From left to right: first row, Stanley Eckles, Carol Heurich, Geoffrey Eckles. Middle row: Corrine Heurich holding Constance Ann, Jan King, Amelia Eckles, Christian Heurich, Charles "Chip" King, Jr., Karla King holding Donald Christian Heurich King. Back row: Connie Young Heurich, Anita Eckles, Leila Stuart (family friend), Charles B. King (courtesy Jan King Evans Houser).

that he canned his beer for overseas shipments. He most likely sold his 15-percent military quota locally—records from immediately after the war show sales to the officers' clubs at nearby Fort Meyer. It was the growth of the local market, however, that proved to be a windfall for Heurich's business. D.C.'s population increased from 486,000 in 1930 to 663,000 in 1940, reaching a peak of over 800,000 in 1950, and while the customer base drastically increased, the products from many rivals from faraway brewers disappeared from the shelves.[77]

At home, Heurich's family grew. He had nine grandchildren and liked to joke that his family came in sets of five, as each child and his or her spouse had three children. Amelia still ruled the family, however, and took the grandchildren shopping for clothing. The youngest daughter Karla and her children escaped some of Amelia's control simply because Karla's husband, U.S. Army Colonel Charles Bowler King, was often stationed away from Washington. Sadly, Colonel King was killed in Normandy, France, on June 22, 1944, leaving behind Karla and their three children.

Near the end of his life, Heurich continued to maintain his moderate lifestyle. His diet remained simple. For breakfast Heurich often had a single egg served in sherry. He

Heurich and his Great Dane, Caesar (courtesy Jan King Evans Houser).

gave up red meat while still middle-aged, and ate fish, turkey, and chicken, finely diced. He loved iceberg lettuce eaten with a dressing of lemon juice with salt, sugar, and water added in. The family would gather together for dinner every Sunday, Christian at the head of the table and Amelia at the other end where she could manage the servers. Children sat at the end with their grandmother, the adults at the other end. There was still the doll, Michael, that would be seated at the table to be a fourteenth diner to prevent the table seating an unlucky thirteen. Heurich ate quietly and sparingly, but his grandchildren were delighted when he mixed cranberry sauce with his mashed potatoes. Wine was served at Christmas dinner, but hard liquor was not, although there was an untouched bottle of whiskey for "medicinal purposes." Heurich drank one bottle of Senate Beer a day, two during his twice-weekly skat games with friends in his *Bierstube*. He refused to use the elevator in his mansion, preferring the stairs. He used a standup desk, although photos taken late in his life show him using a stool as well. Every weekday morning he'd get up at 5:30, have breakfast, and get dressed, and then his chauffeur would drive him down New Hampshire Avenue to the brewery. He'd work there from 8:00 and return home at 9:30. He'd go to bed early, by 9:30 most nights, except for Wednesday and Sunday nights, which were reserved for skat with Dr. Carl S. Keyser and Dr. Frederick Morhart. Summers during the war were always spent at his farm, Bellevue. Heurich wrote his autobiography, *Aus meinem Leben*, in German in 1934, but began a longer version in English about 1942. Titled *I Watched America Grow*, it was written with the assistance of local writer W.A.S. Douglas. Unfortunately he only got through the first three of four planned books, and never completed the section covering 1922–1942, so *Watched* was never published. Heurich continued working until late February 1945, when he fell ill with bronchitis. He died in his home on March 7, 1945, at age 102.[78]

Heurich's funeral service was held at his home, conducted by the Rev. Charles Enders of Concordia Lutheran Church, one of the capital's longtime German congregations. He was buried at Bellevue Farm. The value of Heurich's estate was set at $3,550,471 at probate (approximately $43,000,000 in 2016), most of which was in the form of property, including the brewery and Bellevue. He left a $5,000 annual annuity to Amelia to operate the mansion, but he underestimated the costs as the mansion aged. He did not forget the orphans' home or the Ruppert Home for the Aged, which he had long supported. He left both $100,000. His family members each received regular payments from the estate for twenty years, after which the remaining portions would be divided evenly between them. In 1951, as D.C.'s suburbs grew and spread, Amelia sold Bellevue to a land developer and the family mausoleum was moved to Rock Creek Cemetery, where Heurich and his wives are now interred.[79]

Heurich had begun brewing as an apprentice ninety years before. As he looked back in his memoirs he reminisced, "That I was six times engaged and three times married, each time happily, is more than good luck.... This is my life, and if it was much, it was trouble and work." The brewery continued after Heurich's death as Chris took over running the family business. It would not, however, last long after its founder's passing.[80] The final chapter will examine how the brewery struggled to meet the changing demands of the industry after the war, and what happened to the business, the brewery complex itself, and the mansion Heurich built.

8

Afterwards: 1946–1962

With his father's death in March 1945, Christian Junior took over as president of the brewery.[1] A graduate of the Wharton School of Business, he had been vice-president and treasurer of the brewery since it reopened in 1933. He was not the natural at brewing that his father had been, however. Family stories recall that he had wanted to go to the Naval Academy rather than Wharton, and that he was more interested in science than business. His main love at the brewery seems to have been promoting its many successful sports teams which promoted the brewery.[2]

Even after the war, D.C. had a large transient population. Government workers came and went. Elections always meant a turnover in both elected officials and in staff. Members of the military rotated in and out of the area. Moreover, with postwar prosperity and the lifting of wartime travel restrictions, the city was also filled with tourists. Most of these people, if they were beer drinkers at all, arrived in D.C. with no knowledge of Heurich Brewing's products. Heurich's problem was still to acquaint them as soon and as favorably as possible with Senate and then Old Georgetown. As a result, the brewery's local advertising had a critical role to play in introducing consumers to the brewery's products.

Senate Beer remained the brewery's main product after the war. In February 1947, Heurich advertised that "Cans Were Back" after World War II rationing had ended and the restrictions on canning beer for civilian use were lifted.[3] They canned Senate Beer, ale and bock, although the latter two were apparently only canned briefly[4] as the brewery concentrated on the beer. Unfortunately for the brewery, they began to have problems with bad batches of beer, which damaged Senate's reputation beyond the point it could be salvaged, and the company's last decade would be spent trying to regain lost market share.

Sales had increased every year from 1933 until 1946. They began to slip in 1947 and then "decreased alarmingly," a trend that continued into 1950. A new brewmaster, Frank Omlor, replaced the previous brewmaster, who had been fired in August 1947. Omlor immediately found that the brewery had "one of the most serious infections that can happen to a beer." Something had come into contact with the beer and was giving Senate a "woody" or "musty" taste. They struggled to find where the infection originated. From late 1946 until August 1949, samples the brewery sent to the Wallerstein Laboratories came back with a report that the beer had normal "analytic characteristics," but that many of the samples had a disagreeable taste. It took fifteen months before they found the contamination that caused the problem was spreading through tanks in Cellar C, one of the five aging cellars in the enormous brewery. From there the infection, which Omlor described as an "odor," spread through other tanks as the beer passed from one to another. The equipment in Cellar C was ripped out and entirely replaced, even down to rubber gaskets and filters. Even the yeast had to be "continuously" replaced because it spread the "bad flavor." Other tanks were recoated and the cellars were repainted. They never did find the "original source for the cause" of the problem. However, it was not until late 1949 that they began to produce Senate Beer that did not have a musty, woody taste.[5]

The brewery's advertising reflects their frantic attempts to counter their declining market share even as they struggled to find the source of the spoiled batches. In 1947 April the brewery ads began asking, "Had a Senate Lately?"—which sounded a bit like pleading after the confident prewar "It Holds its Head High in Any Company." In July 1947 they started a campaign asking customers to compare Senate to other premium beers and to "Make This Test," taste-testing Senate with other beers, including imports. Such advertising themes were common with brands that feared they were losing ground to other brands, and Senate sales were plummeting.[6]

The brewery also expanded its presence as a local radio advertiser. The Washington, D.C., audience grew used to hearing, "It's noon in our nation's capital, and this is your Senate Beer reporter with a roundup of the news to the moment ... worldwide, national and local ... presented by the Christian Heurich Brewing Company, makers of extra-fine Senate Beer— now, better than ever," six times every weekday over WMAL radio in the late 1940s. At 7:00 a.m., 12 noon, 4:30 p.m., 6:00 p.m., 11:00 p.m., and at midnight every day, Monday through Saturday, Senate news was on the air and

We are supplying our dealers with Senate Beer in the space economizing, disposable cans once again, as fast as possible from our newly received stock.

Enjoy Senate—whether its tingly small bubble carbonation reaches you in the tin or in the friendly, familiar bottle. Ask for Senate Beer— it's the brew that

"Holds Its Head High in Any Company"

CHR. HEURICH BREWING CO. • WASHINGTON, D. C.

February 24, 1947. With wartime metal rationing ending, beer cans for civilian use return (author collection).

Senate Beer reporter Ken Evans was assigned the task of presenting the Heurich message along with last-minute news and a comprehensive roundup of sports events. The brewery continued Heurich Senior's habit of not advertising on Sunday.[7]

Beginning with this schedule of news programs, in November 1947 the Heurich Brewery added a battery of other programs to create what was then one of the largest radio campaigns ever offered on the air. They added twelve shows a week on station WRC, a National Broadcasting Company outlet, which at the time was considered one of the leading stations in the country. As a result, Heurich reserved for itself a generous portion of a very large listening audience. The brewery created a variety of programs designed to appeal to numerous types of customers, and they tailored their commercials to fit each specially built show.[8]

Echoing the pre–Prohibition Home Brew campaign with the cookbook and the free place settings, a significant part of the advertising aimed at the morning audience, composed at the time chiefly of the housewives who generally were responsible for the family's grocery shopping. There was a Monday, Wednesday, and Friday show called *Tips and Tunes*, starring a woman known simply as "Gail." She gave a recipe on each program for a dish like spaghetti sauce, Welsh rarebit, or anything else that would go with beer, hopefully Senate. Each show started with popular music, and at the end of each program, Gail gave a phone number for anyone who wanted the recipe of the day repeated. In the early afternoon every Tuesday and Thursday, Heurich sponsored *Ripley's Believe It or Not*. Timed so it came on the air just before the most popular soap operas, this spot was appropriate to reach the at-home audience. Commercials for Senate Beer were featured at the beginning and end of the program with the slogan "Better buy extra-fine Senate Beer–now, better than ever." The ads included facts about the brewing industry, such as the brewer's exclusive use of female hops, which fit the *Believe It or Not* theme.[9]

At 6:30 p.m. on Mondays, Wednesdays, and Fridays, Heurich aimed at a dinnertime family audience with a ten-minute show titled *Senate Serenade*. After a brief sign-on, the program featured three recorded musical numbers. The show had a pianist on Monday, a singer on Wednesday, and a small orchestra on Friday. Nothing interrupted the music except an eight-second reminder between records, an announcer reading something fitting a dinner crowd such as "Senate Beer with curried shrimp, delicious! Better buy Senate Beer–now better than ever." On Thursdays from 7:30 to 8:00 p.m. on WRC, Senate sponsored *The Sweetest Music This Side of Heaven* by Guy Lombardo, a show aimed at an adult audience. Finally, at 11:15 p.m. also on Mondays, Wednesdays, and Fridays, Senate presented the news on WRC with Morgan Beatty, senior reporter at NBC, who hosted *Radio News of World* from 1946 to 1967. Commercials were geared to the program's pace by featuring the history of Washington and the part played in that history by the Christian Heurich Brewing Company.[10] Besides these regular shows, the brewery created "specks," which were ten- to fifteen-word announcements like the ones used on *Senate Serenade*. Ten of these quick mini-advertisements were broadcast every weekday on a third radio station, Mutual Network station WOL. They were carefully placed next to the highest-rated programs, especially mystery and sports shows. Finally, Senate Beer had minute-long spots on another local station, WINX. These ads were strategically placed to fill out all all-around radio schedule.[11]

While radio and print advertising tried to convince consumers to keep drinking Senate, the brewery also radically redesigned the label that had been in use since before

Prohibition. In the fall of 1948, the brewery abandoned the traditional blue label. The new Senate Beer label was white and blue with an eagle-and-shield logo, copying the eagle and shield found in the United States Senate since the 1830s. Their ads bragged that Senate was now lighter and "sparkling, new … in white, gold, and blue." One local liquor store ad referred to the "new Senate."[12] In March 1949, the label underwent a small change, adding a "250" over the eagle. It doesn't appear to have actually meant anything: perhaps it just sounded good. The white cans with the 250 appeared in a new ad campaign; "Triplets." These ads showed a trio of pretty girls in casual settings enjoying the beer. The ads read "Try Senate's 'Triplet-Test' for Beer at its Best!" The girls note that Senate "Looks Right!" "Smells Right!" and "Tastes Right!"[13] Gone were the references to the brand's long history in Washington, or to the family patriarch's extensive experience. The World's Exposition Medals from Paris, Liège, and Jamestown disappeared from the labels too. The brewery was desperately tossing out anything having to do with the brand's past but the name. The "smells right" was clearly a reference to what the brewmaster called the bad "odor" that was affecting the beer.

Sales continued to drop precipitously. In 1945 Heurich sold 203,000 barrels of beer, the most the brewery ever sold. That dropped to 184,000 in 1946, 169,000 in 1947, 107,000 in 1948, and declined further to 97,000 in 1949. The company went from making a profit to losing well over $200,000 each year from 1948 through 1950. Total losses for those three years added up to over $750,000.[14] Christian Heurich's old company was bleeding capital. How did this disaster happen?

Brewmaster Omlor said the brewery was not at fault, but it is hard to dismiss their responsibility so easily. Why was the disagreeable taste not discovered before the beer had reached the consumer? The elder Heurich drank his own beer regularly. A trained brewer with over seventy years' experience, he would have likely detected the problem immediately. His son, Chris, however, was not a trained brewer. His degree was in business. Moreover, he liked to drink hard liquor, not beer. Sadly, he developed a drinking problem and family members note that he became an alcoholic. There is even less excuse for the brewmaster to have failed to notice the problem. Brewery management's failure to notice the problem quickly enough arose out of what seems to have been simple carelessness, something exceptionally difficult to imagine happening under Christian Heurich Senior's management.[15]

Frantically trying to stop the brewery's decline, in late 1948 the brewery hired Albert J. Bates, formerly president of Jacob Ruppert Brewing in New York, as general manager. Bates immediately began to modernize the brewery and to fix the problem of continuing bad batches of beer with new aging tanks, new vats, and improved quality standards. He also shifted the brewery's advertising campaigns to new brands and away from Senate, a recognition that Senate's brand was too badly damaged. In August 1949 they began promoting Champeer, a sparkling malt liquor, as "America's New Taste Thrill." The brewery claimed that the formula was created by Christian Heurich Senior for personal use, but that he never felt it was economically viable to sell. Champeer was aimed at a new market, "sophisticated" drinkers, and the packaging showed a man and woman dressed in formal evening clothes for a night out. With a higher alcohol content, 7 percent ABV, it was sold in 8-ounce bottles that were shaped more like small champagne bottles than beer bottles. The brewery intended to sell it nationwide, not for home use, but for customers enjoying a night on the town. "You'll find Champeer," advertising copy noted, "served in the better hotels, night clubs, restaurants, private clubs, and fine cocktail lounges." It was more

Advertisement from *The Evening Star* October 1949 for Heurich's short-lived Champeer. The map of D.C. would be used on the Old Georgetown label as well.

expensive than regular beer, but less expensive than mixed drinks or champagne. Moreover, by setting up nationwide distribution for Champeer, the brewery could also expand distribution of Senate beyond its normal D.C.-Maryland-Virginia area, far beyond any area that might associate the brewery name with bad batches of Senate.[16]

Champeer never got a chance to catch on because it sparked an immediate lawsuit with New Jersey's Metropolis Brewing Company, which had been selling their own sparking malt liquor, Champale, since 1939. Metropolis won an immediate injunction over Heurich's use of the word "Champ" for their product. Heurich responded that since Metropolis did not sell in D.C. or Virginia, there would not be any consumer confusion over the two products. The court agreed, and the injunction was lifted. Champeer's victory was short-lived, however. Almost immediately Metropolis announced that they would began selling Champale nationwide. The Heurich brewery agreed to stop selling Champeer after the initial production run was sold. The last newspaper advertisements for it appeared in February 1950.[17]

With Champeer gone and Senate's reputation in tatters, in March of 1950 Heurich introduced Old Georgetown Beer. It was sold at first in draft only and then in cans. Old Georgetown Beer (there were also an ale and a bock) would replace Senate as the brewery's flagship brand. Old Georgetown a lighter, drier lager than Senate, reflecting the popular tastes of the period. Senate Beer continued to be produced after 1950 (it's listed among available brands in local liquor store ads from 1951 to 1953), although it became a minor brand for the brewery. The brewery also tried reviving Senate Ale and Senate Bock in 1951, although the efforts appear to have been short-lived. This may reflect the damage done to the Senate name, but it might also reflect the decreasing popularity of ales, which continued to lose ground to lagers as the U.S.'s favorite style. On the other hand, Ram's Head Ale was one of the best-selling brands in Washington. The brewery that produced it, Adam Scheidt, bragged in local newspaper advertisements that its main two brands, Ram's Head Ale and Valley Forge (a lager), were the best-selling brands in Washington.[18] Chris Heurich even attempted to buy Adam Scheidt's brands in 1954.[19] This suggests that the problem with Senate Ale and Senate Bock was not their styles, but the "Senate" part of their name.

With Champeer gone and Senate a damaged brand, Old Georgetown became Heurich's mainstay. A lager, it was probably lighter and drier than Senate Beer had originally been, because lighter, drier beers were becoming increasingly popular. Heurich Senior probably would have described it as bland compared to what he had produced before Prohibition, but the market was changing. Continuing the brewery's long practice, Old Georgetown's label played up the brewery's D.C. connection in as blatant as way as possible. It featured a map of Washington, D.C., with numerous local points of interest marked:

- Dumbarton Oaks
- The Georgetown University "castle"
- The Francis Scott Key Home
- The Cumberland Canal
- Rock Creek
- Pennsylvania Avenue
- The White House
- The Hagerstown-Frederick Turnpike
- The Potomack [sic] River
- The Christian Heurich Brewery!

Old Georgetown was more widely distributed than Senate had been only a decade before, being sold throughout Maryland and Virginia, well beyond the twenty-mile radius *The American Brewer* had reported in 1938.[20] Of course, the brewery's advertising was heavily weighted towards Old Georgetown as well. Newspaper ads, point-of-sale pieces, ads, coasters, wall signs, etc., all were designed to sell Old Georgetown. They even put out a bumper sticker. They also used radio advertisements with an Old Georgetown radio jingle:

> (Man) *Did you say Old Georgetown Beer?*
> (Chorus) *Yes, we said Old Georgetown Beer!*
> *Premium Brew, costs less too.*
> *Dry and Light, Always right.*
> *Custom made, Old Georgetown Beer!*
> *Yes, By George, Good Old Georgetown*
> *Best of All, Old Georgetown Beer.*[21]

Old Georgetown was the featured brand when Heurich sponsored Washington Senators' (also referred to as the Nationals) games on TV in the early 1950s. Listeners were sometimes advised to buy a case of Old Georgetown and relax and listen to a game or to watch it on their new TV.[22]

The postwar market was, however, taking its toll on small breweries like Heurich's. Only the biggest nationals could afford the big nationwide advertising campaigns, or could take advantage of the cost savings of large-scale production. The expanding and improved highway system freed shipping brewers from locating along rail lines to reach more parts of the country. Furthermore, consumption had dropped from pre–Prohibition, leading to overproduction as the numbers of barrels produced increased from 32.2 million barrels in 1934 to 85.5 million in 1955. Per capita consumption of beer peaked in 1914 at 21 gallons a year. The highest figure for the 1930s was 12.6 in 1937. By 1955 it was still only 15.7 gallons a year.[23] The number of brewers open post–Prohibition peaked at 766 in 1935. By 1950 that number had dropped to 350.[24]

Many smaller brewers attempted to shore up their market share by coming out with special beers that did not fit the popular light, dry lager style of the 1950s. Heurich tried in 1955 with Heurich's Lager, which was based on a pre-Prohibition formula. Released in April 1955, the lager was advertised as "a beer that tasted like beer." The ad copy quoted Heurich: "I felt that modern beers had just gone too far from the great old beers I remembered so well." The following advertisements promoted Heurich's Lager as "beer as beer was meant to be" and "the beer your father used to drink." They featured Heurich Senior, showing him in 1879 and 1884, and accepting a medal at the 1900 Paris World's Fair for his beer. "I knew," Chris was quoted as saying in one example, "you were tired of the thinned-out beer taste of modern beers." Heurich's Lager was a hit. Sales increased. Heurich claimed that sales in 1954 were 8 percent higher than in 1953, making 1954 the best sales year in the past three years. He hoped, he told the *Washington Post* and *Times Herald*, that 1955 would be the best sales year since 1945, when they topped 200,000 barrels a year.[25]

Heurich's Lager was a success, but the brewery continued to lose market share. They stopped making Senate in late 1955, concentrating on Heurich's Lager and Old Georgetown. The loss of market share was a familiar story for the period, as was their perhaps inevitable decision to close. Most breweries in the United States were caught by the same factors, and they were closing at an alarming rate. By 1956 the number of remaining American breweries was reduced to 239, a third the number that were open in 1935.[26] As 1955 turned to 1956, Heurich's board of directors decided the brewery would close before it started losing money. In early January 1956, they announced that they would shut down on January 31. Amelia Heurich, a member of the board since her husband had died in

The Heurich Brewing in January 1956, its last month in operation. The outside sign still promotes Senate Beer, which the brewery no longer produced (courtesy the D.C. Public Library, Star Collection © *Washington Post*).

1945, reportedly told her son, "If you think Poppa would do that, go ahead." Mrs. Heurich did not live to see the end. She passed away on January 24, 1956, aged 89, exactly one week before the scheduled closure. Chris Heurich blamed high beer taxes in neighboring states, the lack of a tax on beer imported into the District from elsewhere, and the many new residents who ordered the national brands. Moreover, the planned Roosevelt Bridge over the Potomac required that part of the brewery be torn down to make way, and it did not make economic sense to move the brewery to another part of the city. Employees were given a week's pay and two weeks' vacation pay, as well as a favorable letter of reference. Chris wrote letters to each employee himself to explain the closure. At least one local liquor store advertised a "Last Chance Sale" to buy Old Georgetown and Heurich Lager, and when the last can of beer rolled down the line at Heurich, it was an Old Georgetown.[27]

After the brewery closed, parts of the buildings were still used. The gymnasium was home to the Arena Stage for several years, beginning in late 1956 with Arthur Miller's *A View from a Bridge*. The temporary 500-seat theater was nicknamed "The Old Vat" after London's famous "Old Vic."[28] In addition, the federal government rented some of the space for offices. According to a retired United State Air Force intelligence officer, some of the offices of the Air Force Assistant Chief of Staff were in the old brewery. The intelligence officers were in the Pentagon, a more secure space, but the officer remembered going up an old freight elevator to "a dismal and dreary office. There was a big heavy metal door to the office I went to. I don't remember it being very secure, certainly not at SCIF [Sensitive Compartmented Information Facility] standards."[29] The use of the brewery would make sense, as there were U.S. military offices just across the street at what is now the U.S. Navy Bureau of Medicine and Surgery buildings on 23d Street NW. The buildings were also used by the Office of Strategic Services—the forerunner to the Central Intelligence Agency (CIA)—during World War II, and by the CIA after it was founded in 1947. The State Department is just on the other side of 23d Street. So the brewery stood in an area along with numerous offices of the American intelligence, military, and diplomatic agencies.

That was not the only connection the brewery had with the intelligence community. According to another story, one with fewer cloak-and-dagger aspects than secret meetings in the night by the OSS in World War II, in 1953 Heurich saw a group of people standing in the rain waiting for a bus. He asked who they were, and one of his staff told him they were CIA employees who worked in that complex of buildings. Heurich had the brewery carpenters out on the street corner the next day to build them a nice, dry bus shelter with benches and even trash cans. It was decorated with an Old Georgetown sign. After the brewery closed, according to some accounts, the CIA stored part of its extensive library of spy fiction in the building. In actuality, the CIA's logistics officers looked at the brewery space for use for storage, a garage, or for a motor pool, but decided that the brewery was not "adaptable for those purposes." Finally, when the CIA was looking to build a new headquarters building, one of the initial suggestions was to build it where the Heurich Brewery stood. President Dwight Eisenhower rejected that idea, as he claimed D.C. was already too crowded.[30]

When Heurich built the brewery in the 1890s, it was in an industrial area along with another brewery, the gas plant, and other businesses normally stuck in undesirable locations. By the 1930s the tourist areas of the National Mall were getting closer, and the U.S. government began looking for a site to put another bridge across the Potomac from Constitution Avenue. The Heurich Brewery took up some of the space most suitable for such a bridge. The ice house was torn down in 1961 to build what is now the Theodore Roosevelt Bridge. Heurich had built it well. The wrecking ball supposedly bounced off the thick, cork-filled concrete walls. Demolition crews had to dynamite the walls one at a time to bring them down.[31] In 1962 the rest of the brewery was demolished. The family still owned the rest of the land, however, which was needed for a proposed new arts center. The trustees for Heurich's estate could not sell the property for less than a fair market value, but the group building the arts center did not have enough to cover the full cost. An arrangement was made whereby the family would be given two permanent boxes in two of the center's new theaters, and their value made up the difference. In 1965 the land was sold for $1,900,000 plus two boxes valued at $150,000 total. to build a new arts center, which is now the John F. Kennedy Center for the Performing Arts.[32]

The Heurich family has continued to prosper in D.C., benefited by the many investments in land Christian had made over the decades. Amelia died in 1956 and left the Heurich mansion to the Columbia Historical Society, later the D.C. Historical Society. When they outgrew the building, it was about to go on the market. Fearing it would be torn down or gutted, the family raised the money to buy the building, and it reopened

The remains of the Heurich icehouse, November 1961 (courtesy the D.C. Public Library, Star Collection © *Washington Post*).

as one of the premier house museums in the city. Chris died in 1979, but lived long enough to see his family's brewery's artifacts become popular collectibles, and he visited breweriana shows as an honored guest. Anita Augusta Heurich Eckles died in 1986. The youngest daughter, Karla Heurich King Harrison, remarried in 1946 to Army officer Eugene L. Harrison. They lived in Japan during the postwar American occupation, and she became a master of *ikebana*, the Japanese art of flower arranging. Karla died in early 2014, aged 106. Several of Heurich's grandchildren are still living. One of them, Gary Heurich, founded the Olde Heurich Brewing Company in D.C. in 1986. Unfortunately it was at the beginning of the growth of microbreweries, and never caught on in D.C. It closed in 2006.[33]

Christian Heurich, Sr., was one of many German immigrants who succeeded in the brewing industry. Unlike many of the others, however, he was based in an area that did not have a large customer base of either German immigrants or industrial workers. While Heurich was able to tap into an existing German immigrant community, and while he certainly used this community as a source of support, it was too small to support his business singlehandedly. Heurich's success was only possible because his product appealed to a wide variety of customers—white and black, native-born and immigrant, white-collar government clerks and blue-collar workers alike.

Christian Heurich also benefited from the fact that Washington was a city of transients built around a small but rapidly growing permanent population. Fellow immigrants, new federal workers, elected officials, African Americans migrating from the South, and even a growing diplomatic corps flowed into the District at such a rate that the population quintupled from 131,000 in 1870 to approximately 800,000 when Heurich died in 1945.

Moreover, Washington was a place where comparatively recent immigrants could move into the ranks of city leaders. In Washington, D.C., earning money through industry did not disqualify one from entering elite society, as was often the case in cities with an older, established society, such as New York or Philadelphia. In 1872, Heurich made the decision to move to Washington, as he felt that the city promised certain opportunities. His instincts obviously proved correct. Washington, D.C., was indeed an excellent place for a recent immigrant to start a new business and move up in society.

Chapter Notes

Preface

1. "Breweriana" is the term for collectibles related to the brewing industry. Collecting beer cans (remember Billy Beer?) was a popular fad in the 1970s.

2. *Leading Them to the Promised Land: Woodrow Wilson, Covenant Theology, and the Mexican Revolution, 1913–1915* (Kent, OH: Kent State University Press, 2010).

3. See, for example, Mark Benbow, "Christian Heurich," in *Immigrant Entrepreneurship: German-American Business Biographies, 1720 to the Present*, vol. 3, edited by Giles R. Hoyt (German Historichemal Institute). Last modified September 25, 2014. http://immigrantentrepreneurship.org/entry.php?rec=38.

Introduction

1. Phil Casey, "Old Heurich Brewery Scene of Blast Mighty in Sound But Only Near Beer," *The Washington Post*, November 26, 1961, B1.

Chapter 1

1. Heurich's family details are available in the Christian Heurich Papers, The Historical Society of Washington, D.C. MS 537. Box 7. Folder 77.

2. Christian Heurich to W.L. Darby (April 13, 1927), The Christian Heurich Papers. Heurich noted that the U.S. Protestant churches supported Prohibition, which, as a brewer, Heurich detested, and he politely refused to make a donation. The letter is in Box 7. Folder 77.

3. John Osborne, *The Meiningen Court Theater, 1866–1890* (Cambridge: Cambridge University Press, 1988), 3.

4. Born 1800, died 1882. He reigned from 1803 to 1866. He was forced to abdicate in favor of his only son, Georg, after backing Austria in its losing war against Prussia in 1866.

5. "1911 Encyclopædia Britannica/Saxe-Meiningen," Wikisource, The Free Library, http://en.wikisource.org/w/index.php?title=1911_Encyclop%C3%A6dia_Britannica/Saxe-Meiningen&oldid=1169056 (accessed June 8, 2012).

6. Ann Marie Koller, *The Theater Duke: Georg II of Saxe-Meiningen and the German Stage* (Stanford: Stanford University Press, 1984), 28–30.

7. Sabine Freitag, *Friedrich Hecker: Two Lives for Liberty*. Edited and translated by Steven Rowan (St. Louis: University of Missouri Press, 2006), 104–109; *I Watched*, 3; Heinrich F. Francke, *The Water-Cure: Applied To Every Known Disease: A Complete Demonstration of the Advan-* tages of the Hydropathic System of Curing Diseases: Showing, Also, The Fallacy of the Medicinal Method … With An Appendix, Containing a Water Diet and Rules For Bathing (N.p.: Fowlers and Wells, 1850).

8. "Response of Mr. Heurich," Association of the Oldest Inhabitants, Washington, D.C. (September 2, 1942), Heurich Papers, Container 2, Folder 19. Diesel was born in Paris, France. His parents were German immigrants who left for London when the Franco-Prussian War began in 1870. However, as a teen, Diesel was sent to Augsburg to live with family and to go to school.

9. "Rektor" is a headmaster of a primary school.

10. Heurich wrote two memoirs, one of which was published: *From My Life, 1842–1934: From Haina in Thuringia to Washington in the United States of America*, translated by Eda Offutt (Washington, D.C.: n.p., 1934). Hereafter it will be referred to as *From My Life*. I will be using the English translation. The unpublished memoir is Christian Heurich, *I Watched: By Christian Heurich as told to W.A.S. Douglas, Book One, 1842 to 1872* (MS in possession of Jan King Evans Houser), hereafter referred to as *I Watched*. The original is in English. Heurich, *I Watched*, 2.

11. W.A.S. Douglas, "Christian Heurich Observes 75th Anniversary Here," *The Washington Times-Herald*, June 7, 1940, 2-C.

12. Heurich, *I Watched*, 3.

13. Francke, *The Water-Cure*, 184.

14. Interview with Jan King Evans Houser, June 13, 2012. The family papers include Xeroxed copies of genealogical information, but the copies often do not have their source indicated. Heurich Papers, Historical Society of Washington, D.C. MS 537, Box 7, Folder 77.

15. Heurich, *From My Life*, 2; *One Hundred Years of Brewing: A Supplement to 'The Western Brewer'* (Chicago: H.S. Rich & Co, 1903), 675–676. The children's ages are computed for when the mother died in May 1856. The father died five years later, but was ill for some time before then. Heurich's memoirs are unclear as to when the siblings left their father's home, but since Heurich left home for apprenticeship in 1857, I am assuming the children left soon after their mother died.

16. Heurich, *I Watched*, 3.

17. Heurich, *From My Life*, 2–5.; Horst Rössler. "Traveling Workers and the German Labor Movement," in *People in Transit: German Migration in Comparative Perspective, 1820–1930*, Dirk Hoerder and Jörg Nagler, eds. (Washington, D.C.: German Historical Institute, 1995), 129.

18. *One Hundred Years*, 680; "The Technical Education of Brewers in Europe," *Brewers Gazette* 11 (January 15, 1881): 12–13.

19. Heurich, *From My Life*, 3; Heurich, *I Watched*, 5–6; Rössler, 133, 143–145; George S Werner, "Travelling Journeymen in Metternichian South Germany," *Proceedings of the American Philosophical Society* 125/3 (June 23, 1981): 209.

20. Werner, 204–206; Andreas Fahrmeir, *Citizens and Aliens: Foreigners and the Law in Britain and the German States, 1789–1870* (New York: Berghahn Books, 2000), 127.

21. Christiane Eisenberg, "Artisans' Socialization at Work: Workshop Life in Early Nineteenth Century England and Germany," *Journal of Social History* 24/3 (Spring 1991): 513.

22. Werner, 206–208, 212–213, 217; Merry E. Wiesner, "'Wandervogels' Women: Journeymen's Concepts of Masculinity in Early Modern Germany," *Journal of Social History* 24/4 (Summer 1991): 772; Fahrmeir, *Citizens and Aliens*, 127.

23. Heurich, *From My Life*, map between pages 5 and 6.

24. "A Meeting of Retail Liquor Dealers," *The Evening Star*, January 15, 1884, 1.

25. Heurich, *From My Life*, 3–5; Heurich, *I Watched*, 5–6.

26. Heurich, *From My Life*, 3–5; Heurich, *I Watched*, 5–6; Douglas, "75th Anniversary Here," 2-C. Heurich never specified which breweries he worked for, or how many there were, nor did he list all the towns and cities he worked in.

27. Interview with Jan Houser, 2012; Rössler, 131.

28. Vienna first installed gas lighting in 1818. Letter from Dr. Martina Nußbaumer, the Vienna Museum, August 29, 2014. This made it one of the earlier cities in Europe with such street lighting.

29. "Response of Mr. Heurich"; interview with Jan Houser, 2012.

30. Amelia Sarah Levetus, *Imperial Vienna: An Account of Its History, Traditions, and Arts* (London: John Lane, 1905), 149, 213–214.

31. Douglas, "75th Anniversary Here," 2-C; Heurich, *I Watched*, 87.

32. Heurich, *From My Life*, 5; and Heurich, *I Watched*, 7. Heurich spelled Jacobsen's first name "Hermann," but it is spelled with only one "n" in the city directory.

33. Walter D. Kamphoefner, Wolfgang Helbich and Ulrike Sommer, eds., *News from the Land of Freedom: German Immigrants Write Home* (Ithaca: Cornell University Press, 1991), 27; *Appleton's Annual Cyclopaedia and Register of Important Events: Embracing Political, Military, and Ecclesiastical Affairs; Public Documents; Biography, Statistics, Commerce, Finance, Literature, Science, Agriculture, and Mechanical Industry*, 6 (New York: D. Appleton, 1867), 375, 684; https://en.wikipedia.org/wiki/Vienna#Austro-Hungarian_Empire (Accessed July 2, 2015); Werner, 198; Andreas K. Fahrmeir, "Nineteenth Century German Citizenship: A Reconsideration," *The History Journal* 40/3 (September 1997); 721–752.

34. Stefan Manz, "America in Global Context: German Entrepreneurs around the World," in *Immigrant Entrepreneurship: German-American Business Biographies, 1720 to the Present*, vol. 3, edited by Giles R. Hoyt. German Historical Institute. Last modified August 28, 2014. http://www.immigrantentrepreneurship.org/entry.php?rec=187.

35. "The Brewing Trade in Russia," *American Brewers' Gazette* 8 (1878), 130. According to an 1878 report in the *American Brewers' Gazette*, the largest brewer in the United States in 1878 was George Ehret's brewery in New York City, which produced 160,000 barrels a year. The remaining breweries that produced over 100,00 barrels in 1878 were Philip Best in Milwaukee, Wisconsin; Bergner & Engel in Philadelphia, Pennsylvania; Peter Ballantine & Son in Newark, New Jersey; and Jacob Ruppert in New York City. "Breweries in the United States" *American Brewers' Gazette* 8 (1878), 113; *Commercial Relations of the United States: Reports from the Consuls of the United States on the Commerce, Manufactures, Etc., of Their Consular Districts* (Washington, D.C.: Government Printing Office, 1886).

36. Heurich, *I Watched*, 7; interview with Jan King Evans Houser, June 2012.

37. Kamphoefner et al., 289.

38. The first lasted from 1816 to 1857, the second from 1864 to 1873, and the third from 1880 to 1893. Each was interrupted by a major economic depression in the U.S. See Klaus J. Bade, "Conclusion: Migration Past and Present—The German Experience," in *People in Transit: German Migration in Comparative Perspective, 1820–1930*, Dirk Hoerder and Jörg Nagler, eds. (Washington, D.C.: German Historical Institute, 1995), 400.

39. Dirk Hoerder. "The Traffic of Immigration via Bremen/Bremerhaven: Merchants' Interests, Protective Legislation and Migrants' Experiences," *Journal of American Ethnic History* 13/1 (Fall 1993), 68.

40. Farley Grubb, *German Immigration and Servitude in America, 1709–1920* (London: Routledge, 2011), 186, Figure 19.4. The exceptions are 1870 and 1871, during the Franco-Prussian War.

41. Heurich, *From My Life*, 6.

42. Keith Pescod, *Good Food, Bright Fires & Civility: British Emigrant Depots of the Century* (Melbourne: Australian Scholarly Publishing, 2001), 33–37. The Emigration exhibit at the Merseyside Maritime Museum, Liverpool, UK, includes a recreation of the dockside in the mid-nineteenth century.

43. Pescod, 33–37; Milton Rubicam, "Mr. Christian Heurich and His Mansion," *Records of the Columbia Historical Society of Washington, D.C. 1960–1962* (Washington, D.C.: Columbia Historical Society, 1963), 171.

44. This would have been the *Vereinsthaler*, worth about three marks.

45. http://www.norwayheritage.com/p_ship.asp?sh=helv1 (accessed 7/3/13); Bowen, 143; *Lloyd's Captain Register*, 1869, M-Z. 514.

46. Heurich, *From My Life*, 8.

47. *The American Annual Cyclopaedia and Register of Important Events of the Year 1869*, vol. 9 (New York: D. Appleton, 1870), 351–352; Klaus J. Bade, "German Emigration to the United States and Continental Immigration to Germany in the Late Nineteenth and Early Twentieth Centuries," *Central European History* 13/4 (December 1980): 358–361.

48. "Cholera," *London Guardian*, May 23, 1866, 541; "Outbreak of Cholera on Board the Steamer *Helvetia*," *Liverpool Mercury* (May 4, 1866), quoted at "Cholera on Board the *Helvetia* 1866." http://www.old-merseyTimes.co.uk/cholerahelvetia.html (accessed October 12, 2014).

49. "Cholera on Board the *Helvetia* 1866."

50. Richard J. Evans, "Epidemics and Revolutions: Cholera in Nineteenth Century Europe," *Epidemics and Ideas*, Terence Ranger and Paul Slack, eds. (Cambridge: Cambridge University Press, 1992), 169.

51. "Cholera on Board the *Helvetia* 1866."

52. *London Guardian*, May 16, 1866, 507; "Cholera on Board the *Helvetia* 1866."

53. Heurich, *I Watched*, 9; "Cholera on Board the *Helvetia* 1866."

54. Heurich claims that the ship was quarantined for six or seven weeks. However, the weekly list of ship departures and arrivals published by Lloyds indicates that the *Helvetia* left for New York on May 2, returned to Liverpool on May 5, and departed again on May 29, 1866. *Lloyds List*, 1866 (Maritime Archives and Library. Merseyside Maritime Museum, Liverpool, UK). The Liverpool

newspapers of the time confirm this shorter timetable. http://www.old-merseyTimes,co.uk/cholerahelvetia.html (accessed October 12, 2014). Heurich's original draft had the time correct with three weeks, but this was crossed out with "six" written in. Heurich, *I Watched*, 9.

55. "To Correspondents," *British Medical Journal* (May 26, 1866), 565. "Cholera mattresses at Crosby," Merseyside Maritime Museum. www.liverpoolmuseums.org.uk/maritime/collections/seized/casestudies/cholera_mattresses.aspx (accessed 1/27/2011), "The Cholera—Question." House of Commons Debate (May 15, 1866), vol. 183, cc 986–90. http://hansard.millbanksystems.com/commons/1866/may/15/the-cholera-question (Accessed 1/27/2011).

56. Stephen Halliday, "Death and Miasma in Victorian London: An Obstinate Belief," *British Medical Journal* (December 22–29, 2001), 1469; Geoff Gill, "Cholera and the Fight for Public Health Reform in Mid-Victorian England," *Historian* (Summer 2000), 16; Michael Worboys, "Medical perspectives on Health and Disease," *A Cultural History of the Human Body in the Age of Empire*, Michael Sappol and Stephen P. Rice, eds. (London: Bloomsbury, 2010), 74–75.

57. Heurich, *From My Life*, 6–7; Heurich, *I Watched*, 8–9; "News of the Day," *New York Times*, May 15, 1866. One particular bank, Overend, Gurney & Company, failed on May 10, sparking the crisis.

58. *Lloyds List*, 1866. Heurich noted that the Inman Line offered free transportation for cholera survivors but that he declined their offer. The Inman Line was a competitor to the National Line, the company that owned the *Helvetia*.

59. George J. Svejda, *Castle Garden as an Immigrant Depot, 1855–1890* (Washington, D.C.: Department of the Interior, 1968), 77–80.

60. Svejda, 83–84.

61. "A Day in Castle Garden," *Harper's New Monthly Magazine* (March 1, 1871), 549.

62. "A Day," 550; Svejda, 85–88.

63. Svejda, 85–88. A telegraph office run by Western Union was also set up, but not until 1867, after Heurich had already passed through.

64. *Ibid.*

65. Out of curiosity, the author timed his walk first across and then around the original circular building in May 2015. It took a man in his mid-50s with arthritic knees 46 seconds to walk across the building from entry to exit, and 2:42 to walk completely around it. Of course, Heurich would have had a lot more to navigate through than the tourists the author saw while visiting it in 2015, but it is a surprisingly small structure.

66. Of course, there was no "Germany" in 1866. In this case, "German" refers to an area dominated by a language group rather than a specific nationality.

67. Heurich, *I Watched*, 9–11.

68. In *I Watched*, Heurich notes that they lived on Alice Anna [sic] Street. However, the Woods City Directories for Baltimore for 1865–66 and 1867–68 note that a "Herman Jacobsen, mariner" lived at 297 Canton Avenue. Canton Avenue was just one block north of Aliceanna. See *Woods Baltimore Directory*, 1865–66 (Baltimore: John W. Woods, 1866); Heurich, *I Watched*, 7, 12–13; and Joseph Garonzik. "The Racial and Ethnic Make-Up of Baltimore Neighborhoods, 1850–1870," *Maryland Historical Magazine* 71.3 (Fall 1976): 396; Harry O. Haughton, *An Introduction to the Port of Baltimore, United States* (Baltimore: n.p., 1878), 24–25 30, 36.

69. Heurich, *I Watched*, 10–11. The woman's name is unknown. The 1870 census lists only Herman and "Lizzie" Jacobsen and their son Charles living in their home. No live-in servant is noted. Of course it's possible the woman was no longer employed by the Jacobsens in 1870,

or that she did not normally live with them, but was house-sitting while they were at sea, perhaps in case Christian finally arrived. "Port of Baltimore May 22, 1866," *Baltimore Sun* (May 23, 1866), 4.

70. *I Watched*, 11–12. In his original draft, Heurich used the word "fortune." He replaced it with "advancement" in the edited draft.

71. "Maryland style" fried chicken is dipped in milk and flour and then pan-fried, rather than deep-fried.

72. John F. Weishampel, Jr., *A Stranger in Baltimore: A New Hand Book Containing Sketches of the Early History and Present Condition of Baltimore with a Description of its Notable Localities and other Information useful to both Citizens and Strangers* (Baltimore: J.F. Weishampel, Jr., Bookseller and Stationer, 1866), 145. The publisher operated out of a space "under the Eutaw Hotel," so its opinion may not have been unbiased. Nonetheless, Heurich remembered the meal fondly seventy years later.

73. "The McDonogh Monument at Baltimore," *New York Times*, August 4, 1865) ; Heurich, *I Watched*, 8.

74. "Port of Baltimore Aug. 4, 1866," *Baltimore Sun*, August 6, 1866, 4.

75. *I Watched*, 16.

76. Dale O. Van Wieren, *American Breweries II* (West Point, PA: East Coast Breweriana Association, 1995), lists forty-five breweries operating, 4–5, 129–36. I counted all the breweries that were listed as being in business in Baltimore in either 1866 or 1867. However, a local guide published in 1866 claimed only eighteen. Weishampel, 70; Richard Wagner, "The Introduction of Lager Beer in the USA, Arranged Chronologically," *The Keg* (Fall 1998): 11, 20–22.

77. William J. Kelley, *Brewing in Maryland From Colonial Times to the Present* (Baltimore: n.p., 1965), 178–182. Baltimore had a population of 212,000 in 1860 and 267,000 in 1870, when it was the sixth largest city in the U.S.; see Alan M. Kraut, "Immigration through the Port of Baltimore: A Comment," in *Forgotten Doors: The Other Ports of Entry to the United States*, M. Mark Stolarik, ed. (Philadelphia: Balch Institute Press, 1988), 77; and Dean R. Esslinger, "Immigration through the Port of Baltimore," in *Forgotten Doors*, 66–67. Unfortunately, Heurich's memoirs are silent on how he found his job, only noting where he began work.

78. John C. Gobright, *The Monumental City Or Baltimore Guide Book* (Baltimore: Gobright & Torsch, 1858), quoted in Kelley, 236–237.

79. Heurich, *I Watched*, 18–19; Heurich, *From My Life*, 9. There were two "Seeger" breweries operating in Baltimore in 1870. The Jacob Seeger Brewery operated from 1854 to 1888, and Stiefel & Seeger was in business from 1857 to 1872 before changing its name to Edw. W. Stiefel. See Van Wieren, *American Breweries*, 135; Heurich, *I Watched*, 20; "Christian Heurich," *Washington Past and Present: A History*, vol. 5, ed. John C. Proctor (New York: Lewis Historical Publishing Co., 1932), 1036; Bob Kay, "The Conrad Seipp Brewing Company, Chicago," *American Breweriana Journal* 163 (November–December 2009): 28–31; Bob Skilnik, *The History of Beer and Brewing in Chicago, 1833–1978* (Saint Paul, MN: Pogo Press, 1999), 20; Van Wieren, 71; "The Formula for Success Heurich Style," *Heurich Employees Association News* (September 12, 1942), 2.

80. Heurich, *I Watched*, 16–17.

81. Ralph Volney Harlow, "The Rise and Fall of the Kansas Aid Movement," *The American Historical Review* 41/1 (October 1935): 3.

82. Heurich, *From My Life*, 9; Heurich, *I Watched*, 20–24; Bruce Garver, "Immigration to the Great Plains, 1865–1914: War, Politics, Technology, and Economic Development," *Great Plains Quarterly* 31/3 (Summer 2011): 180–188.

83. Heurich, *I Watched*, 57; "Christian Heurich," *Washington Past and Present*, 1036. For the changing rules on voting and naturalization, see Reed Ueda, "Naturalization and Citizenship," *Harvard Encyclopedia of American Ethnic Groups*, Stephan Thernstrom, ed. (Cambridge: Harvard University Press, 1980), 734–748, particularly pages 737–740.

84. http://en.wikipedia.org/wiki/United_States_presidential_election,_1868 (accessed October 12, 2014).

85. Heurich never specified which relatives he stayed with, or if they were from either his mother or father's side of his family.

86. James McGrath Morris, *Pulitzer: A Life in Politics, Print, and Power* (New York: Harper, 2010), 43–46.

87. Heurich, *I Watched*, 27, 30; "Christian Heurich," *Washington Past and Present*, 1036.

88. Jacobsen switched from the *Lucy W. Alexander* to the *Franklin* in April 1867, according to the shipping reports in the *Baltimore Sun*. "Port of Baltimore Apr 15, 1867," *Baltimore Sun*, April 16, 1867, 4. By 1869 he was captain of the schooner *Speculator*. Both the *Speculator* and the *Franklin* ran similar routes to those of the *Lucy W. Alexander*, between the northeast, Baltimore, and the West Indies. In 1870 he was master of the *Jennie*. Judging from the lists of ship departures and arrivals in the *Baltimore Sun*, such switching between ships was common.

89. "Port of Baltimore May 28, 1869," *Baltimore Sun*, May 29, 1869, 4; "Port of Baltimore July 5, 1869," *Baltimore Sun*, July 6, 1869, 4; "Port of Baltimore August 28, 1869," *Baltimore Sun*, August 29, 1869, 4. It's possible Heurich set sail from Baltimore after the *Speculator* returned in late August or early September, but there are no records in the *Baltimore Sun* regarding the *Speculator* after August, which strongly suggests the ship did not sail from Baltimore during that time period.

90. Heurich, *I Watched*, 31. *American Breweries* does not list any breweries operating in Ripley, Ohio, prior to 1874, but if the brewery where Heurich worked was only open a few months, it might not have been listed. Heurich. *From My Life*, 10; "The Formula for Success Heurich Style," *Heurich Employees Association News*, September 12, 1942, 2.

91. Ruth Ritter Runner, *Paul Hugo Ritter and Related Families: Rottweil Germany to Cumberland, Maryland* (Morgantown, WV: n.p., 1995), 62–65.

92. Frank Gutheim, *Worthy of the Nation: The History of the Planning for the National Capital* (Washington, D.C.: Smithsonian Institution Press, 1977), 84–86; Heurich, *I Watched*, 33.

Chapter 2

1. Stanley Baron, *Brewed in America: A History of Beer and Ale in the United States* (New York: Little, Brown, 1962), 223, 258.

2. Van Wieren, *American Breweries*, 220–225, 236–247. The numbers are inexact because the historic record if often unclear when breweries before 1900 opened and closed. Brooklyn was separate from New York City until 1898.

3. Heurich, *I Watched*, 10, 32.

4. 131,700 vs. 267,354, according to the 1870 federal census.

5. Van Wieren, *American Breweries*, 59–60, 374–75. These figures should be taken as close estimates, as small breweries may have opened and closed without leaving much evidence of their existence in the surviving public records such as city directories.

6. Heurich, *I Watched*, 32.

7. Alexandria County (later Arlington County), was the only county in Virginia outside of the new state of West Virginia to vote to reject secession in May 1861. Arlington Ridge is high ground overlooking Washington and was the site of almost two dozen forts guarding the capital. Reattaching Alexandria County to the District of Columbia would have made strategic sense, and its largely pro-Union population might have welcomed the move.

8. Alan Lessoff, *The Nation and Its City: Politics, "Corruption," and Progress in Washington, D.C., 1861–1902* (Baltimore: Johns Hopkins, 1994), 57–61.

9. Lessoff, 24, 37; Gutheim, 84–86.; *I Watched*, 33.

10. See, for example, "Alexander R. Shepherd," *Evening Star*, September 27, 1887, 2; "Gov. Shepherd Talks," *Evening Star*, September 29, 1887, 1.

11. *I Watched*, 33; "Advertisement," *Washington Post*, August 5, 1942, 7; Lessoff, 65–66.

12. Kathleen Neils Conzen, "Die Residenzler: German Americans in the Making of the Nation's Capital," in *Adolf Cluss, Architect: From Germany to America*, Alan Lessoff and Christof Mauch, eds. (Washington, D.C.: Historical Society of Washington, D.C., 2005), 58–63; John Clagett Proctor, "The Schuetzen Park and the home of Asda Whitney," in *Proctor's Washington and Environs* (Washington, D.C.: n.p., 1950).

13. "Christian Heurich at Home," unsigned and undated typed manuscript. In the possession of Mrs. Jan King Evans Houser. Mrs. Houser is Heurich's granddaughter, and the manuscript is among the family papers she has preserved.

14. Heurich, *I Watched*, 40–41.

15. Map of Washington, D.C., showing wood, concrete, and stone street pavements. Library of Congress, Geography and Map Division, g3851p ct001355. http://hdl.loc.gov/loc.gmd/g3851p.ct001355; Heurich, *I Watched*, 43.

16. Joseph J. Varga, *Hell's Kitchen and the Battle for Urban Space: Class Struggle and Progressive Reform in new York City, 1894–1914* (New York: Monthly Review Press, 2013), 122–125.

17. *One Hundred Years of Brewing* (Chicago: H.S. Rich, 1903), 400; Heurich, *I Watched*, 40–41; Milton Rubincam, "Mr. Christian Heurich and His Mansion," *Records of the Columbia Historical Society of Washington, D.C. 1960–1962* (Washington, D.C.: Columbia Historical Society, 1963), 173. Rubincam claims that the company was named "Ritter and Heurich," whereas *American Breweries* lists it as "Heurich and Ritter." Candace Shireman, "The Rise of Christian Heurich and His Mansion," *Washington History* 5.1 (Spring/Summer 1993): 10–11; W.A.S. Douglas. "Christian Heurich Observes 75th Anniversary Here," *Times Herald*, June 7, 1940, C-3.

18. "Christian Heurich at Home," 8.

19. Joe Coker, *Liquor in the Land of the Lost Cause* (Lexington: University Press of Kentucky, 2007), 18–19; Glenn R. Carroll and Anand Swarminathan, "Density Dependent Organizational Evolution in the American Brewing Industry from 1633–1988," *Acta Sociologica* 34 (1991): 155–175.

20. Carroll and Swarminathan, 161; operational dates taken from Van Wieren, *American Breweries*, 59–60, 375–376. Van Wieren's data only lists years, so a brewery listed as in operation in 1874–1875 may have been open two years, or slightly more than one. To keep my figures consistent, I credited each brewery for a full year for each year listed. So a brewery listed as being in business in 1880–1882 would be credited with operating for three years.

21. Van Wieren, 59–60.

22. Garrett Peck, *Capital Beer: A Heady History of Brewing in Washington, D.C.* (Charleston: The History Press, 2014), 44.

23. Peck, *Capital*, 44–46; *One Hundred Years of Brewing*, 250.

24. *One Hundred Years of Brewing*, 401–402; Peck, 47–48.

25. Peck, *Capital*, 52.
26. Peck, *Capital*, 52–65.
27. Peck, *Capital*, 65–68.
28. Amelia Heurich Diary, August 2, 1923.
29. Heurich, *I Watched*, 42. Ritter moved to Cumberland, Maryland, where he bought out the Washington Brewery. The Paul Ritter brewery operated from 1872 to 1894. Runner, 64–65.
30. Hermann Schlüter, *The Brewing Industry and the Brewery Workers' Movement in America* (Cincinnati: International Union of the United Brewery Workmen of America, 1910), 90–93; Peter Hernon and Terry Ganey, *Under the Influence: The Unauthorized Story of the Anheuser-Busch Dynasty* (New York: Avon, 1991), 43.
31. Hernon, 43; K. Austin Kerr, "The American Brewing Industry: 1865–1920," in *The Dynamics of the International Brewing Industry Since 1800*, R.G. Wilson and T.R. Gourvish, eds. (London: Routledge, 1998), 181; Schlüter, 90–93.
32. Cindy R. Lobel, *Urban Appetites: Food and Culture in Nineteenth-Century New York* (Chicago: University of Chicago Press, 2014),179–182.
33. Heurich, *I Watched*, 41.
34. Heurich, *I Watched*, 42; Jon M. Kingsdale, "The 'Poor Man's Club': Social Functions of the Urban Working-Class Saloon," *American Quarterly* 25.4 (October 1973): 476; Shireman, "The Rise of Christian Heurich," 12.
35. Stanley Nadel, *Little Germany: Ethnicity, Religion and Class in New York City, 1845–80* (Urbana: University of Illinois Press, 1990), 83–84.
36. These figures come from Walter Kamphoefner, "The German Component to American Industrialization," in *Immigrant Entrepreneurship: German-American Business Biographies, 1720 to the Present*, vol. 2, edited by William J. Hausman (German Historical Institute). Last modified May 30, 2014. http://www.immigrantentrepreneurship.org/entry.php?rec=189
37. Heurich described how he proposed to his wife in *I Watched*, 43; Rubincam, "Mr. Christian Heurich and His Mansion," 175; "Christian Heurich at Home," 9.
38. Letter from Carl Keyser, December 1, 1981, 41. Copy in author's possession. Keyser, a nephew of Christian Heurich, wrote a long series of letters to family members describing the family history. A copy of the letters were given to the author by Ms. Jan King Evans Houser.
39. Heurich, *I Watched*, 51, 54; Clarence Dickenson Long, *Wages and Earnings in the United States, 1860–1890* (New York: Arno Press, 1975), 48; Shireman, "Rise of Christian Heurich," 12.
40. John Clagett Proctor, "The Schuetzen Park and the Home of Asa Whitney" *Proctor's Washington and Environs* (Washington, D.C.: n.p., 1950).
41. Schade defended Captain Henry Wirz, commander of the Andersonville Prison. He was convinced Wirz was innocent, but was unable to spare his client. He claimed Witz's body for burial for the man's family, as well as that of one of those hanged for involvement in the assassination of President Abraham Lincoln, George Atzerodt. Ironically, Schade later owned the Peterson House, where Lincoln was taken to die after being shot in Ford's Theater across the street. http://boothiebarn.com/2012/08/26/louis-schade-esquire/ (accessed 25 January 2014); *National Republican*, 1 June 1875; "The Coming Schuetzenfest," *Evening Star*, July 16, 1875, 4.
42. Harman Wiley Ronnenberg, *Material Cultural of Breweries* (Walnut Creek, CA: Left Coast Press, 2011), 66; *One Hundred Years of Brewing*, 147.
43. *Reports of Cases Argued and Adjudged in the Supreme Court of the District of Columbia Sitting in General Term, From May 25, 1882 to October 29, 1883* (Washington, D.C.: John L. Ginck, 1884), 204–209.

44. *Evening Star*, July 5, 1878; *Evening Star*, August 17, 1878; "City News in Brief," *Washington Post*, July 18, 1878, 4.
45. Heurich, *I Watched*, 55–56; "Elections of Bank Officers," *Washington Post*, January 9, 1878, 4; Heurich is listed among the bank's managers in an advertisement in 1876. See "German American Savings Bank," *Evening Star*, April 21, 1876. Heurich is also listed among the directors of the bank in both the 1877 and 1878 Boyd's city directories.
46. "The Suspended Banks," *Washington Post*, November 6, 1878, 1; Heurich, *From My Life*, 12.
47. Heurich claims that the bank episode took place either before or during 1877 in *I Watched*, 55–56. However, articles in the *Washington Post* indicate that it occurred in 1878. See "Elections of Bank Officers," *Washington Post*, January 9, 1878, 4; "The Suspended Banks," *Washington Post*, November 6, 1878, 1; "The Broken Banks," *Washington Post*, November 8, 1878, 4. For Heurich's quote "nor endorse for others," see his scrapbook using a 1908 desk diary. The entry is undated, but is located on the page for November 14, 1908. However, he used the diary for articles and quotes dating at least as late as 1926. Scrapbook property of Jan King Evans Houser.
48. The author's own definition based upon outside readings.
49. John R. Logan and Harvey L. Molotch. *Urban Fortune: The Political Economy of Space* (Berkley: University of California Press, 2007), 30.
50. Heurich, *From My Life*, 12–13.
51. Jonathan Levy, *Freaks of Fortune: The Emerging World of Capitalism and Risk in America* (Cambridge: Harvard University Press, 2012), 147.
52. "A Great Big Desk for Gen. Grant," *The News*, May 5, 1955. Clipping in collection of the Christian Heurich House. The desk bears the date 1872. Schultze made other large pieces of furniture that he sold in Washington. An 1874 news story noted that he had sold "the elegant cabinet made exclusively of Rocky Mountain wood, which created so much admiration in Washington, and which was eventually purchased of him by Senator [William M.] Stewart [R–NV] for $1,500." The story also noted that "he now has under construction another piece of work, which, when completed, will far out rival in beauty the cabinet in question, and for which he expects to realize a handsome sum." This raises the interesting possibility that Mr. Schulze regularly made expensive furniture to sell to powerful politicians in Washington. *Helena Weekly Herald*, October 15, 1874, 7.
53. Heurich, *I Watched*, 71; Emily Apt Geer, *First Lady: The Life of Lucy Webb Hayes* (Fremont, OH: The Rutherford B. Hayes Presidential Center, 1995), 149–155; "The God Gambrinius," *Washington Post*, July 30, 1878, 4.
54. "The New Schuetzen Building," *Washington Post*, January 7, 1880, 1; "The Sports of the Schuetzen Fest Covered with a Wet Blanket," *Washington Post*, July 31, 1878, 4. Wolf continued to be active in Jewish and German groups in Washington, and lobbied against Prohibition until the passage of the 18th Amendment. Marni Davis, *Jews and Booze: Becoming American in the Age of Prohibition* (New York: New York University Press, 2012), 131–132, 143–144.
55. Heurich, *I Watched*, 76.
56. "Sale of Real Estate," *Evening Star*, June 22, 1877; "Building Permits," *Evening Star*, October 11, 1877; *One Hundred Years*, 400–401; 1888 Sanborn Map, Library of Congress, http://hdl.loc.gov/loc.gmd/g3851gm.g01227001.
57. "Georgetown Gossip," *Washington Post*, July 12, 1878, 4.
58. John R. Logan and Harvey L. Molotch, *Urban Fortune: The Political Economy of Space* (Berkley: University of California Press, 2007), 32–39.

59. *The Statues at Large of the United States of America* (Washington, D.C.: Government Printing Office, 1879), 20:7. 136.

60. Elizabeth J. Miller, "Dreams of Being the Capital of Commerce: The National Fair of 1879," *Records of the Columbia Historical Society* 51 (1984): 73–75.

61. "The National Fair," *Evening Star*, October 23, 1879, 2; "Gaining Ground," *Washington Post*, October 23, 1879, 4; Miller, 75–76.

62. Miller, 78–81.

Chapter 3

1. *Historical and Commercial Sketches of Washington and Environs* (Washington, D.C.: E.E. Barton, 1884), 152.

2. Heurich, *I Watched*, 55.

3. Christian Heurich, "Looking Backward and Looking Forward," *Washington Post*, March 4, 1929, 23.

4. *Historical and Commercial Sketches*, 152–153.

5. Alexandria's Tivoli Brewery (Portner's) used cars of this type to ship their product throughout the South.

6. http://en.wikipedia.org/wiki/Refrigerator_car (accessed 3 June 2014).

7. http://www.chosi.org/bottles/washington.htm (Accessed June 1, 2014). Local D.C. collector and historian Mike Cianciosi complied these dates using D.C. city directories.

8. Cochran, 124.

9. Two were also brewers at other times: Julius Eisenbeiss had his own brewery from 1890 to 1893, and William Zanner from 1875 to 1879.

10. "Breweries," *Washington Post*, February 2, 1881, 2.

11. There were undoubtedly other active bottlers, so this list should be interpreted as a sample and not a complete list.

12. https://www.census.gov/population/www/documentation/twps0027/tab11.txt (accessed June 12, 2014); Cochran, 173.

13. Martin Stack, "Local and Regional Breweries in America's Brewing Industry, 1865–1920," *Business History Review* 74 (Autumn 2000): 440.

14. Cochran, 111–112.

15. Stack, "Liquid Bread," 138.

16. Many also did establish their own tied saloons, as well, but newspaper advertisements for the shipping brewers at the time indicate a push to sell to better-off consumers outside the traditional saloon.

17. C.C. Pearson and J. Edwin Hendricks, *Liquor and Anti-Liquor in Virginia, 1619–1919* (Durham, NC: Duke University Press, 1967), 288–289.

18. Stack, 140.

19. James D. Norris, *Advertising and the Transformation of American Society, 1865–1920* (New York: Greenwood Press, 1990), 26. Cited in Jib Fowles. *Advertising and Popular Culture* (London: Sage, 1996), 37.

20. See, for example, the ad from James Butler, bottler in the *Evening Star* for May 12, 1883, p. 4.

21. David M. Higgins, "'Forgotten Heroes and Forgotten Issues': Business and Trademark History during the Nineteenth Century," *Business History Review* 86 (Summer 2012): 284.

22. In the late 1940s, after Heurich had died, the brewery carried the connection even further, adding an eagle to the brand's label, copying a famous sculpture of an eagle that is in the U.S. Senate's chamber. Unfortunately, there are no surviving records that indicate the specific differences between Senate and Heurich's Lager, which were both of the lager style and apparently not dark beers like Maerzen. However, in private conversations with the author, several local brewers who recreated Heurich's Lager believe it had a higher BTU and a higher alcohol content than Senate.

23. Stack, 140.

24. Stack, 140; Heurich, *I Watched*, 96.

25. Stack, 140–141. Pabst and Blatz were also both in Milwaukee, which would equalize shipping costs.

26. Anna Watkins, "To Help a Child: The History of the German Orphan Home," *Washington History* 18/1, 2 (2006): 121–124.

27. The article describing the ceremony does not list what each individual placed inside the cornerstone. "The New Schuetzen Buildings," *Washington Post*, January 7, 1880, 1.

28. "The Union Veteran Corps," *National Republican*, January 8, 1881, 4; "Fun on Runners," *National Republican*, January 5, 1881, 4; "The October Celebration Here," *Evening Star*, September 3, 1881, 4; "Beer and Temperance," *Washington Post*, May 11, 1882, 2; Gary Heurich, "The Christian Heurich Brewing Company," *Records of the Columbia Historical Society, 1973–1974* (Charlottesville: University Press of Virginia, 1976), 607.

29. "A Brewery Badly Burned," *Washington Post*, May 2, 1881, 1. The story in the *National Republican* claims that it started in the engine house. "Two Sunday Fires," *National Republican*, May 2, 1881, 4.

30. Heurich, *I Watched*, 81–82; "The Conflict at a Fire," *Washington Post*, May 5, 1881, 2; "An Official Apology," *National Republican*, May 6, 1881, 4; Heurich, *From My Life*, 21; "Christian Heurich," *Washington Past and Present: A History*, vol. 5, John Clagett Proctor, ed. (New York: Lewis Historical Publishing, 1932), 1036.

31. http://www.maggieblanck.com/Blanck/Bremen Sailors.html (Accessed January 8, 2015).

32. Heurich, *I Watched*, 82; Rubicam, "Mr. Christian Heurich and His Mansion," 192, 195; Heurich, *My Life*, 64.

33. Heurich, *I Watched*, 82.

34. Proctor, 1036; W.A.S. Douglas. "Christian Heurich Observes 75th Anniversary Here," *Times Herald* (Washington, D.C.), June 7, 1940, C-3.

35. Heurich, *I Watched*, 82; J.O. Webster, "The Malarial Cachexia," *The Boston Medical and Surgical Journal* 101 (July–December 1879): 180–185. Webster was a physician in Maine, and his article was focused on Union veterans who had contracted malaria in the American South during the Civil War.

36. Arthur Latham and T. Crisp English, eds., *A System of Treatment in Four Volumes*, vol. 3: *Special Subjects* (New York: Macmillan, 1914), 144. The same or similar treatments were recommended in medical books from the 1870s, 1880s and 1890s. See, for example, Herman Weber and F. Parkes Weber, *The Spas and Mineral Waters of Europe* (London: Smith, Elder & Co, 1896), 295, and H. von Ziemssen, ed. *Cyclopedia of the Practice of Medicine*, vol. 2: *Acute Infectious Diseases* (New York: William Wood & Co., 1875), 677–678; Horatio C. Wood and Robert Meade Smith, eds. *The Therapeutic Gazette: A Monthly Journal of the Physiological and Clinical Therapeutics*, Whole Series, vol. 9; Third Series, vol. 1, no. 1 (January 15, 1885): 560.

37. Karl E. Wood, "Spa Culture and the Social History of Medicine in Germany," Ph.D. diss., University of Illinois at Chicago, 2004, 147–149.

38. Merrylees, 28–47, 56.

39. Heikki Lempa, "The Spa: Emotional Economy and Social Classes in Nineteenth-Century Pyrmont," *Central European History* 35/1 (2002): 42.

40. Merrylees, 50–52.

41. Lempa, 61. The upper classes did not stop going to spas, but while they remained an important clientele, they were no longer the most numerous.

42. The same standards did not apply to women, and would not do so until the twentieth century. Katherine

Vester, "Regime Change: Gender, Class, and the Invention of Dieting in Post-Bellum America," *Journal of Social History* 44/1 (Summer 2010), 39–43. This was not universal, as some wealthy men, such as "Diamond Jim" Brady, became famous for their size as a sign of their success.

43. Lempa, 58–61.

44. Lempa, 62–64.

45. Wood, 178; Merrylees, 49.

46. Heurich, *From My Life*, 15–16; Heurich, *I Watched*, 83; John Merrylees, *Carlsbad and its Environs* (New York: Scribner's, 1885), 24; Peter Gay, *Schnitzer's Century: The Making of the Middle Class, 1815–1914* (New York: W.W. Norton, 2002), 234.

47. Heurich, *I Watched*, 82–83; http://en.wikipedia.org/wiki/Parsifal (accessed June 6, 2014); Heurich, *From My Life*, 15.

48. Letter from Carl Keyser, December 1, 1981, 42, 44; Heurich, *I Watched*, 85; "Heurich," *Baltimore Sun*, September 26, 1884, 2.

49. Heurich, *I Watched*, 85–88; Candace Shireman, "The Rise of Christian Heurich and His Mansion," *Washington History* 5/1 (Spring/Summer 1993): 10.

50. In *From My Life*, Heurich claims it was 1883, but the press coverage indicates it was 1885.

51. Dorothee Schneider, *Trade Unions and Community: The German Working Class in New York City, 1870–1900* (Urbana: University of Illinois Press, 1994), 156–158; Hermann Schlüter, *The Brewing Industry and the Brewery Workers' Movement in America* (Cincinnati: International Union of United Brewery Workmen of America, 1910), 114–116.

52. Daniel R. Ernst, "Free Labor, the Consumer Interest, and the Law of Industrial Disputes, 1885–1900," *The American Journal of Legal History* 36/1 (January 1992), 21–23; Schlüter, 238–240.

53. Probably Charles Walter (c. 1824–c. 1894), a lawyer, justice of the peace, and notary.

54. "The News at Washington," *New York Times*, August 20, 1885, 5; "Mr. Heurich and the Unions," *Evening Star*, June 2, 1885, 1.

55. "Mr. Heurich and the Unions," *ibid*.

56. "A Meeting of Retail Liquor Dealers," *Evening Star*, January 15, 1884, 1; "The Union Men Win," *Washington Critic*, August 15, 1885, 3; "Mr. Heurich's Alternative," *Washington Post*, August 15, 1885, 4; "Heurich's Boycott," *National Republican*, August 15, 1885, 1; "The Saloons and the Workingman," *Evening Star*, August 15, 1885, 1.

57. "Mr. Heurich's Alternative," *ibid*.; "Mr. Heurich Accepts," *Washington Post*, August 16, 1885, 8; "80, Works for His Uncle Who is 98."

58. One contemporary newspaper article claims that he refused to sign, but the unions were unwilling to restart the boycott. "A Serious Phase of Boycotting," *The American Settler*, London, Middlesex, UK, January 16, 1886, 26.

59. Heurich, *From My Life*, 17.

60. It may have been late 1885. Heurich is not clear about the date in his memoirs. Heurich, *From My Life*, 19. See also "Christian Heurich at Home," 11.

61. Julius Thausing, *The Theory and Practice of the Preparation of the Malt and the Fabrication of Beer* (Philadelphia: Henry Carey Baird & Co., 1882), 661–662. Quoted at http://blackcreekbrewery.wordpress.com/2010/06/22/history-byte-barrel-pitching/ (Accessed June 14, 2014); Heurich, *From My Life*, 19; "Hints in Regard to the Prevention of Explosions When Pitching Casks, etc.," *The Brewer's Journal* 29 (September 1, 1904): 494–496.

62. Heurich, *From My Life*, 19.

63. "Mrs. Mathilde Heurich Dead," *Washington Post*, (January 21, 1895), 5; Carl A. Keyser, *Leatherbreeches: Hero of Chancellorsville* (Rye Beach, NH: Amherst Press, 1989), 158.

64. *Washington Life* 2/17 (April 23, 1904): 8; Letters to John G. Meyers, March 2, 1889, and April 2, 1889, Heurich Papers, Container 9, Folder 113.

65. It is now known as Mariánské Lázně. http://en.wikipedia.org/w/index.php?title=Mari%C3%A1nsk%C3%A9_L%C3%A1zn%C4%9B&oldid=590656354 (accessed June 14, 2014).

66. Heurich, *From My Life*, 19–20; Heurich, *I Watched*, 100; Candace S. Shireman, "The Rise of Christian Heurich's Mansion: A Study of the Interior Design and Furnishings of the Columbia Historical Society's Christian Heurich Mansion, Washington, D.C., 1892–1914," Master's thesis, George Washington University, 1989; "City Personals," *Washington Post*, July 23, 1888, 2.

67. Oscar E. Anderson, *The Health of a Nation: Harvey W. Wiley and the Fight for Pure Food* (Cincinnati: University of Cincinnati Press, 1958), 70–73.

68. C.A. Crampton, *Fermented Alcoholic Beverages, Malt Liquors, Wine, and Cider* (Washington, D.C.: Government Printing Office, 1887), 280.

69. Crampton, 281.

70. "Purity of Lager Beer," *Washington Post*, October 18, 1891, 5. I have not found a specific connection between Heurich and the Representative from Ohio; however, since Romeis was also a native of Germany, it is possible that they met at events hosted by one of the city's many German societies. "Jacob Romeis," *Magazine of Western History* 4.1 (May 1886): 850–52. Romeis was one of only four German-born members of the U.S. House of Representatives at the time. Willi Paul Adams, *Ethnic Leadership and the German-Born Members of the U.S. House of Representatives, 1862–1945: A Report on Research in Progress* (Berlin: John F Kennedy-Institut für NordAmerikastudien, 1996), 56, 58.

71. Crampton, C.A, *ibid.*; advertisement, "It Stands Unrivaled," *Washington Post* November 8, 1891, 3; "Christian Heurich," *Washington Past and Present*, 1038; "How Heurich Forced U.S. to Show Purity of His Beer," *Times-Herald*. June 7, 1914, Special section.

72. "Report of the Secretary of Agriculture," *United States Congressional Serial Set, Issue 2732* (Washington, D.C.: Government Printing Office, 1890), 58.

73. Named after German microbiologist Robert Koch, who proved that tuberculosis was an infectious disease and not hereditary. He won the Nobel Prize in Physiology or Medicine in 1905. Buckingham (1870–1963), was later Dean of the School of Veterinary Medicine at George Washington University and served as White House Veterinarian.

74. "Tracing Tuberculosis," *Evening Star*, June 7, 1894, 8; "Tuberculosis in Cattle," *Washington Times*, June 7, 1894, 2; Kate Field, "Making Milk Wholesome," *Kate Field's Washington*, July 4, 1884, 68–69. The accounts differ on how many of the cattle were tested at first, but they each agree that five with the disease were destroyed at the demonstration and that most of the ninety-odd cattle on Heurich's farm were clean of the disease. "Display Ad," *Washington Post,* June 17, 1894, 16.

75. *Fiscal Relation Between the United States and the District of Columbia*, vol. 2: *Joint Select Committee to Investigate the Fiscal Relation Between the United States and the District of Columbia, 1912*, 1660. Lancaster was a local lawyer and active on the Washington Board of Trade and Chamber of Commerce and long advocated for great self-rule for the District.

76. Edgar Sydenstriker, *A Brief History of Taxation in Virginia* (Richmond: Legislative Reference Bureau of Virginia, 1915), 39–41.

77. In some press accounts it's spelled "Coopes."

78. "Frank Hume," *A History of the City of Washington, Its Men and Institutions*, Allan Slauson, ed. (Washington,

D.C.: The Washington Post, 1903), 257–259; "Charles Jacobson," Slauson, 287; "Hon. L.G. Hine" Slauson, 48, 377–378; *Boyd's Directory of the District of Columbia, 1897* (Washington, D.C.: William H. Boyd, 1897), 371; Shireman, "The Rise of Christian Heurich and His Mansion," 13; "Charles E. Meyer," *Washington Post,* January 9, 1914, 4; Lyon G. Tyler, "Frank Hume," *Men of Mark in Virginia,* vol. 4 (Washington, D.C.: Men of Mark Publishing Company, 1908), 202–207.

79. "Diverse" within the context for 1890, since they were all wealthy white men. There were no women or persons of color included.

80. William D'Arcy Haley, ed., *Philp's Washington Described: A Complete View of the American Capital, and the District Of Columbia; with Many Notices, Historical, Topographical, and Scientific, of The Seat of Government* (New York: Rudd & Carleton, 1861), 37; Joseph J. Varga. *Hell's Kitchen and the Battle for Urban Space: Class Struggle and Progressive Reform in New York City, 1894–1914* (New York: Monthly Review Press, 2013), 122–125.

81. Shireman, 33, 37; Walter Albano, "History of the DuPont Circle Neighborhood, Washington, D.C., 1880–1900," Master's thesis, University of Maryland, 1982, 113. Quoted in Shireman, 37.

82. It was renamed DuPont Circle in 1882 after Rear Admiral Samuel Francis DuPont.

83. Shireman, 32–37; Heurich, *I Watched,* 98–99.

84. Heurich, *I Watched,* 100; Jonathan Reinarz, *Historical Perspectives on Smell* (Urbana: University of Chicago Press, 2014), 145–147.

85. Heurich, *From My Life,* 20.

86. "Heurich's Brewery Gone," *Washington Post,* July 23, 1892, 1; "To Rise from the Ashes," *Washington Post,* July 24, 1892, 3.

87. Gary F. Heurich, "The Christian Heurich Brewing Company, 1872–1956," *Records of the Columbia Historical Society, 1973–1974* (Washington, D.C.: Columbia Historical Society, 1976), 607; Heurich, *I Watched,* 100.

88. Heurich, *I Watched,* 103; Charles Hoffman, *The Depression of the Nineties: An Economic History* (Westport, CT: Greenwood, 1970), 109.

89. Heurich, *I Watched,* 103–104. He crossed off this latter part in the typed draft, perhaps because he thought it too immodest.

90. R. Reid Badger, *The Great American Fair: The World's Columbian Exposition and American Culture* (Chicago: Nelson Hall, 1979), 47–52.

91. Robert Herrick, *Memoirs of an American Citizen* (Cambridge: Harvard University Press, 1963), 147. Originally published in 1905. Quoted in Robert H. Rydell, *All the World's a Fair: Visions of Empire at American International Expositions, 1876–1916* (Chicago: University of Chicago Press, 1984), 38.

92. Heurich, *I Watched,* 103.

93. Rydell, 38–71.

94. *One Hundred Years of Brewing,* 401.

95. John Clagett Proctor, "'Foggy Bottom' or Hamburg," *Proctor's Washington and Environs* (Washington, D.C.: n.p., 1950), 305–308.

96. Heurich, *I Watched* 100, 112; Suzanne Berry Sherwood, *Foggy Bottom, 1800–1975: A Study in the Uses of an Urban Neighborhood,* G.W. Washington Studies, #7 (Washington, D.C.: George Washington University, 1978), 11–18.

97. Susan Tilghman Mason, "John Granville Meyers, Architect," Master's thesis, George Washington University, 1979, 4–19, 25.

98. Heurich, *I Watched,* 114.

99. Mark Twain and Charles Dudley Warner, *The Gilded Age: A Tale of Today* (New York: Penguin Books, 2001), 236–237.

100. Twain, 232.

101. Mason, 33–34; in Elizabeth Jane Miller's 1977 master's thesis on the dry goods merchants in Washington in the 1880s, she found 39 of the 259 total such merchants were from "Germanic" areas. That was only fifteen percent, but the German-born population made up about eight percent of the total population of the city, so they were over-represented among dry goods merchants. Elizabeth Jane Miller, "The Dry Goods Trade in Washington, D.C., 1880–1889," Master's thesis, George Washington University, 1977, 14; *1880 United States Census Report,* Table XVI, 538–539.

102. Mason, 73–75.

103. J.G. Meyer to Christian Heurich, May 26, 1893. Letter in the archives of the Christian Heurich House.

104. *History of the City of Washington,* 447–448.

105. Katzenjammer, the wailing of cats, is a wonderfully descriptive term for a hangover.

106. Rubicam, "Mr. Christian Heurich and His Mansion," 184–86.

107. Letter from Carl Keyser, December 1, 1981, 45; "Two Ladies in a Runaway," *Washington Post,* January 27, 1893, 6.

108. "Christian Heurich," *Washington Past and Present,* 1037. For more on the role of the D.C. Board of Trade, see Lessoff, *The Nation and Its City.*

109. Kathryn Allamong Jacob, "High Society in Washington During the Gilded Age: 'Three Distinct Aristocracies,'" Ph.D. diss., Johns Hopkins University, 1986, 197–199; John Rhodehamel to Mrs. Benjamin Evans (11 March 1985), copy in the author's possession. Mr. Rhodehamel was the Mount Vernon archivist; "Lady Regents in Session," *Washington Post,* June 3, 1893, 8.

Chapter 4

1. Heurich, *I Watched,* 112.

2. "Building Permits Issued," *Washington Post,* May 11, 1894, 8.

3. "Corner-Stone of Heurich Brewing Company's Plant Laid," *Washington Post,* July 5, 1894, 8.

4. "On The Blacklist Now," *Washington Post,* February 22, 1895, 8.

5. "Big Crap Game Broken Up," *Washington Post,* May 6, 1895, 6.

6. "May Be a Boycott on Beer," *Washington Post,* July 6, 1896, 2.

7. *Ibid.;* "Union Against Union," *Washington Post,* January 7, 1896, 2.

8. *Ibid.;* "To Boycott Home-Made Beer," *Washington Post,* January 8, 1896, 2.

9. Eugene Debs, "Industrialism Unionism," *International Socialist Review* Vol. X, No. 6 (December 1909), https://www.marxists.org/archive/debs/works/1909/industrial.htm (Accessed 12/23/2014).

10. Portner's usually went its own way and was the brewery in which unions had the smallest foothold. Winning the boycott battle against the other area breweries would help local brewery workers organize Portner's, while a loss would weaken their position.

11. "Boycott May Spread," *Washington Post,* January 10, 1896, 2.

12. "Brewers will meet Them," *Washington Post,* January 14, 1896, 2.

13. "Divided Against Themselves," *Washington Post,* January 17, 1896, 4; "Gambrinius is Getting Groggy," *Washington Post,* January 18, 1896, 2.

14. "Boycott the Saloons," *Washington Post,* January 19, 1896, 4.

15. "First Carload of Union Beer," *Washington Post,* January 23, 1896, 4.

16. "Saloons Want Peace," *Washington Post*, January 21, 1896, 2.

17. "Brewers Will Arbitrate," *Washington Post*, January 31, 1896, 2.

18. "Opposed by the Officers," *Washington Post*, February 1, 1896, 5.

19. "Cannot Accept Terms," *Washington Post*, February 3, 1896, 5; "May Split the Labor Forces," *Washington Post*, February 4, 1896, 8; "Brews More Trouble," *Washington Post*, February 6, 1896, 8; "A Break in the Ranks," *Washington Post*, February 7, 1896, 3.

20. "A New Central Union," *Washington Post*, February 24, 1896, 4; "To Work For Brewers," *Washington Post*, March 3, 1896, 9; "News of the Labor Unions," *Washington Post*, March 15, 1896, 5; "To Break the Combine," *Washington Post*, March 25, 1896, 9.

21. "To Lift All the Boycotts," *Washington Post*, April 1, 1896, 10; "Labor Unions at Odds," *Washington Post*, April 21, 1896, 2; "All on the Fair List," *Washington Post*, May 18, 1896, 2; "Vital Work Omitted," *Washington Post*, August 19, 1896, 2; "May Cause Worse Boycott," *Washington Post*, September 25, 1896, 10; "Invited to Dine at New Brewery," *Washington Post*, October 28, 1896, 2.

22. "Headlong Down and Elevator Shaft," *Washington Post*, April 11, 1896, 11; "Overtook and Stopped a Runaway," *Washington Post*, July 30, 1896, 7. The newspaper article does not note whether the driver who lost control of the wagon kept his job.

23. "Slight Wound Results Fatally," *Washington Post*, September 4, 1896, 10; "Sites Struck the Blow," *Washington Post*, September 5, 1896, 10; "Murder is Now the Charge," *Evening Times*, September 3, 1896, 8. The *Evening Times* was uncertain how to spell Sites's name, referring to him as "Henry Seitz" and then John Seitz; "Light Sentence for Plonk's Slayer," *Washington Post*, May 4, 1897, 2.

24. "Sites Struck the Blow," 10; "Detectives Fail to Find Sites," *Washington Post*, September 6, 1896, 8; "Plonk's Murderer Caught," *Washington Post*, September 12, 1896, 2; "Sites Admits His Guilt," *Washington Post*, September 13, 1896, 4.

25. Quoted in Chalmers McGeagh Roberts, *The Washington Post: The First One Hundred Years* (New York: Houghton Mifflin, 1977), 71.

26. http://www.streetsofwashington.com/2015/08/the-slaughtering-sun-brutal-heat-wave.html (accessed August 10, 2015).

27. This seems unlikely. Insurance companies were encouraging the design of factories less prone to fires, and Heurich's brewery would certainly have qualified. For more on insurance companies and factory design, see John R. Stilgoe, "Moulding the Industrial Zone Aesthetic: 1880–1928," *Journal of American Studies* 16/1 (April 1982): 12–13.

28. *One Hundred Years of Brewing*, 401.

29. Stilgoe, 7.

30. "Sights of a Brewery," *Washington Post*, November 10, 1896. 8.

31. *Ibid.*

32. "A New Brewery," *Evening Star*, November 19, 1896, 12.

33. *Ibid.*

34. David E. Nye, *American Technological Sublime* (Cambridge: MIT Press, 1994), 126.; Karen Dubinsky, "'The Pleasure is Exquisite but Violent': The Imaginary Geography of Niagara Falls in the Nineteenth Century," *Journal of Canadian Studies* 29/2 (Summer 1994): 64–88.

35. "Thousands Tested the Beer," *Washington Post*, November 11, 1896, 4; "Viewed the New Brewing Plant," *Washington Post*, November 12, 1896, 2; "German Day at Heurich's," *Washington Post*, November 13, 1896, 9; "Thousands Watch Gambrinius Work," *Washington Post*, No-

vember 14, 1896, 9; "A Brewery Advertisement," *Printers Ink*, December 23, 1896.

36. "Ladies Day at the Brewery," *Washington Post*, November 12, 1896, 1.

37. "Ladies' Day at Gambrinius' Shrine," *Washington Post*, November 16, 1896, 7.

38. "Ladies' Day at the Brewery," *Washington Post*, November 17, 1896, 2.

39. As Leo Marx, one of the pioneer theorists of the role of technology in American culture has noted, the term "technology" itself was not in common usage before World War I. Leo Marx, "Technology: The Emergence of a Hazardous Concept," *Social Research* 64/3 (Fall 1997): 966–967.

40. "Sights of a Brewery," *Washington Post*, November 10, 1896, 8.

41. William Littmann, "The Production of Goodwill: The Origins and Development of the Factory Tour in America," *Perspectives in Vernacular Architecture* 9 (2003): 73.

42. Advertisement, *Washington Post*, July 12, 1896, 4; advertisement, *Washington Post*, October 4, 1896, 4; advertisement, *Washington Post*, August 16, 1896, 4; advertisement, *Washington Post*, August 30, 1896, 4; advertisement, *Washington Post*, August 2, 1896, 4; advertisement, *Washington Post*, October 13, 1896, 4.

43. Advertisement, *Washington Post*, July 12, 1896, 4.

44. Jonathan Zimmerman, "'The Queen of the Lobby': Mary Hunt, Scientific Temperance, and the Dilemma of Democratic Education in America, 1879–1906," *History of Education Quarterly* 31/1 (Spring 1992): 1–30

45. Mary Foote Henderson, *The Aristocracy of Health: A Study of Physical Culture, Our Favorite Poisons, and a National and International League for the Advancement of Physical Culture* (Washington, D.C.: Colton, 1904), 410.

46. http://en.wikipedia.org/wiki/Mary_Foote_Henderson (Accessed October 14, 2014). She was not only a temperance activist, she also promoted vegetarianism.

47. "Trade Marks," *The Western Brewer* (July 15, 1897), 1299; "Trade Marks," *The Western Brewer* (June 15, 1897), 1110k.

48. *The Western Brewer* 26, 2248. Quoted in Stanley Baron, *Brewed in America: A History of Beer and Ale in the United States* (Boston: Little, Brown, 1962), 268.

49. Peter J. Buckley and Brian R. Roberts, *European Direct Investment in the USA before World War I* (New York: St. Martin's Press, 1982), 53–56.

50. Richard A. Hawkins, "American Boomers and the Flotation of Shares in the City of London in the Late Nineteenth Century," *Business History* 49/6 (November 2007): 802–810.

51. "Albert Carry's Brewery Not Sold," *Washington Post*, May 4, 1889, 3; "In the Hands of Englishmen," *Washington Post*, May 5, 1889, 7; "Looks Like a Swindle," *Washington Post*, May 6, 1889, 8; "Carry's Brewery Sold," *Washington Post*, June 4, 1889, 8; "Legal Fight over Carry's Brewery," *Washington Post*, July 7, 1889, 2; "Carry's Brewery as a Campaign Issue," *Washington Post*, September 23, 1889, 7; "Brewer Carry's Explanation," *Washington Post*, September 11, 1889, 2; "Carry's Brewery Sold," *Washington Post*, August 23, 1889, 5; Peck, *Capital*, 43.

52. "Beverage for Summer" display ad, *Washington Post*, July 26, 1891, 2; Peck, *Capital*, 43–46.

53. Heurich, *I Watched*, 119.

54. Keyser, 161. Em did not marry the doctor either, and never married.

55. Letter from Carl Keyser, 27 October 1981, 6. This is one of a series of letters that Carl Keyser, Amelia Heurich's nephew, wrote to relatives about the family history. Copy in the author's possession.

56. These dates are based upon letters in the Christian

Heurich Papers, Historical Society of Washington, D.C., MS 537. Folder 878.

57. Letter: Amelia Keyser to Christian Heurich, March 11, 1898, Heurich Papers, Folder 878; Letter, Amelia Keyser to Christian Heurich, March 15, 1989, *ibid*.

58. "Science against Superstition," *Washington Post*, December 12, 1898, 2.

59. Amelia Louise Keyser Heurich Diary. Entries for January 8, 1899; January 11, 1899; January 22, 1899; January 23, 1899; and January 24, 1899. Oscar must not have remained in the Heurich's employ. In her diary entry for May 5, 1900, Amelia refers to a butler named Dabney.

60. "Mrs. Mathilde Heurich Dead," *Washington Post*, January 21, 1895, 5; Rubicam, "Mr. Christian Heurich and His Mansion," 183–85; Heurich, *I Watched*, 119; http://www.erh.noaa.gov/lwx/winter/storm-pr.htm (accessed October 10, 2014); http://www.srh.noaa.gov/images/bro/research/pdf/Great_Arctic_Outbreak_1899.pdf. That also means his sister-in-law from his first wife was now his mother-in-law.

61. Frank Crane, "The Ship Cure," April 10, 1926. It appears in Heurich's scrapbook using a 1908 desk diary. The clipping is pasted on the page for November 4, 1908. Scrapbook property of Jan King Evans Houser.

62. Amelia Louise Keyser Heurich Diary. Entries for July 13, 1899, and July 15, 1899; http://www.navsource.org/archives/12/174040.htm (accessed October 10, 2014); http://archiver.rootsweb.ancestry.com/th/read/The ShipsList/1999–03/0920467412 (accessed October 10, 2014); John Malcolm Brinnin, *The Sway of the Grand Saloon: A Social History of the North Atlantic* (New York: Delacorte Press, 1971), 318; Drew Keeling, *The Business of Transatlantic Migration Between Europe and the United States, 1900–1914* (Zurich: Chronos, 2012), 229.

63. Mark A. Russell, "Picturing the Imperator: Passenger Shipping as Art and National Symbol in the German Empire," *Central European History* 44 (2011), 233.

64. Brinnin, 310–320, 387–388.

65. Amelia Louise Keyser Heurich Diary. Entries for August 1, 1899; August 2, 1899; and August 8, 1899. Amelia listed two dozen cities and towns they visited. Heurich, *From My Life*, 23; http://en.wikipedia.org/wiki/SS_F%C3%BCrst_Bismarck_(1890), (Accessed October 10, 2014); Brinnin, 326.

66. *From My Life*, 23–24.

67. Central Europe was then in the midst of the Thirty Years War (1618–1648), which not only spread the usual destruction of wars, but diseases such as the plague as well.

68. http://en.wikipedia.org/wiki/Oberammergau_Passion_Play (Accessed September 23, 2014).

69. Robert Rydell, John E. Findling, and Kimberly D. Pelle, *Fair America: World's Fairs in the United States* (Washington, D.C.: Smithsonian Books, 2000), 133.

70. See, for example, Robert W. Rydell and Rob Kroes, *Buffalo Bill in Bologna: The Americanization of the World, 1869–1922* (Chicago: University of Chicago Press, 2005); and Robert H. Rydell, *All the World's A Fair: Visions of Empire at American International Expositions, 1876–1916* (Chicago: University of Chicago Press, 1984).

71. Alexander C.T. Geppert. *Fleeting Cities: Imperial Expositions in Fin-de-Siècle Europe* (New York: Palgrave-Macmillan, 2010), 65, 74.

72. Geppert, 78–79.; Barrett Eastman and Frederick Mayer, Paris, *1900: The American Guide to the City and Exposition* (New York: Baldwin & Eastman, 1899), 86.

73. Geppert, 84.

74. Ferdinand W. Peck, "The United States at the Paris Exposition in 1900," *The North American Review* 168/506 (January 1899): 26–27, 32–33.

75. http://exposition-universelle-paris-1900.com/MEDAILLES_ET_BIJOUTAILLERIE (accessed 9/30/2014).

76. *Catalogue of Exhibitors in the United States Sections of the International Universal Exposition, Paris, 1900* (Paris: Société Anonyme Des Imprimeries Lemercier, 1900), 303–305; *Report of the Commissioner-General for the United States to the International Universal Exposition, Paris, 1900*, vol. 5 (Washington, D.C.: Government Printing Office, 1901), 16, 484. Schuller's report did not indicate the standards used to judge the entries.

77. "Chr. Heurich Brewing Co.: The Model Brewing Plant of the Twentieth Century," *Washington Times*, January 28, 1906.

Chapter 5

1. *I Watched*, 120.

2. Heurich spoke German with his family up until World War I, at which point he switched entirely to English. Near the end of Heurich's life, however, his family switched back to German. He was hard of hearing, and found it easier to understand his native language. Interview with Jan King Evans Houser, 2014.

3. Karla Louise Harrison's interview with Sarah Heald, December 30, 1987; Karla Harrison and Jan Evans's interview with Sarah Heald, August 1, 1985. Transcripts at the Christian Heurich House Museum.

4. Family stories come from the staff of the Heurich House museum staff, and from multiple talks with the Heurichs' granddaughter, Jan King Evans Houser. It is not known how old Christian Junior was when he was given a copy of the house key.

5. "The Last Day of Smoke," *Washington Times*, August 1, 1899, 5.

6. "The Smoke Nuisance," *Evening Star*, February 21, 1898, 4.

7. Adam W. Rome, "Coming to Terms With Pollution: The Language of Environmental Reform, 1865–1915," *Environmental History* 1/3 (July 1996): 6, 15; Heurich, *I Watched*, 100.

8. "Mr. Heurich Acquitted," *Evening Star*, March 8, 1902, 16.

9. Heurich crossed out "real" in the original draft, suggesting that he was ill at other times, but did not consider those instances to be serious.

10. Heurich did not specify which sisters-in-law, or which friends, in his memoirs. *I Watched*, 120.

11. Heurich, *From My Life*, 25. The Heurichs usually took the most prestigious German liners, and in 1902, for the Hamburg-Amerika Line, that meant the *Deutschland*, which the Heurichs took to Europe in 1900 when it was brand-new. It was the only Hamburg-Amerika Line ship to hold the Blue Riband, the unofficial award for the passenger liner with the record highest speed crossing the Atlantic Ocean in regular service (1830–1952). The *Deutschland* held the record in 1900, 1901 and 1903. It's possible that the Heurichs were on either the second of the ship's record-breaking runs in 1900 or its 1903 voyage, as each took place in August and September, the time of year the Heurichs commonly returned home to the United States from Europe. Unfortunately, neither Heurich nor his wife noted the specific ships they took on their trips those years.

12. http://www.hindawi.com/journals/ecam/2013/521879/ (Accessed October 10, 2014); Heurich, *From My Life*, 25.

13. Heinrich Lahmann, *The Airbath as a Means of Healing and Hardening the Body* (Stuttgart: A. Zimmer, 1901), 4–6, 13; Alison F. Frank, "The Air Cure Town: Commodifying Mountain Air in Alpine Central Europe," *Central European History* 45 (2012): 197–198, 201–202.

14. Lahmann. 4–6, 13.

15. Heurich, *From My Life*, 26; Lahmann, 13.

16. Pamela K. Gilbert, "Popular Beliefs and the Body: 'A Nation of Good Animals,'" *A Cultural History of the Human Body in the Age of Empire*, Michael Sappol and Stephen P. Rice, eds. (London: Bloomsbury, 2010), 128–129.

17. http://www.measuringworth.com/uscompare/relativevalue.php (Accessed 10/30/2014).

18. http://memim.com/romhild.html (Accessed 10/29/2014); "Disastrous Fire," *Stevens Point Daily Journal*, May 2, 1891, 2. In *From My Life*, Heurich claimed the fire was in 1890, but he was off by one year. *From My Life*, 25.

19. Heurich, *I Watched*, 120, 128.

20. Peter Blinkle, *Heimat: A Critical Theory of the German Idea of Homeland* (Rochester, NY: Camden House, 2002).

21. Andreas Fahrmeir, *Citizenship: The Rise and Fall of a Modern Concept* (New Haven: Yale University Press, 2007), 66.

22. "Response of Mr. Heurich," Association of the Oldest Inhabitants Washington, D.C. (September 2, 1942), Heurich Papers, Container 2, Folder 19.

23. "President to Open Fair," *Washington Post*, November 15, 1903, E3; "Monster Celebration Planned by Germans," *Washington Times*, November 15, 1903, 8; "At President's Touch," *Washington Post*, November 24, 1903, 2; "German Fete to Continue," *Washington Post*, November 29, 1903, 2; Frank H. Pierce III, *The Washington Saengerbund: A History of German Song and Culture in the Nation's Capital* (Washington, D.C.: n.p., 1981), 53.

24. Stefan Manz, "Diaspora and Weltpolitik in Wilhelmine Germany," in Panikos Panayi, *Germans as Minorities uring the First World War: A Global Comparative Perspective* (Burlington, VT: Ashgate, 2014), 27.

25. Portner's in Alexandria, Virginia, was not included. Robert Portner was part owner of Capital Brewing with Albert Carry and they divided the market between their two companies: Portner's did not sell in D.C., and Capital Brewing did not sell in Virginia. Portner was also more adamantly anti-union than were the other five area companies, which may have impacted his decision not to participate in their pact with local unions. Peck, *Capital*, 59, 86.

26. "Seek a Blanket Injunction," *Washington Post*, July 22, 1904, 2; "Men Struck At Noon," *Washington Post*, July 22, 1904, 2.

27. *The Western Brewer*, May 15, 1901, 196; Peck, *Capital*, 86.

28. Peck, *Capital*, 86–87; Roger J. Calantone, Cornelia Droge, David S. Litvack and C. Anthony di Benedetto, "Flanking in a Price War," *Interfaces* 19/2 (March–April 1989): 4–6.

29. Peck, *Capital*, 86–87. Keep in mind that Carry also denied that he had sold his brewery to British investors when he had, in fact, done so.

30. "No Strike Ordered," *Evening Star*, July 19, 1904, 16.

31. "Brewery Firemen Serve a Notice on Mr. Heurich," *Washington Times*, July 20, 1904, 1.

32. "No Strike Ordered," *Evening Star*, July 19, 1904, 16.

33. *Ibid.*

34. *Ibid.*

35. "Order for a Strike," *Washington Post*, July 20, 1904, 2; Judith Stepan-Norris and Caleb Southworth, "Rival Unionism and Membership Growth in the United States, 1900–2005: A Special Case of Inter-organizational Competition," *American Sociological Review* 75/2 (April 2010): 244–245. The authors discuss the effects such competition between unions have upon union growth, noting that it may in some circumstances help the union movement.

36. Daniel R. Ernst, "Free Labor, the Consumer Interest, and the Law of Industrial Disputes, 1885–1900," *The American Journal of Legal History* 36/1 (January 1992): 23.

37. "Begin Strike at Noon," *Washington Post*, July 21, 1904, 2; "Fifteen Workmen Surrender Jobs at Noon Hour," *Washington Times*, July 21, 1904, 9.

38. "Firemen on Strike," *Evening Star*, July 21, 1904, 1; "Against Beer Trust," *Evening Star*, July 21, 1904, 5.

39. Perry R. Duis, *The Saloon: Public Drinking in Chicago and Boston, 1880–1920* (Urbana: University of Chicago Press, 1983), 25–26.

40. Quoted in Peck, *Capital*, 87.

41. *The Western Brewer* 21 (May 15, 1896): 917.

42. Madelon Powers, "The 'Poor Man's: Saloonkeepers, Workers, and the Code of Reciprocity in U.S. Barrooms, 1870–1920," *International Labor and Working-Class History* 45 (Spring 1994): 2.

43. Powers, 4–5.

44. "Men Struck at Noon," *Washington Post*, July 22, 1904, 2.

45. "Who Makes the Profit?" *Western Brewer* 23 (July 15, 1898): 1248.

46. *Ibid.*; "How It Will be Done," *The Liquor Trade Review*, May 31, 1898.

47. It was renamed Arlington County in 1920 to avoid continuing confusion between Alexandria County and neighboring (but legally separate) Alexandria City.

48. Michael Lee Pope, *Shotgun Justice: One Prosecutor's Crusade Against Crime and Corruption in Alexandria and Arlington* (Charleston: The History Press, 2012), 53–54.

49. Pope, 33–37.

50. Pope, 66–71. A painting depicting the raid currently decorates a wall in the main branch of the Arlington County Library.

51. "Petitioners Without Right," *Washington Times*, July 26, 1904, 2; "Firemen Will Remain Out Indefinitely," *Washington Times*, July 27, 1904, 9; "Brewery Strike Off," *Washington Post*, July 28, 1904, 9; "Firemen Are At Work," *Evening Star*, July 28, 1904, 6.

52. This raises the question of why the Heurichs did not remain at one of those spas. Heurich does not note his absence in his memoirs, but it may simply have been the very human desire to be at home, in familiar surroundings with friends and family during a crisis.

53. Heurich, *I Watched*, 125–126; http://www.shipsonstamps.org/Topics/html/bremen.htm (accessed October 30, 2014); https://heurichhousecollectionscorner.wordpress.com/ (Accessed June 30, 2015). The stories about the nanny and the knockings were related to me by Kimberly Bender, director of the Christian Heurich House, October 30, 2015. They are also recorded in a letter from Amelia's nephew, Carl Keyser, December 1, 1981, 31. Copy in the author's possession.

54. "Liège 1905," John E. Findling and Kimberly D. Pelle, eds., *Historical Dictionary of World's Fairs and Expositions, 1851–1988* (New York: Greenwood Press, 1990), 187–188.

55. *Report of the Commissioners to the Liege Exposition*, U.S. House of Representatives, 59th Congress, Document #454, January 29, 1906, 1–2. Heurich also donated money to Gore's university.

56. *Report of the Commissioners*, 2,5; "French and American Art at Liège," *Brush and Pencil* 16/3 (September 1905): 99; "Chr. Heurich Brewing Co. The Model Brewing Plant of the Twentieth Century," *Washington Times*, January 28, 1906. For examples of the labels see Bob Kay, *U.S. Beer Labels, 1950 and Earlier*, vol. 2: *Eastern & Southern States* (self-published, 2007), 19.

57. "The Pure Beer Craze," *The Western Brewer* 22 (March 15, 1897): 489; "Pure Beer Bills," *The Western Brewer* 24 (March 15, 1899): 123; "Beer in Chunks," *The Liquor Trade Review* (September 15, 1899), 5; "Pure Beer Bills," *The Western Brewer* 24 (February 15, 1899): 76.

58. Donna J. Wood, "The Strategic Use of Public Policy:

Business Support for the Pure Food and Drug Act," *The Business History Review* 59/3 (Autumn 1985): 410.

59. Wood, 415.

60. *Journal of Proceedings of the National Pure Food and Drug Congress* (Washington, D.C. 1898), 2–5.

61. "Chr. Heurich Brewing Co. The Model Brewing Plant of the Twentieth Century," *Washington Times*, January 28, 1906.

62. "District Leaders Raise Large Sums for Sufferers," *Washington Times*, April 20, 1906, 3: http://www.measuringworth.com/uscompare/relativevalue.php (Accessed 24 February 2015); "For New Auditorium," *Evening Star*, February 26, 1906, 2; "Ice for the Babies," *Evening Star*, July 06, 1906, 1.

63. Christian Heurich to the W.H. Moon Company, October 18, 1908, *Heurich Notebook*, n.p.; "A Neutral Tinted Autumn," *Washington Post*, November 12, 1905, SM1.

64. Heurich did not list the breweries he worked in from 1857 to 1866 in his memoirs.

65. At least, there is no mention in either the professional brewery journals or in the D.C. newspapers of his doing so.

66. Baltimore tried to create a world's fair in 1914 for the centennial of the War of 1812 and the writing of "The Star-Spangled Banner," but failed to get enough support. Findling and Pelle, 403.

67. *Official Guide: Jamestown Ter-Centennial Exposition* (n.p.: Jamestown Official Publication Company, 1907), 51, 75.

68. "Historical Census Browser," University of Virginia Library. http://mapserver.lib.virginia.edu/ (Retrieved October 27, 2014).

69. Carl Abbott, "Dimensions of Regional Change in Washington, D.C.," *The American Historical Review* 95/5 (December 1990): 86–87, 96.

70. "Jamestown 1907: Jamestown Tercentennial Exposition," in Findling and Pelle, 200–201; Robert T. Taylor, "The Jamestown Tercentennial Exposition of 1907," *The Virginia Magazine of History and Biography* 65/2 (April 1957): 190, 198.

71. *The Official Blue Book of the Jamestown Ter-Centennial Exposition*, Charles Russel Keiley, ed. (Norfolk: Colonial Publishing, 1909), 489–493; Marc T. Law, "How do Regulators Regulate? Enforcement of the Pure Food and Drug Act, 1907–38," *Journal of Law, Economics, & Organization* 22/2 (October 2006): 483–486.

72. *Official Blue Book*, 489–493, 650.

73. "Gold Medal for Heurich's Beers," *Washington Post*, November 9, 1907, 5.

74. Heurich, *From My Life*, 30; Edmund Morris, *Theodore Rex* (New York: Random Books, 2001), 497–498; Robert Bruner and Sean Carr, *The Panic of 1907: Lessons Learned from the Market's Perfect Storm* (Hoboken, NJ: John Wiley and Sons, 2007), 141–142; Stanley Lebergott, *Annual Estimates of Unemployment in the United States, 1900–1957* (Washington, D.C.: NBER, 1957), 215.

75. Heurich, *From My Life*, 29.

76. Amelia Heurich Diary, entries for June 15–23, 1909; notes from interview with Jan Evans Houses (undated), Christian Heurich papers, Container 19, Folder 179. Ms. Houser told the author the same things in an interview in 2014.

77. Heurich, *From My Life*, 30.

78. The figures on the wall include those listed in the paragraph, as well as William Shakespeare, Raphael, Herodotus, Friedrich Schiller, the Marquis de Lafayette, and Amadeus Mozart. They are still there and may be seen on special house tours.

79. http://www.theshipslist.com/ships/descriptions/ShipsK.shtml#kav (Accessed March 24, 2015).

80. Heurich, *From My Life*, 34; Amelia Heurich Diary, entry for July 22, 1912.

81. Amelia Heurich Diary, entries for July 22, 28, 29, September 2, September 12, 1912. The offer by Georg II comes from the typed transcript of a 1985 tour of the Heurich mansion given by a granddaughter, Jan King Evans Houser, Christian Heurich Papers, Series III, Container 19, Folder 184.

82. The letter was initialed by Amelia, Heurich's wife.

83. Heurich, *From My Life*, 29; "Letter to Miss Grace Hubbard Bell," March 13, 1910, *Heurich Notebook*.

84. Alfred Bennett Iles, *The Log of a Sea-Going Pioneer* (n.p.: n.d.), 127–128; Walter Harvey Weed, *The Mines Handbook* (Tuckahoe, NY: The Mines Handbook Company, 1922); The National Park Service, "Nugget Creek Cabin," *Wrangell-St. Elias*.

85. Heurich's involvement is detailed in several letters to the First Mortgage Guarantee Trust Company, dated November 14, 1910, December 14, 1910, and January 14, 1911. See also A.(?)J. Stewart to Henry Brehm, November 10, 1910, Henry Brehm to Christian Heurich (n.d.), and Christian Heurich to Henry Brehm, November 16, 1910, *Heurich Notebook*.

86. The cartoon has been trimmed so the artist and date are gone. The editorial accompanying it has no byline. A search of various newspaper databases does not locate it either. The cartoon and article clippings appear in Heurich's scrapbook, which used a 1908 desk diary. It is located on the pages for November 27 and 28, 1908. Heurich used the diary for articles and quotes dating at least as late as 1926, and most of the clippings are from the 1920s, so the cartoon and editorial likely date from that period as well. Scrapbook property of Jan King Evans Houser.

87. Amelia Heurich Diary, entry for March 6, 1913; "Modify Excise Bill," *Washington Post*, March 2, 1913, 4; "Liberal Excise Bill," *Washington Post*, March 3, 1913, 4.

88. Heurich advertisement, *Washington Herald*, January 7, 1914. Emphasis in the original.

89. When the title differed from *Recipes of Quality*, I noted the differing title. Christian Heurich Brewing Co., Washington, D.C.; German-American Brewing Co., Buffalo, NY; McAvoy Brewing Co., *Malt Marrow Cookbook*, Chicago; Rock Island Brewing Co., Illinois; Oakland Brewing & Malting Co., *The Blue and Gold Cook Book*, Oakland, CA.; Indianapolis Brewing Co., Indianapolis, IN; Pilsener Brewing Co., Cleveland, OH; Geo. Wiedemann Brewing Co., Cincinnati, OH; S. Liebmann's Sons Brewing Co., *Rheingold Recipes*, New York, NY; and the Huebner-Toledo Breweries Co., Toledo, OH. There are undoubtedly others.

90. Christian Heurich Brewing Company, *Recipes of Quality* (n.p.: 1912). Emphasis in the original.

91. *Recipes*, 3–11.

92. Heurich's Lager, Senate, and Maerzen were the brewery's other three regular products. A Bock beer was sold only in the spring.

93. T.B. Benson, *A Treatise on the Virginia Prohibition Act* (Charlottesville: L.F. Smith and W.F. Souder, Jr., 1916), 14–15.

94. His was not the only D.C. brewer making a temperance beer, either. Abner-Drury made a brand named Progressive. Washington Brewery produced Noalco, and Robert Portner's made Small Brew. None of them caught on.

95. Amelia Heurich Diary, entries for July 2, July 17, August 18, August 22, September 1, September 4, September 11 and September 15, 1913.

96. Brinnin, 387–388.

97. "Weather in Various Cities," *Evening Star*, February 13, 1914, 17; "Earth is Turned at Memorial Site," *Evening Star*, February 12, 1914, 1.

Chapter 6

1. Stuart received 92 percent of the vote against two token socialist candidates.

2. Robert A. Hohner, "Prohibition Comes to Virginia: The Referendum of 1914," *Virginia Magazine of History and Biography* 75 (1967): 78–79; *Acts and Joint Resolutions of the General Assembly of the State of Virginia* (Richmond 1914), 23.

3. Pearson, 271–272; Hohner, 78–79; Cannon, 154.

4. *Daily News-Record* (Harrisonburg, VA), January 21, 1914; February 19, 1914; August 11, 1914; October 19, 1914.

5. Quoted in Hohner, 80.

6. Hohner, 476–478.

7. Hohner, 479; Pearson, 279–280.

8. Quoted in Hohner, 80.

9. *Alexandria Gazette*, September 21, 1914.

10. Hohner, 487. Wilson was born in Virginia and attended law school at the University of Virginia as a young man, but he grew up in Georgia and South Carolina and lived most of his adult life in New Jersey.

11. United States Census, 1910.

12. "Prohibition in Virginia," *American Brewers' Review* (December 1916): 366.

13. "Charles E. Meyer is Dead," *Evening Star*, January 8, 1914, 24. Meyer was sixty years old. The cause of death was not listed.

14. "Teamster Tries to Assassinate Veteran Brewer," *Washington Times*, April 2, 1912, 1.

15. "W.F. Dismer Funeral Set for Monday," *Washington Post*, 19 May 1945, 5.

16. Amelia Heurich Diary, March 11, March 16, and April 7, 1914.

17. Amelia Heurich Diary, June 27, July 4, July 9, and July 10, 1914. On the *Imperator*; see https://en.wikipedia.org/wiki/SS_Imperator (Accessed July 6, 2015).

18. Amelia Heurich Diary, July 25, 1914.

19. Amelia Heurich Diary, July 26, July 27, July 28, and July 29, 1914.

20. Amelia Heurich Diary, July 31 and August 1, 1914.

21. Amelia Heurich Diary, August 1, 1914.

22. Ezra Schabas, *Sir Ernest MacMillan: The Importance of Being Canadian* (Toronto: University of Toronto Press, 1994), 34; "Consular Nominations: Senate Also Asked to Ratify President's Postmaster Appointments," *Washington Post*, June 20, 1914, 2.

23. Amelia Heurich Diary, August 3, August 4, and August 5, 1914.

24. Amelia Heurich Diary, August 6, 1914.

25. Michael S. Neiberg, *Dance of the Furies: Europe and the Outbreak of World War I* (Cambridge: Harvard University Press, 2011), 165.

26. Amelia Heurich Diary, August 11, August 12, and August 16, 1914.

27. James W. Gerard, *My Four Years in Germany* (New York: George H. Doran, 1917), 143; Heurich, *I Watched*, 127–29.

28. Amelia Heurich Diary, August 17 and August 18, 1914.

29. Heurich, *I Watched*, 131; Amelia Heurich Diary, August 20, August 21, August 23, and August 25, 1914.

30. Amelia Heurich Diary, September 7, 1914; Arthur Link, *Wilson: The Struggle for Neutrality, 1914–1915* (Princeton: Princeton University Press, 1960), 75; *Report on Operations of United States Relief Commission in Europe* (Washington: Government Printing Office, 1914), 2, 7, 83.

31. Heurich, *I Watched*, 130–31; Amelia Heurich Diary, September 12, 1914.

32. Amelia Heurich Diary, September 12, September 14, September 16, September 17, September 18, and September 21, 1914, end notes in 1914 diary.

33. H. Schuyler Foster, Jr., "How America Became Belligerent: A Quantitative Study of War News, 1914–1917," *The American Journal of Sociology* 40:4 (January 1935): 464–475; "Local News Briefs," *Washington Post*, February 12, 1916, 14.

34. It was not just a sore point for the Germans, but also for Americans from Austria-Hungary and the other Central Powers as well. However, the German community in the United States took the lead on this issue simply because it was the largest and most influential of the immigrant communities from the Central Powers.

35. Clifton James Child, *The German-American in Politics, 1914–1917* (Madison: University of Wisconsin Press, 1939), 44–46, 52.

36. "Deutsche Heraus!" *Washington Journal*, January 23, 1915, translation by Stefan Manz; "The Neutrality Question," *Washington Journal*, January 23, 1915.

37. "Statement of Horace L. Brand," February 3, 1915; *Records of the Department of State Relating to World War I and its Termination, 1914–1929*, RG 59 NARA M367; "In Germany's Cause," *Washington Post*, January 31, 1915, 8.

38. Child, 54–55; "German-American League Organizes," *New York Tribune*, February 21, 1915, 2.

39. "Hear Bartholdt Warn," *Washington Post*, February 9, 1915, 3; Heurich, *I Watched*, 131–132.

40. Carl Wittke, *German Americans and the World War* (Columbus: The Ohio State Archaeological and Historical Society, 1936), 67–69.

41. "Remarks at a Press Conference," February 2, 1915; *The Papers of Woodrow Wilson*. ed. Arthur S. Link (Princeton: Princeton University Press, 1980), 30:174 (hereafter referred to as *PWW*); "Remarks at a Press Conference," February 2, 1915, *PWW* 30:200; Woodrow Wilson to Edward Mandell House, January 28, 1915, *PWW* 30:145.

42. "Report of the Labor Committee," *Yearbook of the United States Brewers Association, 1915* (New York City: United States Brewers Association, 1915), 65.

43. "Threaten to Close All Local Breweries," *Evening Star*, March 24, 1915, 2; "The Jones-Works Excise Law," *The Western Brewer* (August 1913), 74.

44. *Annual Report of the Secretary of Labor* (Washington D.C.: Government Printing Office, 1916), 36.

45. Brewery closing dates taken from Dale P. Van Wieren, *American Breweries II* (West Point, PA: East Coast Breweriana Association, 1995), 374–377; Danny Morris and Jeff Johnson, *Richmond Beers: A Directory of the Breweries and Bottles of Richmond, Virginia*, 2nd edition (Richmond: n.p., 2000), 19.

46. Wilson Press Conference, January 15, 1917, *PWW* 50:771.

47. Gavit to Wilson, November 22, 1916, *PWW* 40:42.

48. Winthrop M. Daniels, *Recollections of Woodrow Wilson* (New Haven: privately printed, 1944), 51–52; Henry Wilkinson Bragdon, *Woodrow Wilson: The Academic Years* (Cambridge: Harvard, 1967), 291; John M. Mulder, *Woodrow Wilson: The Years of Preparation* (Princeton: Princeton University Press, 1978), 13.

49. Ray Stannard Baker, *Woodrow Wilson Life and Letters: Governor, 1910–1913* (Garden City: Doubleday, Doran, 1931), 63.

50. Kerr, 194.

51. *Washington Times*, March 2, 1917; *Washington Herald*, February 27, 1917.

52. *The Bee*, February 17, 1917; *The Bee*, March 3, 1917.

53. "District Swings into 'Dry Column,'" *Evening Star*, March 1, 1917; "Sheppard Bill May Become Law Today," *Evening Star*, March 2, 1917.

54. "Rubber, Beer and Iron Pole Get Together in Smash-Up," *Washington Herald* (March 2, 1917), 3. The reader might take the symbolism to mean that Heurich's business (the beer wagon), was about to crash into the Drys (rubber

is used to keep things dry). That's stretching things a bit, though.

55. Diary entry by Thomas W. Brahany, March 4, 1917, *PWW* 41:329. Brahany was the White House Chief Clerk; Wilson is quoted in Kerr, p. 195.

56. "Sheppard Dry Law is Upheld by Court," *Evening Star*, October 24, 1917, 1.

57. "D.C. Prohibition Bill Signed by President," *Evening Star*, March 5, 1917; "Prohibition," *The Bee*, March 10, 1917.

58. Heurich, *I Watched*, 134.

59. "King Booze Quits Throne in Capital," *Evening Star*, November 1, 1917, 1.

60. "Ghosts to Claim Old Barleycorn at 12 Tonight," *Washington Times*, October 31, 1917; *The Bee*, October 20, 1917.

61. "To Record the End of Liquor Selling," *Evening Star*, October 31, 1917; "Liquor's Last Day in Washington," editorial, *Evening Star*, October 31, 1917.

62. Ding Darling, "The Kaiser's Submarines Haven't Begun to Wreck as Many Lives," *Washington Herald*, October 31, 1917; "Another Fall Drive," *Washington Herald*, November 1, 1917; "Good-By John," *Washington Herald*, November 1, 1917.

63. Heurich, *From My Life*, 133–34; Heurich, *I Watched*, 135.

64. Heurich, *I Watched*, 135. President Woodrow Wilson was not a prohibitionist although some members of his cabinet were.

65. George W. Lillard, "In Re Construction of Foundations for Large German Guns," October 25, 1915. O.G. 402. RG 65, NARA; "Bellevue Farm: Heurich's Estates," Christian Heurich Papers, The Historical Society of Washington, D.C. MS 0537, Series II, Subseries E.

66. Lillard, *Ibid*.

67. Who was, incidentally, distantly related to Heurich through marriage.

68. Robert Koenig, *The Four Horsemen: One Man's Mission to Wage The Great War in America* (New York: Public Affairs, 2006), 201–203; Theodore Kornweibel, Jr., *Investigate Everything: Federal Efforts to Compel Black Loyalty during World War I* (Bloomington: Indiana University Press, 2002), 200.

69. Heurich noted these stories in one of his scrapbooks which used a 1908 desk diary. The entry is undated, but is located on pages for December 31, 1908, and the following page "Memoranda." The Mountain Lake Park where Heurich's friend heard the rumor was most likely the one in nearby Maryland and not the one in San Francisco, California. Scrapbook property of Jan King Evans Houser.

70. F.S. Underhill, "Christian Heurich, Neutrality," March 21, 1917. O.G. 402. RG 65, NARA.

71. Heurich began the process of becoming a citizen in 1867, and the five-year gap between 1867 and 1872 fits with the practice at the time.

72. F.S. Underhill, "Christian Heurich, Neutrality," March 21, 1917. O.G. 402. RG 65, NARA.

73. George W. Lillard, "RE: Chris. Heurich: Neutrality Matter," April 2, 1917. O.G. 402. RG 65, NARA.

74. "Germans Here Safe If They Obey Law; No General Internment, Baker Announces," *New York Times*, March 27, 1917, 1; Heurich, *From My Life*, 48; Heurich, 133.

75. Tomatso Shibutani, *Improvised News* (Indianapolis: Bobbs-Merrill, 1966), 133; Ellen Maury Slayden, *Washington Wife: Journal of Ellen Maury Slayden from 1897–1919* (New York: Harper & Row, 1962), entry for February 10, 1917, 292.

76. "Rev. Dr. Martin Tells Veterans City is Filled With Spies," *Evening Star*, March 26, 1917, 3; "Planning to Block German Partisans," *Evening Star*, March 26, 1917, 1; "Ground Glass Found in Bandages, He Says," *Evening Star*, March 29, 1917, 1; "Another German 'Plot' Comes to The Surface,"

Evening Star, March 30, 1917, 9; "U.S. Probing Activities of Spies, It Is Believed," *Evening Star*, April 4, 1917, 2; "German Plotters Joining Red Cross," *Washington Times*, March 29, 1917, 3.

77. "Germans Try to Incite Negroes Against U.S.," *Evening Star*, April 5, 1917, 18; "Knows of No Plot to Destroy Capitol," *Evening Star*, April 9, 1917, 1; "Flood of Spy Data," *Evening Star*, April 8, 1917, 16; "War Scare at Great Falls," *Evening Star*, April 8, 1917, 3.

78. "Back Wilson in War Crisis With Pledge," *Washington Times*, March 20, 1917, 1; "Loyalty Pledge is Signed by Hundreds," *Washington Times*, March 29, 1917, 11; "In Justice to Some Germans in Washington," *Washington Times*, March 27, 1917, 1.

79. "In Words of One Syllable," *Washington Times*, April 7, 1917, 8.

80. "Allegiance Only to United States," *Evening Star*, March 28, 1917, 2; "Pledge Loyalty to U.S.," *Washington Post*, March 29, 1917, 5.

81. "Pledge Loyalty to U.S.," *Washington Post*, March 29, 1917, 8; Heurich, *In My Life*, 133–134; Heurich, *I Watched*, 135.

82. Nicholas DiFonzo and Prashant Bordia, "Rumor, Gossip and Urban Legends," *Diogenes* 213 (2007): 19–20, 25; Ralph L. Rosnow and Gary Alan Fine, *Rumors and Gossip: The Social Psychology of Hearsay* (New York: Elsevier, 1976), 55. How is a rumor different from gossip? DiFonzo and Bordia define gossip as "evaluative social talk about individuals … that arises in the context of social network formation" and helps maintain "group norms … and group membership." Gossip in a personal story about someone violating local norms for interpersonal relationships in some way, such as having an extramarital affair, and so is a lesson in how not to behave. Moreover, rumors are not verified, but gossip may or may not be true.

83. Charles J. Walker and Bruce Blaine, "The Virulence of Dread Rumors: A Field Experiment," *Language and Communication* 11: 4 (1991): 291, 296.

84. DiFonzo and Bordia, 24; Slayden, 291.

85. DiFonzo and Bordia, 24.

86. Anthony Lyons and Yoshihisa Kashima, "How Are Stereotypes Maintained Through Communication? The Influence of Stereotype Sharedness," *Journal of Personality and Social Psychology* 85:6 (2003): 990; interview with Gary Heurich, 2006.

87. Allport and Postman, 10–13. In their study of rumors during the Second World War, they found that sixty-six percent of all rumors fell into this category. Twenty-five percent were "fear rumors," including those involving internal subversion. The remainder were "pipe dream" rumors, including those of an imminent peace agreement, and "miscellaneous" rumors that fit no category.

88. Allport and Postman, 12; Slayden, 291. Anti-Jewish rumors made up over thirteen percent of all rumors in those areas. In contrast, they constituted five percent of rumors in the South.

89. Slayden, 292; 1910 Census. There were few than 500 Austrian natives living in D.C. There were three foreign language publications issued by the Pan American Union in D.C., but they were not newspapers.

90. Rosnow and Fine, 58.

91. "Capital Spies to be Arrested at Once," *Washington Times*, April 9, 1917, 1; Prashant Bordia and Nicholas DiFonzo, "Problem-Solving in Social Interactions on the Internet: Rumor as Social Cognition," *Social Psychology Quarterly* 67:1 (March 2004): 34; Roberts, 139; "Another German 'Plot' Comes to the Surface," *Evening Star*, March 30, 1917, 9.

92. "Allegiance Only to United States," *Evening Star*, March 28, 1917, 2; "Mob Wrecks Car; Sent On Wild Run," *Evening Star*, March 28, 1917, 2.

93. "District to be Military Zone," *Washington Post*, November 18, 1917, 2; John Clagett Proctor, ed., *Washington Past and Present: A History*, 4 vols. (New York: Lewis Historical Publishing, 1930), 1:39; "Ice Cream Plants Resume Business," *Washington Post*, August 20, 1918, 10.

94. William Gibbs McAdoo to Robert Lansing, February 6, 1917, *PWW* 41:132; Robert Lansing, "A Statement," February 8, 1917, *PWW* 41:157–158.

95. "Wilson Issues Proclamation: Aliens Warned to Obey Laws," *Washington Herald*, April 7, 1917, 5; "Germans Must Surrender Arms By Tomorrow Noon," *Washington Herald*, April 22, 1917, 8.

96. "By the President of the United States of America A Proclamation," *Washington Post*, November 20, 1917, 4.

97. "Ousts 1,000 Germans," *Washington Post*, November 20, 1917, 1.

98. Dingle, 131–132; Pierce III, 77–79.

99. Heurich, *I Watched*, 138.

100. Heurich, *In My Life*, 133–134; Heurich, *I Watched*, 135. As an American citizen, Heurich could remain in the city.

101. "Intoxicating Liquors. Eighteenth Amendment. Interpretation of the Volstead Act," *Harvard Law Review* 34.4 (1921): 437.

102. Heurich, *I Watched*, 148.

103. Amelia Heurich Diary, January 16, 1920.

Chapter 7

1. Letter from Carl Keyser, December 1, 1981, 32, 60.

2. Chris began school in September 1919, and had spent Christmas break at home as well as making other trips to see his parents, so he was already writing an average of over two letters a week.

3. Amelia Heurich Diary, entries for September 20 and September 27, 1919; April 13, April 19, and April 21, 1920.

4. *The Record* (University of Pennsylvania yearbook) 1920, 252.

5. Amelia Heurich Diary, entries for October 6 and October 11, 1920.

6. Amelia Heurich Diary, entries for February 6 through February 15, 1921.

7. B.C. Forbes, "Sons of Rich men Carry On; Instances Pointed by Forbes," 1922. The clipping does not indicate a date or which paper it appeared in. It is copyrighted 1922. It is in Heurich's scrapbook, which used a 1908 desk diary. The entry is undated, but is located on the page for April 4, 1908. However, he used the diary for articles and quotes dating at least as late as 1926. Scrapbook property of Jan King Evans Houser.

8. Amelia Heurich Diary, entries for February 12 and February 22, 1921.

9. Peck, *Capital*, 82.

10. Letter from Carl Keyser, December 1, 1981, 32.

11. Interview with Jan King Evans Houser (2014)

12. "Sir Arthur Conan Doyle," *Evening Star*, April 26, 1922, 23; "Conan Doyle Says Spiritualism Rids Death of All Horrors," *Evening Star*, April 29, 1922, 28.

13. Amelia Heurich Diary, July 26, 1923.

14. Amelia Heurich Diary, December 2, 1918.

15. "Church Notice," *Washington Times*, May 6, 1900, 2.

16. Emma Dorothy Eliza Nevitte Southworth (1819–1899) was a popular American novelist.

17. "Spirit Pictures," *Evening Star*, February 3, 1900, 14. Thank you to Kimberly Bender, director of the Heurich House Museum, and to Erika Goergen, their collections manager, for pointing me to this article.

18. D. Alan Bensley, "Why Great Thinkers Sometimes Fail to Think Critically," *Skeptical Inquirer* 30/4 (July/August 2006): 49.

19. Brinnin, 450–451; Heurich, *I Watched*, 145.

20. S. William Halperin, *Germany Tried Democracy: A Political History of the Reich from 1918 to 1933* (New York: Norton, 1965), 243–246.

21. https://en.wikipedia.org/wiki/Hyperinflation_in_the_Weimar_Republic (Accessed October 1, 2015). For the chart, see Heurich's scrapbook using a 1908 desk diary. The chart is pasted on the page for July 10, 1908. Scrapbook property of Jan King Evans Houser.

22. Heurich, *I Watched*, 145–146; Heurich, *From My Life*, 49–52; Amelia Heurich Diary, July 4, July 18, and August 21, 1922; Modris Eksteins, *Rites of Spring: The Great War and the Birth of the Modern Age* (New York: Mariner Books, 1989), 270–271.

23. Amelia Heurich Diary, August 20, 1922.

24. Gerald D. Feldman, *The Great Disorder: Politics, Economics, and Society in the Inflation, 1914–1924* (New York: Oxford University Press, 1993), 565–566.

25. Amelia Heurich Diary, entries for July 21 and August 29, 1922.

26. Amelia Heurich Diary, entries for September 12, September 22, and September 27, 1922. Goucher moved to Towson, Maryland, in the late 1930s.

27. Amelia Heurich Diary, entries for July 22, August 4, and September 28, 1925; Heurich, *From My Life*, 51–52.

28. Amelia Heurich Diary, entries for December 5 and December 7, 1925.

29. Heurich, *From My Life*, 53.

30. Heurich, *From My Life*, 54.

31. The museum was still in operation as of 2015. http://www.thueringen.info/roemhild-steinsburgmuseum.html.

32. Robert B. Kane, *Disobedience and Conspiracy in the German Army, 1918–1945* (Jefferson, NC: McFarland, 2002), 69–75.

33. https://en.wikipedia.org/wiki/German_federal_election,_1930 (accessed November 27, 2015).

34. Heurich, *From My Life*, 56–57.

35. Heurich, *From My Life*, 57.

36. Heurich, *From My Life*, 57–59.

37. Letter from Carl Keyser, December 1, 1981, 24. Ironically, Adam Scheidt's brands were some of the strongest competitors for Heurich in D.C. after Prohibition ended. Christian Heurich, Jr., tried without success to buy their brands in the early 1950s.

38. This story was told to the author by one of Heurich's grandson's, Gary Heurich, in 2005. The other details about his health come from interviews with Jan King Evans Houser and the staff at the Christian Heurich mansion. The painting was created by Detlef Sammann (1857–1938), a German immigrant who also painted murals at the White House for the Harrison administration (information from the Heurich House). At least one observer said the story about lying on the floor looking at the pretty girls in the painting sounded more like Christian Jr. than Christian.

39. Amelia Heurich Diary, January 20, 1920.

40. Christian Heurich, "Looking Backward and Looking Forward," *Washington Post*, March 4, 1929, 23.

41. Georgia, Kansas, Louisiana, Mississippi, Nebraska, North Dakota, Oklahoma, and South Dakota.

42. https://en.wikipedia.org/wiki/Twenty-first_Amendment_to_the_United_States_Constitution (Accessed December 19, 2015).

43. Theoretically, had the 21st Amendment not been ratified, the country could still have enjoyed low-alcohol beer and wine because they no longer met the legal definition of "intoxicating." "Bill Signed; Capital Gets Beer To-

night," *Washington Post*, April 6, 1933, 1; "Capital Celebrates Beer's Return After 16 Years of Drought," *Washington Post*, April 7, 1933, 1.

44. "Oldest Brewer Thanks F.D.R," unaccredited clipping, collection of the author; Mark Benbow, "The Prohibition Two-Step: Two Steps In, Two Steps Out," *American Breweriana Journal* 166 (July–August 2010): 35; Kay, U.S. Beer Labels, 19–20.

45. Peck, *Capital*, 118.

46. Peck, *Capital*, 117–119; "Brewery Property Deed is Put on File," *Washington Post*, February 11, 1933, 17; display ad, *Washington Post*, February 22, 1933, 3. Home Brew is not mentioned in Heurich's advertisements, but the November 1936 issue of *The Western Brewer* (p. 104) notes that Heurich registered their label for that brand on October 20, 1936.

47. "Engineer's Act Averts Serious Brewery Blaze," *Washington Post*, August 19, 1933, 20.

48. Peck, *Capital*, 121; "Bandit Slashed Woman: Four Rob Brewery," *Washington Post*, October 6, 1933, 1; "Dunn, Berlin, Found Guilty by D.C. Jury," *Washington Post*, November 29, 1934, 1; "Court is Arsenal as Misunas Tells of Holdup Here," *Washington Post*, November 27, 1934, 1.

49. Selden Richardson, *The Tri-State Gang in Richmond: Murder and Robbery in the Great Depression* (Charleston: The History Press, 2012), 38, 131; Peck, *Capital*. The two gang leaders who escaped from a Richmond jail were caught and executed in Virginia's electric chair in 1935. Misunas served sixteen years for his part in the Union Station robbery and was released.

50. Display ad, *Washington Post*, September 17, 1933, 4.

51. http://www.salemil.us/pages/SalemIL_About/museum (Accessed October 9, 2016); "Christian Heurich at Home," 21.

52. Maureen Ogle, *Ambitious Brew: The Story of American Beer* (New York: Harcourt, 2006), 206. Acme Brewing in California was one of the most notable examples of a brewery trying to overcome beer's reputation as fattening. Their early beer cans in the mid–1930s claimed their beer was "Dietetically Nonfattening" and "Non-Fattening Refreshment." The author has several examples in his collection.

53. Ogle, 204, 217–218.

54. Display ad, *Washington Post*, December 4, 1934, 6.

55. Display ad, *Washington Post*, October 25, 1934, 17; display ad, *Washington Post*, August 27, 1934, 11; display ad, *Washington Post*, July 23, 1934, 13; display ad, *Washington Post*, September 10, 1934, 15; display ad, *Washington Post*, September 24, 1934, 15; display ad, *Washington Post*, June 7, 1934, 18.

56. Display ad, *Washington Post*, June 22, 1936, 17.

57. "Senate Ale Advertisement," *Washington Post*, 15 December 1938, 8.

58. Paul P. Walsh, "How Heurich Holds Washington Market," *The American Brewer* (August 1938): 40–41. Point-of-sale items included signs, lights, clocks, etc., for stores, restaurants, and bars.

59. Constance McLaughlin Green, *Washington Capital City, 1879–1950* (Princeton: Princeton University Press, 1963), 2:399.

60. George M. Adams, Jr., "Radio Waves and Ripples," *Washington Post*, October 8, 1934, 22.

61. John Strausbaugh, *Black Like You: Blackface, Whiteface, Insult & Imitation in American Popular Culture* (New York: Penguin, 2006), 225.

62. Green, 2:401–402.

63. James S. Thomas to Eugene Davidson (November 3, 1939); Eugene Davidson to the Christian Heurich Brewing Company (November 8, 1939); Eugene Davidson to the Christian Heurich Brewing Company (December 1, 1939); "Alliance Opens 140 Job Opportunities," n.d. All in

Christian Heurich Papers, The Historical Society of Washington D.C., Series I, Sub-Series B, Folder 7.

64. "Brewers Maintain Advertising Pace Through Late Summer," *Modern Brewery Age* (September 1949): 56.

65. http://ww2propaganda.eu/art01.htm (Accessed 12/1/2015); "Heurichs Return to Grandest Sight in World—The U.S. Flag," *Evening Star*, October 17, 1939, 1; "Heurichs to Sail Soon for America," *Washington Post*, September 9, 1939, 15.

66. "Hindus, Back, Sees Soviet-Reich War: Here For The New York Season," *New York Times*, October 15, 1939, 42; "Heurichs Return to Grandest Sight in World—The U.S. Flag," *The Evening Star*, October 17, 1939, 1.

67. Hearing before the Appeals Board of the National Production Authority (October 11, 1951), NARA-CP, RG 277. UD, Entry30-NPA Appeals Dkt, Box 23.

68. Brewers around the country began "de-Germanifying" their labels and product names. Germanic eagles became American eagles, and umlauts began to disappear. In Columbus, Ohio, for example, "Noch-Eins Pale Beer" became "Washington Pale Beer," and the little German Burgermeister mascot was replaced by an American eagle. Michigan's Goebel Brewing replaced their Germanic eagle with an American one.

69. Special Section, *Times-Herald* (June 7, 1940).

70. Letter from Carl Keyser, December 1, 1981, 57; "Marines Called Out, Firemen Too, When 56 Monkeys Escape," *Washington Post*, September 22, 1940, 1.

71. Advertisement, *Washington Post*, May 31, 1944, 5; "Civilian Volunteers Needed To Aid Mailing of Ration Books," *Washington Post*, May 15, 1943, B1.

72. The story about the rathskeller was told by a visitor to the staff of the Christian Heurich House, who relayed it to me. E. Howard Hunt and Greg Aunapu, *American Spy: My Secret History in the CIA, Watergate and Beyond* (New York: Wiley, 2007), 9.

73. See advertisements in the *Washington Post*, "The Far West," September 3, 1941, 4.; "Dixie," September 10, 1941, 7; "Middle West," September 17, 1941, 11; "New England," September 24, 1941, 4; "Coal Belt," October 1, 1941, 6; "Oil Fields," October 14, 1941, 2; "Cotton Country," October 23, 1941, 6; "Down East," November 21, 1941, 6; and "The Northwest," *Evening Star*, November 12, 1941, A-9.

74. "Prosit! Heurich to Give Party Marking 74th Year as Brewer," *Washington Post*, June 5, 1940, X3; "Christian Heurich, Brewer, Feted On Anniversary," *Washington Post*, June 7, 1940, 21; Special Section, *Washington Times-Herald*, June 7, 1940.

75. Robert A. Crandall, "Beer in the Army Camps," *Modern Brewery Age* (April 1941): 21–22, 97.

76. The author has several in his collection, including one from a New York brewery that was found by a European relic hunter in an old foxhole in Italy. It had been opened with a knife or bayonet.

77. According the one account from a native Washingtonian, some of the big national shipping breweries continued to ship to D.C. because members of the U.S. Congress wanted to have their favorite beer still. I have not found any documentation for this as yet. Population figures are from the official U.S. census results. The population of Arlington County, Virginia, just across the Potomac from D.C., increased from 27,000 to 135,000 in the same period.

78. "Funeral Rites for Heurich Set Tomorrow," *Washington Post*, March 9, 1945, 2; "Christian Heurich," *Records of the Columbia Historical Society* 46–47 (1944/1945): 416; "Heurich, 99, Believes in 'Live and Let Live,'" *Evening Star*, September 12, 1941, n.p.

79. "C. Heurich, D.C. Brewer, Dies at 102," *Washington Post*, March 8, 1945; "Christian Heurich's Estate Set At

$3,550, 471 for Probate," *Evening Star*, April 10, 1945; Peck, *Capital*, 122.

80. Heurich, *From My Life*, 65. Quoted in Peck, *Capital*, 122.

Chapter 8

1. From this point, "Chris" refers to Christian Jr. When I am referring to his father I will use "Heurich" or "Heurich, Senior."

2. Undated manuscript, Christian Heurich Papers, The Historical Society of Washington D.C., Series III, Folder 189.

3. Display ad, *Washington Post*, February 24, 1947, 10.

4. This is based upon the dating codes on cans made for all three brands. The Ale and Bock cans only have codes for 1947 and are exceptionally scarce. They could have been sold in 1948 (the date code only indicates where the can was made, not when it was filled), and it's possible that the brewery ordered a large batch of the cans and filled a portion when necessary.

5. "Hearing before the Appeals Board of the National Production Authority" (October 11, 1951), NARA-CP, RG 277. UD, Entry30-NPA Appeals Dkt, Box 23, 15–18. The same folder contains multiple reports from the Wallerstein Laboratories on their tests of Senate Beer dating from December 20, 1946, through August 23, 1950.

6. Display ad, *Washington Post*, April 24, 1947, 2; display ad, *Washington Post*, July 10, 1947, 15; display ad, *Washington Post*, August 7, 1947, 6.

7. "Frequency Keynotes New Heurich Radio Campaign," *Modern Brewery Age*, February 1948, 37.

8. "Frequency," 38.

9. *Ibid.*

10. *Ibid.*, 38, 108.

11. *Ibid.*, 108.

12. Display ad, *Washington Post*, October 15, 1948, B5; Calvert Liquor Store display ad, *Washington Post*, March 22, 1949, 13.

13. Display ad, *Washington Post*, May 24, 1949, 18.

14. Hearing before the Appeals Board.

15. For details on Chris Heurich see letters from Carl Keyser, November 10, 1981, 16; December 1, 1981, 31; December 29, 1981, 60. Copy in author's possession.

16. "Champeer," *Tide* (August 5, 1949): 12; undated, uncredited advertisement. Christian Heurich Papers, The Historical Society of Washington, D.C. MS 537. Container 3, Folder 30; "Albert Bates Dies: Managed Heurich's," *Washington Post*, February 15, 1955, 26.

17. "Holiday Season Passes Unnoticed in Many Brewers' Ads," *Modern Brewery Age* (January 1950): 40; Gary Heurich, 612.

18. "Brewers Maintain Advertising Pace Through Late Summer," *Modern Brewery Age* (September 1949): 56.

19. Letter from Christian Heurich to Chris Zeller, July 9, 1954. Copy in author's possession.

20. Paul P. Walsh, "How Heurich Holds Washington Market," *American Brewer* (August 1938): 40.

21. Copy of the jingle recording in the author's possession.

22. Display ad, *Washington Post*, July 4, 1951, 11. Unfortunately the Senators never finished higher than 5th in the 1950s, hitting rock bottom in 1955, losing 101 games

and finishing dead last in the American League. Hopefully the beer was better than the team.

23. A.M. McGahan, "The Emergence of the National Brewing Oligopoly: Competition in the American Market, 1933–1958," *The Business History Review* 65 (Summer 1991): 230, 239.

24. The numbers continued to decrease, reaching an all-time low of 89 breweries operating in the United States in 1978. https://www.brewersassociation.org/statistics/number-of-breweries/ (Accessed January 8, 2016).

25. "Heurich Moves Against Trend," *Washington Post*, April 7, 1955, 28. For the ads, see the *Washington Post*, April 20, 1955, 26; May 4, 1955, 44; May 18, 1955, 30; June 1, 1955, 42; June 15, 1955, 46; and July 3, 1955, 44. Heurich's Lager was reverse engineered by Michael Stein, Joshua H. Hubner, and Pete Jones, Washington-area home brewers, and reintroduced by Washington's, D.C., Brau in cans in March 2016.

26. https://www.brewersassociation.org/statistics/number-of-breweries/ (Accessed January 8, 2016).

27. "Mrs. Heurich Dies: Widow of Brewery Head," *Washington Post*, January 25, 1956, 28; "A Farewell from the Chr. Heurich Brewing Co.," *Washington Post*, January 11, 1956, 18. Calvert Liquor Shop display advertisement, *Washington Post*, January 17, 1956, 8; "Old Heurich Brewery to Close January 31," *Washington Post*, January 10, 1956, 3.

28. Richard L. Coe, "'Intermission's' Over for Arena," *Washington Post*, September 30, 1956, H3; Richard L. Coe, "Arena Reborn Triumphantly," *Washington Post*, November 9, 1956, B10.

29. Letter from Mr. James Getty to the author, December 15, 2015. Mr. Getty was not certain which brewery it had been, only that it had been a brewery, that it was in the early 1960s, and that he walked across the street to attend meetings there. The only other brewery in the area at that time was the Arlington brewery in Rosslyn. However, it was torn down in 1958, and it was not across the street from any U.S. military offices at the time, being somewhat isolated.

30. "Excerpts from an Interview with Former CIA Executive Director Lawrence K. "'Red' White," *50 Years in Langley: Recollections of the Construction of CIA's Original Headquarters Building, 1961–2011* (Washington, D.C.: Center for the Study of Intelligence, 2012), 1. http://www.bibliotecapleyades.net/sociopolitica/esp_sociopol_secret gov_5g.htm (Accessed 8 January 2016); Paolo Caponi, "'ALHS! ALHS! Why are You So OSINT?' Reading Books During Office Hours," *Other Modernities* 11 (2014), 42. On the CIA's decision not to use the brewery space, I am relying on a letter from a CIA librarian to the author, January 21, 2016. The same letter notes the CIA's thank-you to Heurich for the bus shelter in August and September 1953.

31. Phil Casey, "Old Heurich Brewery Scene of Blast Mighty in Sound But Only Near Beer," *Washington Post*, November 26, 1961, B1.

32. Ralph E. Becker, *Miracle on the Potomac* (Silver Spring, MD: Bartleby Press, 1990), 93–96.

33. Tim Carmen, "The Olde Heurich Brewing Company: Where is it Now?" and "Young and Hungary," *Washington City Paper*, September 28, 2010. http://www.washingtoncitypaper.com/blogs/youngandhungry/2010/09/28/the-olde-heurich-brewing-co-where-is-it-now/ Accessed January 8, 2016.

Bibliography

Primary Sources

Christian Heurich Brewing Company Records, 1883–1913. Archives Center, National Museum of American History.

Christian Heurich Collection, 1844–2001. MS 537. The Historical Society of Washington, D.C. Kiplinger Research Library.

Heurich, Amelia. Diaries. 1899, 1900, 1909, 1912–1914, 1918–1924, 1925. Collection of the Various records, Maritime Archives and Library. Merseyside Maritime Museum, Liverpool, UK.

Heurich, Christian, Sr. The Excelsior Diary, n.d. (A scrapbook dating from the 1910s through the 1920s).

_____. From My Life, 1842–1934: From Haina in Thuringia to Washington in the United States of America. Translated by Eda Offutt. Washington, D.C.: n.p., 1934.

_____. From My Life, 1842–1934: From Haina in Thuringia to Washington in the United States of America. New translation from the Christian Heurich House. Washington, D.C.: n.p., 1934.

_____. I Watched America Grow. Unpublished memoirs, circa 1942.

_____. Notebook. N.p., n.d.

_____. Scrapbook of stories and advertisements, 1896–1899.

Various records and papers owned by Jan King Evans Houser.

Government Documents and Contemporary Sources

The American Annual Cyclopaedia and Register of Important Events of the Year 1869, vol. IX. New York: D. Appleton, 1870.

Appleton's Annual Cyclopaedia and Register of Important Events: Embracing Political, Military, and Ecclesiastical Affairs; Public Documents; Biography, Statistics, Commerce, Finance, Literature, Science, Agriculture, and Mechanical Industry, vol. 6. New York: D. Appleton, 1867: 375, 684.

Ayer & Sons, N.W. American Newspaper Annual and Directory. Philadelphia: N.W. Ayer & Sons, 1913–1920.

Blakemore, Arthur W. National Prohibition: The Volstead Act Annotated and Digest of National and State Prohibition Decisions. Albany, NY: Matthew Bender, 1923.

The Boston Medical and Surgical Journal 101 (July–December 1879).

Boyd, James P. The Paris Exposition of 1900. Philadelphia: P.W. Ziegler, 1900.

Catalogue of Exhibitors in the United States Sections of the International Universal Exposition, Paris, 1900. Paris: Société Anonyme Des Imprimeries Lemercier, 1900.

"The Cholera—Question." House of Commons Debate 183 (May 15, 1866): 986–90.

Crampton, C.A. Fermented Alcoholic Beverages, Malt Liquors, Wine, and Cider. Washington, D.C.: Government Printing Office, 1887.

"A Day in Castle Garden." Harper's New Monthly Magazine (March 1, 1871): 547–556.

Eastman, Barrett, and Frederick Mayer. Paris, 1900: The American Guide to the City and Exposition. New York: Baldwin & Eastman, 1899.

Gibson, Hugh. A Journal from Our Legation in Belgium. New York: Doubleday, Page, 1917.

Haughton, Harry O. An Introduction to the Port of Baltimore, United States. Baltimore: n.p., 1878.

Henderson, Mary Foote. The Aristocracy of Health: A Study of Physical Culture, Our Favorite Poisons, and a National and International League for the Advancement of Physical Culture. Washington, D.C.: Colton, 1904.

Hind, H. Lloyd. Brewing Science and Practice. 2 vols. New York: John Wiley & Sons, 1940.

"Hints in Regard to the Prevention of Explosions When Pitching Casks, etc." The Brewer's Journal 29 (September 1, 1904): 494–496.

Historical and Commercial Sketches of Washington and Environs. Washington, D.C.: E.E. Barton, 1884.

"Intoxicating Liquors. Eighteenth Amendment. Interpretation of the Volstead Act." Harvard Law Review 34.4 (1921).

Kaufman, Stuart B., ed. The Samuel Gompers Papers, vol. 4: A National Labor Movement Takes Shape, 1895–98. Urbana: University of Illinois Press, 1991.

Lahmann, Heinrich. The Airbath as a Means of Healing and Hardening the Body. Stuttgart: A. Zimmer, 1901.

Latham, Arthur, and T. Crisp English, eds. A System of Treatment In Four Volumes, vol. 3: Special Subjects. New York: Macmillan, 1914.

Maple, Col. Dick. Palaces of Sin, or, The Devil in Society. St. Louis: National Book Concern, 1902.

Miron, Jeffrey A., and Jeffrey Zwiebel. Alcohol Consumption During Prohibition. NBER Working Paper

Series. Working Paper No. 3675. Cambridge, MA: National Bureau of Economic Research, 1991.

Official Guide: Jamestown Ter-Centennial Exposition Jamestown Official Publication Company, 1907.

Proctor, John Clagett, ed. *Washington Past and Present: A History*, 4 vols. New York: Lewis Historical Publishing, 1930.

R.C. "French and American Art at Liège" *Brush and Pencil* 16/3 (September 1905): 98–100.

Report of the Commissioner-General for the United States to the International Universal Exposition, Paris, 1900, vol. 5. Washington, D.C.: Government Printing Office, 1901.

Report of the Commissioners to the Liege Exposition. House of Representatives. Document #454. 59th Congress.

Report on Operations of United States Relief Commission in Europe. Washington: Government Printing Office, 1914.

Reports of Cases Argued and Adjudged in the Supreme Court of the District of Columbia Sitting in General Term, From May 25, 1882 to October 29, 1883. Washington: John L. Ginck, 1884.

Rutter, Frank R. *South American Trade of Baltimore.* Baltimore: Johns Hopkins Press, 1897.

The Statutes at Large of the United States of America. Washington, D.C.: Government Printing Office, 1879, 20:7.

Sydenstriker, Edgar. *A Brief History of Taxation in Virginia.* Richmond: Legislative Reference Bureau of Virginia, 1915.

Thausing, Julius. *The Theory and Practice of the Preparation of the Malt and the Fabrication of Beer.* Philadelphia: Henry Carey Baird, 1882.

"To Correspondents." *The British Medical Journal* (May 26, 1866): 565.

Tyler, Lyon G. "Frank Hume." *Men of Mark in Virginia*, vol. 4. Washington, D.C.: Men of Mark Publishing Company, 1908, 202–207.

United States Senate. *Brewing and Liquor Interests and German and Bolshevik Propaganda: Report of the Subcommittee on the Judiciary, Pursuant to Senate Resolutions 307 and 436: Sixty-fifth Congress: Relating to Charges Made Against the United States Brewers' Association and Allied Interests.* Washington, D.C.: Government Printing Office, 1919.

Walsh, Gerard P., Jr. *Federal Food, Drug, and Cosmetic Act with Amendments.* Washington, D.C.: Government Printing Office, 1981.

Weishampel, John F. *A Stranger in Baltimore: A New Hand Book Containing Sketches of the Early History and Present Condition of Baltimore with a Description of its Notable Localities and other Information useful to both Citizens and Strangers.* Baltimore: J.F. Weishampel, Jr., Bookseller And Stationer, 1866.

Western Brewer. *One Hundred Years of Brewing: A Supplement to "The Western Brewer."* Chicago: H.S. Rich, 1903.

Wolman, Leo. "The Extent of Labor Organization in the United States in 1910." *The Quarterly Journal of Economics* 30/3 (May 1916): 486–518.

Woods Baltimore Directory, 1865–66. Baltimore: John W. Woods, 1866.

Books

Adams, Willi Paul. *Ethnic Leadership and the German-Born Members of the US House of Representatives, 1862–1945: A Report on Research in Progress.* Berlin: John F Kennedy-Institut für NordAmerikastudien, 1996.

Allport, Gordon W., and Leo Postman. *The Psychology of Rumor.* New York: Henry Holt, 1947.

Anderson, Benedict. *Imagined Communities.* London: Verso, 1991.

Anderson, Oscar E. *The Health of a Nation: Harvey W. Wiley and the Fight for Pure Food.* Cincinnati: University of Cincinnati Press, 1958.

Badger, R. Reid. *The Great American Fair: The World's Columbian Exposition and American Culture.* Chicago: Nelson Hall, 1979.

Baker, Ray Stannard. *Woodrow Wilson Life and Letters: Governor, 1910–1913.* Garden City: Doubleday, Doran, 1931.

Baron, Stanley. *Brewed in America: A History of Beer and Ale in the United States.* New York: Little, Brown, 1962.

Becker, Ralph E. *Miracle on the Potomac: The Kennedy Center from the Beginning.* Silver Spring, MD: Bartleby Press, 1990.

Bragdon, Henry Wilkinson. *Woodrow Wilson: The Academic Years.* Cambridge: Harvard, 1967.

Brinnin, John Malcolm. *The Sway of the Grand Saloon: A Social History of the North Atlantic.* New York: Delacorte Press, 1971.

Bruner, Robert, and Sean Carr. *The Panic of 1907: Lessons Learned from the Market's Perfect Storm.* Hoboken, NJ: John Wiley and Sons, 2007.

Buckley, Peter J., and Brian R. Roberts. *European Direct Investment in the USA before World War I.* New York: St. Martin's Press, 1982.

Cawelti, John G. *Apostles of the Self-Made Man: Changing Concepts of Success in America.* Chicago: University of Chicago Press, 1965).

Chambers, Thomas A. *Drinking the Waters: Creating an American Leisure Class at Nineteenth-Century Mineral Springs.* Washington, D.C.: Smithsonian Institution Press, 2002.

Child, Clifton James. *The German-American in Politics, 1914–1917.* Madison: University of Wisconsin Press, 1939.

Chudacoff, Howard P. *The Age of the Bachelor: Creating an American Subculture.* Princeton: Princeton University Press, 1999.

Clark-Lewis, Elizabeth. *Living In, Living Out: African-American Domestics in Washington, D.C., 1910–1940.* Washington, D.C.: Smithsonian Press, 1994.

Cluss, Adolf von. *Erinnerungen an Amerika und siene Brauindustrie.* Munich: R. Oldenbourg, 1911.

Coker, Joe. *Liquor in the Land of the Lost Cause.* Lexington: University Press of Kentucky, 2007.

Coppin, Clayton A., and Jack High. *The Politics of Purity: Harvey Washington Wiley and the Origins of the Federal Food Policy.* Ann Arbor: University of Michigan Press, 1999.

Cox, Robert S. *Body and Soul: A Sympathetic History of American Spiritualism.* Charlottesville: University of Virginia Press, 2003.

Craig, Gordon. *Knowledge and Power: Essays on Politics, Culture and War.* Edited by Bruce Thompson, Carolyn Halladay and Donald Abenheim. Palo Alto, CA: Society for the Promotion of Science and Scholarship, 2013.

Daniels, Winthrop M. *Recollections of Woodrow Wilson.* New Haven: privately printed, 1944.

Davis, Marni. *Jews and Booze: Becoming American in*

the Age of Prohibition. New York: New York University Press, 2012.

Detjen, David W. *The Germans in Missouri, 1900–1918: Prohibition, Neutrality, and Assimilation.* Columbia: University of Missouri Press, 1985.

Douglas, Paul H. *Real Wages in the United States, 1890–1926.* Boston: Houghton Mifflin, 1930.

Downard, William L. *Dictionary of the History of the American Brewing and Distilling Industries.* Westport, CT: Greenwood Press, 1980.

Duis, Perry R. *The Saloon: Public Drinking in Chicago and Boston: 1880–1920.* Urbana: University of Chicago Press, 1983.

Eighmey, Rae Katherine. *Food Will Win the War: Minnesota Crops, Cooks, and Conservation During World War I.* Minneapolis: Minnesota Historical Society Press, 2010.

Ekrich, A. Roger. *At Day's Close: Night in Times Past.* New York: W.W. Norton, 2005.

Eksteins Modris, *Rites of Spring: The Great War and the Birth of the Modern Age.* New York: Mariner Books, 1989.

Elfenbein, Jessica I. *Civics, Commerce, and Community: The History of the Greater Washington Board of Trade, 1889–1989.* Dubuque, IA: Kendall/Hunt Publishing, 1990.

Erenberg, Lewis A. *Steppin' Out: New York Nightlife and the Transformation of American Culture, 1890–1930.* Chicago: University of Chicago Press, 1981.

Fahrmeir, Andreas *Citizens and Aliens: Foreigners and the Law in Britain and the German States, 1789–1870.* New York: Berghahn Books, 2000.

_____. *Citizenship: The Rise and Fall of a Modern Concept.* New Haven: Yale University Press, 2007.

Feldman, Gerald D. *The Great Disorder: Politics, Economics, and Society in the German Inflation, 1914–1924.* New York: Oxford University Press, 1993.

Findling, John E., and Kimberly D. Pelle, eds. *Historical Dictionary of World's Fairs and Expositions, 1851–1988.* New York: Greenwood Press, 1990.

Foster, Gaines M. *Moral Reconstruction: Christian Lobbyists and the Federal Legislation of Morality, 1865–1920.* Chapel Hill: University of North Carolina, 2002.

Fowles, Jib. *Advertising and Popular Culture.* London: Sage Publications, 1996.

Freitag, Sabine. *Friedrich Hecker: Two Lives for Liberty.* Edited and translated by Steven Rowan. St. Louis: University of Missouri Press, 2006.

Fulwider, Chad R. *German Propaganda and U.S. Neutrality in World War I.* Columbia: University of Missouri Press, 2016.

Gabaccia, Donna R. *We Are What We Eat: Ethnic Food and the Making of Americans.* Boston: Harvard University Press, 2000.

Geer, Emily Apt. *First Lady: The Life of Lucy Webb Hayes.* Fremont, Ohio: The Rutherford B. Hayes Presidential Center, 1995.

Geppert, Alexander C.T. *Fleeting Cities: Imperial Expositions in Fin-de-Siècle Europe.* New York: Palgrave Macmillan, 2010.

Gerard, James W. *My Four Years in Germany.* New York: George H. Doran, 1917.

Goode, James M. *Capital Houses: Historic Residences of Washington, D.C., and Its Environs, 1735–1965.* New York: Acanthus Press, 2015.

Goodwin, Lorine Swainston. *The Pure Food, Drink, and Drug Crusaders, 1879–1914.* Jefferson, NC: McFarland, 1999.

Green, Constance McLaughlin. *Washington Capital City, 1879–1950.* Princeton: Princeton University Press, 1963.

Grier, Katherine C. *Culture & Comfort: Parlor Making and Middle-Class Identity, 1850–1930.* Washington, D.C.: Smithsonian Institution Press, 1988.

Grubb, Farley. *German Immigration and Servitude in America, 1709–1920.* London: Routledge, 2011.

Gutheim, Frank. *Worthy of the Nation: The History of the Planning for the National Capital.* Washington, D.C.: Smithsonian Institution Press, 1977.

Haley, William D'Arcy, ed. *Philp's Washington Described: A Complete View of the American Capital, and the District of Columbia; with Many Notices, Historical, Topographical, and Scientific, of the Seat of Government.* New York: Rudd & Carleton, 1861.

Halperin, S. William. *Germany Tried Democracy: A Political History of the Reich from 1918 to 1933.* New York: Norton, 1965.

Hamlin, Christopher. *Cholera: The Biography.* Oxford: Oxford University Press, 2009.

Hansen, Stephen A. *A History of Dupont Circle: Center of High Society in the Capital.* Charleston, SC: The History Press, 2014.

Harvey, David. *The Urban Experience.* Baltimore: Johns Hopkins University Press, 1989.

Hastings, Max. *Catastrophe: 1914: Europe Goes to War.* New York: Alfred Knopf, 2013.

Helbich, Wolfgang, and Walter D. Kamphoefner, eds. *German-American Immigration and Ethnicity in Comparative Perspective.* Max Kade Institute for German-American Studies. Madison: University of Wisconsin, 2004.

Hernon, Peter, and Terry Ganey. *Under the Influence: The Unauthorized Story of the Anheuser-Busch Dynasty.* New York: Avon, 1991.

Himer, Kurt. *75 Jahre Hamburg Amerika Linie.* Hamburg: Petermann, 1922.

Hoffman, Charles. *The Depression of the Nineties: An Economic History.* Westport, CT: Greenwood, 1970).

Ironmonger, Elizabeth Hogg, and Pauline Landrum Phillips. *History of the Woman's Christian Temperance Union of Virginia and a Glimpse of Seventy-Five Years, 1883–1958.* Richmond: Cavalier Press, 1958.

Josephson, Matthew. *Union House, Union Bar: The History of the Hotel & Restaurant Employees and Bartenders International Union, AFL-CIO.* New York: Random House, 1956.

Kamphoefner, Walter D., Wolfgang Helbich, and Ulrike Sommer, eds. *News from the Land of Freedom: German Immigrants Write Home.* Ithaca: Cornell University Press, 1991.

Kane, Robert B. *Disobedience and Conspiracy in the German Army, 1918–1945* Jefferson, NC: McFarland, 2002.

Karau, Mark D. *Germany's Defeat in the First World War: The Lost Battles and Reckless Gambles that Brought Down the Second Reich.* Santa Barbara: Praeger, 2015.

Kasper, Rob. *Baltimore Beer: A Satisfying History of Charm City Brewing.* Charleston, SC: History Press, 2012.

Kay, Bob. *U.S. Beer Labels,* vol. 2: *East & Southern States.* Batavia, IL: self-published, 2007.

Kazal, Russell A. *Becoming Old Stock: The Paradox of German-American Identity.* Princeton: Princeton University Press, 2004.

Keeling, Drew. *The Business of Transatlantic Migration between Europe and the United States, 1900–1914.* Zurich: Chronos, 2012.

Kelley, William J. *Brewing in Maryland from Colonial Times to the Present*. Baltimore: n.p., 1965.

Kerr, K. Austin. *Organized for Prohibition: A New History of the Anti-Saloon League*. New Haven: Yale University Press, 1985.

Koller, Ann Marie. *The Theater Duke: Georg II of Saxe-Meiningen and the German Stage*. Stanford: Stanford University Press, 1984.

Koshar, Rudy. *German Travel Cultures*. New York: Oxford, 2000.

Koslofsky, Craig. *Evening's Empire: A History of the Night in Early Modern Europe*. Cambridge: Cambridge University Press, 2011.

Latour, Bruno. *Reassembling the Social: An Introduction to Actor-Network-Theory*. Oxford: Oxford University Press, 2005.

Lender, Mark Edward, and James Kirby Martin. *Drinking in America: A History*. Revised and expanded. New York: Free Press, 1987.

Lessoff, Alan. *The Nation and Its City: Politics, "Corruption," and Progress in Washington, D.C., 1861–1902*. Baltimore: Johns Hopkins, 1994.

_____, and Christof Mauch, eds. *Adolf Cluss: Architect from Germany to America*. Historical Society of Washington, D.C., and Stadtarchiv Heilbronn in association with Berghahn Books: New York, 2005.

Lebergott, Stanley. *Annual Estimates of Unemployment in the United States, 1900–1957*. Washington, D.C.: NBER, 1957.

Levetus, Amelia Sarah. *Imperial Vienna: An Account of Its History, Traditions, and Arts*. London: John Lane, 1905.

Levy, Jonathan. *Freaks of Fortune: The Emerging World of Capitalism and Risk in America*. Cambridge: Harvard University Press, 2012.

Link, Arthur S. *Wilson: The Struggle for Neutrality, 1914–1915*. Princeton: Princeton University Press, 1960.

Lobel, Cindy R. *Urban Appetites: Food and Culture in Nineteenth-Century New York*. Chicago: University of Chicago Press, 2014.

Logan, John R., and Harvey L. Molotch. *Urban Fortune: The Political Economy of Space*. Berkley: University of California Press, 2007.

Long, Clarence Dickenson. *Wages and Earnings in the United States, 1860–1890*. New York: Arno Press, 1975.

Luebke, Frederick C. *Bonds of Loyalty: German Americans and World War I*. DeKalb: Northern University Press, 1974.

_____. *Germans in the New World: Essays in the History of Immigration*. Urbana: University of Chicago Press, 1990.

Maddex, Diane. *Historic Buildings of Washington, D.C.* Pittsburgh: Ober Park Associates, 1973.

Mandel, Bernard. *Samuel Gompers: A Biography*. Yellow Spring, Ohio: Antioch Press, 1963.

Mandell, Richard D. *Paris 1900: The Great World's Fair*. Toronto: University of Toronto Press, 1967.

Manz, Stefan. *Constructing a German Diaspora: The "Greater German Empire," 1871–1914*. London: Routledge, 2014.

Massey, Doreen. *Spatial Divisions of Labour: Social Structures and the Geography of Production*. New York: Macmillan, 1984.

McGarry, Molly. *Ghosts of Futures Past: Spiritualism and the Cultural Politics of Nineteenth-Century America*. Berkeley: University of California Press, 2008.

McGirr, Lisa, *The War on Alcohol: Prohibition and the Rise of the American State*. New York: Harper, 2015.

Mills, Eric. *Chesapeake Rumrunners of the Roaring Twenties*. Centreville, MD: Tidewater, 1999.

Mohl, Raymond A., and Neil Betten, eds. *Urban America in Historical Perspective*. New York: Weybright and Talley, 1970.

Morris, Danny, and Jeff Johnson. *Richmond Beers: A Directory of the Breweries and Bottles of Richmond, Virginia*. 2d edition. Richmond: n.p., 2000.

Morris, James McGrath. *Pulitzer: A Life in Politics, Print, and Power*. New York: Harper, 2010.

Morton, Frederic. *Thunder at Twilight: Vienna 1913–1914*. (Cambridge, MA: De Capo Press, 2001).

Mulder, John M. *Woodrow Wilson: The Years of Preparation*. Princeton: Princeton University Press, 1978.

Nadel, Stanley *Little Germany. Ethnicity, Religion and Class in New York City, 1845–80*. Urbana: University of Illinois Press, 1990.

Neiberg, Michael S. *Dance of the Furies: Europe and the Outbreak of World War I*. Cambridge: Harvard University Press, 2011.

Norris, James D. *Advertising and the Transformation of American Society, 1865–1920*. New York: Greenwood Press, 1990.

Nye, David E. *American Technological Sublime*. Cambridge: MIT Press, 1994.

Ogle, Maureen. *Ambitious Brew: The Story of American Beer*. New York: Harcourt, 2006.

Osborne, John. *The Meiningen Court Theater, 1866–1890*. Cambridge: Cambridge University Press, 1988.

Panayi, Panikos. *Germans as Minorities during the First World War: A Global Comparative Perspective*. Burlington, VT: Ashgate, 2014.

Pearson, C.C., and J. Edwin Hendricks. *Liquor and Anti-Liquor in Virginia, 1619–1919*. Durham: Duke University Press, 1967.

Peck, Garrett. *Capital Beer: A Heady History of Brewing in Washington, D.C.* Charleston: The History Press, 2014.

_____. *Prohibition in Washington, D.C.: How Dry We Weren't*. Charleston: The History Press, 2011.

Penny, H. Glenn. *Objects of Culture: Ethnology and Ethnographic Museums in Imperial Germany*. Chapel Hill: University of North Carolina Press, 2002.

Pescod, Keith. *Good Food, Bright Fires & Civility: British Emigrant Depots of the 19th Century*. Melbourne: Australian Scholarly Publishing, 2001.

Pierce, Frank H. III. *The Washington Saengerbund: A History of German Song and Culture in the Nation's Capital*. Washington, D.C.: The Washington Saengerbund, 1981.

Pope, Michael Lee. *Shotgun Justice: One Prosecutor's Crusade against Crime and Corruption in Alexandria and Arlington*. Charleston: The History Press, 2012.

Porter, Roy, ed. *The Medical History of Waters and Spas*. Medical History, Supplement No. 10. London: Wellcome Institute for the History of Medicine, 1990.

Proctor, John Clagett. *Proctor's Washington and Environs*. Washington, D.C.: n.p., 1950.

Read, James M. *Atrocity Propaganda, 1914–19*. New Haven: Yale University Press, 1941.

Reinarz, Jonathan. *Historical Perspectives on Smell*. Urbana: University of Chicago Press, 2014.

Richardson, John. *Alexander Robey Shepherd: The Man Who Built the Nation's Capital*. Athens: Ohio University Press, 2016.

Richardson, Selden. *The Tri-State Gang in Richmond: Murder and Robbery in the Great Depression*. Charleston: The History Press, 2012.

Rieger, Bernhard. *Technology and the Culture of Modernity in Britain and Germany, 1890–1945*. Cambridge: Cambridge University Press, 2005.

Roberts, Chalmers. *The Washington Post: The First 100 Years*. Boston: Houghton Mifflin, 1977.

Robertson, Craig. *The Passport in America: The History of a Document*. New York: Oxford University Press, 2010.

Ronnenberg, Herman W. *Material Culture of Breweries*. Walnut Creek, CA: Left Coast Press, 2011.

_____. *The Politics of Assimilation: The Effect of Prohibition on the German-Americans*. New York: Carlton Press, 1975.

Rosnow, Ralph L., and Gary Alan Fine. *Rumors and Gossip: The Social Psychology of Hearsay*. New York: Elsevier, 1976.

Runner, Ruth Ritter. *Paul Hugo Ritter and Related Families: Rottweil Germany to Cumberland, Maryland*. Morgantown, WV: n.p., 1995.

Rydell, Robert H. *All the World's a Fair: Visions of Empire at American International Expositions, 1876–1916*. Chicago: University of Chicago Press, 1984.

Rydell, Robert H., John E. Findling, and Kimberly D. Pelle. *Fair America: World's Fairs in the United States*. Washington, D.C.: Smithsonian Books, 2000.

Rydell, Robert H., and Rob Kroes. *Buffalo Bill in Bologna: The Americanization of the World, 1869–1922*. Chicago: University of Chicago Press, 2005.

Sappol, Michael, and Stephen P. Rice, eds. *A Cultural History of the Human Body in the Age of Empire*. London: Bloomsbury, 2010.

Schivelbusch, Wolfgang. *Disenchanted Night: The Industrialization of Light in the Nineteenth Century*. Trans. Angela Davies. Berkley: University of California Press, 1995.

Schlüter, Hermann. *The Brewing Industry and the Brewery Workers' Movement in America*. Cincinnati: International Union of the United Brewery Workmen of America, 1910.

Schneider, Dorothee. *Trade Unions and Community: The German Working Class in New York City, 1870–1900*. Urbana: University of Illinois Press, 1994.

Seale, William. *The Imperial Season: America's Capital in the Time of the First Ambassadors, 1893–1918*. Washington, D.C.: Smithsonian, 2013.

Sherwood, Suzanne Berry. *Foggy Bottom, 1800–1975: A Study in the Uses of an Urban Neighborhood*. G.W. Washington Studies, #7. Washington, D.C.: George Washington University, 1978.

Shibutani, Tomatso. *Improvised New*. Indianapolis: Bobbs-Merrill, 1966.

Sismondo, Christine *America Walks into a Bar: A Spirited History of Taverns and Saloons, Speakeasies and Grog Shops*. New York: Oxford University Press, 2011.

Skilnik, Bob. *The History of Beer and Brewing in Chicago, 1833–1978*. Saint Paul, MN: Pogo Press, 1999.

Slayden, Ellen Maury. *Washington Wife: Journal of Ellen Maury Slayden from 1897–1919*. New York: Harper & Row, 1962.

Smith, Andrew F. *Drinking History: Fifteen Turning Points in the Making of American Beverages*. New York: Columbia University Press, 2013.

Strasser, Susan. *Satisfaction Guaranteed: The Making of the American Mass Market*. Washington, D.C.: Smithsonian Institution Press, 1989.

Strausbaugh, John. *Black Like You: Blackface, Whiteface, Insult & Imitation in American Popular Culture*. New York: Penguin, 2006.

Svejda, George J. *Castle Garden as an Immigrant Depot, 1855–1890*. Washington, D.C.: Department of the Interior, 1968.

Sydenstriker, Edgar. *A Brief History of Taxation in Virginia*. Richmond: The Legislative Reference Bureau of Virginia, 1915.

Thompson, Margaret Susan. *The 'Spider Web': Congress and Lobbying in the Age of Grant*. Ithaca: Cornell University Press, 1985.

Tolzmann, Don Heinrich. *The German-American Experience*. Amherst, NY: Humanity Books, 1999.

Tremblay, Victor J., and Carol Horton Tremblay. *The U.S. Brewing Industry: Data and Economic Analysis*. Cambridge, MA: MIT Press, 2005.

Trommler, Frank, and Joseph McVeigh, eds. *American and the Germans: An Assessment of a Three-Hundred-Year History*, vol. 2: *The Relationship in the Twentieth Century*. Philadelphia: University of Pennsylvania Press, 1983.

Twain, Mark, and Charles Dudley Warner. *The Gilded Age: A Tale of Today*. New York: Penguin Books, 2001.

Unrau, Harland D. *Historical Resource Study: Chesapeake & Ohio Canal*. Washington, D.C.: Department of the Interior, National Park Service, 2007.

Van Wieren, Dale O. *American Breweries II*. West Point, PA: East Coast Breweriana Association, 1995.

Varga, Joseph J. *Hell's Kitchen and the Battle for Urban Space: Class Struggle and Progressive Reform in New York City, 1894–1914*. New York: Monthly Review Press, 2013.

Voss, Kim. *The Making of American Exceptionalism: The Knights of Labor and Class Formation in the Nineteenth Century*. Ithaca: Cornell University Press, 1993.

White, Luise. *Speaking with Vampires: Rumor and History in Colonial Africa*. Berkley: University of California Press, 2000.

Wittke, Carl. *German Americans and the World War*. Columbus: The Ohio State Archaeological and Historical Society, 1936.

Zimmerman, Jonathan. *Distilling Democracy: Alcohol Education in America's Public Schools, 1880–1925*. Lawrence: University Press of Kansas, 1999.

Articles

Abbott, Carl. "Dimensions of Regional Change in Washington, D.C." *The American Historical Review*. 95/5 (December 1990): 1367–1393.

_____. "Norfolk in the New Century: The Jamestown Exposition and Urban Boosterism" *The Virginia Magazine of History and Biography* 85/1 (January 1977): 86–96.

_____. "Urban Economic Planning: The Case of Washington, D.C. Since 1860." *The Public Historian* 11/2 (Spring 1989): 5–21.

Anderson, Timothy G. "On the Pre-Migration Social and Economic Experience of Nineteenth-Century German Immigration." *Yearbook on German-American Studies* 36 (2001): 91–108.

Anthony, Susan. "Anxiety and Rumor." *The Journal of Social Psychology* 89 (1973): 91–98.

Bade, Klaus J. "Conclusion: Migration Past and Present—The German Experience." In *People in Transit: German Migration in Comparative Perspective, 1820–1930*. Dirk Hoerder and Jörg Nagler, eds. Washington, D.C.: German Historical Institute, 1995, 399–412.

_____. "German Emigration to the United States and

Continental Immigration to Germany in the Late Nineteenth and Early Twentieth Centuries." *Central European History* 13/4 (December 1980): 348–377.

Badenhausen, Carl W. "The Brewing Industry's Program of Action." *The Public Opinion Quarterly* 4/4 (December 1940): 657–663.

Benbow, Mark. "The Old Dominion Goes Dry: Prohibition in Virginia." *Brewery History* 138 (Winter 2010).

_____. "The Prohibition Two-Step: Two Steps In, Two Steps Out." *American Breweriana Journal* 166 (July–August 2010): 35.

Bensley, D. Alan. "Why Great Thinkers Sometimes Fail to Think Critically." *Skeptical Inquirer* 30/4 (July/August 2006): 47–52.

Blackbourn, David. "'Taking the Waters': Meeting Places of the Fashionable World." In Martin H. Geyer and Johannes Paulmann, *The Mechanics of Internationalism: Culture, Society, and Politics from the 1840s to the First World War*. London: German Historical Institute, 2001, 435–457.

Bordia, Prashant, and Nicholas DiFonzo. "Problem-Solving in Social Interactions on the Internet: Rumor as Social Cognition." *Social Psychology Quarterly* 67:1 (March 2004).

Brown, Sterling A. "Negro Character as Seen by White Authors." *The Journal of Negro Education* 2/2 (April 1933): 179–203.

Browne, Joseph L. "Adolph Cluss, from Communist Leader to Washington, D.C., Architect, 1848–68." *Yearbook on German-American Studies* 46 (2011).

Buenker, John D. "Sovereign Individuals and Organic Networks: Political Cultures in Conflict During the Progressive Era." *American Quarterly* 40/2 (June 1988): 187–204.

Bungert, Heike. "'Feast of Fools': German-American Carnival as a Medium of Identity Formation, 1854–1914." *Amerikastudien/American Studies* 48/3 (2003): 325–344.

Calantone, Roger J., Cornelia Droge, David S. Litvack, and C. Anthony di Benedetto. "Flanking in a Price War." *Interfaces* 19/2 (March–April 1989): 1–12.

Capozzola, Christopher. "The Only Badge You Need is Your Patriotic Fervor: Vigilance, Coercion, and the Law in World War I America." *The Journal of American History* 88/4 (March 2002): 1354–1382.

Carnevali, Francesca. "Social Capital and Trade Associations in America, c. 1860–1914: A Microhistory Approach." *Economic History Review* 64 (2011): 905–928.

Carroll, Glenn R., and Anand Swarminathan. "Density Dependent Organizational Evolution in the American Brewing Industry from 1633–1988." *Acta Sociologica* 34 (1991): 155–175.

Chickering, Roger. "Patriotic Societies and German Foreign Policy, 1890–1914." *The International History Review* 1/4 (October 1979): 470–489.

Conzen, Kathleen Neils. "Die Residenzler: German Americans in the Making of the Nation's Capital." In *Adolf Cluss, Architect: from Germany to America*, ed. Alan Lessoff and Christof Mauch. Washington, D.C.: Historical Society of Washington, D.C., 2005, 58–63.

DiFonzo, Nicholas, and Prashant Bordia. "Rumor, Gossip and Urban Legends." *Diogenes* (2007).

Dingle, Mona E. "Gemeinschaft und Gemütlichkeit: German American Community and Culture, 1850–1920." In *Washington Odyssey: A Multicultural History of the Nation's Capital*, edited by Francine Curro Cary. Washington: Smithsonian Books, 1996, 113–134.

Dobbert, G.A. "German-Americans Between New and Old Fatherland." *American Quarterly* 19/4 (Winter 1967): 663–680.

Drescher, Nuala McGann. "The Workmen's Compensation and Pension Proposal in the Brewing Industry, 1910–1912: A Case Study in Conflicting Self-Interest." *Industrial and Labor Relations Review* 24/1 (October 1970): 32–46.

Dubinsky, Karen. "'The Pleasure is Exquisite but Violent': The Imaginary Geography of Niagara Falls in the Nineteenth Century." *Journal of Canadian Studies* 29/2 (Summer 1994): 64–88.

Eisenberg, Christiane. "Artisans' Socialization at Work: Workshop Life in Early Nineteenth Century England and Germany." *Journal of Social History* 24/3 (Spring 1991): 507–520.

Ekirch, A. Roger. "Sleep We Have Lost: Pre-Industrial Slumber in the British Isles." *The American Historical Review* 106/2 (April 2001): 343–386.

Ernst, Daniel R. "Free Labor, the Consumer Interest, and the Law of Industrial Disputes, 1885–1900." *The American Journal of Legal History* 36/1 (January 1992): 19–37.

Esslinger, Dean R. "Immigration through the Port of Baltimore." In *Forgotten Doors: The Other Ports of Entry to the United States*, ed. M. Mark Stolarik. Philadelphia: Balch Institute Press, 1988.

Evans, Richard F. "Epidemics and Revolutions: Cholera in Nineteenth Century Europe." *Epidemics and Ideas*. Terence Ranger and Paul Slack, eds. Cambridge: Cambridge University Press, 1992, 149–173.

_____. "The 19th Century High-Tech Systems of Christian Heurich's Mansion." *Washington History* 8/1 (Spring/Summer 1996): 39–53.

Fahrmeir, Andreas K. "Nineteenth Century German Citizenship: A Reconsideration." *The History Journal* 40/3 (September 1997): 721–752.

Farr, James R. "The Disappearance of the Traditional Artisan." In *A Companion to Nineteenth-Century Europe, 1789–1914*. Stefan Berger, ed. Malden, MA: Wiley-Blackwell, 2009, 98–108.

Fine, Gary Alan. "Cokelore and Coke Law: Urban Belief Tales and the Problem of Multiple Origins." *The Journal of American Folklore* 92/366 (October–December 1979): 477–482.

_____. "Tiny Publics: Small Groups and Civil Society." *Sociological Theory* 22/3 (September 2004): 341–356.

Foster, H. Schuyler, Jr. "How America Became Belligerent: A Quantitative Study of War News, 1914–1917." *The American Journal of Sociology* 40:4 (January 1935): 464–475.

Frank, Alison F. "The Air Cure Town: Commodifying Mountain Air in Alpine Central Europe." *Central European History* 45 (2012): 185–207.

Garonzik, Joseph. "The Racial and Ethnic Make-Up of Baltimore Neighborhoods, 1850–1870." *Maryland Historical Magazine* 71/3 (Fall 1976).

Garver, Bruce. "Immigration to the Great Plains, 1865–1914: War, Politics, Technology, and Economic Development." *Great Plains Quarterly* 31/3 (Summer 2011): 179–203.

George, Alexander L. "The 'Operational Code': A Neglected Approach to the Study of Political Leaders and Decision-Making." *International Studies Quarterly* 13/2 (June 1969): 190–222.

Gill, Geoff. "Cholera and the Fight for Public Health Reform in Mid-Victorian England." *Historian.* (Summer 2000): 10–16.

Greer, Douglas F. "The Causes of Concentration in the

US Brewing Industry." *Quarterly Review of Economics and Business* 21/4 (Winter 1981): 87–106.

Griesinger, Karl Theodor. "From *Land und Leute in Amerika: Skizzen aus dem Amerikanischen Leben* (1857)." In *Empire City: New York Through the Centuries.* Kenneth T. Jackson and David S. Dunbar, eds. New York: Columbia University Press, 2002, 240–243.

Gross, Stephen J. "'Perils of Prussianism': Main Street German America Local Autonomy, and the Great War." *Agricultural History* 78/1 (Winter 2004): 78–116.

Gusfield, Joseph R. "Status Conflicts and the Changing Ideologies of the American Temperance Movement." In *Society, Culture, and Drinking Patterns.* David J. Pittman and Charles R. Snyder, eds. New York: John Wiley & Sons, 1962, 101–120.

Halliday, Stephen. "Death and Miasma in Victorian London: An Obstinate Belief." *British Medical Journal* (December 22–29, 2001): 1469–1471.

Hanlon, James. "Unsightly Urban Menaces and the Rescaling of Residential Segregation in the United States." *Journal of Urban History* 37/5 (2011): 732–756.

Harlow, Ralph Volney. "The Rise and Fall of the Kansas Aid Movement." *The American Historical Review* 41/1 (October 1935): 1–25.

Hatcher, Ed. "Washington's Nineteenth-Century Citizens' Associations and the Senate Park Commission Plan." *Washington History* 14/2 (Fall/Winter 2002/2003): 70–95.

Hawkins, Richard A. "American Boomers and the Floatation of Shares in the City of London in the Late Nineteenth Century." *Business History* 49/6 (November 2007): 802–822.

Heron, Craig. "Boys Will Be Boys: Working Class Masculinities in the Age of Mass Production." *International Labor and Working Class History* 69 (Spring 2006): 6–34.

Hershman, Robert R. "Gas in Washington." *Records of the Columbia Historical Society* 50 (1948/1950): 137–157.

Heurich, Gary F. "The Christian Heurich Brewing Company, 1872–1956." *Records of the Columbia Historical Society, 1973–1974.* Washington: Columbia Historical Society, 1976, 604–615.

Hiatt, Shon, Wesley D. Sine, and Pamela S. Tolbert. "From Pabst to Pepsi: The Deinstitutionalization of Social Practices and the Creation of Entrepreneurial Opportunities." *Administrative Science Quarterly* 54/4 (December 2009): 635–667.

Higgins, David M. "'Forgotten Heroes and Forgotten Issues': Business and Trademark History during the Nineteenth Century." *The Business History Review* 86/2 (Summer 2012): 261–285.

Hoerder, Dirk. "The Traffic of Immigration via Bremen/Bremerhaven: Merchants' Interests, Protective Legislation and Migrants' Experiences." *Journal of American Ethnic History* 13/1 (Fall 1993): 68–101.

Hohner, Robert A. "Prohibition Comes to Virginia: The Referendum of 1914." *Virginia Magazine of History and Biography* 75 (1967): 476–478.

Holian, Timothy J. "Cincinnati and Its Brewing Industry: Their Parallel Development through the German Community." *Yearbook on German-American Studies* 38 (2003).

_____. "'Des Arbeiters Stärke': German-American Brewery Owner-Worker Relations, 1860–1920." *Yearbook on German-American Studies* 29 (1994): 69–82.

Huberman, Michael. "Working Hours of the World Unite? New International Evidence of Worktime,

1870–1913." *The Journal of Economic History* 64/4 (December 2004): 964–1001.

Hummel, Richard L., and Gary S. Foster. "Germanic/American Shooting Societies: Continuity and Change of *Schuetzenvereins*." *The International Journal of the History of Sport* 15/2 (August 1998): 186–193.

Ingham, John N. "Rags to Riches Revisited: The Effect of City State and Related factors on the Recruitment of Business Leaders." *The Journal of American History* 63/3 (December 1976): 615–637.

Jacobson, Lisa. "Beer Goes to War: The Politics of Beer Promotion and Production in the Second World War." *Food, Culture and Society* 12 (September 2009): 275–312.

Jimenez, Mary Ann. "Concepts of Health and National Care Policy: A View from American History." *Social Science Review* 71/1 (March 1997): 34–50.

Jones, Bartlett C. "Nullification and Prohibition, 1920–1933." *The Southwestern Social Science Quarterly* 44/4 (March 1964): 389–398.

Kamphoefner, Walter. "The German Component to American Industrialization." In *Immigrant Entrepreneurship: German-American Business Biographies, 1720 to the Present,* vol. 2, edited by William J. Hausman. German Historical Institute. Last modified May 30, 2014. http://www.immigrantentrepreneurship.org/entry.php?rec=189.

Kastoryano, Riva. "Codes of Otherness." *Social Research* 77/1 (Spring 2010): 79–100.

Kay, Bob. "The Conrad Seipp Brewing Company, Chicago." *The American Breweriana Journal* 163 (November–December 2009): 28–31.

Keire, Mara L. "Dope Fiends and Degenerates: The Gendering of Addictions in the Early Twentieth Century." *Journal of Social History* 31/4 (Summer 1998): 809–822.

Kerr, K. Austin. "The American Brewing Industry: 1865–1920." In *The Dynamics of the International Brewing Industry Since 1800.* R.G. Wilson and T.R. Gourvish, eds. London: Routledge, 1998, 176–191.

_____. "The Rebirth of Brewing and Distilling in the United States in 1933: Government Policy and Industry Structure." *Business and Economic History On-Line* 3 (2005). Online at http://www.thebhc.org/BEH/05/kerr.pdf. Accessed June 1, 2014.

Keyser, Carl A. *Leatherbreeches: Hero of Chancellorsville.* Rye Beach, NH: Amherst Press, 1989.

_____. *Leatherbreeches' Legacy.* Rye Beach, NH: Amherst Press, 1990.

Kingsdale, Jon M. "The 'Poor Man's Club': Social Functions of the Urban Working-Class Saloon." *American Quarterly* 25/4 (October 1973).

Kraut, Alan M. "Immigration through the Port of Baltimore: A Comment." In *Forgotten Doors: The Other Ports of Entry to the United States,* ed. M. Mark Stolarik. Philadelphia: Balch Institute Press, 1988.

Kyvig, David E. "Women Against Prohibition." *American Quarterly* 28/4 (Autumn 1976): 465–482.

Lait, Jack, and Lee Mortimer. *Washington Confidential.* New York: Crown Publishers, 1951.

Lamme, Margot Opdycke. "Tapping into War: Leveraging World War I in the Drive for a Dry Nation." *American Journalism* 27/4 (Fall 2004): 63–91.

Law, Marc T. "How do Regulators Regulate? Enforcement of the Pure Food and Drug Act, 1907–38." *Journal of Law, Economics, & Organization* 22/2 (October 2006): 459–489.

Law, Marc T., and Gary D. Libecap. "The Determinates

of Progressive Era Reform." In *Corruption and Reform: Lessons from America's Economic History*. Chicago: University of Chicago Press, 2006, 319–342.

Lee, Alfred McClung. "Techniques of Social Reform: An Analysis of the New Prohibition Drive." *American Sociological Review* 9/1 (February 1944): 65–77.

Lempa, Heikki. "The Spa: Emotional Economy and Social Classes in Nineteenth-Century Pyrmont." *Central European History* 35/1 (2002): 37–73.

Lessoff, Alan. "Washington, D.C.: Worthy After All." *Journal of Urban History* (March 2010).

Lewis, Michael. "Access to Saloons, Wet Turnout, and Statewide Prohibition Referenda, 1907–1919" *Social Science History*. 32/3 (Fall 2008), 373–404.

Littmann, William. "The Production of Goodwill: The Origins and Development of the Factory Tour in America." *Perspectives in Vernacular Architecture* 9 (2003): 71–84.

Loomis, Seymour C. "The Legal and Constitutional Aspects of the Proposed Prohibition Amendment to the Federal Constitution." *The Scientific Monthly* 8/4 (April 1919): 335–350.

Lorenz-Meyer, Martin. "United in Difference: The German Community in Nativist Baltimore and the Presidential Elections of 1860." *Yearbook on German-American Studies* 35 (2000): 1–26.

Low, George S., and Ronald A. Fullerton. "Brands, Brand Management, and the Brand Manager System: A Critical-Historical Evaluation." *Journal of Marketing Research* 31/2 (May 1994): 173–190.

Lyons, Anthony, and Yoshihisa Kashima. "How Are Stereotypes Maintained Through Communication? The Influence of Stereotype Sharedness." *Journal of Personality and Social Psychology* 85/6 (2003).

Manz, Stefan. "America in Global Context: German Entrepreneurs around the World." In *Immigrant Entrepreneurship: German-American Business Biographies, 1720 to the Present*, vol. 3, edited by Giles R. Hoyt. German Historical Institute. Last modified August 28, 2014. http://www.immigrantentrepreneurship.org/entry.php?rec=187 (Accessed September 2, 2014).

_____. "Nationalism Gone Global: The *Hauptverband Deutscher Flottenvereine im Auslande* 1898–1918." *German History* 30/2 (2012): 199–221.

Marx, Leo. "Technology: The Emergence of a Hazardous Concept." *Social Research* 64/3 (Fall 1997).

McDonagh, Eileen L., and H. Douglas Price. "Woman Suffrage in the Progressive Era: Patterns of opposition and Support in Referenda Voting, 1910–1918." *The American Political Science Review* 79/2 (June 1985): 415–435.

Meikle, Jeffrey L. "*Leo Marx's The Machine in the Garden*." *Technology and Culture* 44/1 (January 2003): 147–159.

Merry, Sally Engle. "Rethinking Gossip and Scandal." In *Toward a General Theory of Social Control*. Donald Black, ed. New York: Academic Press, 1984: 271–302.

Mezvinsky, Norton. "Scientific Temperance Instruction in the Schools." *History of Education Quarterly* 1/1 (March 1961): 48–56.

Miller, Elizabeth J. "Dreams of Being the Capital of Commerce: The National Fair of 1879." *Records of the Columbia Historical Society* 51 (1984): 71–82.

Miller, Michael B. "The Business Trip: Maritime Networks in the Twentieth Century." *The Business History Review* 77/1 (Spring 2003): 1–32.

Montgomery, David. "The 'New Unionism' and the Transformation of Workers' Consciousness in Amer-

ica, 1909–22." *Journal of Social History* 7/4 (Summer 1974): 509–529.

Muessdoerffer, Franz. "Beer and Beer Culture in Germany." Wulf Schiefenhovel and Helen Macbeth, eds. In *Liquid Bread: Beer and Brewing in Cross-Cultural Perspective*. New York: Berghahn, 2011, 63–70.

Mullen, Patrick B. "Modern Legend and Rumor Theory." *Journal of the Folklore Institute* 99/2–3 (August–December 1972): 95–109.

Nelson, Frank. "The German-American Immigrants Struggle." *International Review of History and Political Science* 10/2 (1973): 37–49.

Neumann, Caryn E. "The End of Gender Solidarity: The History of the Women's Organization for National Prohibition Reform in the United States, 1929–1933." *Journal of Women's History* 9/2 (Summer 1997): 31–51.

Olson, Erik L. "How Magazine Articles Portrayed Advertising from 1900–1940." *Journal of Advertising* 24/3 (Autumn 1995): 41–54.

Pabst, Frederick. "The Brewing Industry." In *One Hundred Years of American Commerce*. Chauncey M. DePew, ed. New York: D.O. Haynes, 1895), II: 413–417.

Parker, Alison M. "'Hearts Uplifted and Minds Refreshed': The Women's Christian Temperance Union and the Production of Pure Culture in the United States, 1880–1930." *Journal of Women's History* 11/2 (Summer 1999): 135–158.

Peck, Ferdinand W. "The United States at the Paris Exposition in 1900." *The North American Review* 168/506 (January 1899): 24–33.

Pennock, Pamela E., and K. Austin Kerr. "In the Shadow of Prohibition: Domestic American Alcohol Policy Since 1933." *Business History* 47/3 (July 2005): 383–400.

Peters, Kim, Yoshihisa Kashima, and Anna Clark. "Talking About Others: Emotionality and the Dissemination of Social Information." *European Journal of Social Psychology* 39 (2009): 207–222.

Peterson, Warren A., and Noel P. Gist. "Rumor and Public Opinion." *The American Journal of Sociology* 57/2 (September 1951): 159–167.

Powers, Madelon. "The 'Poor Man's Friend': Saloonkeepers, Workers, and the Code of Reciprocity in U.S. Barrooms, 1870–1920." *International Labor and Working-Class History* 45 (Spring 1994): 1–15.

Proctor, John C., ed. "Christian Heurich." *Washington Past and Present: A History*, vol. 5. New York: Lewis Historical, 1932, 1036–1038.

Rennelle, Mark, and Whitney Walton. "Planned Serendipity: American Travelers and Trans-Atlantic Voyage in the Nineteenth and Twentieth Centuries." *Journal of Social History* 38/2 (Winter 2004): 365–383.

Renner, Andrew. "A Nation That Bathes Together: New York's Progressive Era Public Baths." *Journal of the Society of Architectural Historians* 67/1 (December 2008): 504–531.

Rippley, La Vern J. "Monumentality: How Post-1871 Germans in the United States Expressed Their Ethnicity." *Yearbook on German-American Studies* 38 (2003): 139–153.

Rosnow, Ralph L., James L. Esposito, and Leo Gibney. "Factors Influencing Rumor Spreading: Replication and Extension." *Language & Communication* 8/1 (1988): 29–42.

Ross, Alice. "Health and Diet in 19th-Century America: A Food Historian's Point of View." *Historical Archaeology* 27/2 (1993): 42–56.

Rössler, Horst. "Traveling Workers and the German Labor Movement." In *People in Transit: German Migration in Comparative Perspective, 1820–1930*. Dirk Hoerder and Jörg Nagler, eds. Washington, D.C.: German Historical Institute, 1995, 127–143.

Rubincam, Milton. "Mr. Christian Heurich and His Mansion." *Records of the Columbia Historical Society of Washington, D.C. 1960–1962*. Washington, D.C.: Columbia Historical Society, 1963, 167–205.

Russell, Mark A. "Picturing the *Imperator*: Passenger Shipping as Art and National Symbol in the German Empire." *Central European History* 44 (2011): 227–256.

Scranton, Philip. "Determinism and Indeterminacy in the History of Technology." *Technology and Culture* 36/2 (1995): S31-S53.

_____. "Diversity in Diversity: Flexible Production and American Industrialization, 1880–1930." *The Business History Review* 65/1 (Spring 1991): 27–90.

Shireman, Candace. "The Rise of Christian Heurich and his Mansion." *Washington History* 5/1 (Spring/Summer 1993): 4–27.

Simmel, Georg. "The Stranger." http://www.infoamerica.org/documentos_pdf/simmel01.pdf. Accessed February 6, 2015.

Stack, Martin. "Local and Regional Breweries in America's Brewing Industry, 1865–1920." *Business History Review* 74 (Autumn 2000): 435–463.

_____. "Was Big Beautiful? The Rise of National Breweries in America's Pre-Prohibition Brewing Industry." *Journal of Macromarketing* 30 (March 2010): 50–60.

Stepan-Norris, Judith, and Caleb Southworth. "Rival Unionism and Membership Growth in the United States, 1900–2005: A Special Case of Interorganizational Competition." *American Sociological Review* 75/2 (April 2010): 227–251.

Stilgoe, John R. "Moulding the Industrial Zone Aesthetic: 1880–1928." *Journal of American Studies* 6/1 (April 1982): 5–24.

Stone, Gregory P. "Drinking Styles and Status Arrangements." In *Society, Culture, and Drinking Patterns*. David J. Pittman and Charles R. Snyder, eds. New York: John Wiley & Sons, 1962, 121–140.

Taylor, Robert T. "The Jamestown Tercentennial Exposition of 1907." *The Virginia Magazine of History and Biography* 65/2 (April 1957): 169–208.

Ueda, Reed. "Naturalization and Citizenship." In *Harvard Encyclopedia of American Ethnic Groups*, ed. Stephan Thernstrom. Cambridge: Harvard University Press, 1980, 734–48.

Vester, Katharina. "Regime Change: Gender, Class, and the Invention of Dieting in Post-Bellum America." *Journal of Social History* 44/1 (Fall 2010): 39–70.

Wade, James B. "Normative and Resource Flow Consequences of Local Regulations in American Brewing Industry, 1845–1918." *Administrative Science Quarterly* 43/4 (December 1998): 905–935.

Wagner, Richard. "The Introduction of Lager Beer in the USA, Arranged Chronologically." *The Keg* (Fall 1998): 11, 20–22.

Walker, Charles J., and Bruce Blaine. "The Virulence of Dread Rumors: A Field Experiment." *Language & Communication* 11/4 (1991): 291–297.

Watkins, Anna. "To Help a Child: The History of the German Orphan Home." *Washington History* 18/1, 2 (2006): 120–138.

Welskopp, Thomas. "Prohibition." In *Immigrant Entrepreneurship: German-American Business Biographies, 1720 to the Present*, vol. 4, edited by Jeffrey Fear. German Historical Institute. Last modified September 23, 2013. http://www.immigrantentrepreneurship.org/entry.php?rec=87.

Werner, George S. "Travelling Journeymen in Metternichian South Germany." *Proceedings of the American Philosophical Society* 125/3 (June 23, 1981): 190–219.

Wiedemann-Citera, Barbara. "The Role of the German-American *Vereine* in the Revitalization of German-American Ethnic Life in New York City in the 1920s." *Yearbook on German-American Studies* 29 (1994): 107–116.

Wiesner, Merry E. "'*Wandervogels*' Women: Journeymen's Concepts of Masculinity in Early Modern Germany." *Journal of Social History* 24/4 (Summer 1991): 767–782.

Wilkins, Mira. "The Free-Standing Company, 1870–1914: An Important Type of British Foreign Direct Investment." *Economic History Review* 41 (1988): 259–282.

Wood, Donna J. "The Strategic Use of Public Policy: Business Support for the 1906 Food and Drug Act." *The Business History Review* 59/3 (Autumn 1985): 403–432.

Wright, Robert. "German Corporate Entrepreneurs in Nineteenth Century America." In *Immigrant Entrepreneurship: German-American Business Biographies, 1720 to the Present*, vol. 2, edited by William J. Hausman. German Historical Institute. Last modified April 1, 2014. http://www.immigrantentrepreneurship.org/entry.php?rec=197 (Accessed September 3, 2014).

Yox, Andrew. "The German-American Community as a Nationality, 1880–1940." *Yearbook on German-American Studies* 36 (2001): 181–193.

Zimmerman, Jonathan. "'The Queen of the Lobby': Mary Hunt, Scientific Temperance, and the Dilemma of Democratic Education in America, 1879–1906." *History of Education Quarterly* 32/1 (Spring 1992): 1–30.

Zukobn, Sharon. "Urban Lifestyles: Diversity and Standardisation in Spaces of Consumption." *Urban Studies* 35/5–6 (1998): 825–839.

Dissertations and Theses

Albano, Walter. "History of the DuPont Circle Neighborhood, Washington, D.C. 1880–1900." Master's thesis, University of Maryland, 1982.

Jacob, Kathryn Allamong. "High Society in Washington during the Gilded Age: 'Three Distinct Aristocracies.'" Ph.D. diss., Johns Hopkins University, 1986.

Mandley, Erin V. "American Come Into Your Own: A Case Study of the Christian Heurich House Museum Regarding the Effects of Nineteenth Century Domesticated Technology." Master's thesis, Sotheby's Institute of Art, 2013.

McLoud, Melissa. "Craftsmen and Entrepreneurs: Builders in Late Nineteenth Century Washington, D.C." Ph.D. diss., George Washington University, 1988.

Miller, Elizabeth Jane. "The Dry Goods Trade in Washington, D.C., 1880–1889." Master's thesis, George Washington University, 1977.

Shireman, Candace S. "The Rise of Christian Heurich's Mansion: A Study of the Interior Design and Fur-

nishings of the Columbia Historical Society's Chris-
tian Heurich Mansion, Washington, D.C., 1892–1914."
Master's thesis, George Washington University, 1989.
Stack, Martin Heidegger. "Liquid Bread: An Examina-
tion of the American Brewing Industry, 1865–1940."
Ph.D. diss., University of Notre Dame, 1989.
Wood, Karl E. "Spa Culture and the Social History of
Medicine in Germany." Ph.D. diss., University of Illi-
nois at Chicago, 2004.

Newspapers and Magazines

Anglo-American Times (New York).
Brewers' Gazette.
Brewers' Journal.
The Evening Star (Washington, D.C.).
The Herald (Washington, D.C.).
London Guardian.
London Illustrated Times.
London Patriot.
Modern Brewery Age.
The New York Times.
The Times (Washington, D.C.).
The Washington Post.
The Western Brewer.

Unpublished Sources

Karla Harrison and Jan Evans's interview with Sarah
Heald, August 1, 1985.
Karla Louise Harrison's interview with Sarah Heald, De-
cember 30, 1987.
Heurich, Christian, Sr. *I Watched America Grow: By
Christian Heurich as told to W.A.S. Douglas, Book One,
1842 to 1872.* MS. in possession of Jan Evans Houser.
Interviews with Jan Evans Houser, 2012, 2013, 2014.
Letters from Carl A. Keyser to family members, 1981–
1982.
Elizabeth Miller, "The Washington Business Commu-
nity in the Nineteenth Century: Dreams and Disap-
pointments."

Websites

"Cholera Mattresses at Crosby" Merseyside Maritime
Museum. www.liverpoolmuseums.org.uk/maritime/
collections/seized/casestudies/cholera_mattresses.
aspx (accessed January 27, 2011).
"Cholera on Board the Helvetia 1866." http://www.old-
merseytimes.co.uk/cholerahelvetia.html (accessed
October 12, 2014).

Index

Numbers in *bold italics* indicate pages with illustrations.
"H." refers to Christian Heurich, Sr.